*Cities and the Rise
of States in Europe,*
A.D. 1000 to 1800

Cities and the Rise of States in Europe, A.D. 1000 to 1800

edited by

Charles Tilly and
Wim P. Blockmans

Westview Press

Boulder • San Francisco • Oxford

Chapters 2, 5, 6, 8, and 9 previously appeared in *Theory and Society* 18, no. 5 (September 1989): 563–755. © 1989 Kluwer Academic Publishers. Reprinted by permission of Kluwer Academic Publishers.

Published in 1994 in the United States of America by Westview Press, Inc., 5500 Central Avenue, Boulder, Colorado 80301-2877, and in the United Kingdom by Westview Press, 36 Lonsdale Road, Summertown, Oxford OX2 7EW

Library of Congress Cataloging-in-Publication Data
Cities and the rise of states in Europe, A.D. 1000 to 1800 / edited by
    Charles Tilly and Wim P. Blockmans.
        p.   cm.
    Some articles previously published in Theory and society, v. 18,
no. 5 (Sept. 1989).
    Includes bibliographical references (p.) and index.
    ISBN 0-8133-8848-1 (hardcover). — ISBN 0-8133-8849-X (pbk.)
    1. Cities—Europe—History.   2. Europe—History—476–1492.
3. Europe—History—1492–1648.   4. Europe—History—1648–1789.
I. Tilly, Charles.   II. Blockmans, Willem Pieter.
D200.C57   1994
940—dc20   94-17378
                                                                              CIP

Printed and bound in the United States of America

The paper used in this publication meets the requirements
of the American National Standard for Permanence of Paper
for Printed Library Materials Z39.48-1984.

10   9   8   7   6   5   4   3   2   1

Contents

Entanglements of European Cities and States

CHARLES TILLY

THE END OF THE fifteenth century brought a major change in European diplomacy and warfare. France (finally restored to vigor after the extenuation of the plague and the Hundred Years' War), Aragon (still an independent kingdom despite the momentous marriage of its monarch, Ferdinand, with Isabella of Castile), and Venice (then a fearsome maritime power with domains scattered from the Adriatic and the Mediterranean to the Black Sea) began bidding for positions on the Italian mainland. At the same time, dealing with the expansive Ottoman Empire preoccupied an increasing number of European potentates. General wars, furthermore, resumed with increasingly expensive artillery, fortifications, and mercenary armies. The rulers of Italian city-states, who for a century had been free to cut each other's throats without vigorous, visible external intervention, found themselves contending continuously with Europe's great powers.

In 1510 and 1511, the pope and Ferdinand of Aragon turned against France, their former ally in the League of Cambrai formed two years earlier to counter Venetian expansion. They threatened France's Italian allies as well. The most steadfast among those allies, the Florentine republic, found its days of independence numbered. As the French retreated in 1512, the conquering powers forced Florence to enthrone the long-exiled Medici, who promptly undertook to eliminate their enemies from the city. One of the republic's major functionaries, Niccolò Machiavelli, suffered torture and expulsion.

During years of exile from his beloved Florence, Machiavelli wrote the books for which we remember him, among them *The Prince*. Chapter 5 of that great guide to Renaissance statecraft bore the title "The Way to Govern Cities or Dominions That, Previous to Being Occupied, Lived Under Their

Own Laws." "When those states which have been acquired are accustomed to live at liberty under their own laws," commented Machiavelli,

> there are three ways of holding them. The first is to despoil them; the second is to go and live there in person; the third is to allow them to live under their own laws, taking tribute of them, and creating within the country a government composed of a few who will keep it friendly to you. Because this government, being created by the prince, knows that it cannot exist without his friendship and protection, and will do all it can to keep them. What is more, a city used to liberty can be more easily held by means of its citizens than in any other way, if you wish to preserve it.[1]

Machiavelli left little doubt about his preference for the third course. Nevertheless, his advice to a prince takes for granted that an effective ruler will conquer new territory, that he will seek to incorporate conquered territories into his domains, that several means of incorporation (direct rule, indirect rule, or annihilation) are feasible, and that the prior existence of a coherent government in a conquered city poses a political problem as well as a political opportunity.

This last Machiavellian insight touches the question before us: In Europe after A.D. 1000, how did the density and organization of cities in a region affect changes in the character of states? Did the histories of states follow different courses in times and places of varying urban density? How did rulers of states negotiate with the city-dwellers in their midst? How did those who ran cities negotiate with the rulers of states? In short, how did urbanization and the transformation of states interact?

The chapters in this book examine that interaction in detail. Our essays survey the variety of transformations European states underwent after A.D. 1000, asking how they intersected with the changing configuration of cities in Europe. More precisely, we want to know how variable processes of urbanization constrained changes in the character of European states. To help answer that question, we examine both (1) how rulers interacted with urban populations in different regions or periods and (2) what correspondences between urban structure and type of state appear at the large scale. Most chapters in the book focus on the first problem. My introduction and the conclusion by Wim Blockmans focus on the second.

Given the salience of Paris, Moscow, Rome, Madrid, and London in the histories of European states, one might have thought these connections would dominate comparative analyses of European political history. Nothing of the sort has happened. The synthetic and comparative literature on states offers surprisingly little guidance in answering our questions. Of course, histories of France tell us much about interactions between Paris and French kings, histories of the Venetian republic follow urban factions in detail, and histories of Muscovy pay plenty of attention to Moscow, its capital.

But general treatments of state structure and change rarely mention state-city relationships. Nor, for that matter, do they give much attention to any variation in the paths along which states travel. In the exemplary recent synthesis by John Hall and John Ikenberry, for example, the question does not come up at all; the authors simply ignore why states take different forms in different times and places.[2] Gianfranco Poggi, in his own ambitious summing up, explicitly declares, "I take little notice of the differences the development [of the modern state] presents in different regions of Western Europe."[3] If variation does not matter, then urbanization does not matter much either.

As a whole, the scholarly literature on states follows Poggi's rule: Varying forms and differing trajectories of change in the organization of states come up for discussion chiefly as major evolutionary stages (e.g., from traditional to modern states), as expressions of different major economic systems (e.g., capitalist versus socialist states), as competing constitutional models (e.g., parliamentary versus presidential systems), or as some combination of the three. Although those bases of variation all deserve analysis, they leave standard questions of comparative politics untouched. Why, for example, should the oil-producing Middle Eastern states of Saudi Arabia, Iraq, and Iran have such disparate political regimes? Why should Latin American states that all acquired independence as the Spanish Empire disintegrated early in the nineteenth century have followed such contrasting trajectories since then? Scholars have occasionally sought to answer questions of this sort by invoking evolutionary stages, contrasting economic systems, or competing constitutional models, but their efforts have remained unconvincing.

The synthetic and comparative literature on states breaks into four rough categories:

1. *geopolitical* analyses, which attach great importance to the international system as the shaper of states within it;
2. *mode of production* analyses, which derive the structures of states from the logic of the productive systems with which they are associated;
3. *world-system* analyses, which trace the histories of states to their changing positions in the world economy; and
4. *statist* analyses, which treat political change as proceeding in partial independence of economic change, chiefly as a consequence of events within particular states.

So far, geopolitical analyses, as exemplified by Kenneth Waltz's neorealist models, have provided possible explanations of various states' diplomatic and military policies, but they have yielded no useful accounts of variation in state organization. Mode of production and world-system analyses, as exemplified by the works of Perry Anderson and Immanuel Wallerstein, offer accounts of change and variation in state structure; they treat states as the creatures and instruments of dominant classes, whose characters vary markedly from one mode of production or one niche in the world system to another. Such accounts, however, almost always reduce cities to expressions of their dominant classes and surrounding economies. They allow no place for the independent effects of cities on states.

Statist analyses have come a little closer, at a great sacrifice of generality. Thus Lisa Anderson clarifies the substantially different histories of Libya and Tunisia through sustained comparison, and Richard Lachmann contrasts the states and class configurations of England and France during the sixteenth and seventeenth centuries. Indeed, hundreds of authors have examined particular states or pairs of states such as England, France, Prussia, Spain, the Dutch Republic, or Russia in order to bring out the particularities of their experiences. The puzzle remains: How can their conclusions be generalized?

In an earlier effort, I thought an improved analysis of "state formation" in Europe would help produce the essential generalizations. Although that inquiry yielded some valuable results in other regards, I confess now to regretting my part in promoting that particular framing of the problem. At the time, it seemed like a good idea. Like the colleagues who joined me in publishing *The Formation of National States in Western Europe* in 1975, I had acquired severe doubts about the teleology of the then-current catchwords *political development* and *political modernization*. In setting up our joint inquiry, we had accepted the definition of the subject matter as "state- and nation-building." The longer the work went on, the more doubtful we became of the engineering metaphor—building, *Bau, edificazione*—with its implications of foresight and directionality. Hence when it came time to put our conclusions into book form to report our findings, I chose what seemed a more neutral, historicist term: *formation*. Anthropologists and archaeologists had occasionally used the term to describe the appearance of states where none had existed before. As far as I know, our book introduced it into the literature on political change in the West.

In context, the term had some justification. We aimed the book at explaining "the emergence of the alternative forms of Western states."[4] We concentrated, furthermore, on how and why the "national" state came to be the dominant form in Europe after 1700. By "national state" we meant one that:

1. controlled a well-defined, continuous territory;
2. was relatively centralized;
3. was differentiated from other organizations;
4. reinforced its claims through moves toward monopolization of coercive means.

I made a mistake in calling such states *national* because of the term's sugges-tion that they embodied *nations,* or homogeneous peoples. From the eigh-teenth century onward, Europeans created an ideology and a practice of the nation-state, arguing that homogeneous peoples deserved their own states, creating origin myths for existing states, and promoting the dominance of one set of cultural idioms within a given state. In fact, almost all states re-mained quite composite, either through their toleration of multiple regional cultures, their reception of large immigrations, or both. Even Norway and Sweden, for example, still have substantial regions of Sami culture, and most European countries remain even more polyglot, religiously divided, and cul-turally various than Scandinavia. The ideology matters since it bolsters the claims of such regions as Croatia, Slovakia, and Georgia to states of their own. Yet it would be much clearer to call the territorially continuous, cen-tralized, differentiated, coercion-monopolizing state *consolidated.*

By state formation, in any case, we meant the whole set of processes whereby this sort of state first appeared among the many other varieties of European states, then became the dominant variety. If the matter had stayed there, our terminological innovation would probably have done no harm. Between 1500 and 1800, the period on which our book concentrated, the "national" state, in this limited sense of the term, really did take form and then begin to prevail in western Europe. If we had managed to restrict the term *state formation* to that shift, the problem would have remained fairly clear.

The trouble lay elsewhere. First, we actually inquired occasionally into how city-states, empires, federations of commercial cities, and other types of states as well as the "national" state formed without insisting that those pro-cesses did *not* constitute state formation. Second, we called attention to a great many activities, such as control of food supplies, that all sorts of states undertook, without reserving the term *state formation* for those that pro-moted the circumscription of territory, centralization, differentiation, and the monopolization of coercive means. Third, once out of its original setting, the term *state formation* suggests either that the "national" state's predeces-sors were not full-fledged states or that the same processes produce all sorts of states in all eras and parts of the world; hence books and articles started appearing on such subjects as state formation in the contemporary Third World, in which authors searched for deliberate analogies with the processes we had identified as crucial in western Europe. Finally, my use of our find-ings to criticize previous theories of political development emphasized the extractive, coercive, war-making side of state activity so strongly as to sub-stitute implicitly a new unilinear model, this one centered on coercion, for the more consensual unilinear models that had gone before. These were all seductive errors, to us and to others after us. Only the success of our efforts in persuading other scholars to follow our lead revealed the trap we had dug for ourselves.

In a more recent effort, I corrected one problem but not the other. *Coercion, Capital, and European States, A.D. 990–1990* (first published, appropriately, in 1990) deliberately examined variation in the trajectories followed by European states over the millennium in question. It continued to employ, however, the vocabulary of state formation rather than *transformation*. Precisely because the book examined a period in which the varieties of viable states multiplied in Europe before eventual convergence on the consolidated state of our own time, the inconsistency in the vocabulary became even clearer than in *The Formation of National States in Western Europe*. The present book, then, adds another corrective to the dialectical chain. For Europe, it explores the possibility that the variable distribution of cities and systems of cities by region and era significantly and independently constrained the multiple paths of state transformation. It argues that states, as repositories of armed force, grow differently in different environments and that the character of the urban networks within such environments systematically affects the path of state transformation.

Why might we suppose that analytically separable effects of urbanization actually exist? We have several reasons for the supposition. First, in Europe, striking correspondences between the geographical distributions of cities and states endured for centuries, with—as we shall see abundantly—very different sorts of states evolving in densely urban regions and in regions with few cities. Second, where distinctive forms of urban organization existed early in the consolidation of major states, they typically survived the growth of state power and played significant roles in subsequent national politics. Third, urban merchants and financiers typically wielded considerable influence in the organization and growth of state facilities, especially armed forces, both because they entered actively into public finance and because they controlled the markets that supplied new institutions with their wherewithal. Where few merchants and financiers existed, on the other hand, a politics of warlords and landlords more often prevailed. These facts give us prima facie reasons for looking hard at city-state relations and their changes in Europe. Let us start at the last millennium, A.D. 1000, and work forward.

CITIES VERSUS STATES

Over most of the past 10,000 years, the world's cultural, political, and economic epicenter has lain somewhere around the Indian Ocean; Europe has generally constituted the westerly periphery of overlapping systems oriented to such centers as Constantinople, Baghdad, Edo, or Hangchow. As of 1000 A.D., most of Europe remained quite peripheral despite the temporarily stronger connections to world trade and communication afforded them by Roman, Byzantine, and Islamic Empires. Muslim navigators, merchants, and rulers then mediated European relations to much of the non-European world. Córdoba (capital of the Umayyad caliphate) and Constantinople (seat of the Byzantine Empire) were Europe's largest cities by far. Within Europe, the Muslim-controlled western Mediterranean and the eastern Mediterranean, increasingly oriented to an axis from old Constantinople to newcomer Venice, contained the most intensive regions of trade. At the millennium, in short, relations to the great Asian-based system of trade and conquest strongly affected the relative prosperity of different European regions.

Maps of the time that divided Europe into neatly distinct countries present a seriously misleading impression of cultural and political interpenetration. In actuality, languages, religions, trading systems, and political jurisdictions overlapped and intertwined to a degree that defies mapping; beyond the scale of a city-state, any territorial sovereign drew tribute from multiple peoples and dealt with members of trade diasporas whose cultural bases lay far away. The closer they lived to the southeast corner of Europe, the more likely it was that these ordinary Europeans were multilingual, engaging in separate tongues for trade, political administration, and domestic affairs.

Within Europe, three basic forms of government proliferated into a vast variety: (1) petty despotisms operated by military specialists, (2) city-states oriented to trade and the exploitation of their agricultural hinterlands, and (3) empires concatenating central military organizations, thin regional administrations, trading networks, and organizations of tribute in which local and regional rulers—often maintaining cultural identities distinct from that of the empire's center—enjoyed great autonomy in return for collaboration in the collection of tribute and support in the empire's military campaigns. In all three forms and their variants, especially the petty despotisms and empires, landlords played crucial parts in supplying nonagricultural populations and the government of local areas; landlords often mobilized their own armed force, from household retainers to private armies. None of the three approximated the sharply demarcated, centrally administered states that have predominated in Europe over the last century or so.

In the year 1000, three different relations between cities and states prevailed in Europe. Over much of the Mediterranean, empires based in opulent capitals ruled cities that were carrying on both commercial and administrative activities. From Catalonia to Italy and in the denser urban clusters across the Alps, sovereignty fragmented into city-states, minor episcopal domains, and similar localized arrangements only nominally connected with great overlords. In the rest of Europe, landlords governing substantial domains and private armies, some of whom had royal titles attached to wispy state structures, coexisted uneasily with the rarer merchant-run cities in their zones of influence.

Looking forward from the year 1000, a European sibyl might therefore have reasonably predicted a number of changes that never occurred:

- increasing subordination of European trade to that of the eastern Mediterranean, the Middle East, the Indian Ocean, and East Asia;
- continued expansion of Muslim power in continental Europe;
- the rise of city-states, city-empires, and religious organizations as the dominant European political structures;
- cyclical destruction of those political structures' power, especially in eastern Europe, by nomadic invaders from the Eurasian steppe; and
- battles among armed tribute-takers and their personal armies as the predominant form of war.

Why none of these became the prevailing pattern is the major unanswered question in European history. In this book, we propose to approach the question by examining the variable articulations of cities and states in different regions of Europe between A.D. 1000 and 1800. We concentrate on the period before 1800, for two reasons: (1) because the small existing literature on city-state interaction has concentrated unduly on the period since 1800, presuming that cities remained relatively insignificant—except as capitals—before the massive urbanization of the last two centuries, and (2) because the variable relations between cities and states prior to 1800 strongly marked the nature of government in different regions of Europe after that point.

Cities shape the destinies of states chiefly by serving as containers and distribution points for capital. By means of capital, urban ruling classes extend their influence through the urban hinterland and across far-flung trading networks. But cities vary in how much capital their oligarchies control; seventeenth-century Amsterdam made once-glorious Bruges look puny. The fact that cities are loci of capital accumulation, furthermore, gives the urban political authorities access to capital, credit, and control over hinterlands that, if seized or co-opted, can serve the ends of monarchs as well.

States, in contrast, operate chiefly as containers and deployers of coercive means, especially armed force. But they, too, vary in how much they control; in the 1630s, for example, Spain's 300,000 troops under arms dwarfed Holland's 50,000 and Sweden's 45,000. Similar inequalities in armed forces have prevailed throughout the history of European states.

Over Europe as a whole, alterations in the state control of capital and of coercion between A.D. 1000 and the present have followed two parallel arcs. Consider capital: At first, European monarchs generally extracted what capital they needed as tribute or rent from lands and populations that lay under their immediate control—often within stringent contractual limits on the amounts they could demand. In a middle period (especially between 1300 and 1700 or so), they relied heavily on formally independent capitalists for loans, for management of revenue-producing enterprises, and sometimes for collection of taxes. By the eighteenth century, however, many sovereigns were incorporating the fiscal apparatus directly into the state structure and drastically curtailing the involvement of independent contractors.

On the side of coercion, a similar evolution took place. During the early period, monarchs drew armed forces from retainers, vassals, and militias who owed them personal service—but again within significant contractual limits. Later (again, especially between 1500 and 1700), they turned increasingly to mercenary forces supplied to them by contractors who retained considerable freedom of action. Finally, sovereigns absorbed armies and navies directly into the state's administrative structure, eventually turning away from foreign mercenaries and hiring or conscripting the bulk of their troops from their own citizenries.

By the nineteenth century, most European states had internalized both armed forces and fiscal mechanisms; they thus reduced the governmental roles of tax farmers, military contractors, and other independent middlemen. Their rulers then continued to bargain with capitalists and other classes for revenues, manpower, and the necessities of war. Bargaining, in its turn, created numerous new claims on the state: pensions, payments to the poor, public education, city planning, and much more. In the process, states changed from magnified war machines into multipurpose organizations. Their efforts to control coercion and capital continued but were now accompanied by a wide variety of regulatory, compensatory, distributive, and protective activities.

Before the nineteenth century, states differed markedly in the relative timing and intensity of the two main processes of change. The Dutch state avoided heavy investment in mercenaries by favoring sea warfare over combat on land, and it created state-managed finances precociously, yet long remained beholden to the capitalists of Amsterdam and other commercial cities. In Castile, on the other hand, land forces—often hired outside Spain—prevailed; there, the monarchy captured the credit of merchants by turning them into rentiers and by relying on colonial revenues for their reimbursement. Portugal, Poland, the Balkans, Italian city-states, and the states of the Holy Roman Empire followed other variations on the two arcs and thereby created distinctly different state structures.

The varying intersections between the processes by which capital and coercion concentrated and came under state control help explain the geographic pattern of European state formation, the differential incorporation of urban oligarchies and institutions into consolidated state structure, and the shift in state power from the Mediterranean to the Atlantic. To understand those processes, we must look at the history of war and its financing.

WARS, STATES, AND CAPITAL

The coercive means controlled by European states have risen almost incessantly over the last millennium, no matter what standard we employ to measure this: the absolute mass of force at the disposition of the average state, the relative bulk of coercive means available to the state and its individual citizens, or the extent to which the state monopolized concentrated force within its own territory. The great increase in stateheld force resulted from an interplay between alterations in the state system and technical changes in war-making. But it depended on a large financial transformation.

Although it was once possible for a monarch to wage war with his own routine revenues and the poorly paid services—voluntary or coerced—of his clients and servitors, it became increasingly necessary to borrow in the short run for the immediate expenses of the military and to tax in the long run for maintenance of the armed forces and repayment of the debt. In both regards, especially the financing of debt, the energetic participation of men (they were usually men, not women) who had access to large amounts of cash and credit became crucial. Thus the concentration of coercion depended in part on the concentration of capital.

Pursuit of war generates many demands: for troops, arms, equipment, transport, lodging, and food. The relative salience and ease of acquisition of these requisites depend on both the type of warfare and the commercialization-capitalization of the ambient economy. Noble cavalry and their retainers, for example, typically received land, booty, and privilege but little money for their services. The shift to a mercenary infantry with siege artillery (which occurred widely in Europe during the fifteenth and sixteenth centuries) greatly increased the financial requirements of war, but it took place without mobilizing large proportions of the national population into armies and navies. Mass warfare of the eighteenth- or nineteenth-century type only occurred with huge outlays of cash and large organizational efforts. Sea warfare, on the whole, cost plenty but required less manpower; a nation that was already mercantile and seafaring could make the conversion to a war footing with relative ease. To the extent that weapons, ammunition, vehicles, and other machines became prominent means of war, the availability of money took on greater importance than the supply of men. States varied greatly in their ability to provide for these different kinds of war-making.

In Europe before 1800 or so, most important changes in state structure stemmed from rulers' efforts to acquire the requisites of war, from resistance to those efforts, and from bargains that ended—or at least mitigated—that resistance. Courts, treasuries, representative assemblies, central administrations, fiscal structures, and much more formed and reformed in response to the creation of military force, the pursuit of war, and the payment of its costs.

How much state structure issued from war-making depended, to be sure, on the interaction between (1) the type of war, (2) the character of the economy, and (3) fiscal strategy. A ruler who wanted to build military power in a relatively uncommercialized agrarian economy, such as Russia, had little choice but to enlist the support of landlords, to conscript peasants, and to tax property—a process that ordinarily created massive bureaucracies. A commercialized maritime state, such as Venice, on the other hand, could rely on customs and excise (which are relatively inexpensive to collect) and emphasize sea power without forming a vast central administration; the strategy could only work, however, with the close collaboration of merchants and financiers. Where merchants and financiers *ran* the state, as in the republics of Venice and Dubrovnik at the peaks of their commercial power, the major problem was to coordinate their domestic commercial interests.

All makers of war on a large scale therefore conquered, co-opted, or otherwise allied themselves with those who had effective competing claims on the potential means of war: other war-makers within their own territories, landlords (who overlapped, of course, with other war-makers), clergy, and capitalists. At first, European monarchs used the influence of these groups to control workers and peasants, who often paid the final bill for war. Eventually, as their demands for taxes and manpower rose, all states turned to at least a modicum of direct bargaining with workers, peasants, and other classes—in the form of either negotiated settlements to rebellions and revolutions or elections, assemblies, referenda, and other consultative devices.

Rulers who could avoid bargaining with the mass of the population by means of external revenues (e.g., from colonies), repression, or (more likely) both, did so. But most found themselves bargaining. With whom they made the strongest bargains depended on the various classes' relative strength and the kind of war the state was preparing. Where landlords predominated and rulers fought with massed infantry, privileged classes of noble officers, often charged with recruiting their own troops, emerged; where capitalists were strong and naval warfare salient—the two often coincided—the crown typically confirmed the privileges of the patricians and of their cities.

After 1300 or so, no ruler who seriously pursued war avoided reliance on capitalists of some sort. The activity of capitalists facilitated the concentration of coercive means in the long run by making them increasingly available through monetized markets and in the short run by making cash and credit available—at a price. But capitalists, when they had a choice, resisted the concentration of the means of coercion, except insofar as it increased the protection of their own uses of capital; in general, they preferred to use their capital in other ways, rather than spending it on war or loaning it to the crown, and rightly feared that a powerful ruler would both tax their proceeds and inhibit their transactions with other capitalists elsewhere.

Hence, rulers faced a dilemma. Every state that mounted a large war apparatus eventually surmounted this dilemma, but the paths past it, as the chapters in this volume show, ran in radically different directions. The variable interaction of capital and coercion significantly affected those paths. Over the long run, almost all European states moved toward greater concentrations of both coercion and capital. But in some, concentrations of coercion grew earlier and more emphatically than concentrations of capital; in others, the reverse was true. Poland provides an example of coercion-intensive history; the Netherlands has a capital-intensive history.

Early paths affected later developments. If a state began by means of brute conquest in rural regions (Castile is a case in point), its successors generally exploited and cramped the cities in its midst. If, in contrast, merchants and cities lay at a state's origins (Barcelona and Aragon come closer to this pattern), cities and citizens usually enjoyed a measure of autonomy or at least of representation. A middle path, combining considerable concentrations of both capital and coercion (London and the rest of England, with their antagonistic synthesis of merchants and landlords, illustrate this trajectory), promoted substantial, rich states. Coercion-intensive, capital-intensive, and capitalized-coercion paths of state transformation differed significantly from each other.

CITY SYSTEMS VERSUS STATE SYSTEMS

These differences divided Europe into contrasting regions. To see the geographic pattern more clearly, we should distinguish between city systems and systems of states. European cities formed a loose hierarchy of commercial and industrial precedence within which, at any point in time, a few clusters of cities (usually grouped around a single hegemonic center) clearly dominated the rest. (The European hierarchy, to be sure, formed only part of a vaster urban network that reached far into Asia at the period's beginning and extended to Africa and the Americas as time went on.) In Fernand Braudel's useful simplification, Venice, Antwerp, Genoa, Amsterdam, London, and New York successively dominated the European system of cities from the fourteenth century to the twentieth.

For dominance, the crucial matter was not so much size as centrality in the European network of trade, production, and capital accumulation. Nevertheless, the concentrations of capital and urban population corresponded closely enough that the dominant *cluster* of cities was always also one of the largest. For example, Jan de Vries's computation of "urban potential" singles out regions centering approximately on Antwerp, Milan, and Naples as the peaks of the European urban system in 1500, but in 1800, the zone around London (including areas across the English Channel) clearly predominated.[5]

One thousand years ago, a tenth of the European population (which totaled perhaps 39 million, excluding Russia) lived in settlements of 5,000 people or more. Today the proportion is around two-thirds of the Continent's population of 475 million (again, excluding Russia). In A.D. 1000, only a few hundred such places existed anywhere in Europe; by 1990, they numbered in the thousands. At the millennium, a threshold of 5,000 inhabitants clearly singled out urban centers: foci of communications for considerable regions, major connectors with distant populations and activities, loci of specialized production, accumulation, distribution, and administration. By the recent past, it brought together not only unquestioned cities but also hundreds of agricultural villages, suburbs, satellite industrial sites, military installations, and recreational communities.

The time between A.D. 1000 and 1800 brought nothing like linear growth in the urban areas of Europe. Even over the Continent as a whole, we must distinguish at least five phases: (1) considerable urban expansion, accompanied by a general population growth that was almost as significant, up to 1300 or so; (2) a dramatic slowdown, punctuated with food shortages and plague epidemics, up to 1500; (3) acceleration of both urban growth and general population increase (resulting in a slight rise in the urban share), accompanying Europe's energetic exploration, conquest, and mercantile expansion outside the Continent, up to the early seventeenth century; (4) another slowdown in the population increase and urban growth, coupled with a proliferation of cottage industries, during the seventeenth and early eighteenth centuries; and (5) unprecedented population increase, outrun by spectacular urban growth associated with the formation of capital-concentrated urban manufacturing, from 1750 onward.

Urban growth was distributed very unevenly over Europe's surface. The Eurasian map of A.D. 1000 clearly showed Europe lying on the periphery of a huge commercial-imperial system extending from the Mediterranean to the Indian Ocean and China and on into the Pacific. Within Europe, cities clustered around the Mediterranean. The two greatest metropolises were Córdoba and Constantinople. They connected directly to the impressive non-European cities of Fez, Cairo, Aleppo, Hasa, Baghdad, Jerusalem, Rayy, and Isfahan. Caravan roads reached east to China; small cities like Sarajevo earned their livings as caravan stops and transshipment points for long-distance trade. Urban tendrils reached north from Mediterranean and Black Sea roots. The most substantial tendrils linked small trading cities of southwestern Germany, Flanders, and northern France to the thriving city-states of Italy. Raiding and conquering Vikings had also managed to establish a connection between such Russian cities as Novgorod and Kiev with the east-west mercantile system to their south.

Up to 1300, the system grew with little change in its overall contours; the greatest alteration was the prosperity of the German-Flemish axis, which spilled over into adjacent areas like the Baltic and southern England. The subsequent depression simply froze that new balance. During the sixteenth-century surge, however, an emphatic recasting of the map to the north and west occurred: Along with imperial power, urban densities actually declined around the Mediterranean as Flanders became the center of a greatly expanded urban field. By 1750, the urban dominance of northwestern Europe left no doubt. The period since then has seen a vast expansion of urban regions and an intense further urbanization within them but no fundamental break with a pattern oriented to the densely packed cities of the Low Countries, western Germany, northern France, and southern England. The great long-term alteration of European urban distribution, then, preserved the axis from Italy to England but gave the northwestern end of that axis greater and greater weight.

The map of states divided Europe up very differently. To understand the map, we must apply the term *state* generously, including any organization that commanded substantial means of coercion and successfully claimed durable priority over all other users of coercion within at least one clearly bounded territory. In the year 1000, relatively large Muslim states dominated much of the western Mediterranean, including southern Spain and Africa's north coast. Other sizable states included the kingdom of France, the Saxon empire, the Danish kingdom, Russia, Poland, Hungary, Bohemia, and the Byzantine Empire. On the whole, the rulers of these political entities drew tribute from the territories nominally under their control, but outside their home regions, they gave them little administrative attention and saw their authority continually contested by rival potentates, including their own putative agents.

Within the ring formed by these weak, ephemeral states, sovereignty fragmented even further, as hundreds of principalities, bishoprics, city-states, and other authorities exercised overlapping control in the small hinterlands of their capitals. Except for the relative urbanity of Muslim lands, the correlation between size of states and density of cities was negative: Where cities swarmed, sovereignty crumbled.

During the following millennium, Europe's political map changed even more fundamentally than did its distribution of cities. By 1500, Muslims were retreating from Spain but building a substantial empire around the eastern Mediterranean and making inroads in the Balkans, states fielding large armies and extending some judicial and fiscal control over good-sized territories were beginning to appear around Europe's edges, and city-states were arming for land war as never before. Europe was starting to consolidate into territorially distinct states organized around permanent military establishments.

But this was only a beginning, to be sure. In 1500, armies consisted largely of mercenaries hired by the campaign, clients of great lords, and citizen militias. Standing armies had displaced urban militias in France and Burgundy but few other realms. Tribute and personal rents still contributed greatly to royal revenues. Within the larger states, communities, gilds, churches, and regional magnates retained wide areas of immunity and self-government. Administration chiefly concerned military, judicial, and fiscal affairs. Europe's central zone continued to teem with tiny jurisdictions. Since city-states, leagues of cities, dynastic empires, principalities having only nominal bonds to larger monarchies or empires, and ecclesiastical entities such as the Teutonic Order all coexisted (however contentiously) on the Continent, it was not clear that consolidated states as we know them would become Europe's dominant organizations.

On a small scale, some type of city-state seemed a viable form of rule; on a large scale, empires held together by tribute-yielding, semiautonomous authorities and backed by the intermittent use of centrally assembled military force continued a pattern that had flourished in Eurasia for thousands of years. Not until the nineteenth century, with Napoleon's conquests and the subsequent unifications of Germany and Italy, did almost all of Europe settle into mutually exclusive states having permanent, professional armed forces and exercising substantial control over the people in areas of 40,000 square miles or more.

These changes in the geographies of European cities and states had strong implications for the interactions of city-dwellers and state-makers. Between 1000 and 1500, roughly speaking, cities were rare, and states were numerous. Many more or less autonomous political entities had no city of any size, and the rulers of most cities of 10,000 or more exercised something resembling sovereignty within their own walls and their immediate hinterlands. Relative to territorial lords, urban oligarchies wielded considerable political power. The situation varied, however, from center to periphery: in the dense urban band, city-states and similar organizations predominated, but on Europe's more rural flanks, princes, sultans, and bishops carried greater weight and more often subordinated any cities that existed to their own jurisdiction.

After 1500, the formation of consolidated states coupled with the proliferation of cities to change the city-state relationship both numerically and politically. Suppose, for purposes of counting, we take any entity having a recognized sovereign, its own distinct armed force, and its own formally designated resident ambassadors as a state. Numerically, the proportion of cities of 10,000 or more grew from about one for every three such states in 1500, to two or three per state in 1800, to roughly 180 per state today. Politically, the odds that the oligarchy of any single city would dominate a state declined drastically. The proliferation of cities facilitated a state-making strategy of divide and conquer, the gradual monopolization of coercive means by consolidated states weakened the defensive positions of cities vis-à-vis national authorities, and the expansion of state administrative apparatus (which was itself largely a consequence of war and the preparation for war) gave those authorities increasing ability to monitor and control the urban population.

Again, how these processes worked varied from one part of Europe to another. The variation sets the problem explored in this volume: How did the character and density of urban organization affect the course of state formation in different parts of Europe? Wim Blockmans and I did not impose the line of reasoning just sketched on our fellow authors. We did, however, ask them a series of questions about city systems, capital, and state formation in different parts of Europe, with special emphasis on the period before 1800. The questions were:

1. What connection, if any, existed between the market positions of late medieval and early modern cities and the forms of their municipal institutions, especially the representative institutions?
2. What power structures did the ruling classes of major trading cities create on a supralocal scale: town leagues, ports-of-trade, city-states, monopolistic commercial companies, or federations? Were their protection costs for inhabitants of the core cities lower than those imposed by consolidated states?
3. What response did cities and their institutions make to the efforts of state-makers to impose control on them, draw capital from them, and tax them?
4. Did the strategies and successes of state-makers vary systematically according to the market positions of cities (e.g., Seville versus Madrid or Danzig versus Berlin)?
5. What effect, if any, did the character of cities in a region have on their relation to those national states that formed and the general structure of those states?
6. What effects, if any, did the imposition of control by consolidated states have on the market position of formerly autonomous trading cities?
7. At what points did the relationship between cities and states change most drastically and why?

We asked these questions of specialists in the history of Scandinavia, Poland, the Low Countries, German Europe, Italy, Spain, Portugal, and the Balkans. We deliberately avoided the classic cases of France and England because their histories are fairly well known, because we wanted to leave room for an exploration of the wide variation in the interactions between cities and states, and because we wanted to resist the ever-present temptation to treat France and England as the "successful" examples of state formation and all others as failures to be explained by features of the French and English experience that they lacked.

Readers can use the individual essays in several different ways. First, they provide succinct, authoritative descriptions of states and their transformations in nine important regions of Europe over several centuries of social change; they provide unconventional documentation of the urban and political history in those regions. Second, they contain evidence bearing on general arguments about the histories of European states, including those that Wim Blockmans and I present in our essays; they therefore provide readers with independent grounds for judging such arguments. Third, they teem with suggestions, implicit or explicit, relevant to the analysis of city-state interaction elsewhere. Traian Stoianovich's treatment of the Ottoman command economy, for example, immediately raises questions and hypotheses concerning the economies of other great empires, including those of China, Persia, India, and Japan. To read Marjolein 't Hart's analysis of fiscal organization in the Dutch Republic is to ask urgently what part the organization of state finances and taxation has had in shaping the states of other continents and eras. In short, a reader who finds the scheme of city-state interaction I have laid out in this essay unconvincing will nevertheless discover material of immediate value in the chapters that follow.

CONTRASTING CASES

What relations between cities and states and between capital and coercion do the essays in this volume describe? Before trying to sort out general patterns, let me highlight some points of the individual chapters.

Giorgio Chittolini on Italy's City-States. If the Dutch fashioned a durable federation of self-interested city-states, Italians created no more than temporary coalitions among their city-states and city-empires. Even in the face of conquest by Spain and repeated military threats from other powers, Italian city-states guarded their sovereignty with greater enthusiasm than they put into joint military efforts. Yet, as Chittolini explains, the equation was not simply 1 city equals 1 state. Larger cities such as Florence and Milan conquered and dominated *contadi* (dependent territories) that included formerly independent cities and their hinterlands, and fifteenth-century Venice shifted, to some extent, from maritime trade, piracy, and overseas colonization to conquest of territory—including many other cities—on the Italian mainland.

The cities of north-central Italy differed from their Dutch counterparts in harboring oligarchies that devoted a significant part of their energy to agrar-

ian and military activity. Many of their states succumbed to Spanish conquest, and others declined in vigor as trade moved from the Mediterranean
to the Atlantic. Still, not until the nineteenth century did a system of small
territorial states each dominated by the oligarchy of a single city give way to
a state resembling the large multicity organizations that had long prevailed
north of the Alps.

Sergij Vilfan on Istria and Dalmatia. Although he covers an even greater
chronological range and includes stubbornly independent Ragusa-Dubrovnik, Vilfan essentially treats the area of the northeastern Adriatic that Venice
controlled during most of the fifteenth to eighteenth centuries. As if to illustrate the changing contours of states in southeastern Europe, the territories
he examines now belong to Italy, Slovenia, Croatia, and Bosnia-Herzegovina (the latter two in fierce contestation with Serbia), but at times, they have
fallen variously under the control of Austria, Hungary, Serbia, and the Ottoman Empire as well as Venice. With their arrangement of port cities having
their own subject territories stretching into the interior mountains, they constitute a fascinating variant of city-state Europe that shares some properties
with northern Italy and others with Switzerland. In their own way, they experienced capital-intensive transformations of state structure.

Creatures of commercial expansion around the Adriatic, cities bustled as
transit points in the export of agricultural products from their hinterlands.
Their governments issued from an interaction between the external jurisdictions that claimed them (the contrast between territories of the Habsburg
Empire and the Venetian republic being exemplary) and their common mercantile organization, which guaranteed that merchants and financiers would
wield significant local power in whatever formal institutions prevailed.
Vilfan points out, however, that from the sixteenth century onward, as monarchies and oligarchies consolidated their holds on the region's dominant
states, regional nobilities likewise gained political strength in each subdivision; the new nobilities merged urban patriciates with rural landlords.

Traian Stoianovich on the Ottoman Balkans. Advancing and receding like a
great glacier, the Ottoman Empire occupied much of European territory
south and east of Venice and Istria for hundreds of years. At its western edge,
the zone studied by Stoianovich overlaps the Dalmatia analyzed by Vilfan.
Within that zone, Stoianovich singles out a distinctive feature of Ottoman
rule: the imposition of a command economy on urban areas. As compared
with the coastal Adriatic, the interior regions on which he concentrates followed coercion-intensive trajectories, with both landlords and armed
countrymen playing major parts in national politics. In the Balkans, the Ottoman Empire generally ruled indirectly through Turkish landlords, military
officers, removable officials, and tax farmers, all of whom enjoyed consider-

able autonomy within their own spheres but remained strictly responsible to the Sublime Porte. The region experienced frequent and violent rebellions, especially in periods when Ottoman power was contracting and the chances of profitable connections with western Europe were expanding.

Adopting the logic of central-place theory, Stoianovich shows that a relatively complete hierarchy of cities, centered on Constantinople-Istanbul, eventually extended into the Balkans. He likewise shows that a centralized (if incomplete) command economy pumped goods out of the countryside, up the hierarchy, and toward the capital. However intentionally, Ottoman authorities accomplished the same thing by imposing taxes and rents in rural areas that forced country people into urban markets and returned part of their income from those markets to the authorities. The state backed its regional representatives with armed force. Over the long run, however, the sheer development of the system made it advantageous for intermediaries to skim off larger portions of revenues nominally due to the central state, gain lifetime or hereditary control over their positions, and divert state power to their own advantage.

The presence of overlapping jurisdictions, the frequent pursuit of war, the position of the Balkans on the great overland route between western Europe and East Asia, and the entrepreneurial activities of Jews, Armenians, and Greeks, however, all attenuated any simple hierarchical action of the sultan's economy. Finally, after 1750, the peripheralization and sabotage of the command economy changed the relation between Istanbul and its hinterland, simultaneously transforming the Balkan economy and weakening the state's capacity to hold on to its possessions in the region. More so than any of our other essays, Stoianovich's analysis reveals the delicate interaction between state power and the organization of capital.

Peter Moraw on the Holy Roman Empire. German-speaking regions, in Moraw's account, had both vigorous cities and strong states. Nevertheless, the fundamental political structures of Germany bore the unmistakable stamp of princes and nobles and only ceded places to the bourgeoisie by drawing them into feudal social relations. Considerable variation, furthermore, appeared within German territory. The early division between the city-rich regions of the Rhine and Danube, on one side, and the more rural lands to the east, on the other, prefigured later maps of sovereignty; relatively autonomous free cities and imperial cities endured to the eighteenth and nineteenth centuries toward the west, and territorial cities holding substantial hinterlands under essentially feudal control prevailed further east. On the whole, cities grew more salient in German life from the thirteenth century on, with 1450–1650 being a crucial period for urban expansion and influence. At that time, urban magnates such as the Fuggers wielded great power in the empire. Still, insists Moraw, German cities never gained the upper hand; princes absorbed them into a system of power that retained its feudal cast.

Anders Andrén on Scandinavia. In the territory that eventually became Norway, Sweden, Denmark, and the Scandinavianized sections of Finland, warrior-monarchs founded many towns and established control over others early on. In many cases, urban settlements came into being as outposts for military and fiscal control of a fractious countryside. Although the expansion of the Baltic trade and the arrival of foreign (especially German) merchants enriched Scandinavian towns, royal agents and vassals maintained their priority in urban life. With commercial activity, however, cities became more interesting to kings as sources of taxes, especially excise and customs. In the process of expanding taxation, cities acquired charters, separate institutions, state-guaranteed monopolies, distinct identities, and a certain amount of power to bargain with the crown. On the whole, the weight of commerce, capital, urban oligarchies, and municipal rights grew lighter with movement north from Denmark. But in the period before 1550, nowhere in Scandinavia did municipal institutions or urban oligarchies wield significant power over the consolidated state.

Andrzej Wyrobisz on the Polish-Lithuanian State. If German states overshadowed their cities, the Polish state barely had any cities with which to contend. Its territory included vast agricultural domains, scattered villages, and few cities of importance. Only Gdánsk participated actively in the great circuits of international trade. Nobles and gentry dominated the state and elected its king. They also controlled most towns—founding, organizing, taxing, and legislating for them at their own convenience. The more perceptive nobles and gentry recognized a contradiction between their desires to draw state revenues from cities and to make cities serve the short-run needs of the aristocracy, but the Polish political system greatly favored the second outcome. The result was a further contradiction: a state under virtually complete control of a military aristocracy that was unable to mobilize a major military effort at a national scale.

Pablo Fernández Albaladejo on Aragon, Castile, and Spain. Pablo Fernández emphasizes the fallacy of treating "Spain" as a unitary state, for, until recent centuries, the Iberian peninsula hosted a conglomerate of dynastically linked monarchies. In Aragon, the great port of Barcelona bore a relation to the crown vaguely similar to the one linking Lisbon to Portugal. In Castile, Madrid remained the headquarters of a fractious landowning nobility, which, like the crown, profited first from the capture of Muslim lands within the peninsula and then from the creation of an overseas empire. Nevertheless, the oligarchies of Madrid and other Castilian cities enjoyed some autonomy, reinforced by their representation in the Cortes. In both Aragon and Castile, royal borrowing for military expenses eventually encouraged merchants to become rentiers rather than entrepreneurs, a change that made the crown all the more dependent on the empire's uncertain revenues.

Antonio Manuel Hespanha on Lisbon and Portugal. Portugal's history conforms more closely to classic models of state formation than do the histories of Italy, Poland, or the Dutch Republic. Yet even in Portugal, the correspondence was not close. An unchallenged metropolis, Lisbon, maintained tenuous relations with an agricultural hinterland and combined maintenance of the bulky national and imperial administrative apparatus with heavy involvement in world-spanning international trade. We should not exaggerate the distinction between administration and trade since such large governmental institutions as the *Casa da India* occupied themselves chiefly with commercial transactions; the monarchy, after all, drew a large share of all its income from profits on overseas trade.

At a pole far removed from Scandinavian or Polish monarchs, Portuguese kings had the great advantage of deriving much of their income and credit from the commerce of a single city, dominated by their agents. By the same token, however, the Portuguese crown remained vulnerable to a decline in Lisbon's commercial vigor, and Lisbon's commercial oligarchy retained power in royal affairs. Portugal's situation—more so than that of Scandinavia, Poland, Germany, Holland, or Italy—resembled the situation of today's oil-producing states: Ready revenue gave its rulers wide autonomy vis-à-vis the population they ruled, but it made them dependent on the continued flow of that revenue and on the people who produced it.

Marjolein 't Hart on Amsterdam, Holland, and the Dutch Republic. What a contrast with Poland and Germany! Marjolein 't Hart describes a contingent federation of city-states that formed in rebellion against Spanish centralization and fiscal pressure, created little durable national state apparatus, yet, on occasion, mounted enormous concerted military efforts. The Dutch drew on a deeply commercialized economy and cities occupying major positions in international trade. Self-renewing patricians who had made their money from trade and manufacturing ran those cities, named the deputies to the States General, took positions on foreign policy directly reflecting their particular commercial interests, and occasionally made war at their own initiative. Above all, Amsterdam (which the revolt turned into the preeminent Dutch city by cutting off the new state from the southern Netherlands and therefore from previously dominant Antwerp) weighed heavily in the republic's deliberations and inspired numerous coalitions among other cities to check its power.

Characteristically, members of the States General acted by unanimous consent and lacked any substantial fiscal power of their own. They chose The Hague as their meeting place precisely because the town was neutral territory, lacking municipal powers and commercial strength. But the superficial resemblance to Poland, with its *liberum veto* (rule of unanimous consent), masked a great difference: Although the Dutch nobility had some power in the interior provinces, a well-connected commercial and industrial bourgeoisie ran the cities and therefore the state.

GENERAL IMPLICATIONS

The geography and timing of changes in Europe's systems of cities and states suggest that the positions of cities within market hierarchies (international markets, regional markets, exclusively local markets, and so on) correlated approximately with their size, their demographic impact on their hinterlands, the extent of their capital accumulation, and their ability to build up and control an extended sphere of influence. It seems that these, in turn, strongly affected the relative attractiveness of different cities as sources of capital for building armies and for state formation, the autonomy of their ruling classes with respect to would-be and actual state-makers, and the strength of their representative institutions.

As a consequence, major trading cities and city-states mounted more effective resistance to the penetration of consolidated states than did cities in mainly agrarian regions. Most often, consolidated states only gained genuine control over major trading cities when the cities had begun to lose their predominant positions in international markets. Even then, important trading cities managed to build into the state apparatus more of their local and regional power structures than did local and regional market centers, and their presence in great numbers generally slowed down the formation of consolidated states.

Our accounts indicate that the focus of bargaining over the wherewithal of war strongly affected the forms of representation that emerged. In Portugal, with its strong reliance on overseas trade for royal income, we see few representative institutions of any kind except for the strong presence of Lisbon's municipal government as interlocutor; in Aragon, we observe Barcelona in a similar relation to the crown; in Castile, we witness the power invested in the Cortes, an instrument of great landlords and of eighteen cities' oligarchies. On the whole, urban institutions themselves seem to have become part of state structure more readily where capitalists predominated.

States in which capitalists and bourgeois institutions played commanding roles had great advantages when it came to the rapid mobilization of capital for expensive wars. But they remained vulnerable to withdrawals of capital, demands for commercial protection, and blockage of the waterways on which they relied so heavily. The Dutch Republic illustrates clearly the costs and benefits of capitalist dominance. The military advantage of such states nevertheless varied with the prevailing type of warfare: It was historically great for naval warfare, less so for artillery and cavalry, and an actual disadvantage in mass-army tactics.

Permanent military forces reduced (but by no means eliminated) surges in the demand for military means and thereby increased the advantage of states having long-term credit and large tax bases. States such as Prussia, France, and Britain—often considered models of effective state formation—combined the co-optation of landlords and merchants and built standing armies (and navies) in the time of mass-army tactics, from the Thirty Years' War to the Napoleonic Wars. The essays in this volume teach us that contrasts among the textbook examples occupied only a narrow band in the whole spectrum of European state formation.

The various combinations of coercion and capital across the European map show us multiple paths of state formation and an ultimate convergence on states with high concentrations of both capital and coercion. The relative availability of concentrated capital and concentrated means of coercion in different regions and periods significantly affected the organizational consequences of making war. Until recently, only those states that held their own in war with other states survived, and over the long run, the changing character of war gave the military advantage to states that could draw large, durable military forces from their own populations, which were increasingly consolidated states.

The coercion-capital reasoning also suggests some possible solutions to a series of historical problems concerning the histories of European states. What, for example, accounts for the roughly concentric pattern of European state formation, with large, autonomous states forming early on the periphery and regions of fragmented sovereignty enduring around the center? This pattern reflects the uneven spatial distribution of capital and therefore sets off the relatively large but capital-poor states that ringed the Continent from the swarm of smaller, capital-rich statelike entities that proliferated near its center. The contrast distinguishes exterior states (such as Sweden and Russia) that went through their formative years with relatively large concentrations of coercion and relatively small concentrations of capital both from interior states (such as Genoa and Holland) for which the opposite was true and from intermediate states (such as England and France) in which concentrations of capital and coercion grew side by side.

Again, why did European states vary so much with respect to the incorporation of urban oligarchies and institutions? States that had to contend from the start with urban oligarchies and institutions generally incorporated those oligarchies and institutions into the national structure of power. Representative institutions generally first appeared in Europe in two circumstances: (1) when local populations undertook difficult cooperative ventures, such as control of the sea in the Netherlands, and (2) when local, regional, or national governments bargained with groups of subjects who had enough power to inhibit the governments' operations but not enough power to take control of them. Where the governments in question were more or less autonomous states and the groups of subjects were urban oligarchies, municipal councils and similar institutions commonly became integral elements of the state structure. Where a single city predominated, a very effective form of state—the city-state or city-empire—emerged. The city-state and city-empire lost out, however, once mass armies recruited from the state's own population became crucial to successful warfare.

Why, despite obvious interests to the contrary, did rulers frequently accept the establishment of institutions representing the major classes within their jurisdictions? In fact, those institutions were the price and outcome of bargaining with different members of the subject population for the wherewithal of state activity, especially the means of war. Kings of England did not *want* a parliament to form and assume ever-greater power; they conceded power to barons and then to clergy, gentry, and bourgeois in the course of persuading them to raise the money for warfare.

Why did political and commercial power slide from the city-states and city-empires of the Mediterranean to the substantial states and relatively subordinated cities of the Atlantic? They lost out not only because the Atlantic and Baltic trade eclipsed that of the Mediterranean but also because control of massive, permanent armed force became increasingly crucial to a state's success in politics and economics alike. When, in the late sixteenth century, Spain, England, and Holland all started to send large, armed vessels into the Mediterranean for trade and piracy (the two were not so distinct), city-states such as Ragusa, Genoa, and Venice found that their previous reliance on speed, connections, and craftiness was no longer enough to evade massive commercial losses. The owners of big ships that were suitable for long ocean voyages won out commercially and militarily as well.

Why did city-states, city-empires, federations, and religious organizations lose their importance as the prevailing kinds of state in Europe? Two things happened in this regard. First, commercialization and capital accumulation in the larger states reduced the advantage enjoyed by small mercantile states, which had previously been able to borrow extensively, tax efficiently, and rely on their own sea power to hold off large, landbound states. Second, war eventually changed in a direction that made their small scale and fragmented sovereignty a clear disadvantage, and they lost to large states. Florentine and Milanese republics crumbled under the weight of the fifteenth and sixteenth centuries' military requirements. Indeed, a professional organizer of mercenary armies, Francesco Sforza, became duke of Milan in 1450 before his descendants lost their duchy to France (in 1499) and then to Spain (in 1535).

In Florence, a revived republic lasted until 1530, but then the combined forces of the pope and Emperor Charles V occupied its contado, forced a surrender of the city (despite fortifications recommended by a commission headed by Niccolò Machiavelli and built under the direction of Michelangelo Buonarroti), and installed the Medici as dukes. With the partial exceptions of Venice and Genoa, which retained some distinction as maritime powers, that era of large armies, heavy artillery, and extensive fortifications relegated all the Italian city-states to extinction, subordination, or perilous survival in the interstices of great powers.

Why did war shift from conquest for tribute and struggle among armed tribute-takers to sustained battles among massed armies and navies? This occurred for essentially the same reasons: With the organizational and technical innovations in warfare of the fifteenth and sixteenth centuries, states with access to large volumes of men and capital gained a clear advantage and either drove back the tribute-takers or forced them into patterns of extraction that built more durable state structures. During the fifteenth and sixteenth centuries, the Russian state made the transition as Ivan III and Ivan IV used awards of land to tie bureaucrats and soldiers to long-term service to the state. During the eighteenth century, the ability of populous states like Great Britain and France to draw mass armies from their own citizens gave them the means to overpower small states.

Prior to 1800, states had, for centuries, followed divergent paths as they fashioned military forces in situations of very different relations between capital and coercion. But if this is true, then standard debates about the transition from feudalism to capitalism and the rise of consolidated states have concentrated too heavily on the experiences of France, England, and a few other massive states, while neglecting a major determinant of the actual character of states. The relative importance of cities, financiers, and capital in a zone of state formation significantly affected the kinds of states that took shape there. Great landlords overwhelmed both capitalists and kings in Poland but were practically nonexistent in Holland. The "feudalism" of Florence and its contado differed so greatly from the "feudalism" of Hungary that it hardly seems worthwhile to cover them both by the same term.

After 1800, to be sure, the directions of change in European states altered considerably. All over the Continent, states converged on the consolidated type, with its centralized organization, direct rule, uniform field administration, circumscription of resources within the territory, and expanded control over cultural practices. Two forms of nationalism became the standard political programs: the *state-led* nationalism, in which rulers deliberately promoted one cultural definition of the nation and demanded that citizens give loyalty to the state priority over other loyalties, and *state-seeking* nationalism, in which the leaders of some population defined it as distinct, coherent, and therefore deserving of separate political status or even an autonomous state. In most states, the military now came under much firmer civilian control than in the past. As the capacity of states to extract and redistribute resources increased and as the very activities of extraction and redistribution involved rulers in bargaining with wider and wider circles of the population, states moved beyond their previous concentration on military activity and material support of rulers toward becoming general instruments of deliberate social intervention. This means they also became objects of struggles for influence over the state, unprecedented before 1800.

The unparalleled post-1800 interventionism of states and hence the increasing incentives for popular struggle to influence state personnel and policy rested on an expanded capacity to monitor, contain, seize, and redistribute resources within national territories. The relevant resources included not only goods and money but also land, natural resources, labor, technology, capital, and information. In recent years, that capacity has been declining. Especially with respect to labor, capital, technology, and information, international flows that baffle state power have increased enormously; the ability of European states to detect and counteract movements of illegal migrants, for example, has declined radically even as capital moves ever more freely from opportunity to opportunity, regardless of state interest. Furthermore, after several centuries in which capital and coercion converged under state command, they now seem to be separating; two of the world's great commercial powers—Germany and Japan—have insignificant military forces under their own command. It therefore seems possible that consolidated states will disintegrate or at least transmute into something very different. Although we have no reason to expect a reversion to states of an eighteenth-century style, the long range of state transformation we have surveyed at least hints at what might be involved in the deconsolidation of European states—or, for that matter, of states elsewhere.

Thus, for the period before 1800, the relative importance of cities, financiers, and capital in a zone of state formation significantly affected the kinds of states that took shape there. Mobilizing for war had significantly different effects, depending on the presence or absence of substantial capital and capitalists. Alternative paths of state formation led to different forms of resistance and rebellion, different state structures, and different fiscal systems. The chapters that follow analyze these alternative paths in fascinating detail.

Notes

Recruited and edited by Blockmans and Tilly, earlier versions of the essays by Andrén, Blockmans, Chittolini, Fernández Albaladejo, 't Hart, Hespanha, Moraw, Tilly, and Wyrobisz appeared in a special issue of *Theory and Society* (vol. 18, no. 5, September 1989). We are grateful to the journal for permission to reprint material from that issue. Having had to compress the papers mercilessly to fit the journal's page limits, we invited the authors to revise and expand their contributions for this volume. Andrén,

Chittolini, Hespanha, and Moraw chose to reprint their papers with no more than minor editorial changes, while Blockmans, Fernández Albaladejo, 't Hart, Wyrobisz, and Tilly undertook major revisions. Aware of an important geographic gap, Blockmans and Tilly persuaded Sergij Vilfan and Traian Stoianovich to write new syntheses on the Balkans. Andrén, Blockmans, 't Hart, Stoianovich, Tilly, Vilfan, and Wyrobisz wrote their papers in English, with Tilly editing them. Blockmans and Tilly translated Chittolini's paper from Italian, Tilly translated Hespanha's paper from French, and Blockmans translated Moraw's paper from German. Tilly translated the early version of Fernández Albaladejo's paper from Spanish, but Javier Rambaud provided English translations of new and altered material.

1. Niccolò Machiavelli, *The Prince and the Discourses* (New York: Modern Library, 1940), p. 18. I will cite specific quotations and facts directly. For more general references to authors and subjects, see the annotated bibliography at the book's end.

2. John A. Hall and G. John Ikenberry, *The State* (Minneapolis: University of Minnesota Press, 1989).

3. Gianfranco Poggi, *The State: Its Nature, Development and Prospects* (Stanford: Stanford University Press, 1990), p. 34.

4. Charles Tilly, ed., *The Formation of National States in Western Europe* (Princeton: Princeton University Press, 1975), p. 12.

5. Jan de Vries, *European Urbanization, 1500–1800* (Cambridge, Mass.: Harvard University Press, 1984), pp. 160–164.

2

Cities, "City-States," and Regional States in North-Central Italy

GIORGIO CHITTOLINI

ITALY PROVIDES A significant, eloquent example of the difficulties encountered by state formation in the midst of numerous and flourishing urban centers.[1] A unitary Italian state only formed in the latter half of the nineteenth century. Although this tardiness was due to many other factors besides the strength of Italy's cities, the roots of a strong municipal tradition dating back to the Middle Ages certainly held back the forces tending toward the country's territorial unification. Most notably during the later Middle Ages and the Renaissance, at precisely the time when the great western monarchies were consolidating, the political system of central and northern Italy was characterized by the city-states' great fragmentation and spirit of autonomy. This situation constituted an insuperable obstacle to any prospect of national unification and a serious barrier even to the formation of smaller state organizations such as the regional states into which Italy later consolidated.

The Italian experience would seem less important if the relation between city system and state formation were conceived as linking (a) urban centers having commercial and financial functions and the political character they imply with (b) various formations, such as principalities, monarchies, and states, having different and conflicting political and economic objectives and intent on expansion, conquest, and territorial unification, sustained not so much by commercial as by agrarian and military social forces.[2]

The extraordinary energy and growing capacity of urban centers led paradoxically to the early elimination from central and northern Italy's political firmament of any *superior*—king, emperor, or prince. The cities transformed themselves precociously into city-states with corresponding territorial dimensions and political functions. In Italy from the twelfth to fifteenth centuries it was the cities that inspired and pursued conquest and state formation, although on a limited scale. They did so partly as a consequence of features that distinguished them from other European cities: they were foci not only of mercantile and artisanal classes and interests but also of "feudal," agrarian, and military ones. Only in a few centers (typically those with the most pronounced commercial and financial character, located geographically on the margins of the city-state system) was the impulse toward the formation of territorial states weak or belated. Nevertheless they, too, heard the call, which generalized through the whole of central and northern Italy during the first decades of the fifteenth century.

The dialectic of city system and state formation thus has peculiar characteristics in Italy, forming less of a contrast than elsewhere in Europe. The role of the Italian city in processes of state unification, and consequently its position within regional states, seems distinctly different from that of cities in other parts of the continent.

The following pages will pursue these questions: (1) What were the distinctive features of Italy's communal cities? (2) What was the place of city-states in the formation of those larger territorial and centralized systems that developed in Italy between the thirteenth and fifteenth centuries? (3) What accounts for the slower and contested development of the choice to establish a state and a dependent territory in some centers (notably Florence and Venice) that were more closely tied than other Italian cities to the medieval commercial system of Europe and the Mediterranean? (4) What position did cities, whether subordinated or "dominant," maintain in the regional states of early modern times?

DISTINCTIVE FEATURES OF ITALY'S CITIES

To evaluate to what degree "the city—a general phenomenon in Europe and elsewhere—could develop a life style in Italy, or a large part of it, so different from that in the cities at the other side of the Alps, less in economic affairs than in regard to politics and justice,"[3] it is important to stress again that in general Italian communes "precociously achieved full autonomy with respect to any higher authority" while "municipalities north of the Alps, whatever their juridical base of self-government or their degree of autonomy, never became totally independent of their lords."[4] Strong or weak, the Empire, kingdoms, and principalities continued to constitute the territorial structures in which cities north of the Alps found themselves embedded. In central and northern Italy, however, these structures did not succeed in imposing themselves or even in acquiring firm roots. Territorial principalities did not succeed because they were hampered and eroded in their consolidation by the smaller lordships that grew from the proliferation of *castra* and the formation of large domains, and by the rapid political growth of the urban centers.[5] Nor did the kingdom of Italy take permanent roots; it was unable to build up structures of sufficient solidity and a dynastic tradition, and never became entirely emancipated but was instead precociously reabsorbed into the empire. The empire itself did not succeed; as early as the second half of the twelfth and first decades of the thirteenth century, after the failure of Barbarossa's and Frederick II's attempted imperial restoration, it was excluded from the peninsula as an effective political force.[6]

It was therefore the cities, grown into strong municipal structures, that came to the fore as the chief, if not the only, actors in north and central Italy's political organization and territorial consolidation. From the twelfth and thirteenth centuries onward, a political system formed that was based on city-states: autonomous, relatively large, and internally compact, each bordering the next without serious discontinuity. As Otto of Freising noted at the time, Italy became "totally divided up among cities"; he further observed that rural lordships did not attain any important weight, being dispersed, uncoordinated by royal or princely structures, relegated to the margins of urban regions, and forced to submit to the *imperium* of cities.[7]

These *civitates* were the few centers, almost all of them ancient in origin, that were able to keep on trying to impose themselves as organizational nuclei for large territories through the high Middle Ages. This vocation was often inherited from their former position as *municipia* in Roman territorial organization. Ecclesiastical functions such as a bishop's chair were added to reinforce their position. From their origins, this mixture of functions, powers, and social classes, both rural and urban, did not oppose Italian cities to the surrounding countryside but instead created a close symbiosis. This was the basis of the cities' strong capacity for influence and for polarization in themselves of interests and social forces that might have furthered the conquest and creation of the *contado*.[8]

The number of *civitates* was limited. In comparison with the rest of Europe, only a few Italian cities developed autonomous municipal institutions and domination over a *contado*—essentially those that had already had such functions in the early days of municipal life in continuation of their traditional positions as Roman *municipia* and bishops' seats. Only these centers had the title of city, in the old and well-established meaning of capital of both a civil and an ecclesiastical district.

During the Middle Ages numerous other centers (such as Monza, Vigevano, and Prato), that achieved demographic and economic importance with thousands of inhabitants, manufacturing establishments, and trade, never obtained the title of city because they found themselves included in districts, *contadi*, and bishoprics headed by another urban center; despite many efforts, struggles, and confrontations, they never acquired the strength to change the old structure of urban districts and create the indispensable requisite for the honor to which they aspired: a space of their own. Promotions to the rank of city, which occurred frequently in Europe as a whole during the late Middle Ages, were extremely rare in Italy. Moreover, the occasional concession of the title *civitas* ran the risk of being only a name and of fading quickly into obsolescence if (as happened in some cases) it was not sustained by its indispensable correlate: the clearly acknowledged and autonomous domination of a substantial territory.

This explains the relatively low number of cities in Italy, and their greater scarcity and dispersion where their political growth was most impressive. In the Po Valley and Tuscany, for example, in a space of nearly 100,000 square kilometers only a few dozen municipalities enjoy the title of city.[9] Accordingly, the urban districts (*contadi*) are large. In that area, average sizes are 1,500 to 2,000 square kilometers, larger in the cases of the biggest cities (Milan, Bologna, and Florence) and with minima that rarely drop below 1,000 kilometers. This situation differed greatly from that beyond the Alps, where only Zurich and Nürnberg exceeded the limit of 1,000 square kilometers while even the strongest other cities had territories of a few hundred kilometers, and many had a few dozen.

It is also characteristic of the great Italian cities that they succeeded in exercising extensive powers in their districts, which were well organized, compact, and controlled in a way that was unthinkable beyond the Alps. It would be hard to find a transalpine equivalent of an Italian city's *contado*. What we might find is a mosaic of small territories in which a city exercised rights concerning taxes and justice, and other territories in which it had minor rights exercised in competition with various claimants. The influence of a transalpine city remained weak vis-à-vis the prerogatives of lords, individual urban families, or ecclesiastical institutions. Still more indirect is the influence that large European cities sought to obtain—sometimes in vast and distant areas—by granting citizenship, enacting commercial and tax agreements, regulations for food supply, protectorates, wardships, and controls over waterways, thus defining what has been called their *Stadtraum*. This influence always remained limited to some kinds of activity: it never excluded the presence and influence in the same area of other powerful lords and potentates, who were sometimes their political and military rivals.

Control over the Italian *contado,* in contrast, was much more firm and complete. Italian cities strove systematically to eliminate all intermediary and indirect forms of government and to organize their territories into lower-level districts run by officials from the city (*podestà, vicari*); the law, the legislation, and the fiscal, juridical, and administrative rules of the city were extended to the whole territory. This process formed a unitary body in which the city was the head (as in the famous image) and the countryside, organically and inseparably linked, the members.[10] Strict economic control paralleled the territorial administration. It extended to matters of commercial and industrial policy and above all to agriculture and landed property.

The *contado* thus became the natural area of expansion for urban property, which underwent continuous expansion under intensive tutelage from the city.[11] Urban landlords, in any case, had contributed to the formation of communes from their very origins.[12] All in all, as has often been pointed out, the city and the city-state represented a set of classes and interests in which, besides mercantile and artisanal actors, other forces were interested in an expansionist policy and strict control of the surrounding territory.

CITY-STATES AND LARGER SYSTEMS

All this helps explain the differences between Italy and Europe in the territorial recomposition of the late Middle Ages—or, in other words, the different place of cities in the formation of the larger and more compact political systems that can be observed in Europe as a whole during that period. North of the Alps, we generally observe antagonism between cities, on one side, and other political forces, sovereigns, and territorial princes. The political entities initiated changes in which smaller and even larger cities did not want to participate, and which they opposed and resisted.

Situations on the two sides of the Alps differed radically. Vis-à-vis the dukes of Burgundy, Flemish cities defended their acquired position of quasi-independence with great energy and determination. Vis-à-vis the king of France, small provincial urban centers could only aspire to somewhat greater autonomy. German cities differed in other ways, perhaps more comparable to Italian ones; but even the *Freie Städte, Reichsstädte,* or *Landesstädte* confronted potentates who were frequently hostile, and who were strongly oriented to policies of extension and consolidation of their authority over urban centers. The German cities did not, as a rule, tend to form analogous and opposed territorial organizations; such a program would in any case have been difficult to realize, and would probably not always have fit the economic and political orientations of their leading classes.

The German situation left to cities the objective of preserving the liberties that the constitution (*Verfassung*) guaranteed them in relation to the other estates (*Stände*). Hence the character of the urban leagues (*Städtebünde*) for the defense of common economic and political interests against rival interests.[13] Hence also the importance of estates and representative assemblies, which were institutional spaces for meeting and dialogue made necessary by the coexistence within the same political system of different forces and interests. In a word, cities tended to oppose the formation of states and did not themselves initiate the process. City and state formation are an opposed pair in the lexicon of European political history.

The construction of states, as they formed in central and northern Italy from the twelfth to the fifteenth century, was on the contrary the work of cities as political organizations imbued with an interest in territorial conquest;

confrontations took place between antagonistic city-states and not, or only marginally, with other political forces such as landlords or the Empire. Urban leagues also appeared in Italy, but as a rule they opposed towns to other towns, not towns to princes and lords. These conflicts, however, had as their object conquest and subordination of the territories of other city-states, which does not differentiate them from conflicts fought elsewhere by aristocrats or feudal actors. Leading classes in the towns were not only interested in commercial and industrial assets, but also aimed at territorial expansion. (Later we shall discuss the few centers that were exceptions to this rule.) Italian political powers did not experiment at all successfully with forms of economic organization that were distinct from political forms. Their means of pursuing commercial objectives, food supply, or the control of production were oriented chiefly to political conquest and subjugation of the territory.

This background helps explain Italian politics, especially in the Po region, from the twelfth to the fifteenth century, with their endless struggles between individual cities or groups of cities; these struggles could only end with the total subjection of one city and its *contado* to a stronger one. From this resulted the formation of territorial aggregates containing several cities, aggregrates that were very labile, predestined to fall into fragments and to recompose in various shapes. It proved difficult to build up a solid system without external actors or determinants, since the existing system resulted from power relations within the urban world as they underwent hundreds of turnovers, alternating and contradictory phases, expressing a changing, uncertain hierarchy of power, hegemony, and alliances among centers.[14]

The same circumstances help account for the unusual position of the *podestà*, a figure whose Italian form did not appear in other European cities, and the peculiarities of the *signoria* within cities.[15] They also lie behind the exhausting, fluctuating struggles over the creation of dynastic states round major urban lordships in the Po region, where all these conditions had their strongest and most durable roots. The *signorie* of the Estensi, Scaligeri, Gonzaga, and Carraresi were among the most enduring. Above all, the Visconti succeeded in adding the energy of a lucky, aggressive dynasty to its base city Milan's old and very strong tradition of widespread influence and capacity to expand. In these dynastic states, the lord was more an organizer, mediator, and coordinator of urban interests than a statemaker aiming at the absorption of cities into his own different territorial organizations.

COMMERCIAL CENTERS AND STATE FORMATION

Some great and strong centers such as Venice and Genoa (and, to a lesser degree, Florence and Pisa) were little involved in these conflicts, considering their importance. Although these centers likewise seem to have been aiming at strong political authority, they aimed less at large-scale territorial conquests than at an expansion appropriate to their commercial and industrial calling and sustained by their secure position within the Mediterranean and European commercial systems. These different aims help explain their interest in broader and more distant targets in southern Italy or the Levant, and their involvement in conflicts and wars that were no less bitter than those fought along the Po or across the Apennines. They fought especially at sea, aiming at commercial hegemony, at colonies and maritime bases, at commercial agreements and pacts rather than at the stable occupation of territory, at least in the peninsula.[16]

The internal political evolution of these cities also differed from that of northern Italy's interior cities. Their republican institutions showed more vitality and capacity to resist, and the *signoria* was weak or absent. They met the need for internal stability by other means, chiefly through oligarchy. Their commercial patriciates were powerful, their corporate structures strong and politically active; in all these ways, these Italian cities more greatly resembled centers elsewhere in Europe.[17]

For a long time, and with relatively little variation from case to case, these cities showed little interest in territorial expansion; instead they pursued a policy of agreements and alliances aimed at the maintenance around their borders of free communes and small urban or rural lordships. Toward the end of the fourteenth century and (especially) the beginning of the fifteenth, however, the formation of robust, aggressive princely states changed the situation suddenly. The situation became more serious when the Visconti, and in particular Gian Galeazzo Visconti, led a determined, effective policy of territorial expansion, aiming to solidify their hegemony over north-central Italy by means of a great state—a new kingdom, some said, in which a stable monarchial order would be imposed on the restless urban world.

More than in the past, a confrontation between a city system and a statemaker seemed to come into the open in Italy in ways that other European regions had already experienced. On the one hand, a prince sought military conquest, the acquisition of new territory, and reorganization in terms of strong monarchial centralization. On the other hand, urban leagues (with Florence in the forefront as the great animator of resistance) formed to defend a system based on the federal order of towns, republican liberties, and the ideals of civic life.[18]

The firm resistance of this urban world and its determined opposition to absorption into state structures that were so different from the old tradition of municipal liberty played a major part in the defeat of the Visconti and in their definitive containment within Lombardy during the early fifteenth century. In similar conflicts, other European urban centers were unable to mobilize equal economic and military force. But the other, possibly even more significant, difference from the situation beyond the Alps was the gradual transformation of some of the same greater commercial centers into territorial states. This did not happen in Lucca or Siena, which were too small. It was only partly true of Genoa, which limited its territorial expansion to the arc of the Ligurian coast; Genoa was favored by its geographical location, protected by the Apennine wall, and sheltered even more by the broad, intense system of relations and alliances in which the city and its aristocracy were embedded.[19]

Florence and Venice, however, displayed the same strong tendency to create large and solidly organized dominions around themselves. In the fourteenth century, Florence had already extended its control over various centers in Tuscany, from Pistoia to Arezzo, from Prato to San Gimignano and Volterra, using forms that stood midway between a true *dominium* and a simple protectorate. Over about thirty years during and just after the period of Milanese expansion under Gian Galeazzo Visconti, however, Florence occupied various other territories, notably the Pisano, Cortona, and some places in the Apennines; it expanded its territory to about 12,000 square kilometers. More important, it launched an administrative and fiscal reorganization designed to secure much more effective control over its state.[20]

For centuries, Venice had felt no need to dominate the Terraferma; it occupied only a small strip of land protecting the lagoons, and from 1339 onward the Trevigiano. During the early fifteenth century, however, it transformed itself into Italy's mightiest territorial power. The decision was painful and controversial. It divided the Venetian ruling class in bitter antagonism because it meant a radical reversal with respect to the secular political orientations of the *Commune Veneciarum*.[21] Yet most people felt the change was inevitable. From 1404 to 1428 Venice conquered Vicenza, Feltre, Belluno, Verona, Padua, the Friuli and, beyond Lake Garda, the provinces of Brescia and Bergamo. These conquests brought Venice's boundaries within fifteen miles of Milan and brought together a territory of some 30,000 square kilometers, which comprised its Terraferma state until the end of the Republic in 1797.

The formation of a large territorial domain did not mean for Florence, much less for Venice, renunciation of their old calling as mercantile centers. On the contrary, it was conceived as a means of supporting the free, unthreatened continuation of their intense commercial activity. The new conditions, however, necessarily changed the character of the great commercial centers as they became capitals of major territorial complexes. New political orientations matured and new economic interests (such as agrarian investment, the exercise of offices in the dominion, and the control of ecclesiastical benefices) came to the fore. During the sixteenth and seventeenth centuries, the weakening of their potential as commercial and industrial centers made this side of the cities' character ever more visible. In fact, these new functions contributed greatly to the prosperity of Venice and Florence during the early modern period; in the case of Venice, they even aided the long preservation of the old republican institutions.

As for relations between Florence and Venice, on the one hand, and the state as it developed during the Renaissance, on the other, these Italian cities followed different trajectories from other great European commercial centers. They were not subordinated, even as privileged cities, to other state structures; that development would be hard to imagine in Italy. Instead, they transformed themselves into large regional states. In the context of the whole continent's experience, this is an unusual outcome, one that is hard to compare with the Helvetic Confederation, the Hanseatic League, German imperial cities, or, later, the United Provinces. But Florence and Venice were able in this peculiar way to acquire firm guarantees for their independence and their potential for economic activity.

CITIES IN REGIONAL STATES

Thus the formation of a system of regional states, which often took the form of principalities, did not mean that cities decayed in the face of rising states. Although the remarkable trajectory of the independent city-state came to an end almost everywhere, its heritage still left a strong imprint on the Renaissance political order. An established historiographical tradition sees the figure of the prince and princely state structures as the most characteristic features of fifteenth- and sixteenth-century Italy. In reality, the Renaissance prince was less the result of a process directed toward the establishment of solid absolutist structures than of a personality capable of holding together a scattered, disaggregated, fragile political order: thanks to personal talent, without the support of specific, consolidated instruments of government. These are the features of Machiavelli's *Prince*.[22] In this political system, old municipalities and their ruling classes actually kept a preponderant influence.

Lamentations about lost "liberties" certainly sounded loudly in the cities. Indeed, the establishment of principalities and regional states implied the creation of new governmental institutions that limited the autonomy of cities. The old free towns found themselves reduced to the status of "subordinate cities," of provinces within regional states. Yet belonging to a princely state did not force the old leading groups to renounce their fundamental interests and objectives or to subordinate them to new political programs. In exchange for the authority they exercised, the prince or the dominant city provided for the old needs of the urban world, such as internal peace, external defense, and a new "Italian equilibrium." It was in fact these needs that, from the thirteenth century onward, had led many cities to seek a more stable and secure order in overlordship.

In fifteenth-century regional states and principalities, what stands out is the division and complementarity of functions between a central authority and local political institutions. The situation was now therefore not so different from that in other European countries having very different traditions.[23] Yet in Italy this "dualism," which we often find in institutions of the early modern state, meant essentially a polarization between prince and cities, while feudal lords and smaller towns had much less weight. The role as full-fledged city-states inherited by cities from the municipal tradition turned out to be strong; it could be maintained to a large degree in the new state systems. The stabilization and legitimation of the preeminent position they had acquired compensated for the loss of independence.[24]

In this sense, the general political orientations of the new states, whether principalities or republics, did not break with the old ways. Especially in matters of local government, old communal institutions, such as statutes, councils, and offices, were maintained beside those of the central power. Legally or practically, large responsibilities were left to cities—a distribution of power that some historians have called a "diarchy." In particular, cities maintained extensive control over their old *contado;* this control was perhaps their greatest bulwark and chief privilege.[25]

Just as the old city-states in all regions became provinces in the new regional states, so the cities gained recognition as so many provincial capitals. They were not simply neutral administrative centers, but organs disposing of their own powers and of the authority to exercise them. In matters of jurisdiction, their statutes, courts, and colleges of jurists held primacy throughout the province. In fiscal affairs, municipal institutions influenced the assessment and collection of rural taxes as they did for food supply, water, roads, and so on. To the preeminence of the city in the *contado* was added the privileged position of citizens by comparison with *comitatini:* in economic activities through the recognized rights of urban corporations; in fiscal matters, "civil" goods were not as heavily taxed as "rural" ones. In judicial action, citizens were favored over the *rustici laboratores terrarum.* As a consequence, urban-landed property penetrated more deeply into the *contado* during the fifteenth and sixteenth centuries.[26]

It was chiefly on these foundations that Italian provincial cities maintained such a strong position in the modern era. They reveal an economic and social organization in which landed, "territorial" interests prevailed. Certainly commercial and industrial activities still constituted a significant component of many cities' economies. Within the new regional states, we can see some reorientations and shifts in productive activities and commercial roles; the cities discussed earlier experienced limits and difficulties,[27] but these problems did not restrain or strongly affect their economic potential.

These important sectors of the urban economy, however, were not by themselves sufficient to make the city, vis-à-vis the state, the interpreter and representative of mercantile or industrial interests alone. Although communal Italy did not have representative assemblies analogous to those Estates that were elsewhere the loci of negotiations with the prince, an intense, continuous dialogue went on between subordinate cities and regional states, especially during the fifteenth and sixteenth centuries.[28] In these contacts, urban councils, merchants' colleges, or various craft organizations often spoke with regard to commercial interests and various artisanal or industrial activities, above all concerning taxation. Problems related to administrative and fiscal control of the territory and to the juridical and fiscal condition of landed property, however, were much more widely discussed. These discussions testified to the strong rural and territorial markings of the urban physiognomy. The crisis of the urban economy in the sixteenth and seventeenth centuries could only accentuate this feature; a dense and still mighty urban network became steadily more inert and lethargic: the "hundred cities of silence" evoked by Gramsci.[29]

CONCLUSIONS

Similar observations apply to cities such as Venice, Florence, Genoa, and Milan, which during the Renaissance retained their places as centers of European trade, and which also carried on vigorous manufacturing activity. These centers (which, not accidentally, found themselves promoted to the rank of state capitals in the new political order) maintained positions of considerable strength, and contributed greatly to the image of the Italian political system as being still dominated by cities. But the sources of their strength were to be found more and more in their preeminence as political capitals rather than in the vitality of their economic role. This position survived without substantial modification, even after the crisis of the early sixteenth century. During the Italian wars, the weak, fragmented political system of the peninsula was confronted by the great European powers, which initiated the period of "foreign preponderance." The pressures and conquests of France, of the Empire, and then, more durably, of Spain had substantial effects and doubtless produced significant reshuffling: the definitive fall of the Florentine republic, the submission of the Sienese republic to the new grand duchy of the Medici, the substantial reduction of Bologna's and Perugia's "liberties" within the papal state.

These episodes could give the feeling of an irreversible crisis of republican and urban liberties, and so they were presented in a long historiographic tradition as the symbolic end of a glorious historical era.[30] After four centuries without *superiores* during which these anomalous and vital city-states could develop, the Italian urban world—with the exception of Venice—found itself subjugated, although in a new organization and a changed context, to the influence or dominion of great foreign political forces: a development not so different from what in previous centuries had happened in other regions of Europe that earlier had an equally fragmented urban tradition.

But even then no serious conflict arose between statemaker and city system in Italy for many reasons: the marginal position of Italian provinces in the whole of the Spanish empire, which a certain international equilibrium guaranteed; the propensity of the Madrid government to do little for effective state integration; the absence of religious or economic antagonisms that might have provoked conflicts similar to those occurring elsewhere (between Spain and the cities of the Netherlands, for example). The lives of great Italian centers, both those entirely absorbed into the Spanish system and those, like Florence, under its influence, could go on in far-reaching autonomy.

A historiographic tradition with distant origins in nationalism and the Risorgimento insisted on the grave consequences of foreign domination: loss of liberty, taxation, economic crisis, hispanization, cultural decadence. Recent research, less conditioned by the "fundamental presuppositions of nineteenth century historiography that claimed an incompatibility in principle between civil progress and national dependence," has pointed out that Italian states enjoyed relatively wide areas of autonomous government and the opportunity to develop their own forms of social and political life.[31]

Foreign domination was not responsible, or at least not solely responsible, for the decadence and the crises. Decline seems rather to have resulted, as some economic historians have pointed out, from the progressive and slow loss of the role played by the great centers in the medieval economic system.[32] They became increasingly inert, marginal, and secondary in the new economic world system, especially in the seventeenth century, and were unable to organize their production in new forms.[33] Venice had increasing trouble maintaining its commercial position between Europe and the Levant, fell outside the great streams of traffic, and could only find partial relief in the renewal of its manufacturing. Florence became ever more wrapped up in itself as its economy weakened steadily. During the seventeenth century Genoa lost the very strong position it had held in the Spanish financial system. Milan turned to new forms of "rural" economy, in both manufacturing and agriculture, but only in the long run did this shift stir innovation.[34] Within Italy of the late Middle Ages the cities had exercised the vital function of mediating between the agrarian economy of the south and centers of manufacturing in the north; even that function gradually wore out.[35]

The prominent position that great Italian urban centers continued to hold throughout the modern period depended on past achievements, on a *rentier* role, one might say, derived from their territorial and agrarian advantages. It did not depend on effective vitality or a capacity to tap new energy from the old resources that had fed urban growth in the past and that continued to sustain the prosperity of other great centers in the continent.

Hence, for example, the difference in economic and social style between Venice and Amsterdam.[36] Hence, again, the frequently mentioned impression of weakness, of "decadence" of Italian city-based states as compared with the place of cities in other European states. In comparison not only with the great monarchies, but even with republican and federal political organizations that had strong urban centers such as those in the Netherlands, Germany, the Baltic, and the Atlantic, Italian city-based states proved poor in capacity and willingness to take the international economic and political initiative, partly because of the lack of commercial stimuli, and partly because of high costs.[37] The case of Venice shows this clearly: it belonged among the most autonomous and active states of its size, yet could not, in the long run, sustain a high-cost, high-obligation role in the Levant. The internal order also offers a picture of relative inertia and passivity, due to the absence of reforms and the heaviness of the mechanisms for social and political change.

The imprint of the city-state, the old capacity of the Italian city to penetrate its territory broadly and deeply, and to construct solid political systems to protect its territory and itself, thus remained clearly visible until the end of the old regime, even when the old, specific forms of economic vitality of towns dwindled and were not replaced (as they were elsewhere in Europe) by other commercial or industrial activities.[38] On the eve of the eighteenth-century enlightened reforms, "agriculture and the countryside formed the heart of the problems which the Italian economy and society were facing" either in the sense that "the major forces of conservatism were nested there," or in the sense that in them "could be found all the dynamics that matured in the course of the eighteenth century."[39]

When the nineteenth century finally brought the constitution of a national monarchy in Italy, the initiative would come from a state, Savoy-Piedmont, whose social and political structure was different, and of less glorious tradition, from that of the city-based states.[40] Inversely, the rapid fall of the city-based states signals the absence of effective power to sustain them, even though their long survival testified for centuries to the vitality of medieval urban civilization.

Notes

1. This article was translated from the Italian by Wim Blockmans and Charles Tilly.

2. See Wim Blockmans, "Economic Network and State Formation: A Comparative View," presented to the conference on "Stadt-Bürgertum-Staat," Bielefeld, November-December 1985, and Charles Tilly, "War Making and State Making as Organized Crime," in Peter B. Evans, Dietrich Rueschemeyer, and Theda Skocpol, editors, *Bringing the State Back In* (Cambridge: Cambridge University Press, 1985).

3. E. Sestan, "La città comunale italiana dei secoli XI–XIII nelle sue note caratteristiche rispetto al movimento comunale europeo," Eleventh International Congress of Historical Sciences, Stockholm, *Rapports, III, Moyen Age* (Göteborg,

Stockholm, & Uppsala: Almquist & Wiksell, 1960), 75–79; reprinted in Sestan, *Italia medievale* (Naples: Edizioni Scientifiche Italiane, 1968), 93.

4. N. Ottokar, "Comuni," in *Enciclopedia Italiana*, XI (1931), and *Studi comunali e fiorentini* (Florence: La Nuova Italia, 1948), 41.

5. G. Sergi, "L'Europa carolingia e la sua dissoluzione," in N. Tranfaglia and M. Firpo, editors, *La Storia, II: Il Medioevo: Popoli e strutture politiche* (Turin: UTET, 1986), 231–262, and especially 250–258.

6. G. Tabacco, *Egemonie sociali e strutture politiche nel Medioevo italiano* (Turin: Einaudi, 1979), 190ff., 266ff.

7. Ottonis and Rehevini (G. Waitz and B. de Simson, editors), "Gesta Friderici I imperatoris," in *Monumenta Germaniae Historica: Scriptores rerum germanicarum in usum scholarium* (Hannover & Leipzig: Hahn, 1912), 116.

8. Sestan, *Italia medievale*, 105ff.

9. For the much denser urban network of some French regions, see the data in Philippe Contamine, "La noblesse et les villes dans la France de la fin du Moyen Age," *Bollettino dell'Istituto storico italiano per il Medioevo* 94 (1985), 467–468.

10. A. I. Pini, "Dal comune città-stato al comune ente amministrativo," in G. Galasso, editor, *Storia d'Italia IV* (Turin: UTET, 1981), reprinted in Pini, *Città, comuni, corporazioni nel medioevo italiano* (Bologna: Il Mulino, 1986), esp. 76ff.; see also Giorgio Chittolini, "Signorie rurali e feudi alla fine del Medioevo," in *Storia d'Italia*, IV, 597–613, and R. Bordone, "La città comunale," in P. Rossi, editor, *Modelli di città* (Turin: Einaudi, 1987).

11. G. Cherubini, *Signori, contadini, borghesi: Richerche sulla società italiana del basso Medioevo* (Florence: La Nuova Italia, 1974), 51–120; P. Cammarosano, *La campagne italiane dell'età comunale (metà sex. XI–metà sec. XIV)* (Turin: Loescher, 1974); F. Bocchi, "Città e campagne ell'Italia centro-settentrionale (sec. XII–XIV)," *Storia della città* 10 (1986), 101–104.

12. Philip Jones, "Economia e società nell'Italia medievale: la leggenda della borghesia," in Ruggiero Romano and C. Vivanti, editors, *Storia d'Italia, Annali, I: Dal feudalismo al capitalismo* (Turin: Einaudi, 1978), esp. 200ff.; cf. Ruggiero Romano, *Fra due crisi: l'Italia del Rinascimento* (Turin: Einaudi, 1971).

13. H. Maurer, editor, *Kommunale Bundnisse Oberitaliens und Oberdeutschlands im Vergleich* (Sigmaringen: Thorbecke, 1978); Bordone, "La città comunale."

14. Sestan, *Italia Medievale*, 116ff.; G. M. Varanini, "Dal comune allo stato regionale," in N. Tranfaglia and M. Firpo, editors, *La Storia, II: Il Medioevo: Popoli e strutture politiche* (Turin: UTET, 1986), 693–724.

15. Sestan, *Italia Medievale*, 117–120; Tabacco, *Egemonie sociali*, 352ff.

16. The process follows the model developed by Charles Tilly, "La dimensione spaziale nella formazione degli stati," *Passato e Presente* 5 (1986), 143; Blockmans, "Economic Network," 7. For the relations between Italy's seafaring centers and the interior see, e.g., A. Vasina, "Ravenna e Venezia nel processo di penetrazione in Romagna della Serenissima (secoli XIII–XIV)," in D. Bolognesi, editor, *Ravenna in età veneziana* (Ravenna: Longo, 1986), 11–29.

17. Lauro Martines, *Power and Imagination: City-States in Renaissance Italy* (New York: Knopf, 1979), 170ff.

18. D. M. Bueno de Mesquita, *Gian Galeazzo Visconti, Duke of Milan (1351–1402): A Study in the Political Career of an Italian Despot* (Cambridge: Cambridge

University Press, 1941); Hans Baron, *The Crisis of the Early Italian Renaissance: Civic Humanism and Republican Liberty in an Age of Classicism and Tyranny* (Princeton: Princeton University Press, 1966); N. Valeri, *L'Italia nel'età dei principati* (Milan: Mondadori, 1966), 208ff.

19. Jacques Heers, *Gênes au XVe siècle: Activité économique et problèmes sociaux* (Paris: SEVPEN, 1961).

20. Giorgio Chittolini, *La formazione dello stato regionale e le istituzioni del contado* (Turin: Einaudi, 1979), 293–352.

21. See G. Cozzi, "Politica, Società, Istituzioni," in G. Cozzi and M. Knapton, *La Repubblica di Venezia nell'età moderna* (Turin: UTET, 1986; vol. XII/1 of G. Galasso, editor, *Storia d'Italia*), 3ff.

22. Federico Chabod, *Del Principe di Niccolò Machiavelli* (Turin: Einaudi, 1964; originally published in 1925), 31ff.; Perry Anderson, *Lineages of the Absolutist State* (London: NLB, 1974), 163–168.

23. G. Chittolini, editor, *La crisi degli ordinamenti comunali e le origini dello stato del Rinascimento* (Bologna: Il Mulino, 1979), introduction, 34–40; Chittolini, *La formazione dello stato regionale*, xxxff.

24. For a comparison with the position of cities in other state structures, see Bernard Guénée, *L'Occident aux XIVe et XVe siècles: Les Etats* (Paris: Presses Universitaires de France, 1985), 235–237; E. Fasano Guarini, "La crisi del modello republicano: patriziati e oligarchie" in *La Storia, III: L'età moderna: I quadri generali* (Turin: UTET, 1987), 553–584.

25. M. Berengo, "Città e contado in Italia dal XV al XVIII secolo" in *Storia della città*, 107–111; Chittolini, *La formazione dello stato regionale*, xxiff.

26. G. Cherubini, "La proprietà fondiaria nei secoli XV e XVI nella storiografia italiana," *Società e Storia* 1 (1978), 9–33.

27. P. Malanima, "La formazione di una regione economica: la Toscana nei secoli XIII–XV," *Società e Storia* 6 (1983), 229–269; M. Knapton, "City Wealth and State Wealth in Northeast Italy, 14th–17th Centuries," paper presented to the meeting on "Stadt-Bürgertum-Staat," Bielefeld, 1985.

28. Wim Blockmans, "A Typology of Representative Institutions in Late Medieval Europe," *Journal of Medieval History* 4 (1987), 189–215.

29. Anderson, *Lineages*, 168–169; see especially Ruggiero Romano, *La storia economica* (Turin: Einaudi, 1974; *Storia d'Italia*, II), 1813–1939.

30. Valeri, *L'Italia*, 544ff., 638ff.; M. Berengo, "Il Cinquecento," in *La storiografia italiana negli ultimi vent'anni* (Milan: Marzorati, 1970), I, 483ff.

31. R. Villari, "La Spagna, l'Italia, l'assolutismo," in *Colloquio internazionale su "Potere e élites" nella Spagna e nell'Italia spagnolu nei secoli XV–XVIII* (Rome: Istituto Storico Italiano per l'Eta moderna e contemporaranea, 1979), 55–77; E. Fasano Guarini, "Gli stati dell'Italia centro-settentrionale fra Quattro e Cinquecento: continuità e trasformazioni," *Società e Storia* 6 (1983), 617–639.

32. Gino Luzzatto, *Storia economica dell'età moderna e contemporanea, I: l'Età moderna* (Padua: CEDAM, 1955); Immanuel Wallerstein, *The Modern World System* (New York: Academic, 1974 & 1980; 2 vols.); M. A. Romani, "Mercantilismo e sviluppo dei traffici," in *La storia*, III, 234–259.

33. Carlo M. Cipolla, "The Economic Decline of Italy," in Cipolla, editor, *The Economic Decline of Empires* (London: Methuen, 1970), 196–214; F. Krantz and Paul M.

Hohenberg, editors, *Failed Transitions to Modern Industrial Society: Renaissance Italy and Seventeenth Century Holland* (Montreal: Interuniversity Centre for European Studies, 1975); Maurice Aymard, "La transizione dal feudalesimo al capitalismo," in *Storia d'Italia, Annali*, vol. I, 1131–1192.

34. Domenico Sella, *Commerci e industrie a Venezia nel secolo XVII* (Venice/ Rome: Istituto per la Collaborazione Culturale, 1961); Domenico Sella, *Crisis and Continuity: The Economy of Spanish Lombardy in the XVIIth Century* (Cambridge: Harvard University Press, 1979); P. Malanima, *La decadenza di un'economia cittadina: L'industria di Firenze nei secoli XVI–XVIII* (Bologna: Il Mulino, 1982); G. Vigo, *Fisco e società nella Lombardia del Cinquecento* (Bologna: Il Mulino, 1979); A. de Maddalena, *Dalla città al borgo: Avvio di una metamorfosi economica e sociale nella Lombardia spagnola* (Milan: Angeli, 1982).

35. Aymard, "La transizione," 1180.

36. Peter Burke, *Venice and Amsterdam: A Study of Seventeenth-Century Elites* (London: Temple Smith, 1974).

37. For a comparison of European city republics in the modern period, see E. Fasano Guarini, "La crisi," 567–573.

38. A. Anzilotti, "Il tramonto dello stato cittadino," in Anzilotti, *Movimenti e contrasti per l'unità italiana* (Milan: Giuffrè, 1964; first published in 1924), 5–32.

39. G. Galasso, *Potere e istituzioni in Italia* (Turin: Einaudi, 1974), 141–142.

40. E. Stumpo, "Finanze e ragion di Stato nella prima Età moderna: Due modelli diversi: Piemonte e Toscana, Savoia e Medici," in A. de Maddalena and H. Kellenbenz, editors, *Finanze e ragion di Stato in Italia e in Germania nella prima Età moderna* (Bologna: Il Mulino, 1984), 181–231; cf. Stein Rokkan, "Dimensions of State Formation and Nation-Building," in Charles Tilly, editor, *The Formation of National States in Western Europe* (Princeton: Princeton University Press, 1975), 576ff.; Anderson, *Lineages*, 170–172.

3

Towns and States
at the Juncture of the Alps,
the Adriatic, and Pannonia

SERGIJ VILFAN

TWO KINDS OF RELATIONS between towns and states from the end of the Middle Ages until the eighteenth century will be considered in this chapter. My analysis focuses on two regions: first, the Adriatic coastal region, where continuity of Roman urban life persisted to an extent even after the fall of the Western empire and where the medieval communal system evolved into city-states; second, the interior regions, where the further development of Roman towns was interrupted and where new urban life arose during the High Middle Ages. The latter towns long conserved their patrimonial status, as they arose within territories belonging to noble landlords. This patrimonial (but nevertheless autonomous) structure will be contrasted in this essay with an urban-communal structure characteristic of coastal regions. The terms *communal* and *patrimonial structures* are not mutually exclusive, but they give an idea of the distinctions that I will make.

Both communal and patrimonial structures belong to western European civilization, but they are connected with different cultural-geographic areas. The communal structure was spread over the east Adriatic coastal area, which formed a part of the much larger Mediterranean world; the patrimonial structure in the southeastern Alpine and peri-Pannonian regions constituted specific groups representing central European historical traditions. By about the year A.D. 600, large portions of these regions were settled by Slavic tribes.

In the early Middle Ages, the east Adriatic coastal towns were occasionally dominated by the Byzantine Empire (most of their agrarian surroundings belonged to the developing Croatian state). But in the period dealt with in this chapter, several regions can be distinguished: the Venetian part of Istria in the north, flanked by two Habsburg harbor towns (Trieste and Rijeka-Fiume); further toward the southeast, a short Croato-Hungarian coastal strip with relatively modest towns, followed by Venetian Dalmatia in the central part of the coast, including the islands; and finally, on the extreme southeast, the rather small state of Dubrovnik-Ragusa. The coastal towns of Istria and their territories had been under Venetian control since the thirteenth century; some towns in Dalmatia had been subdued by Venice as early as the thirteenth and fourteenth centuries, but most came under Venetian control in the fifteenth century. In both Istria and Dalmatia, Venetian power—together with the Venetian state itself—was destroyed by the Campoformio peace in 1797. Dubrovnik-Ragusa was a virtually independent city-state from 1358 until 1806 (the period of French occupation) and again after 1808, when its independence was formally abolished.

In the east Adriatic coastal region, towns were of Roman, Greek, or early medieval origin, and the continuity of their development was seldom interrupted. Each town possessed a relatively large rural territory, analogous to the *contado* in Italy. As a result, the rural economy—including the salt basins—and urban life were intensely connected within the same area. The economic power was naturally (and not by chance) concentrated in the chief towns, which were also important harbors. Commerce between the Continent and overseas countries formed the basis of other economic activities. Furthermore, the economy of dependent towns was subordinated to the interests of the metropolis. Venice, for example, imposed its monopoly in the production of salt on the town of Piran in Istria. Agrarian production in the urban territories was important but not sufficient to feed big urban settlements like Venice, which depended on imports from overseas and from a vast hinterland reaching far into the empire. Venice regarded its east Adriatic towns as essential for the safety and control of navigation but watched just as surely over fiscal interests and benefits resulting from its control over these towns.

In the southeastern Alps and in the immediately adjacent peri-Pannonian region, a variation of central European types of states and towns appeared. In the period covered in this chapter, the region constituted inner Austria (i.e., the provinces of Styria, Carinthia, Carniola, and Gorice) as part of the Holy Roman Empire. The group of provinces was ruled by the Habsburg dynasty from the late Middle Ages until 1918. Today, almost the entire inner Austrian territory is divided between Slovenia in the south and Austria in the north.

Occasionally, I shall look still further east into the Pannonian region, where Croatia-Slavonia (the latter is clearly distinguished from Slovenia!), united from about 1100 until 1918 with Hungary, represents a further variation—that is, the east-central European type of states and towns.

Unlike those in the Adriatic region, towns and similar settlements (smaller and nonfortified "markets") in the interior of the Continent—in the Alps and Pannonia—did not grow directly from ancient urban roots. Roman *civitates* (municipalities) had existed here as well, but they were destroyed about the year A.D. 600. The continuity of urban life was interrupted even if many late medieval towns arose on the same location where civitates had existed in antiquity. It was especially during the twelfth and thirteenth centuries, when provinces were still being formed, that new urban settlements appeared within territories belonging to feudal lords.

The Alpine provinces imported overseas goods through the intermediary of Adriatic towns and in return sent foods, metals, and other raw materials. Their economy was preponderantly agrarian. Towns were centers for transit commerce; their own production was not very important for export. In the sixteenth and seventeenth centuries, towns contributed one-quarter of the provincial taxation of Styria. In Carniola, the towns' share in the provincial taxation was no more than 10 percent, about 40 percent of which was paid by the chief town of Ljubljana. (In Carinthia, a few prelates who were also town lords paid the bulk of the cities' contribution to provincial taxation.) By the end of the Middle Ages, some burghers possessed relatively large capital holdings and had good connections with south German financiers. But during the sixteenth century, the importance of indigenous capital seems to have diminished. In the seventeenth century, Italian and especially Venetian businessmen were active in commerce, and in the second half of the century, Ljubljana became a relatively important financial center.

The general economic character of Croatian-Slavonic towns did not differ significantly from the pattern just described for Alpine provinces, but it seems that the agrarian character of smaller towns or markets was even stronger than in the mountain regions. Economic differences between Adriatic and interior towns combined with differences in city-countryside relations to create distinctively different social patterns in the two regions, which affected state-city interactions as well.

THE EAST ADRIATIC COMMUNES
AND THEIR OLIGARCHIES

Along the whole east Adriatic coast, relatively large rural areas belonged to urban territories, and agrarian lands and salt basins thus constituted a relatively stable basis for the wealth of the urban upper classes. Later, membership in the town oligarchy (in the leading councils) became hereditary: A member of the upper class was simultaneously nobleman and burgher, knight and businessman, landlord and urban dweller—in a word, a patrician. Towns on the east Adriatic coast eventually replaced their general assemblies, consisting of free citizens, with great councils composed of urban elites. As with the shrinking of the council in Venice around 1300, the east Adriatic towns prohibited new families from becoming members of these councils. As a result, the circle of patrician families was fixed, and newly rich families (who rarely succeeded in entering this circle) enjoyed fewer legal and political rights than the old privileged patricians. Even when a town was subordinated to a city-state or to a monarch, its great council was composed of local patricians. Its structure and autonomous powers were very similar to those of corresponding bodies in the chief towns. The great councils, normally composed of male patricians of a certain age, were cumbersome entities; therefore, day-to-day affairs were managed by smaller committees. The authorities of city-states and of subordinated towns also controlled some lower, autonomous local units in rural areas.

This, then, was the general pattern and structure of the higher social strata in Adriatic towns and local autonomies. Some examples will provide a more concrete idea of the nature of town-state relations that developed on this basis.

After establishing its domination in Istria, Venice was represented in each urban commune by its own patrician, appointed by the *Signoria* (ranking executive) for a limited period. He functioned as *potestas et capitaneus* (ruler and military governor), both the head of the jurisdiction and the commander of the urban territory's defensive forces. Other functions were performed by autonomous committees and functionaries (e.g., four *consules,* or judges) elected or appointed by a kind of drawing of lots (*ballotage*) by the great council of the town itself. The autonomous structure was a simplified adaptation of the Venetian system of collective bodies.

In the immediate neighborhood of Venetian Istria, Trieste recognized Habsburg domination in 1382. The monarch was represented by his capitaneus (chosen from the nobility of nearby provinces), but the autonomous government was directed by committees led by patricians. However, even into modern times, Trieste did not belong to any province. The consequences of such a status persisted until the beginning of the twentieth century: Although other Habsburg towns were parts of realms, provinces, and so on, Trieste and its hinterland continued to have the judicial status of a province. This indicates that in state-town relations, each town remained within its original, historically developed group, even when an Adriatic town came under the dominance of a continental prince.

The governmental structure was similar in Dalmatian towns, where the representative of Venice was normally designated as a *comes,* or rector. Through their great councils, the privileged citizens in Istrian and Dalmatian towns (even when exceptionally dependent on a monarch) enjoyed rather broad autonomy. Zadar (initially known as Zara) exemplifies a communal town that became the chief town of a Venetian province. It had an excellent harbor, a central position on the east Adriatic coast, and a large, fertile contado with villages that enjoyed the benefits of organized, local autonomy, at least until the beginning of modern times. Venice established its power over Zadar in 1409; eleven years later, it consolidated its dominance in Dalmatia—a dominance that would last nearly 400 years. Beginning in 1305, Venice modified the Statute of Zadar to represent that quasi-imperial control of the region. Previously autonomous institutions were integrated into the Venetian system of control: The *Serenissima* (that is, Venice) was represented in the town by two rectors—the count and the (military) captain, both appointed by the Signoria. Since the civil and military functions were normally united in a single person in other Venetian towns, the doubling of functionaries indicates the particular importance Zadar already enjoyed in the fifteenth century. The great council of patricians was convoked by the count. The latter was also president of the Court of First Degree, whose four councillors were appointed by the Great Council of Zadar. The most remarkable limitations of economic liberty were the Venetian control of navigation and its salt monopoly.

During the sixteenth and seventeenth centuries, the structure of communal administration in Zadar did not change much formally, but the strength of the great council diminished gradually in favor of the Signoria of Venice, and the nonnoble burghers obtained elected representation through *procuratores* (deputies). The important constitutional changes in Zadar occurred by the end of the sixteenth century, when the provincial town became the residence of the Venetian governor-general (*provveditore*) and his staff for Dalmatia. Besides fulfilling administrative functions, the governor-general administered justice on appeal. The autonomy of the town was certainly not enhanced by the prestige Zadar gained as the chief town of an important province, for important administrative centers were more vulnerable to state control than were less important towns. Nevertheless, Zadar's late medieval communal structures—in the town and in nearby villages—were not abolished.

Like Venice, Dubrovnik also belonged to the Mediterranean group of city-states. When Dubrovnik had been under Venetian rule, the comes were appointed by the Signoria, and collective bodies—except the community of all recognized citizens—were appointed from above. After Dubrovnik became independent from Venice in 1358, the great council, constituted on the basis of noble birth, acted as an electoral body. The comes, formerly appointed by the Signoria, was now elected by the Great Council of Dubrovnik for a very short period in order to prevent the concentration of power in the hands of one person or family. The main collective bodies were the great council (which displaced the community of all recognized citizens), the council of requested members (the *pregadi,* with forty-five members), and the small council (with about eleven or twelve members, including the comes)—each of which had some governmental power. The territory of the state of Dubrovnik was not very large, but certain smaller communes, which enjoyed some autonomy, were part of it.

In a very simplified way, then, four main patterns of state-town relations on the east Adriatic coast can be identified: (1) direct Venetian control over communes and their territories, especially in Istria; (2) the similar but smaller city-state, Dubrovnik, with dependent communes, in the eastern coastal region; (3) the provincial system ruled by the Venetian bureaucracy, with its center in Zadar, which permitted the autonomy of subordinate units; and (4) communal autonomy under a foreign prince outside the provincial structure.

THE CENTRAL EUROPEAN MONARCHIC STATES AND
THE LEADING GROUPS IN THEIR TOWNS

The southeastern provinces of the Holy Roman Empire came into being during the High and late Middle Ages. They took the place of earlier territorial units (e.g., marches or border countries) that had been substantially weakened or even dismembered into territorial manors ruled by lords who developed their own patrimonial power. The formation of provinces resulted from an opposite process—the merging of small territories. The process typically involved a peaceful or forced concentration of dismembered units in the hands of a lord belonging to the highest nobility—the provincial prince (*Landesfürst*) *in statu nascendi* (aborning, nascent). Eventually, this prince became a member of the Habsburg dynasty.

Toward the end of the Middle Ages, most of the urban settlements in Styria and Carniola, as well as some towns in Carinthia—together with the manorial (*grundherrschaftlich*) and judicial territories from which they originated—became the property of the Habsburg provincial princes and turned into "princely towns and markets." In these urban settlements, the monarchic power of the prince was united to his patrimonial power. A few other towns and markets remained the property of bishops or members of the high nobility. In the sixteenth century, central offices of the provincial prince became the supreme judicial authorities for such "private" urban settlements as well.

In the inner Austrian provinces under discussion, no cities depended directly on the empire. Although the towns and markets belonged to the Habsburg dynasty, they did not become imperial cities because they belonged directly to the royal family. In this region, nobility remained closely connected with the rural society. Towns and markets were islands with a special legal status inside surrounding manorial structures, and the urban upper class continued to depend on income from nonagrarian origin. This economic basis was precarious and even risky, so the privileged position of a merchant or a distinguished workman in a town was frequently transitory. Further, there was no legal basis for keeping the wealth in the hands of one person or family. (This is notably different from a scenario in which wealth is based on property ownership.) Consequently, in urban settlements, where burghers were not a hereditary privileged class, there were no patricians in the Mediterranean sense of the word. And even when noblemen dwelt in a town, they continued to belong to the provincial nobility (predominantly based on a rural economy) and did not share the autonomous rights of the burghers. On the other hand, townspeople were often able to acquire minor manorial rights (though not always legally), especially the right to collect rents. In certain circumstances, they also could be made noble by the monarch, but if they were, they became part of the provincial nobility and thereby lost their rights as burghers.

In the inner Austrian provinces, the first stage of the administration of towns was similar to that in the coastal towns. The town's lord—the provincial prince or somebody else—was represented in his own town by a judge (*judex* or *richter*), who was originally appointed by the lord himself. Later, as in coastal towns, smaller councils superseded local lords. But in contrast to coastal governments, no great council of patricians was formed. The leading autonomous body became the council, sometimes called the interior council, composed of no more than twelve members. The members were appointed and changed via yearly electoral proceedings that guaranteed the appointment of councillors recruited from wealthy groups. In the seventeenth century, positions on the councils of some towns were granted for life.

The Croatian-Slavonian urban social and legal structure, which was similar to the structure in Hungary, had more in common with that of the central European towns than that of the Mediterranean area, but it had some distinguishing features. Bigger towns were founded primarily in the thirteenth century, as they had been in Prussia, Poland, and Bohemia (i.e., *locatio*, or by a systematic colonization of foreign settlers). These settlers (*hospites*) retained or received special rights, partially like those of the urban systems thriving in their country of origin but also adapted to local circumstances. The colonists and their successors—still organized according to their places of origin—enjoyed some autonomy. A few important towns in Slavonia were founded by the king of Hungary as free royal towns, and they depended directly on the king, which gave them privileged constitutional statuses. Other towns and markets belonged to their own ecclesiastical or noble founders and their successors.

Free royal towns were ruled by an elected council composed of a judge, eight to twelve jurors, and about twenty councillors. From the beginning of the seventeenth century on, jurors were elected for life. As in the Alpine provinces—or perhaps even more strictly—the difference between burghers and noblemen was respected in Croatia-Slavonia. Important consequences for the position of towns in the general constitutional structure proceeded from that fact.

TOWNS AND HIGHER REPRESENTATIVE BODIES

In the east Adriatic area, the great councils of towns governed in at least two ways. In a city-state, the council of the principal town acted as the supreme assembly both for the town and—in the most important affairs—for subordinated autonomous towns. The great council as the supreme authority symbolized the independence of the city-state, even though, in practice, smaller councils decided on current political and legal affairs and had more effective power. On the other hand, the great council of a subordinated town legally constituted only a leading committee of an autonomous unit, even if it exercised considerable power. In other words, from the constitutional point of view, the great council of a town was either a supreme authority or a subordinated one, according to the town's position in the city-state. The subordinated great council did not send delegates to the collective bodies of the principal town.

As mentioned earlier, the towns in the interior of the Continent formed relatively small judicial and administrative areas within much larger territories, such as the inner Austrian provinces or the kingdoms of Croatia-Slavonia. In inner Austria before the fifteenth century, towns did not participate directly in the provincial government because each town was represented by its lord (a prince, a bishop, or a member of the high nobility). After 1400, when provincial diets began to evolve, only the princes' towns were invited to attend these meetings of nobles and clergy; other towns, however, were still represented at the diets by their lords and taxed through them. These diets were summoned by the prince exclusively to deliberate about the personal participation of the nobles in the defense of the province and about financial contributions of the clergy and towns for the same purpose. The special topic of these diets was the growing and, for a long time, continual danger posed by the Ottoman Empire—especially the frequent Turkish raids that lasted from about 1470 until the end of the sixteenth century. After about 1500, diets were typically summoned every year. Members of four estates took part: prelates, lords (magnates), gentry (low nobility, knights), and representatives of towns belonging to the prince. Because financial participation of towns in general provincial taxation was modest, the political importance of towns in diets was never very great, and it actually diminished from the sixteenth to eighteenth centuries.

In the fifteenth and sixteenth centuries, when a prince wanted to coordinate defensive efforts, he convoked general diets of representatives or deputies sent by the invited provinces. Such extraordinary diets, though they brought together more provinces (e.g., the four provinces of inner Austria), had more in common with the French Etats Généraux than with the diets of Croatia-Slavonia or Hungary.

For nearly 100 years, especially in the second half of the sixteenth century, the secular estates of the Alpine provinces, in opposition to the Catholic prince, belonged to the Augsburg Confession. But on the basis of patrimonial rights, Protestantism was prohibited, first in towns and manors belonging to the prince and bishops; nobles who were unwilling to convert were expelled about the year 1630. Clearly, fidelity to the dynasty was an important result of the Ottoman threat. (In the Mediterranean region and in Croatia-Slavonia, however, Protestantism had some success.)

The diets of inner Austrian provinces were strictly distinguished from the judicial assemblies of the privileged groups (lords, gentry, prelates) in a particular province. In judicial assemblies, towns were not admitted as members because they had their own autonomous courts of initial jurisdiction and their own appellate courts before their lord or his representative. (Only the supreme courts before the prince became general for all social groups.)

In Croatia-Slavonia, the representative system was an adaptation of Hungarian institutions. It was dominated by the nobility even more than that in inner Austria. Assemblies of the nobility took place on three levels. The county (*comitatus*) assembly was a regular judicial meeting that occurred several times each year. The united diet of the kingdoms of Croatia-Slavonia was a more frequent judicial meeting, in which issues of defense and taxation were also deliberated. The common diet of Hungary (including Croatia) was a similar meeting at the highest level. It included county deputies and magnates who belonged by hereditary right. The hierarchic structure of assemblies and the principle of representation were consequences of the relatively centralized governmental structure in Hungary, particularly the specific structure of the Croato-Hungarian nobility, consisting of a few very mighty magnates (who acted to block the establishment of a strong royal power) and a rather numerous gentry. In the Alpine provinces, the nobility comprised less than 1 percent of the total population, but the Hungarian and Croatian nobility included numerous rather poor knights (light cavalry) and comprised about 5 percent of the total population. Obviously, the principle of representation, rather than the personal presence of the gentry, was more developed in the higher levels of meetings. In this structure, only the very rare, free royal towns were represented in the assemblies of Croatia-Slavonia and Hungary. It seems that towns as members of representative bodies were even less important here than in the southeastern provinces of the empire.

Otto Hintze compared the Hungarian and Polish representative systems and the English two-house system. He designated the common type, a bicameral legislature, as the *Zweikammersystem*. Even if the name given by Hintze to the opposite system—the *Dreikuriensystem*, a three-court or three-chamber system—is surely not appropriate (the number of *curiae* [chambers or courts] varies and is not essential to defining this phenomenon), his distinction between the two systems is basically correct. The bicameral legislature enjoys distinctive collective powers; the other type of legislature is a series of bodies existing more autonomously from each other, with each enjoying its own relationship to the sovereign. Hungary-Croatia's system resembled the second type. Two further distinctions mark the latter system: Namely, the provincial diet normally exists only on one level (the provincial), and the knights are its personal members. There is another rather important difference within the system of two houses: The share and political role of the royal towns in Hungary and Croatia in the common assembly cannot be compared with the English House of Commons.

The constitutional and political position of towns (except urban settlements belonging to bishops or lords) in relation to the representative bodies of different types of states may be illustrated in the simplified manner shown in Figure 3.1.

STRUCTURAL CHANGES IN STATES FROM
THE FIFTEENTH TO THE EIGHTEENTH CENTURIES

By the end of the Middle Ages, Venice and Dubrovnik were important commercial and political powers. On the other hand, inner Austria was a rather uncohesive union of mostly agrarian provinces inside the Holy Roman Empire, and Croatia-Slavonia was an even more agrarian but nevertheless legally more compact kingdom united with Hungary. By the middle of the fifteenth century, all these countries were confrontational neighbors of the offensive and expansive Ottoman Empire, but they sometimes also fought among themselves.

In the early 1500s, Emperor Maximilian had only very modest success in his eight-year war against Venice. This illustrates the decisive importance of financial resources in wars. The support given to the emperor by the Augsburg financier Jakob Fugger was important, but even coupled with the military and financial participation of the provinces (and in spite of occasional alliances with other powers), it was not sufficient to enable the emperor to defeat Venice and its mercenaries. Ultimately, the republic composed of merchants and bankers was able to resist the oppression of the agrarian-feudal empire.

Two and a half centuries later, the situation was quite different. Interior Austria had become a compact group of provinces whose autonomy was declining but whose economy was expanding, partly due to the Austrian penetration into the Pannonian Plain at the expense of the weakening Ottoman Empire. As in Hungary and Croatia-Slavonia, the oligarchy, reviving the

	Eastern Adriatic Coast	Empire: Inner Austria	Croatia-Slavonia
Supreme Power	chief town	prince	king
Intermediate Powers	city-states: Great Council smaller councils	multiple provinces: general diet (exceptional)	united realms: assemblies of two houses
Regional Powers	dependent towns: Great Council smaller councils	province: diet of four estates	single realm: diet of four estates county: assemblies

←← urban element predominant ←←

FIGURE 3.1 Constitutional Positions of Towns in the Adriatic and Adjacent Regions

centrifugal tendencies of the magnates and in opposition to the Habsburg king, succumbed (at least temporarily) to the absolutist monarch by the end of the eighteenth century. Meanwhile, the economic power of Venice and Dubrovnik had declined. About 1800, the two city-states yielded to France and Austria. In the Adriatic region, it seems as if the city-state was destroyed by its more agrarian hinterland.

Does this mean that the more developed urban society was defeated by less developed agrarian countries? In reality, the answer to this question is complex. The transfer of trade toward the Atlantic coast of Europe might be assumed to have caused the decline of city-states: Surely, the opening of new sea routes and markets after the discovery of America had reduced the importance of the Adriatic Sea for international traffic. But in relation to the hinterlands, this change was not as abrupt as one might suppose. Venice still dominated the economy of southern inner Austria during the entire seventeenth century. (The so-called Carniolan value, for example, was a special exchange rate for Venetian coins in these regions.) And Dubrovnik remained an important window onto the western Balkans. Thus, a weakening economy alone does not explain the debacle. Besides, the decisive blow to urban society came not from naval forces but from continental powers.

The contrast between agrarian and urban states had already begun to disappear by the end of the Middle Ages. In Venice, the policy of controlling and exploiting the mainland prevailed by the fifteenth century. The elites in coastal towns enjoyed stability during this time, but disruptions were to be felt later. The oligarchy of city-states had never been a pure financial-commercial oligarchy, and after the expansion of city-states into their hinterlands near the end of the Middle Ages, the nobility in such states became increasingly similar to that in more agrarian countries. Indeed, since they had no monarch to finance, the leading families perhaps became even more independent or "feudal" than most of the nobles in Habsburg provinces. It may be sufficient to mention the impressive villa Manin, which belonged to the last Venetian doge (duke), or the villas of Dubrovnik's patricians on the Ombla River bay. On the other hand, the nobility in the Habsburg provinces had changed considerably. The Protestant opposition of the sixteenth century had been defeated. The new nobility emerged partially from more urbanized north Italian regions and from indigenous financial circles. Members of the Eggenberg family, for example, entered the highest bureaucracy in the seventeenth century and became the new "princes" (*Fürsten*). Although the high nobility in Austria remained faithful to the dynasty, the Hungarian and Croat magnates opposed the rising absolutism; the result, however, was different from that in Poland—a country that ceased to exist by the eighteenth century due to successive divisions by absolutist neighbors. The chief difference between Poland and the city-states Venice and Dubrovnik was that the agony of the city-states was brief.

As a matter of fact, the Adriatic city-states and the east-central European realms (such as Hungary, with its united kingdoms, and Poland) had one feature in common: a strong noble oligarchy at the head of state. That means conservative forces placed obstacles to the advance of their own absolute monarchs. But once these states were faced with more centralized foreign powers, their resistance could not be successful. The decline of noble oligarchic power in favor of concentrated structures seems to have been a general trend all over Europe at this time.

The new powers that put an end to the oligarchic states were of two kinds: absolutist monarchies, with highly developed bureaucracies serving the monarch, and the newly established bourgeois-centralistic France, which left its mark on the east Adriatic city-towns. By the end of the eighteenth century, the Habsburg monarch had returned to a conservative policy, but he had little responsibility for the collapse of the city-states, even if he eventually gained thereupon. The new power that decisively intervened when Venice and Dubrovnik began to falter was France.

The new centralized empire had turned the page of history. Austria could only profit from the changing alliances and the final victory over Napoleon. Austria seized Venice's immediate terraferma (the Venetian territory closest to Venice itself), Istria, Dalmatia, and Dubrovnik, holding the latter three until 1918. The victory of these powers was not a victory of an agrarian society over towns but rather of new governmental forms over the old centrifugal oligarchy that existed both in city-states and in agrarian countries.

One more phenomenon contributed to the end of city-states: the rise of new military systems. Instead of using mercenaries, the absolute monarchs had introduced the obligatory military service of their own citizens; it was, however, a selective service, and not all males had to serve. Postrevolutionary France did so on an even larger scale. The city-states could not keep pace with this development.

THE ROLE OF TOWNS IN THE TRANSFORMATION

Does this mean that the absolutist and centralized state made its progress without the support of towns or even in conflict with them? As a rule, it certainly did not.

The role of towns in the development of economic connections and thus in the growth of the power of a state had never been unilateral. To characterize city-state and agrarian economies as two neat opposites may have been appropriate for those existing at the end of the Middle Ages, but it was not at all apt regarding those of the sixteenth and eighteenth centuries. At least by the beginning of modern times, the urban nonagrarian economy represented two opposite tendencies: protected local economy versus free trade. The old coercive economic structures, on one side, met the capitalist liberal elements, on the other. The latter were sometimes even more well represented outside the towns: in mines, ironworks, and the production of linen. Conservative coercive elements (such as guilds), together with *connected* protective urban institutions (such as the obligatory sale of merchandise), were nearly abolished by coercion exercised by the absolutist state in favor of its own finances. Capitalists supported the increasing power of the monarch not only by loans and other fiscal transactions (e.g., the *appalto,* or leasing, of monopolies) but also by assuming administrative functions. The new capitalist element was almost independent from the old urban leading structures. And as the old economic privileges of towns lessened, the financial functions of the bourgeoisie increased. The Habsburg absolutism in the old Austrian provinces, in spite of its conservative political regime, could not or did not want to prevent the growth of a new bourgeoisie that recruited new members only partially in the old towns. From an economic perspective, the emphasis was now more on nonagrarian activities than on the towns as such.

From the fifteenth to the eighteenth centuries in the Alpine provinces, both agrarian and urban autonomous bodies were forced to withdraw before the advancing bureaucratic system. Together with the old economic privileges, the corresponding "autonomous" institutions in the inner Austrian towns died faster than the provincial estates. After the functions in town councils were made hereditary, elections increasingly became a mere formality and were later almost completely abolished. In the Adriatic towns, collective bodies and other autonomous structures seemed to be more persistent, but that was only due to the conservative spirit of their leading groups, which ultimately were unable to prevent the complete destruction of the system from outside. Retrospectively, the romantic and, later, the liberal historiographers considered such relics of councils and other collective bodies as expressions of democratic mentalities. But in reality, these were very conservative societies.

From the sixteenth century on, rich burghers from interior towns invested greater sums of money in manorial property. Some of the new landlords became noblemen. But the number of simple burghers who acquired rural rents—but did not change their status—increased after the first half of the eighteenth century. In coastal towns, a similar merging of rural and urban activities was particularly noticeable among the patricians.

As the interior towns gradually lost their autonomy and their importance as members of the provincial estates, they took on new functions in the monarchic state. Though new residential towns were not founded in this area (as they were in German principalities), at least the existing towns were enlarged by residences belonging to the high nobility. Bureaucrats became a considerable part of the towns' population, not only in residential towns such as Vienna but also in other administrative centers. Garrison towns (e.g., Karlovac in Croatia) and quarters were built, nonagrarian production—manufactures—increased, and the improvement of commercial ways between towns, especially toward Trieste, reinforced the connections between them. However, all this happened under the control of the monarchic government and its administrative authorities. The legal position of towns did not profit substantially from this development.

At our starting point, state-city relations varied as a function of previous involvement in the Roman Empire, other historical experiences, culture, geography, and institutions. In the interior, further features differentiated central European from east-central European regions (i.e., inner Austria from Croatia-Slavonia). Such differences persisted until the end of the eighteenth century. But one can also observe some growing similarities, such as the installation of a kind of province in Dalmatia and the penetration of town elites into rural property. When the progress of absolute monarchies—united in the last phase with the appearance of new state forms—had led to the extinction of the old Adriatic city-state, as well as of the autonomy of its subordinated towns, the ancient distinction between two systems of state-town relations came to an end. Certainly, differences in the townscape, in ethnic structure, and in other cultural phenomena remained, but the legal position of towns in the state became much more uniform after about 1800.

Bibliographic Note

This chapter gives a succinct survey of comparative conclusions based on local monographs and several works of synthetic character. Almost every sentence ought to have special documentation, but it would be very difficult to distribute the numerous titles in particular footnotes. Moreover, a simple bibliographic list would hardly serve for the documentation of details. Therefore, the bibliography will be limited to some brief information about both general and specific titles.

Writings and publications about sources concerning the history of the political and institutional framework of the regions discussed in this chapter are cited in S. Vilfan, "Jugoslawien," in H. Coing, ed., *Handbuch der Quellen und Literatur der neueren Europäischen Privatrechtsgeschichte 3/5* (München 1988): Slovenian regions (as a part of interior Austria) on pp. 346–347, 350, 353–355; Croatia-Slavonia on pp. 345, 349, 367; Dalmatia and Dubrovnik on pp. 344, 348, 355; Istria on pp. 344, 348; and urban statutes in all regions on pp. 358–360. More concentrated on towns is an earlier survey: S. Vilfan, "Yougoslavie," in Ph. Wolff, ed., *Guide international d'histoire urbaine*, I, *Europe* (Paris, 1977), 506–528.

Special attention should be paid to some synthetic works, such as, for Croatia-Slavonia and Dalmatia, N. Klaić, "Prilog pitanju postanka slavonskih varoši" (The Origins of Slavonic Towns), in *Zbornik radova Filozofskog fakulteta 3* (Zagreb, 1955), 41–59; idem, *Povijest Hrvata u razvijenom srednjem vijeku* (History of the Croats in the Late Middle Ages) (Zagreb, 1976); M. Gross, ed., *Društveni razvoj u Hrvatskoj od 16. st. do početka 20. st.* (Social Development in Croatia, 16th–20th Centuries) (Zagreb, 1981); I. Beuc, *Povijest institucija državne vlasti kraljevine Hrvatske, Slavonije i*

Dalmacije (Governmental Institutions in Croatia, Slavonia, and Dalmatia) (Zagreb, 1985).

Relations among the Alpine provinces, estates, and towns are dealt with in S. Vilfan, *Rechtsgeschichte der Slowenen* (Graz, 1968). Concerning the area of Slovenia, I have presented and developed a comparison between Adriatic and interior towns, e.g., in the article "Die mittelalterliche Stadt zwischen Pannonien und der Nordadria" (The Medieval City Between Pannonia and the North Adriatic), in *Internationales kulturhistorisches Symposion Mogersdorf* 4 (Szombathely, 1974), 125–141. As for towns in some other Austrian provinces, see idem, "Die Land- und Stadtgemeinden in den habsburgischen Ländern" (Rural and Urban Community Governments in Habsburg Regions), in P. Blickle, ed., *Landgemeinde und Stadtgemeinde in Mitteleuropa* (München/Oldenburg, 1991), 145–167.

For Styria in particular, the most detailed synthesis on provincial administration is still A. Mell, *Grundriß der Verfassungs- und Verwaltungsgeschichte des Landes Steiermark* (Elements of the Constitutional and Administrative History of Steiermark) (Graz, 1929). Short comparative studies in foreign languages include S. Vilfan, "Les états particuliers et leurs réunions" (Individual States and Their Constitutions), in *XVe Congrès international des Sciences Historiques,* Rapports III (Bucharest, 1980), 193–203; idem, "Crown, Estates and the Financing of Defence in Inner Austria, 1500–1630," in R.J.W. Evans and T. V. Thomas, eds., *Crown, Church and Estates* (Houndmills/Macmillan, 1991), 70–79.

For Istria, besides the titles listed in the bibliographies just mentioned, a recent critical edition of the statutes of Piran has been published by M. Pahor and J. Šumrada, *Statuti piranskega komuna od 13. do 17. stoletja* (The Statutes of the Commune of Piran from the Thirteenth to the Seventeenth Century) (Ljubljana, 1987).

For Dubrovnik, see V. Foretić, *Povijest Dubrovnika do 1808* (History of Dubrovnik Until 1808), 1–2 (Zagreb, 1980); B. Stulli, "Dubrovačka republika" (The Republic of Dubrovnik), in *Enciklopedija Jugoslavije* 3 (Zagreb, 1984); idem, *Povijest Dubrovačke republike* (History of the Republic of Dubrovnik), Biblioteka "D" (Zagreb/Dubrovnik, 1989); I. Mitic, *Dubrovačka država u medjunarodnoj zajednici (od 1358–1815)* (The State of Dubrovnik in the International Community, 1358–1815) (Zagreb, 1988).

For Piran, see M. Pahor, *Socialni boji v občini Piran od 15. do 18. stol.* (Social Struggles in the Commune of Piran, Fifteenth to Eighteenth Centuries) (Ljubljana/Piran, 1972).

For Trieste, see A. Tamaro, *Storia di Trieste* 1–2 (Rome, 1924).

For Venice and the east Adriatic towns, see J. C. Hocquet, *Le sel et la fortune de Venise* (Salt and Venetian Wealth) 1 (Lille, 1979).

And for Zadar, see M. Suić, T. Raukar et al., "Zadar," in *Enciklopedija Jugoslavije* 8 (Zagreb, 1971), 564–570; N. Klaić, *Zadar u Srednjem vijeku do 1409* (Zadar, 1976); and T. Raukar et al., *Zadar pod mletačkom upravom 1409–1797* (Zadar, 1987).

4

Cities, Capital Accumulation, and the Ottoman Balkan Command Economy, 1500–1800

TRAIAN STOIANOVICH

THE HISTORY OF CITIES in the Balkans goes back several thousand years. Here, I shall confine my observations to the urban structures set in place during the fifteenth and sixteenth centuries, only to fall apart during the eighteenth and first half of the nineteenth centuries under the pressure of European models. The precise subject of my inquiry is the command-economic cities. The nature of such cities and the meaning of the term *command-economic* will become evident as the analysis proceeds.

To appreciate the Ottoman command-economic urban economy, a brief description and analysis of the immediately preceding urban economy may be of some value. One consequence of the Avaro-Slavic invasions of the sixth and seventh centuries and of the first great pandemic of the same period was the destruction or decline of the smaller Danubian and Balkan cities. The occupation of large portions of the Balkan peninsula by the Slavs also led to less direct involvement by Byzantium in the administration of the cities of the eastern Adriatic littoral. The ability of the Adriatic communes to preserve Roman law thus was less the product of a continuing Byzantine administration than of the acts of their Roman Catholic bishops.

By the twelfth century, if not earlier, the further weakening of Byzantine authority, along with the general European cultural propensity for corporate association, led to the formation of privileged, often self-governing communes on and near the Adriatic and even in several deeply inland locations, including Curzola (Korčula), Zara (Zadar), Varaždin, Vukovar, Virovitica, Sombor, Gradec, Bihać, Traù (Trogir), Spalato (Split), Sebenico (Šibenik), Lastovo, Mljet, Cattaro (Kotor), Bar (Antivari, Trivari), Ulcinj (Ulocin, Dulcigno), Shkodër (Skadar, Scutari), Budva, Drivost, Krujë (Krue,

Croia), and perhaps Durazzo. (Balkan and Adriatic cities—e.g., Dubrovnik-Ragusa—frequently have multiple names because of the changing administrative and linguistic regimes under which they have lived.) The consolidation of communal autonomies promoted the mingling and acculturation of neighboring cultural-ethnic groups: Latins and Slavs, Latins and Albanians, Albanians and Slavs, Greeks and Albanians. One of the Adriatic communes, Ragusa (Dubrovnik), was able to maintain its urban autonomies and political identity until the Napoleonic Wars.

Even in territories where Byzantine political authority was fully restored after the Avaro-Slav invasions, a trend toward acknowledging municipal franchises set in after the partition of Byzantium by the crusaders. Thus, in 1319, Emperor Andronicus II issued a chrysobull (an imperial edict) exempting Janina from state taxes, freeing residents from military service beyond the city and from the obligation to quarter imperial troops, and relieving the city's merchants of the onus of duties on goods exported to other parts of the fragmented Byzantine state. Although expressly forbidden to harbor fugitive pareques, Janina won the right to maintain its own separate judicial administration and communal police. In 1332, Andronicus III issued a chrysobull of franchises to Peloponnesian Monembasia, forbidding duties on the goods of Monembasiot merchants. Soon thereafter, the despot of Morea freed Monembasia of the obligation to return escaped pareques to their lords.

Byzantine rulers also granted municipal privileges to Salonika (Thessaloniki), Adrianople, Melinikon (Melnik), Mesembria, and Anchialus (Pomor'e), and to several cities in Asia Minor (Nicaea and Philadelphia). By chrysobulls, by prostagmas (extensions of rights on a ruler's own authority), and by Serbia's new law code (*Zakonik*), Stephen Dušan of Serbia confirmed the privileges of occupied Byzantine towns, allowing their citizens to be tried in their own law courts even in cases where one of the contestants was a rural dweller.[1] Dušan's recognition of such rights was not an aberration. It conformed, in fact, to the custom of granting communal rights, known in medieval Serbia as *pravine,* to villages, clans, monasteries, and the inhabitants of various other territorial units, including Saxon-Serbian mining towns.[2]

Between the twelfth and fourteenth centuries, communal rights and autonomies were a reality in the western, eastern, and southern Balkans, as well as in the territories of Croatia and Hungary, in which there were both free royal cities—*liberae et regiae civitates*—and privileged market places—*oppida privilegiata.* Free from the jurisdiction of the lords of seigneurial county (*comitatus, vármegye, županija*), the free royal cities had their own courts of civil and criminal law. The oppida privilegiata possessed varying privileges, depending on the relative bargaining power of each particular town and local lord.[3]

As we have seen, even the principle of the liberating function of town air—*Stadtluft macht frei*—was partially and occasionally honored in several cities under Byzantine authority. Indeed, in the strife between feudal and state power, the state often supported the towns against the lords. All three forces—state, lords, and towns—were much weakened by the struggle, however. The Ottoman conquest of the Balkans thereby was made easier.

To persuade them to yield without a bitter fight, the Ottoman Turks may have enticed several cities by promises to grant charters of privilege. A striking example of a city that took advantage of such an offer is Janina. In return for its prompt surrender, Sinan Pasha agreed not to destroy the citadel and to allow Janina's inhabitants to continue to reside within its ramparts and practice their orthodox faith without hindrance. He also confirmed the judicial attributes of the bishop and exempted Janina citizens from the *devşirme* requirement (tribute in Christian children). Not until the local jacquerie of 1611 were the Christians of Janina expelled from the citadel.[4]

After 1500, however, no new municipal franchises were granted in the Balkans. In the Adriatic, Aegean, and extra-Balkan territories north of the Sava and Danube, as in much of the rest of Europe, franchises thereupon assumed a more limited character, or they were held in check, fragmented, or abolished.

Virtually all Balkan, Adriatic, and Pannonian cities of the late medieval era had fewer than 10,000 inhabitants and generally less than 5,000 or even 2,000, again as in the rest of Europe. But the total number of places of commerce grew, especially after the mid-thirteenth-century Mongol invasion. Welcomed in Rascia (Serbia), Saxon miners stimulated the development of mining towns, most notably the silver mining town of Novo Brdo. Silver and other mining towns arose also in Bosnia, Macedonia, and Bulgaria. An anonymous observer wrote of Serbia in 1308 that it possessed, along with many citadels and other fortified places, some large unwalled towns, at least a few of which contained 300 to 400 wooden houses: "*multa castra, fortalicia et magne ville de tricentis et quadricentis domibus de lignis et asseribus edificatis sine aliqua clausura*" ("many military bases, forts, and large towns of 300 to 400 houses built of wood and posts, without any walls").[5] The concurrent expansion of Italian commerce on the Black Sea and lower Danube, the development of Saxon mining and trading towns in Transylvania, and urban growth in Hungary furthered the growth of towns along the left bank of the Danube (previously limited to the higher right bank).

The larger and older pre-Ottoman Balkan towns generally included a citadel-agora or political-religious upper city and a commercial lower town. Known as a *kastron, castrum,* or *grad* (a possible cognate of *agora*), the primary function of a kastron or grad was to serve as a place of assembly for protection and communion. Comprising princely garrisons, officials, and monks and priests, the military-religious citadel, fortress, or castle communities drew itinerant merchants and artisans; these included foreigners from the Adriatic, Black Sea, and Aegean coastal cities, who often settled in a growing lower town—or what was known in western Europe as a *suburbium* or *burgus*. Termed an *emporium* in Byzantium, the lower town was usually called *podgradie* (under-citadel) in Bosnia; it was sometimes designated by the name of the citadel preceded by the prefix *pod* (under), as in Podzvonik (today's Zvornik).

A suburb was sometimes known to the Balkan Slavs and Romanians as a *trg* or *tîrg*. Often, however, a *trg*, or cluster of wooden booths and huts, was simply a market town situated at the crossroads of two or more important trade routes or near a physically or culturally vital commodity, such as salt or silver. The growth of such market towns characterized thirteenth- and fourteenth-century Balkan and Pannonian urban or semiurban development, as did the decline in population of the formerly great cities of Constantinople and Thessaloniki.[6]

AN EXPANDING BUT NONGENERATIVE
URBAN SYSTEM

Historians have overlooked the impact of the second great pandemic of bubonic plague on Balkan urban development. Like the Ottoman conquest of the central and western Balkans between the 1420s and 1470s, it caused a hiatus in urban growth between the 1340s and the 1470s. Clear evidence of a general urban recovery was not seen until after 1520. The Ottoman Empire was constituted as a vast territorial state between 1420 and 1470, and after 1470 (and increasingly after 1520), it was committed to the pursuit of an urbanization policy. It therefore instituted a system of command-economic arrangements in the interest of its armed forces, its capitals—Istanbul or Konstantiniyya (the former Constantinople and its suburbs) and Adrianople (Edirne)—and its other cities. In those cities, Muslims—chief supporters of Ottoman rule and chief threats to a government ignoring their needs and interests—tended to concentrate.

Every kind of economy is a system for determining which individuals and groups receive an opportunity—and to what extent—to enjoy and dispose of property in prescribed ways. Every economy functions in the framework of a social or political authority that is able to deploy a certain moral and physical coercive force and thereby allow various persons and groups to enjoy the use of things in certain definite ways and to forgo their use in other ways.

In loose Gramscian vocabulary,[7] one may identify a social or political authority that works in this way as a *hegemonic force*. A hegemonic force consequently is present in every society, existing as much in demand economies as in command economies. Wealth is reallocated in both types of economy in the same four ways—by gift, by legal or customary devolution, by violence, and by exchange.[8]

Nevertheless, a difference exists between these two forms of economy. A demand economy embraces the notion that exchange is the ideal means of circulating wealth. A command economy, on the other hand, uses exchange (like gifts) as a complement to the principle of devolution, its ideal mode of passing wealth from one person or group to another. The command economy may be more prone to violence than the demand economy, but excessive violence tends to undermine all authority. Unless it is both limited and used with caution, violence may undermine a command economy no less than a demand economy.

Neither type of economy is inherently superior to the other as a system of techniques. But to maintain its efficacy, a command economy must always be almost closed. To achieve the same end, a demand economy must become increasingly—if not ever wholly—open.

Eighteenth-century orientalist Abraham-Hyacinthe Anquetil Duperron wavered between two views of the relationship between merchants and the Ottoman, Persian, and Indian states of the sixteenth, seventeenth, and eighteenth centuries. Although often associated with the view that these states were not (Asiatic) despotisms, he argued, in his more subtle moments, less against the existence of Asian despotisms than against the customary eighteenth-century definitions of despotism.

One may infer from the conceptions presented thus far that a despotic government lacks an interest in protecting the technical and social institutions that foster trust (without which credit tends to evaporate) and promote production and communication—that is, conditions of security.[9] The term *despotism* thus has acquired a pejorative sense. I shall opt, therefore, for such terms as *command, command economy,* and *command-economic structures.*

The guiding principle of the *command economy,* a term put into circulation by economist Sir John Hicks,[10] is what economic anthropologist Karl Polanyi called "centricity."[11] Under institutions governed by centricity, control patterns are defined not by autonomous markets but by administration and political decisions.

A command economy cannot exist without a central-place settlement model and "its hierarchical assembly of internally determined and transformed confluctive units."[12] Centricity requires a center of command or a central city and a system of dependent centers in a hierarchical arrangement with each other.

To maintain a command economy near a maximum level of efficiency is therefore difficult, for the dependent cities tend to subvert command in two ways. They can, first of all, subvert it by contesting the authority of the old highest-order central place. They can also weaken and despoil it by their propensity to sell to other political-economic systems, in return for envied products of foreign manufacture, the raw materials and semifinished products that they obtain by property management and devolution. They thereby open the largely closed command system at critical points.

No sixteenth-century European state was better able to organize, finance, and equip a larger number of effectively armed soldiers than the Ottoman Empire. Nor was any European state of the time better able to administer the machinery needed to govern such vast and culturally heterogeneous territories as the Asian, European, and African dominions of the Ottoman Empire. No European state was then more powerful nor more centrally organized.

Marc'Antonio Pigafetta of Vicenza placed the "court" of Selim II in 1567 at 40,000 persons.[13] Several decades later, the Italian sociologist Giovanni Botero set the number of horsemen and footmen in the Ottoman court at "not lesse than thirty thousand very well appoynted."[14] This may have represented 10 percent of the population of Istanbul, where the sultan usually resided when he was not off to war or to hunt. The secondary residence of the Ottoman sultans was Adrianople (Edirne). These two capital cities would have shrunk to half their size if they had not been centers of officialdom—the chief European command posts of the empire, with their numerous soldiers, slaves, lackeys, and bevies of women (the prerogative of political overlords). After Adrianople was abandoned as a customary residence of the sultans and the secondary capital toward the end of the seventeenth or early eighteenth century, the commerce of the city fell off, and many merchants withdrew to other places.[15] In 1717, according to Lady Mary Wortley Montagu, wife of the new British ambassador to the Sublime Porte, Adrianople was "full of people." She hastened to add that "most [were] such as follow the Court, or Camp, and when they are remov'd, I am told, 'tis no populous City."[16]

From Botero's time to the present,[17] scholars have repeatedly estimated the population of Istanbul during the second half of the sixteenth and in the seventeenth centuries at 700,000. The layout and circumference of the city do not, however, support this claim. According to Gabriel de Luïtz (Baron d'Aramon), the mid-sixteenth-century French ambassador to the Sublime Porte, Istanbul *intra muros* had a perimeter of thirteen to fifteen miles.[18] In 1573, estimating the perimeter of Istanbul at sixteen *miglia* (miles), the Venetian senator and envoy Costantino Garzoni attributed to the Ottoman capital a population of "more than 300,000."[19] Reducing the perimeter to ten to twelve miles, the mid-seventeenth-century French ambassador Jean Thévenot concluded that both Paris and Cairo were more populous than Istanbul.[20]

Gazing at the city from the Janissary Tower in the time of Napoleon, John Cam Hobhouse (Lord Broughton) was "convinced of the exaggeration in

which most writers have indulged in speaking of the size and population" of
Istanbul and its suburbs:

> The base of the triangle on which the city is built, and which extends from the
> Seven Towers to the port, is perhaps one-fifth less than the side towards the Sea
> of Marmora, and about a sixth larger than that towards the harbour; and it ap-
> pears from this height of so inconsiderable an extent, that, having heard of a
> comparison between Constantinople and Paris, and even of London, I was in-
> duced to time myself in passing under the walls from one point to another, and
> found the walk to have lasted one hour and seventeen minutes. This will give
> about five miles for the breadth of the city on the land quarter, and will reduce
> the extent of the three sides to fifteen miles. ... It should be added that the walls,
> which are treble on the land-side and eighteen feet apart from each other, take
> away from the real dimensions of the town, and that the gardens of the Seraglio
> and a multitude of other palaces, the large courts of the royal moscks, and the
> vacant spaces of the Hippodrome and other open spots, diminish considerably
> the extent of the ground actually covered with houses. There is no such determi-
> nate way of judging the size of the suburbs of Galata, Pera, and Scutari [Üskü-
> dar, in Asia], which, if they were not interspersed with vast burying-grounds,
> would be at least one-fourth as large as the city within the walls, but cannot be
> said at present to be in the proportion of more than one-fifth to the capital itself.

But persuaded by the registers for 1796 showing 88,185 houses in Istanbul
without the suburbs, Hobhouse concluded that a population of "five hundred thousand does not appear too large an estimate for the population of
Constantinople and its environs."[21] This might have been a reasonable conclusion if one could be sure that houses destroyed in frequent fires were subtracted from the registers as such events occurred. But we have no assurance
of this, and furthermore, we know that the principal bazaars occupied a
fairly extensive area devoid of residences. Fountains, promenades, wooded
zones, meadows, public baths, and burying grounds also took up much
space. As in Paris, the streets of Istanbul were very narrow. In contrast to
seventeenth- and eighteenth-century Paris, however, the houses were built
low.

Made mainly of wood and earth, as in other Ottoman cities, the house of
the typical Stambouliot (Istanbul resident) comprised a ground floor and an
upper story. A smaller number of houses had two stories in addition to the
ground floor. In 1725, to reduce the risk of fire, regulations fixed the maximum authorized height for a Muslim house, recognizable by its authorized,
gay colors (white, yellow, pale blue, rose, and red), at 12 *zira'*, or about 9
meters. Confined to colors of a dark hue (black, dark brown, or gray), the
houses of non-Muslims were restricted to a height of 9 *zira'*, or 6.75 meters.[22]

Distorting Hobhouse's calculations in order to visualize Istanbul *intra
muros* as an isosceles triangle with 5 miles to each side, one obtains an area

of 10.825 square miles, or 28 square kilometers. Recent historical research further reduces that area. Often likening it to a Phrygian bonnet, Byzantinists estimate the perimeter of Constantinople *intra muros*—hence, Istanbul—at 18 kilometers (5.5 kilometers along the Great Wall of Theodosius, 8 kilometers along the southern and eastern shores, and 4.5 kilometers along the northern seawall).[23] Istanbul *intra muros* thus comprised an area of 12 square kilometers, corresponding exactly to Ferdinand Lot's estimate of 1,200 hectares.[24]

If private dwellings and their appendages, such as gardens and dependent structures, occupied 60 percent of the city's surface and if each dwelling and its dependencies covered an average surface of 200 square meters, one could estimate the city had a total of 36,000 to 39,000 houses. Indeed, 36,000 houses is the number that orientalist François Pétis de la Croix (d. 1713) ascribed to it.[25] An estimate of 200 square meters per individual dwelling may not be much off the mark if one notes that, except in the densely populated area by the water, Stambouliot houses generally had a yard and were relatively spacious, comprising a ground floor with a kitchen, a stable, a washhouse, storerooms, and a guest room.

It was also "a very unusual thing for two [Muslim] families to live in one house"—something that was regarded as "an indecency"; the practice was confined to the poor, and even then, only the families of a father and son or of two brothers could inhabit one house.[26] But well-to-do Muslims had concubines and other servants and sometimes more than one wife. I therefore shall multiply the number of houses by seven to obtain the probable total urban population. Adding 30,000 to 40,000 for the imperial establishment, I estimate the total stable population of Istanbul during large portions of the 1600–1780 period at 300,000, almost certainly not more than 350,000 ([36,000–39,000] × 7 + [30,000–40,000] = 282,000–313,000); consequently, there was a relatively stable population density of about 250 persons per hectare.

If we add to this total a floating population engaged in policing, retail trade, and service activities, we arrive at a combined stable and floating population on the order of 350,000 to 400,000. Clearly, then, the estimate of 700,000 made by many distinguished historians, not to mention one Islamicist's suggestion that the population of Istanbul may have reached 1.2 million in 1593,[27] is absurd.

According to William Eton, the number of dead carried through the gates of Istanbul between 1770 and 1777, when there was no serious plague in the city, reached an average annual total of 5,000. In addition, 1,000 dead were buried in the city itself and in the burial grounds of Pera-Galata and Üsküdar. If one accepts Eton's figures (which perhaps are too low) and his estimate of an average life span of 36 years (perhaps too high), the total population of Istanbul *intra muros* could barely have exceeded 216,000. Thus, if I have erred in my estimate, I have erred on the high side.

Subscribing to Hobhouse's view that the total population of the suburbs did not exceed a fifth of the stable population of the capital itself,[28] one may attribute to Greater Istanbul, or Konstantiniyya, a further population of 60,000 to 70,000. A check on this estimate may be made by reference to the average number of houses in a neighborhood and the number of neighborhoods (*mahalles*) in each suburb.

In the mid-seventeenth century, there were 93 neighborhoods (70 Greek, 17 Muslim, 3 Frankish or western European, 2 Armenian, and 1 Jewish) in Pera-Galata, 82 (70 Muslim, 11 Greek, and 1 Jewish) in Üsküdar, and an unknown number in Eyyub.[29] In 1477, Üsküb (Skoplje, Skopje) comprised 33 Muslim mahalles of 20 houses each and 12 Christian mahalles of 25 houses each.[30] With only 3 mahalles in 1489 and 15 in 1516, by the middle of the seventeenth century Sarajevo had 4,000 houses in 104 wards, or an average of 38.6 houses to a ward.[31] A usual Balkan Ottoman mahalle thus contained 25 to 50 houses. At an average of 40 houses to a ward, one may set the population of Galata-Pera in the mid-seventeenth century at 26,000 (93 × 40 × 7) and that of Üsküdar at 23,000 (82 × 40 × 7). It is therefore unlikely that the total population of the three suburbs exceeded 60,000 to 70,000, precisely the estimate derived on the basis of Hobhouse's criteria. If, moreover, one accepts Evliya Çelebi's estimate of 1,004 mahalles for Istanbul *intra muros* in A.H. 1044 (A.D. 1634), one may give it (excluding the court and suburbs) a total population of 281,000 (1004 × 40 × 7), close to my estimate of 252,000 to 273,000.[32]

To diminish the estimated population of Istanbul is not to deny the city's role as a highest-order central place, with a superior concentration of political and military power and religious and cultural authority. But it also functioned as the highest-order central place for portions of the three subsystems of the world continent (Asia, Africa, and Europe). Consequently, in analyzing its function as the highest-order Ottoman central place, with Europe as the locus, one is dealing with no more than one-third to one-half its population.

If rank-size regularities among cities are a necessary criterion of an urban system, one must conclude that no all-Ottoman, Eurasian-Ottoman, or Balkan-Ottoman urban system has ever existed. Indeed, even regional rank-size regularities were rare in the Balkans. As late as 1800, only one such system existed: Bosnia-Herzegovina.

The towns of the dual province showed the traits of a harmonic series: an ordering in terms of rank-size regularities in which the second city is half as large as the first, the third is one-third the size of the first, and the smallest has a population equal to the largest divided by its own rank in the system.[33]

TABLE 4.1   Estimated Population and Theoretical Harmonic-Series Population of the Towns of Bosnia-Herzegovina, 1807

	Estimated Population	Harmonic-Series Population
Sarajevo	60,000	30,000–40,000[a]
Novi Pazar	15,000	15,000–20,000
Mostar	12,000	10,000–13,333
Maglaj	7,500	7,500–10,000
Travnik	7,000	6,000–8,000
Zvornik	6,000	5,000–6,667
Banjaluka	5,000	4,286–5,714
Višegrad	5,000	3,750–5,000
Jajce	4,000	3,333–4,444
Bihać	3,000	3,000–4,000
Srebrenica	3,000	2,727–3,636
Skoplje	3,000	2,500–3,333
Trebinje	2,000	2,308–3,123
Vranduk	1,000	2,143–2,857
Average population of 38 market towns	1,000	
Highest-level market town		2,000–2,667
Lowest-level market town		577–769

[a] Probable population.

In 1807, Amédée Chaumette des Fossés ranked the cities of the dual province (Table 4.1).[34]

Not yet fully formed was a harmonic series along the Aegean coast of Macedonia and Thessaly, where French consul Félix de Beaujour observed the urban ordering displayed in Table 4.2.[35]

In addition, one or more of the following towns may have reached the 3,000 to 5,000 level of five of the eight missing harmonic-series places: Orphanos, Drama, Avret-Hisar, Elasona, Servia, Trikkala, and Moscholouri.

The rarity of a rank-size ordering of cities of 10,000 or more at even a regional level until the eighteenth century may be explained by the scarcity of cities of that size: only four in the 1520s (Istanbul, Thessaloniki, Adrianople, and Athens); six or seven in 1580 (with the addition of Sarajevo, Belgrade, and perhaps Galata-Pera); eleven to thirteen in 1660 (with the addition of Üsküb, Sofia, Chalkis [Negropont], Philippopolis, perhaps Priština, and soon thereafter Moschopolis, whose population declined to well under 5,000 between 1769 and 1788); and eighteen in 1800 (with the falling away of Üsküb, Priština, Moschopolis, and perhaps Chalkis and the addition of Ruse, Vidin, Novi Pazar, Mostar, Serres, Patras, Candia [Herakleion], Larissa, and Vodena). Up to nine other places—Svishtov, Selimno (Sliven),

TABLE 4.2 Estimated Town Population and Theoretical Harmonic-Series Population of Coastal Macedonia and Thessaly, c. 1800

	Estimated Population	Harmonic-Series Population
Thessaloniki	60,000	60,000
Serres	30,000	30,000
Larissa	20,000	20,000
Missing Place[a]		15,000
Vodena (Edessa)	12,000	12,000
Missing Place		10,000
Kara-Verroia	8,000	8,571
Missing Place		7,500
Yenidje-Vardar	6,000	6,667
Tyrnavos	6,000	6,000
Pharsala	5,000	5,454
Ambelakia	5,000	5,000
Missing Place		4,615
Missing Place		4,286
Zeitoun (Lamia)	4,000	4,000
Missing Place		3,750
Missing Place		3,529
Missing Place		3,333
Kavalla	3,000	3,158
Volos	3,000	3,000

[a] Refers to place theoretically expected but nonexistent.

Silistra, Shumen, Užice, Monastir (Bitolj, Bitola), Janina, Gallipoli, and Kirk-Kilisse (Kirklareli)—may have approached that level. A regional ordering of cities therefore had to await the formation of cities in the 10,000 category—a product of the growth of cities in the 5,000 to 10,000 category, of which there were as many as forty to fifty in 1800.

The lateness of rank-size urban ordering also stemmed from the fact that cities were part of a command structure. With uniform administrative structures, all cities performing functions at a stated territorial level in a given command-economic system should be of the same size. Provincial, or *sanjak,* cities should be of a uniform provincial size; subprovincial, or *kaza,* cities should be of a uniform subprovincial size; great-county, or *nahiye,* towns should be of a uniform great-county size, and palanques (*palanka,* from *phalanx*), or palisaded command posts, along the routes of war should be of a uniform palanque size.

The construction of a pure command economy is virtually impossible, however, because of the unequal and unlike distribution of resources. To come close to achieving a pure command economy, the unit of command must be an isolated state. But the human craving—and especially the yearning of the agents of command—for rare or otherwise prestigious goods makes isolation difficult and, in the long term, impossible. Moreover, an isolated state should be a small state. Only in that way can effective control be exercised from the command center without the use of many ambitious agents. But the desire for power drives states to relinquish the advantages of isolation.

Both demand-economic and command-economic structures are old, going back to classical antiquity and beyond, and they coexist. Consequently, the Ottoman state lacked the option of fashioning a political-economic structure without a demand-economic sector. Indeed, in the world before planned economies, an exchange economy was almost a necessary aspect of redistribution: Devolution could win more allegiance if, prescribing devolution from producers to the beneficiaries of redistribution, the overall system subsequently allowed goods to enter a partly regulated exchange system.

Two sets of central-place hierarchies—command-economic and demand-economic—thus coexisted in the Ottoman Empire,[36] often overlapping. The same dependent cities performed both devolutionary and exchange functions. The hegemonic mode, however, was the redistributive mode. In some places—in market towns with a minimal administrative structure—the exchange function was more important. Such places began to play a significant role in the overall Ottoman economy, however, only as the command-economic system began to founder.

South of the Sava and Danube, the aggregate population of all cities with 10,000 or more residents (excluding Istanbul) grew from 60,000 in the 1520s to 125,000 in 1580, 200,000 in 1700, and 400,000 in 1800.[37] But though the cities facilitated the mobilization of labor, capital, and information, they failed to produce an economically generative urban system that was capable of articulating achievements to the general advantage of producers and consumers alike.[38]

In 1820, according to geographer-statistician Adriano Balbi, European Turkey (including Wallachia, Moldavia, and Bessarabia) comprised 573,605 square kilometers.[39] Ottoman territories south of the Sava and Danube therefore embraced 440,000 square kilometers. The total population of that area rose from 5 or 6 million in 1520 to 7 or 8 million in 1580, fell to 6 million in 1700, and rose again to 7 million by 1800.[40] Population density south of the Sava and Danube stood at 11.4 to 13.6 persons per square kilometer in 1520, 15.9 to 18.2 in 1580, 13.6 in 1700, and 15.9 in 1800.

By using the available data for cities with a population of 10,000 or more and applying to the whole of Balkan-Ottoman Europe south of the Danube and Sava the Bosnia-Herzegovina ratio between cities of 2,000 to 10,000 and total population, one may guesstimate an urban population in 1800 of 1 to 1.2 million, distributed as shown in Table 4.3.

TABLE 4.3   Estimated Populations of Balkan-Ottoman Cities: 1800

Istanbul as a Balkan-Ottoman city	
(about half the population of the city)	200,000
Other cities of 10,000 or more	400,000
Forty to fifty towns of 5,000–10,000	300,000
About thirty towns of 2,000–5,000	100,000
Several hundred market towns and palanques	
with a population of 300–2,000 each	200,000

TABLE 4.4   Estimated Population Growth of Balkan-Ottoman Cities, 1520, 1580, 1700, 1800

Population Component	*1520*	*1580*	*1700*	*1800*
Istanbul as a Balkan-Ottoman city				
(about half the population)	50,000	100,000	175,000	200,000
Other cities of 10,000 or more	60,000	125,000	200,000	400,000
Towns of 2,000–10,000	150,000	250,000	300,000	400,000
Market and palanque towns	75,000	125,000	150,000	200,000
Total including market				
and palanque towns	335,000	600,000	825,000	1,200,000
Total excluding market				
and palanque towns	260,000	475,000	675,000	1,000,000

TABLE 4.5   Percentage of Urban Dwellers in Balkan-Ottoman Europe South of the Sava and Danube, 1520, 1580, 1700, and 1800

Categories of Cities Included Under "Urban"	*1520*	*1580*	*1700*	*1800*
All	5.6–6.7	7.5–8.6	13.8	17.1
All except market towns and				
palanques	4.3–5.2	5.9–6.8	11.2	14.3
Cities of 10,000 and more (but only half the				
population of Istanbul)	1.8–2.2	2.8–3.2	6.2	8.6

Between 1520 and 1800, the urban population of the area may have grown as illustrated in Table 4.4.

One may also guess the probable growth in the percentages of urban dwellers (see Table 4.5).

Between 1520 and 1800, urban population grew faster than rural population. In an economically generative urban system, the cost of such growth need not be borne wholly by rural producers. But in the Ottoman case, the urban growth was not generative: It was realized, at least in part, by the increasing diversion of resources from peasants to cities and landlords.

During the second half of the sixteenth century, the annual per capita cereal production in some twenty villages of the Kravari district of Aetolia was about 320 kilograms. Of that amount, only 11.5 kilograms directly entered a commercial circuit, the rest being used for seed, consumption, and devolution.[41] Two centuries later, the usual wheat production in the commercialized maritime sanjaks of Salonika, Volos, and Kavalla was almost 75,000 metric tons.[42] In 1833, in the far less commercialized vassal principality of Serbia, the cereal production totaled 50,000 metric tons,[43] all produced for home use. Serbian cereal production therefore stood at 200 kilograms per capita then, a third below the earlier Kravari level. Since per capita production in the Aegean sanjaks exceeded the Kravari level, the Kravari estimate may be a good Balkan average during a long period of minor technological change in the rural sector. If rural dwellers south of the Danube and Sava (mostly peasants) numbered 4.6 to 5.6 million in 1520, 6.4 to 7.4 million in 1580, 5.2 million in 1700, and 5.8 million in 1800, their hypothetical annual cereal production in good years, on the basis of the Kravari data, should have been 1,472,000 to 1,792,000 metric tons in the 1520s, 2,048,000 to 2,368,000 metric tons in the 1580s, 1,664,000 metric tons around 1700, and 1,856,000 metric tons around 1800.

Annual cereal consumption per capita varied from 250 kilograms in Istanbul to 200 in other cities.[44] Consequently, one may suppose there was a rise in urban cereal requirements from 55,500 metric tons in 1520 to 100,000 in 1580, 173,750 in 1700, and 250,000 in 1800. On the basis of the Kravari multiplier of 11.5 kilograms, the amount of peasant-produced cereals directly entering a commercial circuit would grow from between 52,900 and 64,400 metric tons in 1520 to between 73,600 and 85,100 in 1580, only to fall to 59,800 in 1700 and 66,700 a century later. Even if the precise figures are arguable, the logic is certainly plausible.

To meet urban needs as less and less of the total peasant cereal product directly entered a commercial circuit, more and more cereals had to enter the market by means of devolution—rising from several thousand tons in the 1520s to 20,000 in 1580, 110,000 in 1700, and 180,000 in 1800; put another way, the volume grew from less than half of 1 percent of the total cereal product in the 1520s to 1 percent in the 1580s, more than 6 percent in 1700, and almost 10 percent a century later. These hypothetical figures include only part of the cereal production accruing by devolution to rural landlords, rural notables, and other country mediators.

SYSTEM OF COMMAND AND DEVOLUTION

The Balkan-Ottoman urban system consequently became less generative as it became more urban. The production of cities of the Ottoman type entailed a high social cost,[45] creating an ever-greater imbalance of wealth and diversity of opportunity between country and city—an increase in the cost of production (mostly protection costs) to the peasantry—as towns became larger and more numerous. This result was not simply the product of the command economy; it also stemmed from the worsening conditions of Ottoman com-

mand structures. This occurred partly in response to the shift from an equilibrium between northern and Mediterranean poles of commercial attraction to the dominance of the northern pole between 1580 and 1650, as the
European-Mediterranean world economy entered the downward phase of a
secular trend that was completed only during the 1740s.[46]

In the Ottoman system of devolution, commerce assumed two forms—retail trade and a linear wholesale trade, almost without depth except at points
where routes converged to form cities, market towns, and fairs. If production for the capital, for provincial administration, and for long-distance
trade (especially with other politicocultural systems) is subtracted from the
total production, what remains, side by side with the household economy or
peasant mode of production, is a mode of production "geared to supply only
the immediate neighboring region, that is, a clearly defined and limited [au-
thority] market."[47] Indeed, the Ottoman state was organized as a succession
of lower central places, each with its own staples or central-place rights but
subordinate to the chief central place or capital. Istanbul routinely took
some staples of nearby Ottoman regions, especially the maritime provinces,
but in an emergency, it had the right to take more; the commodities from
these regions were conveyed to the central place by sea—in the case of
wheat, from Volos, Thessaloniki, Rodosto, Karaağaç, and Varna—more
easily and cheaply than by land.

In elementary or small societies, devolution is imposed by moral authority. Generally implicit in such authority, however, is the threat of physical
force. The devolutionary systems of large states or ethnically complex
societies have usually been organized as command economies—protection-
producing political enterprises with monopoly rights to the instruments of
major violence. The object of command is to assure the redistribution of
goods in prescribed ways and to prevent reallocation in other ways. One of
its specific aims is to prevent popular disorder by assuring the constant provisioning of authorized market places. Therefore, one may describe a command economy as a *moral economy,* a term made famous by Edward P.
Thompson. But to do so would be to overlook a more fundamental aspect of
its raison d'être—its close association with a policy known in eighteenth-
century France as *économie de police* (supervised or policed economy).

Almost at its inception, the Ottoman command system took form as a
"gunpowder empire": It had monopoly rights to powder and shot within its
own widening territorial limits; and it had the power to resist foreign enemies, demand domestic support, and crush domestic rebellion,[48] conforming
to Sir John Hicks's maxim that a command economy almost inevitably
possesses, at first, "a military character." But a "pure, or almost pure, command economy," adds Hicks,

can hardly exist excepting in an emergency, for it is only in the emergency that a wide range of orders will be accepted. The case is the same as that in the firm ... some "belowness" as well as some "aboveness" is bound in the end to be a necessary part of its organization. In the emergency the community has become, to all intents and purposes, an army; but the time will come when the army has to be transformed into an instrument of civil government. This (many instances confirm) is a very difficult stage; it may happen that the empire fails to pass it, so that the central power, save perhaps in nominal terms, just disappears. But even if the central power disappears, there may be consolidation at a lower level. Failure may not be complete failure; but success may not be complete success.

The multitude of systems of social organization to which the term "feudalism" has been applied—including those to which many would say it is misapplied—have no more than one thing in common: They are a low degree of success in the transmutation of an army into a civil government. The generals are made governors of provinces, the captains their district officers. They retain some memory of the positions from which they have sprung, so they have some feeling of allegiance to the centre; but the power of the centre to enforce its commands upon them has become very limited, so that hardly more authority over them is retained than is expressed in some customary rights.[49]

From the 1590s to the mid-eighteenth century, provincial attempts to divert emphasis from one Ottoman center to a multitude of centers did not produce "the transmutation of an army into a civil government." But central authority *was* weakened. During most of the period between 1580 and 1830, yearly revenues accruing to the central government ceased to grow or declined, while the revenues of the European states grew almost without interruption. By the 1780s, perhaps no more than a quarter of the Ottoman tax levies reached the state treasury. The rest accrued to prebends, tax collectors, and local notables.[50] The central government also lost control over the expenditure of military funds, for army commanders kept a smaller military force than could have been sustained by the pay coupons allotted to them, which they sold to buyers at a discount.

Finally, during the Russo-Turkish war of 1768–1774, the government had to extend official recognition to the provincial notables known as *ayans*, many of them members of *ulema* (Muslim religious families), in order to get them to assemble the manpower and supplies needed for waging war. Effective control of kaza military districts, or territorial units with a city of nearly 10,000 or more, thus slipped into the hands of ayan notables. Obtaining control of kaza and provincial councils, the ayans assumed responsibility for local security, the apportionment and collection of taxes, the provisioning of towns, the training and commitment of troops, and the assignment of transport to military use. As merchants, wealthy artisans, landlords, possessors of revenue rights, and tithe collectors, the town-based ayan notability became the paramount local military authority, with access to the manpower of the local janissaries.[51]

Decentering—the partial shift from a centrally based command economy to provincial and kaza command—was advantageous for long-distance commerce. Ayans owned considerable livestock and derived rents from properties in and around towns, and their interests coincided with the goals of the European market economy and European states—to make Ottoman raw materials available to Europe and to place European manufactures and colonial products in the hands of Ottoman notables.

The object of kaza and provincial protection and violence production (i.e., military organization), however, continued to be devolution. The Ottoman command system has been correctly described as "a redistributive economy with state [and some degree of provincial] control over the supply of basic cereals and raw material for crafts."[52]

As a system of reallocating wealth to the more highly trusted and privileged sectors of Ottoman society, the command economy was temporally and spatially coterminous with the Ottoman state. Not until the conquest of Constantinople—and, indeed, not until the deliberate undertaking, in the 1520s, of a politics of urbanization and reurbanization—was there a command economy that was more than a tribute collection of human and other resources and a manifestation of military power. Between the 1520s and the latter decades of the eighteenth century, the Ottoman command economy was produced and reproduced in at least five different ways: (1) by the payment of tithes (*öşr*), as in the earlier era, to timariots, or *sipahis*, who, in turn, had to provide the state with a prescribed number of armed horsemen (or perform some other designated service) during the ordinary fighting season of the year; (2) by the farming out (*iltizam*) of the right to revenues (including those from salt, copper, iron, and other mineral resources), granted on a lifetime basis (*malikâne*) from 1695 onward; (3) by the issuance of temporary grants of exclusivity rights to certain sylvicultural, agricultural, and pastoral products; (4) by the forced contribution to the state of labor, capital, or other resources; and (5) by a capitation tax (*cizye*) on non-Muslim males that had to be paid in cash.

To pay the head tax, Christian peasants normally had to sell a portion of their products in town—presumably, the city to whose decisions they were subject. If they lacked a surplus in some year (not an unusual occurrence), they had to borrow money at usurious rates of interest. If they possessed a surplus, they had little freedom to choose the time of sale since they had to market their products when other peasants were offering similar goods for the same reason and thus at a time of depressed prices.

The Ottoman command economy also commissioned buyers to purchase certain staples at low prices determined by the government. Abusing their authority, the privileged buyers often bought such commodities at even lower prices. Several kinds of forced purchases were common. In the vassal principalities of Wallachia and Moldavia, purveyors known as *kapanlis* were authorized to buy designated quantities of cheese, butter, honey, beeswax, tallow, and smoked beef and mutton at prices set by the government (in practice, at prices yet lower); these goods were delivered to the Imperial Palace, to the Ottoman armed forces, and to the *kapan,* or wholesale food market of Istanbul. In the same principalities and in the Ottoman core territories in Europe, the government had designated (sometimes coerced) buyers known as *celeps*—many of them wealthy sheep-raisers—to purchase specific quantities of sheep (and sometimes cattle and dairy products) at a very low price; these, too, were delivered to the capital or the armed forces. Other buyers were forbidden to buy such goods until the celeps completed their devolutionary business. In 1591, forced sales in Moldavia added 141,000 sheep to the meat supplies of Istanbul. During some years of the eighteenth century, the celeps drove from Bulgaria to Istanbul or diverted to the armed forces as many as 440,000 sheep. Forced purchases and sales of sheep ceased only at the end of the century.

Other government purchasing agents—*iştiracis*—were commissioned to buy a tenth of the wheat production of the Black Sea coasts of Bulgaria, Wallachia, and Moldavia, of the Aegean coasts of Thrace, Macedonia, Thessaly, and Morea, and of several maritime districts in Asia Minor, again destined for the capital and its protection-producing monopoly. Forced to sell the wheat at a low price set by the government, peasants had to deliver it to the nearest port or *iştira* storage granary. Purchasing agents were authorized to buy for private gain, at the same low fixed price, an additional quantity equal to 10 percent of the iştira collection. As the result of both official authorizations and abuses, 12 percent of the wheat production of the eastern Balkan maritime provinces—and, combined with the tithe, well over a fifth of the total wheat production of these areas—entered the economy by means of devolution. Additional cereals were obtained by other devolutionary means. Similarly, kapanlis and celeps were authorized to buy for private gain, at the low price of purchases made for the government, some quantities of cattle, sheep, or dairy products.[53]

In an almost Physiocratic vein, Baron de Tott made the following critique of the iştira form of *Zwangswirtschaft* (command economy):[54]

The Grand Signior publicly monopolizes the corn, and with it furnishes the capital. He receives this commodity from the maritime Provinces, which are subject to a kind of tax called *Ichtirach*. It consists in an obligation to deliver to the Sultan [in fact, to the *Defterdar,* or grand treasurer], at a very low rate, a certain quantity of corn, which he causes to be conveyed to his magazines by vessels hired at his expense; he afterwards sells it out retail to the Bakers, who are obliged to take it at a price which his Highness thinks proper to fix. The consequence of this management is, that Corn is forbidden to be exported, that the officers elude the Prohibition by every species of Knavery, that a great part of the Grain, laid up in the magazines, and taken little care of, is frequently spoiled and the remainder rendered unwholesome, and that Famine concludes the long catalogue of Evils produced by this wretched Policy.

The seraglio of Istanbul claimed priority rights to the resin of the mastic evergreens of Chios, used by the ladies as chewing gum and prized as an oral freshener and whitening and cleansing dental agent. Indeed, hardly an item of rural production was exempt from some monopoly right, some command precluding it from immediate entry into a market economy (as opposed to an authority market).

Off limits to foreign merchants until the eighteenth century, the Ottoman domestic market lying beyond the authorized rivers and seaports was organized almost wholly as a command economy. It was committed to protecting the staples rights (the rights of the chief place of each territorial subdivision to a portion or the rural product of its dependent territory) of the second-, third-, and fourth-level central places after the staples rights of the supreme central place and armed forces were assured. Rural populations were subject alike to central command and to the partly complementary but ultimately rival systems of provincial (sanjak), military-judicial (kaza), and great-county (nahiye) systems of staples or devolutionary rights. Towns obtained part of the products through peasant payments of tithes to the local cavalry of sipahis, who wanted to convert the tithes into cash or exchange them for other commodities.[55] Town rights to the rural product of their constituent territories were reinforced by the hardships of transportation, which dissuaded families of modest means from directing surpluses to more distant centers of consumption.

An administrative city was primarily a retailing city—a place of residence for rentiers and a center of consumption. Possessing a legally defined hinterland, it enjoyed certain hegemonic rights—a right to the surplus product of its dependent territory, presumably the right to forbid the diversion of local surpluses except to the city at the next level of territorial command and to the capital and armed forces, and a practical right to part of the staples belonging to numerous beneficiaries of revenue rights residing in the city.

Some rural communities had to bring to the central place of immediate jurisdiction a designated portion or quantity (that is, a proportion or the absolute amount) of some particular local product. Charcoal-producing villages at the edge of the Ihtiman basin, for example, had to deliver to the iron-manufacturing town of Samokov a specified quantity of charcoal.[56]

THE PERIPHERY AND THE MOBILIZED DIASPORAS

With few exceptions, commercial cities were located in coastal areas and along the main routes of trade. They were the seaports and rivers—the emporia where commodities were unloaded, stored, and transferred from one form of carriage and one set of merchants to another. As entrepôt cities, they were the "unraveling points" of the wholesale trade.[57]

But the main Ottoman trade routes were also war routes, and most Ottoman commercial towns and cities reflected this ambiguous status. As dependent cities, they were an outward projection of the state itself—often the means by which the state declared its identity *as* a state. Both sharing in and acting as agents of the redistribution of wealth, the cities promoted the circulation of money and goods, at least to the extent that benefits might accrue to them from such circulation.

One must nonetheless distinguish between the retail and wholesale functions of cities and between retailing and wholesaling cities. Craft production and the retail trade were subject to state regulation regarding weights and measures, style, quality, prices, and methods of production (although the regulations varied from place to place). In contrast, the business of domestic merchants (*tüccar* or *tüjjar*) engaged in intra-imperial long-distance trade was both privileged and highly remunerative.[58] It was also highly vulnerable. As in Byzantium, where the obligation had been known as *leitourgia* (public services),[59] it was the duty of the rich to serve the state. The wealth of intra-imperial merchants (*bazirgan başis*), like that of (other) public servants, was therefore always subject to state confiscation.

Commerce with the states of Europe presented a special problem. As Christian states, they were not simply politically but also culturally alien. Moreover, they were not only part of the "house of war" (*darülharb*) of the nonbelievers[60] but also the most threatening part of that house, both because of their common frontiers with Turkey, shielded culturally from other parts of the darülharb by other Muslim states, and because of the very closeness (and therefore the more apparent differences) between Muslim and Christian beliefs. Consequently, a special system had to be devised to facilitate commerce between Turkey and Europe.

An ad hoc invention initially designed to foster commerce between the Ottoman Empire and Venice and Ragusa, the system was later regularized. In 1535, Süleyman the Magnificent's grand vizier, Ibrahim, and Francis I's envoy to the Sublime Porte, the abbé Jean de la Forest, a knight of the order of Saint John of Jerusalem, concluded the first of the agreements called capitulations. Among the guarantees extended to French subjects by that accord, affirms a twentieth-century scholar, were "freedom of trade, security against extraordinary duties, immunity from Ottoman law, release from imprisonment or slavery, and the right to practise their own religion and to protect the Holy Places of Palestine."[61] Later in the century, especially during the seventeenth and eighteenth centuries, other European states obtained similar privileges. The scope of the capitulations was made increasingly comprehensive.[62]

From an Ottoman viewpoint, the purpose of the capitulations was not to extend privilege to the European states but to take advantage of the services of Europeans so that Muslim merchants would not have to enter the polluting darülharb of the Christian states. Simultaneously, the Turks confined the European merchants to designated seaports and rivers along the main routes of trade, excluding them from Ottoman internal commerce.

Between 1731 and 1783, however, the system was altered drastically—first by the right won by the French in 1731 to share in the direct purchase of wool in Macedonia and Thessaly (hitherto a monopoly of the Jews of Thessaloniki) and then by the Russo-Turkish commercial treaty of June 10–21, 1783. The latter accord recognized the right of Russian subjects to trade anywhere in the Ottoman Empire, to wear the dress of their own country, and to remain in Ottoman lands for an unlimited time. By allowing Russian traders to sell goods to any Ottoman buyer, the treaty divested celeps, kapanlis, and iştiracis of their monopoly rights to raw materials at low, state-determined prices. By authorizing Russians to buy rice, coffee, olive oil, and silk anywhere in Turkey except Istanbul and to ship grains of Russian origin through Istanbul's straits, the accord also undermined Istanbul's monopoly rights to the products of the Black Sea and radically reduced its rights of special access to the goods of the Aegean. Between 1784 and 1806, similar rights were granted to Austria, the United Kingdom, France, and Prussia. In 1802, foreign merchants won the right to buy goods in one place and sell them in any other part of the empire.[63]

The very nature of commerce between the two economic systems, one of which was a command economy, required the use of intermediaries—compradors who understood both the European and Ottoman economies and had easy access to the internal Ottoman market. The intermediaries were the three mobilized diasporas that had well-articulated networks of kinship and religious and business associations both in many European cities and in most of the cities and unraveling points of the Ottoman Empire: Jews, Armenians, and Greeks.

A mobilized diaspora is an ethnoreligious collectivity whose elite members are communication specialists—individuals who possess skills that the dominant ethnic group of the command economy prizes in others but does not seek to promote in its own members.[64] Charged with a territorial redistribution of money and goods, diasporas engage in international commerce as insurance against the political risks of privilege in a single polity, especially one constituted as a command economy.

The Ottoman-mobilized diasporas took advantage of grants of privilege—in return for provisioning the capital and armed forces—to serve as intra-imperial merchants as well as compradors. But as changes occurred in both the Ottoman command economy and the European periphery, the diasporas redefined their relationships with the two systems. As the European states became more powerful, for example, and Muslim-Ottoman urban populism grew more influential, many enterprising Jews realigned themselves more closely with the more highly mixed economies of the European states. The realignment was not too difficult: Long-distance commerce involves a network of information and correspondence, of communication and transaction, between two or more modes of production, two or more economic or political systems, or two or more differently endowed geographic regions.[65]

An early manifestation of the realignment was the departure from the Ottoman Empire of an undetermined number of Jews after the mid-seventeenth century, including many of the enterprising Portuguese Jews. As a result, the Jewish mobilized diaspora—by definition, a system of long-distance commerce and, indeed, "the foremost mercantile network in the world"—was redistributed spatially.[66] The center of Jewish population and economic action, which had moved eastward between 1200 and 1600, shifted westward after 1670, from the Russian and Ottoman Empires to Moldavia, Wallachia, Hungary, Venice, Livorno, Trieste, Hamburg, Vienna, Frankfurt, Amsterdam, Bordeaux, London, and the Americas. The revival of Jewish commerce in Turkey after 1800, partly by means of the Leipzig fairs, was itself a reflection of that readjustment.[67]

Jews continued to play an important role in the Ottoman economy even during the eighteenth century. But many Constantinopolitan Jews diverted their wealth to conspicuous consumption.[68] A portion of the Armenian mobilized diaspora similarly opted for conspicuous consumption or for realignment with the mixed economies of Europe, in which demand would play an increasingly important role. In Aegean and Balkan Turkey, more frugal merchants, packmen, and forwarding agents—ethnic and cultural Greeks—replaced some of the Jews and Armenians.

In fact, Greek merchants fashioned strong links with both the Ottoman command economy and the European economies.[69] But their conception of economic action embraced a growing preference for the bold entrepreneurship of European commerce. In 1836, an English traveler, Julia Pardoe, noted how their business behavior differed from that of members of the other diasporas, especially the Armenians—a difference probably already manifest a half century or century earlier:

> All the steady commerce on a great scale in the capital may be said to be, with very slight exceptions, in the hands of the Armenians, who have the true, patient, plodding, calculating spirit of trade; while the wilder speculations of hazardous and ambitious enterprise are grasped with avidity by the more daring and adventurous Greeks, for which it is at first sight difficult to account, that the most wealthy and the most needy of the merchants of Stamboul are alike of that nation: while you rarely see an Armenian either limited in his means, or obtrusive in his style.[70]

The identification of an increasing number of Ottoman merchants, mainly Greeks and Jews, with European conceptions of commerce impaired the Ottoman command economy. At the same time, with the initial complicity of the Ottoman government itself, a group of compradors—Jews, Greeks, and Armenians—was formed to facilitate the business of European merchants. Known to the French as *barataires* or *drogmans barataires,* these compradors—interpreters and specialists in commercial correspondence and intelligence—held patents (*berats*) of privilege, presents from the sultan to new European ambassadors. Each European ambassador distributed fifty new patents among the consuls of his nation in the authorized ports of trade. The consuls, in turn, granted the patents to Greek, Jewish, and Armenian brokers whose aid and collaboration they valued.

In the final decades of the eighteenth century, the consuls put such patents up for sale. By 1800, a berat was worth 5,000 or 6,000 French francs.[71] Local merchants were eager to purchase the patents, which not only exempted holders from the head tax but also declared their status as protégés of a European state. Benefiting from the extraterritorial rights granted to Europeans by the capitulations treaties, the barataires continued to enjoy the right to engage in intra-imperial commerce. They thus undercut the competition of Ottoman merchants who, lacking a berat, continued to be subject to imperial command.

The consuls also created numerous subbarataires (presumably, false barataires), who received similar rights. The Ottoman government occasionally checked the berats, as it did in 1793, and withdrew those that were unauthorized, but the number of barataires grew to many tens of thousands. By 1800, Austria alone was reputed to have distributed 200,000 berats (mostly without Ottoman authorization) in Moldavia and 60,000 in Wallachia. Moreover, the barataires claimed a hereditary right to protection, a belief the European consulates did little to dispel. And the Ottoman government was too weak to undo what had been done.[72]

The peripheralization of the Ottoman economy proceeded apace through the increasing access of the European merchants to internal commerce—buying and selling beyond the ports. Until 1731, for example, the wool farm (*beylik*) of the Jewish cloth manufactures of Thessaloniki enjoyed the right to purchase a fifth of the wool product of Macedonia and Thessaly at a low price—a third to a sixth of the market price—before other buyers entered the market. Holding a monopoly more lucrative even than the privileges of the kapanlis, iştiracis, and celeps, the Jews of Thessaloniki bought wool far in excess of their manufacturing needs and resold it to the merchants and commission agents of wool-buying firms in Marseilles, Livorno, Genoa, Venice, and Ancona. On June 25, 1731, however, France's ambassador, the marquis de Villeneuve, obtained a government order requiring the beylik of Thessaloniki to limit wool purchases to the amount needed for its manufacturing.

European merchants in Thessaloniki then negotiated a series of agreements with the beylik Jews allowing the Europeans to buy wool at the same time as the Jews, as long as they offered the beylik a certain proportion of their purchases—20 percent in the French case—at a fixed low price.[73]

European merchants did, however, suffer some reverses. In 1740, for example, soap dealers and manufacturers in Canea (a port on the island of Crete) and holders of revenue rights to the oil of the district protested vehemently when two French merchants directly purchased olive oil from peasant cultivators and paid a higher price than the privileged local dealers were ready to pay. On this occasion, staples rights and command carried the day.[74]

The market economy made further inroads during the 1770s, however, when several Austrian firms set up *comptoirs* (trading posts) along the middle and lower Danube and dispatched their own factors—mostly Greeks and Hellenized Arumanians (Macedo-Vlachs)—to Serres, Larissa, and other towns of the Balkan interior. As European merchants and their Balkan factors obtained control of the unraveling points of Balkan wholesaling, they sought to expand the demand for European manufactures. By the 1770s, indeed, French and Austrian merchants transformed the growing number of active Balkan fairs into "a mechanism for the distribution of European imported goods."[75]

ACCUMULATION AND DISPERSION OF CAPITAL

The increase in the number and activity of Balkan fairs and the partial integration of these fairs with the state-encouraged market economies of the European periphery depended, in fact, on the diminished Ottoman interest in protecting domestic manufactures and on the growing desire of Ottoman landlords and urban notables to place local products on the international market in order to obtain higher prices, the wherewithal for more luxuries. In 1703, for example, France's ambassador to the Porte, the marquis de Ferriol, executed his government's instructions to block grand vizier Rami Mehmed Pasha's project to improve old Ottoman textile manufactures and found new ones. Rami Mehmed fell from power before the end of the year, and subsequent Ottoman efforts to amend their manufactures were half-hearted. The establishment of new cotton manufactures in the small Thessalian town of Ambelakia was therefore not the product of privilege and government support but of the private, local, and communal enterprise of the Greek and Greco-Vlach diaspora.[76]

On the other hand, the attempt of Sarando Papadopoulo, a barataire under French protection, to found soap factories in Coron (Koroni) and Navarino met resistance from French consuls. The latter had orders to impede all manufactures that might push up the price of olive oil, needed for the soap-making businesses of Marseilles and Provence. In 1779, moreover, after his inspection tour of France's consulates in the Levant, Baron de Tott advocated continued opposition to the promotion and protection of Ottoman industry—that is, the closing of what had become a half-open command economy.[77]

Until about 1770, however, Turkish soap manufactures had modest success. Toward the end of the seventeenth century, for example, after the Ottoman conquest of Crete and before Europe embraced a systematic policy of hindering the further development of Ottoman manufactures, a Marseillais established a soap factory on Crete. Because soap was a staple in great demand in the Ottoman capital, it was easy to apply to the soap manufactures of Crete the command principle of staples rights. By 1723, Crete had more than 20 soap factories, 6 of them in Herakleion (Candia). The number of soap factories in Herakleion then grew to at least 12 in 1748, 15 in 1763 and 18 in 1787. In Canea, the number rose from 40 in 1745 to 50 in 1772 but declined to 25 in 1794. Rethymno then had 8, all run by Jewish barataires under French protection.

From an annual average of 675 metric tons between 1735 and 1737, the soap production of Crete rose to 6,000 metric tons between 1787 and 1789. Half the total production was for Istanbul, and two-fifths was for Izmir (Smyrna), Thessaloniki, and Syria. By 1772, however, the production of Canea alone was 5,500 to 6,000 metric tons.[78] But between 1772 and 1794, the soap production of Canea declined precipitously.

New soap factories founded by Greeks in the Ukraine and Russia's new Black Sea ports explain that decline, in part.[79] In 1800, Greeks owned 54 percent of the total capital of 113,720 rubles of the ten merchants in the first guild of the new Russian port of Odessa (shippers, bankers, and insurers). In the second merchant guild of small Odessa merchants (which, like the first guild, enjoyed the right to both internal and international trade), Greeks owned 61 percent of the capital.[80] Greek capital thus was diverted from Ottoman to Russian territories.

The perceptions of Orthodox Christians that property was more secure in Russia than in Turkey may partially account for that diversion. Also important, however, was the existence of a growing Russian market not only for soap but also for the shipping and mercantile services that Greeks could provide. Istanbul, Thessaloniki, Izmir, and Syria, on the other hand, may have been unable to consume more than 6,000 metric tons of Cretan soap unless Ottoman producers obtained protection against the soap manufactures of Italy and Provence. Ottoman abandonment of mercantilism thus probably encouraged the flight of Greek capital.

Some capital was also lost to Ottoman cities when a small number of enterprising Ottoman Jews departed for Europe. For a full century, however, Greeks filled the vacuum caused by the loss of Jewish talent and capital.

During the latter half of the seventeenth and throughout the eighteenth centuries, Chiot, Smyrniot, and Constantinopolitan Greeks, often called Phanariots, challenged the banking monopoly of the Jews and Armenians and won control of much of the provisioning of Istanbul. As dispensers of credit, advisers and secretaries to high government officials, administrators of the civil and fiscal affairs of the Greek Orthodox Church, governors of the principalities of Wallachia and Moldavia, and holders of the posts of dragoman of the Porte (undersecretary of the grand vizier), dragoman of the fleet, and chargé of Aegean affairs,[81] they created a foundation on which less wealthy Greeks could build.

In need of public support against the unruly janissaries and other urban sectors dismayed by the loss of Istanbul's monopoly rights to Black Sea resources, Selim III yielded to Demetrios Mouroutsis's suggestion that Greeks be allowed to constitute themselves as a company or guild of "European merchants."[82] In 1795, the three mobilized diasporas—the Greeks, Jews, and Armenians—obtained a firman (imperial order) legitimating the charging of interest, an act that was previously denounced, albeit tolerated in practice. Ordering the imprisonment of debtors who neglected their obligations to creditors, the firman declared that whatever was good for the state was legitimate and desirable. Moneylenders, it held, supplied needed funds to the tax farmers and other state agents, but if they failed to receive interest, they could not render necessary services. The charging of interest was consequently deemed appropriate.[83]

By the time of Napoleon, the comprador moneylenders lent funds even to Muslim landowners in return for mortgages on their properties. If the latter defaulted, lenders laid claim to the landlords' surpluses at prices below current market levels.[84] This triumph of money and trade, however, encouraged an alliance between landlordism and an anticapitalist and antimarket urban populism.

The Greek commercial diaspora attained the pinnacle of success just before and during the Napoleonic era. The rise of a Greco-Orthodox-Albanian merchant marine by the 1750s allowed Greek merchants and shippers to amass much wealth in the carrying trade between Black Sea ports and the Aegean and between the eastern and western Mediterranean, especially by bringing wheat and other cereals to Marseilles during the French Revolution and the Napoleonic Wars. Some Greeks even became millionaires.[85]

Acting within the framework of the Ottoman command economy, other Greeks controlled the Danube River traffic between Vidin and Orsova. "Every day," wrote a contemporary observer, "the Greeks, and especially those of Vidin, conjointly with the Pasha [Pasvanoğlu, rebel governor of Vidin], make ... a true monopoly of the passage of poorly laden boats and frequently spoiled goods, increasing their cargoes at will, overloading the boats." As customs officials and tax farmers, they hindered the trade of foreign (and perhaps rival domestic) merchants, altering cargoes, opening bales, appropriating a portion of the goods moving between Turkey and Austria, and exacting arbitrary tolls and customs duties. By such practices, common also at Belgrade and Svishtov (Sistova), some of the merchants of the command economy, too, became "*in breve tempo, miglionari*" ("in little time, millionaires").[86]

The partly Hellenized Arumanian Sina family of Moschopolis settled in the Bosnian provincial capital of Sarajevo around 1750, proceeded to the unraveling point of Slavonski Brod, and finally set up headquarters for trade with Turkey in Vienna. In Vienna, Simon G. Sina (1753–1822) became the foremost importer of Ottoman cotton (mainly Macedonian) and wool (mainly Thessalian) during the British blockade of Napoleonic Europe. Soon he formed a banking enterprise of European renown, and three years before his death, he was ennobled.[87]

In 1763, the total capital of Ottoman merchants in Vienna (mostly Greeks but also Hellenized Arumanians, Jews, Armenians, and Serbs) amounted to 2 million florins. Equal to the total value of current Austrian imports from Macedonia and Thessaly and to an eighth of the total capital of the "most distinguished" native and naturalized merchants of Vienna,[88] it was a sizable amount.

Diaspora means dispersion. Using the word in that sense, one may say that, along with three main ethnic diasporas, there was a diaspora of capital in the Ottoman Empire—material and nonmaterial wealth (including talent) with which more wealth could be created.

Of diminished importance in the Ottoman Balkans during the eighteenth century, the Jewish diaspora recovered its losses after 1800. The Armenian commercial diaspora remained more or less intact until after 1800. Of only minor importance until after the 1660s, the Greek commercial diaspora grew rapidly thereafter. In 1800, taken together, the three commercial diasporas were greater in size and probably wealthier than in any previous period.

As Charles Tilly has shown, however, the accumulation of capital does not necessarily result in the concentration of capital.[89] The capital of the Ottoman diasporas thus was both ethnically and territorially dispersed.

Greek capital, for example, was invested in the construction of Greek ships (often flying the Russian colors), the building of attractive homes, the promotion of education (philanthropy), as was done at Chios and Kydoniai, and even the encouragement of manufactures, as at Ambelakia and Kydoniai (Ayvalik). Situated in the Aegean coast of Asia Minor, Kydoniai (Quinces) grew, between 1770 and 1820, from a simple village to a town with a famous "college," 40 oil mills, 30 soap manufactures, and a Greek population of 15,000, many living in stone houses.[90] But in the 1820s, the Greeks were unable to finance their revolution without foreign (political) financial aid. They could not achieve a concentration of capital in the poorly developed rebel territories, where money was scarce and from which it was prone to flee.[91]

By rejecting mercantilism, the Ottoman government itself had fostered the dispersion of wealth, including the investment of commercial capital in other countries. Russian policies, on the contrary, drew the wealth of the Ottoman diasporas to its Black Sea ports. For a time, Austrian policies, too, benefited the Greek diaspora and other Balkan merchants. After 1780, however, Austria pressured them to become Habsburg subjects. Some diaspora members thus acquired a new identity—by the fusion of cosmopolitan interests and *Kaisertreue* (imperial allegiance).[92] The denationalizing and assimilation of the diasporas were under way by 1800. Where a diaspora was of the same faith as the group in whose midst it lived, assimilation was not too difficult. Marriage with the dominant ethnic group and conversion were other paths to assimilation. The creation of Balkan nation-states between 1805 and 1878 similarly promoted assimilation. But assimilation also assured that the capital of the diasporas would remain dispersed.

CONCLUSION

The foregoing changes depended on the assertion of a European-centered world market economy.[93] The contact between two adjacent world political-economic systems, Ottoman and European (the first governed mainly by a command economy and the second by a mercantilist demand economy) required the use of commercially mobilized diasporas. The secular stagnation of the European world economy between 1620 and 1720 was paralleled by a decline in the market value of Ottoman commerce with the not yet fully formed European world economy between 1620 and the mid-eighteenth century. This temporarily relieved the Ottoman diasporas of any pressing need to realign more firmly with the peripheral European world economy. Between 1730 and 1780, however, aided by the export orientation of the urban-based but landowning Ottoman notabilities, the realignment was made—a realignment that can be understood as peripheralization.[94]

Until the 1770s or 1780s, the Ottoman government regarded the exportation of goods as an exceptional affair, for exports could deprive the command authority of strategic and consumer goods alike. Exports might also make prices soar, thereby fomenting urban riots. The Ottoman government allowed European ships to remove goods from Ottoman ports but only under the fiction that the goods would be transported to some other part of the empire—in other words, that the Europeans would perform the useful function of an internal exchange confined to the ports of trade. From time to time, the government took steps to prevent the export of grains, wool, cotton, cotton yarn, leather, beeswax, copper, gold, and silver, but local authorities executed related orders only in time of war: Beneficiaries of tax farms and other revenue rights and men of wealth in general were drawn to the export market by the desire to negotiate the highest possible price for their staples, rarely obtainable in the internal trade.

Selective by staple, peripheralization was favored in particular by tax farmers, by producers of wheat, wool, and cotton; by owners of livestock; and, exceptionally, by the lessees of olive groves. It also was favored by importers and consumers of cloth, fezzes, furs, sugar, West Indian coffee, dyes, hardware, and glassware.[95]

Peripheralization was the result of two facts—that the Ottoman Empire was never a totally closed command economy and that its particular form of command economy or devolution gave rise to an economically nongenerative urban system. The latter occurred, in part, because (1) the Ottoman Empire increasingly opened itself to Europe during a downward economic secular trend—during the shift, between 1580 and 1720, from an equilibrium between a northern European and a Mediterranean pole of commercial attraction to the emergence of northern Europe as the core of a European-Mediterranean and Atlantic world economy—and (2) the empire nonetheless remained a separate world economy, confining its contacts with Europe to some forty seaports and several rivers of trade, in which no more than 1,000 Europeans resided, if one excludes the protected diasporas.[96]

Ottoman cities and landlords consequently shifted the cost of urbanization to the peasantry. Once the secular trend turned around after 1720, cities and landlords were eager to place an increasing share of the products that they acquired by means of devolution into the markets of Europe, for European buyers paid a higher price than was available locally. In accord with the views of the European states, therefore, these cities and landlords forced the Ottoman government to abandon its mercantilist policies.

At the same time, the diasporas that had been mobilized to serve mainly as agents of intra-imperial trade reduced the ever-present risks to merchants in a command economy by making themselves necessary in international trade, especially exchange between Europe and the Ottoman Empire. Two main forces thus undermined the Ottoman command economy—urban and rural notables who succeeded in effecting a partial shift from a centrally based command economy to a multiple-centered one and a portion of the mobilized diasporas. Notables increased their accumulation of capital largely by promoting diminished consumption by the peasantry, that is, by favoring cities of an economically nongenerative type. The diasporas, on the other hand, at least partly encouraged capital accumulation by means of increased business revenues. In either case, however, even when capital was not diverted to nongenerative ends, it was widely dispersed territorially and ethnically.

Consequently, both the concentration of capital and the difficult process of creating economically generative cities or an effective capital accumulation in the Balkans had to await the emergence of nation-states and the restructuring of the Ottoman Empire. Decisively weakened between 1730 and 1780, the Ottoman command economy was further undermined between 1780 and 1830. Full integration with the European world economy was then accomplished—but the results were not entirely positive.

Notes

For their comments on a preliminary version of this chapter, I am grateful to Michael Adas, Rudolph M. Bell, the Rutgers Social History Group, and the editors of this book.

1. D. A. Zakythinos, "Crise monétaire et crise économique à Byzance du XIIIe au XVe siècle," in *L'Hellénisme contemporain,* ser. 2, Vol. I (Athens, 1947), 572, and (for the continuation of the monograph), Vol. II (1948), 57–81, 150–167; Peter Charanis, "Internal Strife in Byzantium During the Fourteenth Century," *Byzantion* (American Series, I), XV (1940–1941), 208–230; Peter Charanis, "A Note on the Population and Cities of the Byzantine Empire in the Thirteenth Century," in *The Joshua Starr Memorial Volume,* Jewish Social Studies, Publication No. 5 (New York: Conference on Jewish Relations, 1953), pp. 146–147; E. Francès, "La Féodalité et les villes byzantines au XIIIe et au XIVe siècles," *Byzantinoslavica,* XVI (Prague, 1955), 91–95; Konstantin [Constantin Josef] Jireček, *Istorija Srba,* trans., with additions, by Jovan Radonić (Beograd: Geca Kon, 1923), p. 183; C[onstantin Josef] Jireček, *La Civilisation serbe au Moyen âge,* trans. from the German under the direction of Louis Eisenmann, Collection historique de l'Institut d'Etudes Slaves, I (Paris: Editions Bossard, 1920), pp. 24–27; Nikola Radojčić, *Dušanov Zakonik* (Novi Sad, Serbia: Matica Srpska, 1950), pp. 55–58, 62–67; Rudolf Horvat, *Povijest Hrvatske* (Petrinja, Croatia: Dragutin Benko, 1904), pp. 217–218; Sima Ćirković, "Unfulfilled Autonomy: Urban Society in Serbia and Bosnia," in Bariša Krekić, *Urban Society of Eastern Europe in Premodern Times* (Berkeley: University of California Press, 1987), pp. 158–184; Bariša Krekić, "Developed Autonomy: The Patricians in Dubrovnik and Dalmatian Cities," in ibid., pp. 185–215; Alain Ducellier, *La Façade maritime de l'Albanie au Moyen âge: Durazzo et Valona du XIe au XVe siècle* (Thessaloniki, Greece: Institute for Balkan Studies, 1981), pp. 104–111, 470, 517–520.

2. Stojan Novaković, *Zakonski spomenici srpskih država srednjega veka,* Srpska Kraljevska Akademija, knj. 5 (Beograd: Državna Štamparija, 1912), pp. VIII–IX, 1–74.

3. Yovan Radonitch [Jovan Radonić], *Histoire des Serbes de Hongrie* (Paris: Bloud et Gay, 1919), pp. 16–17; Jireček, *Istorija Srba,* p. 185.

4. D. A. Zakythinos, "La Commune grecque: Les conditions historiques d'une décentralisation administrative," *L'Hellénisme contemporain,* ser. 2, Vol. II (Athens, 1948), 415; François-Charles-Hugues-Laurent Pouqueville, *Voyage dans la Grèce,* 5 vols. (Paris: Firmin Didot, 1820–1821), V, 282–291.

5. Olgierd Górka, ed., *Anonymi Descriptio Europae Orientalis (Imperium Constantinopolitanum, Albania, Serbia, Bulgaria, Ruthenia, Ungaria, Polonia, Bohemia) Anno MCCCVIII Exarata* (Cracow: Gebethner, 1916), p. 32.

6. Traian Stoianovich, "Model and Mirror of the Premodern Balkan City," in Institut d'Etudes Balkaniques of the Académie Bulgare des Sciences, *Studia Balcanica,* III, *La Ville balkanique, XVe–XIXe siècles* (Sofia: Editions de l'Académie Bulgare des Sciences, 1970), pp. 86–88, 207–208.

7. Jacques Rueff, *L'Ordre social,* 3d rev. ed., with a new preface (Paris: Editions M. Th. Génin, 1967), pp. I–III, X–XIII.

8. Ibid., p. 21.

9. Abraham-Hyacinthe Anquetil Duperron, *Législation orientale, ouvrage dans lequel, en montrant quels sont en Turquie, en Perse et dans l'Indoustan, les principes fondamentaux du gouvernement, on prouve, I. Que la manière dont jusqu'ici on a représenté le despotisme, qui passe pour être absolu dans ces trois Etats, ne peut qu'en donner une idée fausse; II. Qu'en Turquie, en Perse & dans l'Indoustan, il y a un code de loix écrites, qui obligent le Prince ainsi que les sujets; III. Que dans ces trois Etats, les particuliers ont des propriétés en biens meubles & immeubles, dont ils jouissent librement* (Amsterdam: chez Marc-Michel Rey, 1778), pp. 15, 18, 25, 30; Bibliothèque Nationale (Paris), cited hereafter as BN, Nouvelles Acquisitions Françaises 453: Anquetil Duperron, "Le Despotisme, considéré dans les trois Etats où il passe pour être le plus absolu, la Turquie, la Perse et l'Indoustan," composed between 1774 and 1776, read in 1776 by the minister of foreign affairs, the comte de Vergennes, bound manuscript, pp. VIII–106. See, in particular, pp. 14–15.

10. Sir John Hicks, *A Theory of Economic History* (London: Oxford University Press, 1969), pp. 9–24.

11. Karl Polanyi, *The Great Transformation,* foreword by Robert M. MacIver (Boston: Beacon Press, 1957), p. 48; Abraham Rotstein, "Karl Polanyi's Concept of Non-Market Trade," *Journal of Economic History,* XXX, 1 (March 1970), 117–126.

12. James E. Vance, Jr., *The Merchant's World: The Geography of Wholesaling* (Englewood Cliffs, N.J.: Prentice-Hall, 1970), pp. 3, 140–143.

13. P[etar] Matković, "Putopis Marka Antuna Pigafette u Carigrad od god. 1567" (re-publication in entirety of "Itinerario di Marc' Antonio Pigafetta, gentil'huomo vicentino," London: John Wolf, 1585), in Jugoslavenska Akademija znanosti i umjetnosti, *Starine,* XXII (1890), 135–136.

14. Giovanni Botero, *A Treatise Concerning the Causes of the Magnificencie and Greatness of Cities, Divided into Three Bookes, by Sig. Giovanni Botero, in the Italian Tongue; Now Done into English,* trans. by Robert Peterson (London: Richard Ockould and Henry Tomes, 1606), p. 81.

15. Haus-, Hof- und Staatsarchiv (Wien), Staatenabteilung (hereafter cited as HHSA, St A.), Türkei V/25, undated memoir in French, c. 1775.

16. Robert Halsband, ed., *The Complete Letters of Lady Mary Wortley Montagu,* 3 vols. (Oxford: Clarendon Press, 1965–1967), I, 354, Lady Mary Wortley Montagu's letter, dated Adrianople, May 17 (O.S.), 1717.

17. Peterson's translation of Botero, *A Treatise Concerning the Causes of the Magnificencie and Greatness of Cities,* pp. 80–81.

18. Fernand Braudel, *La Méditerranée et le monde méditerranéen à l'époque de Philippe II,* 2 vols. (Paris: Armand Colin, 1966), I, 319.

19. "Relazione dell' Impero Ottomano del Senatore Costantino Garzoni stato all' ambascieria di Costantinopoli nel 1573," in Eugenio Albèri, ed., *Relazioni degli Ambasciatori Veneti al Senato,* ser. IIIa, Vol. I (Firenze, 1840), 389.

20. François Billaçois, ed., *L'Empire du Grand Turc vu par un sujet de Louis XIV, Jean Thévenot* (Paris: Calmann-Lévy, 1965), pp. 54–55.

21. [John Cam Hobhouse] Broughton, *Travels in Albania and Other Provinces of Turkey in 1809 and 1810,* new ed., revised and corrected, 2 vols. (London: John Murray, 1858), II, 264–266.

22. Stoianovich, "Model and Mirror," pp. 90–91, 97–100; Robert Mantran, *La Vie quotidienne à Constantinople au temps de Soliman le Magnifique et de ses successeurs (XVIe et XVIIe siècles)* (Paris: Hachette, 1965), p. 46; Ignatius Mouradgea d'Ohsson, *Tableau général de l'Empire othoman,* 7 vols. (Paris: Firmin Didot, 1788–1824), IV, première partie (Paris: Imprimerie de Monsieur, 1791), pp. 233–242; Otto und Gertrud Rudloff, "Die Stadt Philippopel in Bulgarien," *Geographischer Anzeiger,* XXXVIII (1937), 351; Peter F. Sugar, *Southeastern Europe Under Ottoman Rule, 1354–1804* (Seattle: University of Washington Press, 1977), pp. 74–77.

23. Dean A. Miller, *Imperial Constantinople* (New York: John Wiley and Sons, 1969), pp. 10–11, and [Raymond] Janin, *Constantinople byzantine: Développement urbain et répertoire topographique,* 2d ed. (Paris: Institut d'Etudes Byzantines, 1964), pp. 3–4 and map 1, an archaeological and topographic map on the basis of which Miller has determined the perimeter of Constantinople *intra muros*. Istanbul was contained within the same walls.

24. Ferdinand Lot, *L'Art militaire et les armées au Moyen âge en Europe et dans le Proche Orient,* 2 vols. (Paris: Payot, 1946), II, 236, n. 2.

25. François Pétis de la Croix gives an all too brief description of Constantinople in M. Langlès, ed., "Extrait du *Journal* du sieur Pétis, fils," which M. de Fienne, trans., joined to his own *Relation de Dourry Efendy [Durri-Efendi], ambassadeur de la Porte othomane auprès du roi de Perse, traduite du turk [by M. de Fienne], et suivie de l'Extrait des Voyages de Pétis de la Croix, rédigé par lui-même* (Paris: chez Ferra, 1810), pp. 160–164, in which the number of houses is not indicated. Cited by Mantran, in *La Vie quotidienne à Constantinople,* p. 44, the figure presumably comes from the *Journal* of Pétis de la Croix. Mantran gives the volume and page—I, 133—but not the title of the work in which it appeared. I have thus far been unable to check the information.

26. W[illiam] Eton, *Survey of the Turkish Empire* (London: printed for T. Cadell, jun., and W. Davies, 1798), pp. 276–278.

27. Bernard Lewis, *Istanbul and the Civilization of the Ottoman Empire* (Norman: University of Oklahoma Press, 1963), pp. 102–103.

28. Eton, *Survey of the Turkish Empire,* pp. 276–278.

29. Alexander Pallis, *In the Days of the Janissaries: Old Turkish Life as Depicted in the "Travel-Book" of Evliyá Chelebí* (London: Hutchinson, 1951), pp. 87–88, 95, 100. In *La Vie quotidienne à Constantinople,* p. 27, Robert Mantran seems to accept Evliya Çelebi's absurdly high figure of 9,800 dwellings for mid-seventeenth-century Eyyub.

30. Metodija Sokolski, "Prilog kon proučavanjeto na tursko-osmanskiot feudalen sistem so poseben osvrt na Makedonija vo XV i XVI vek," *Glasnik na Institutot za Nicionalna Istorija,* II, 1 (Skopje, 1958), 220.

31. Nedim Filipović, "Neki novi podaci iz ranije istorije Sarajeva pod Turcima," *Pregled: Časopis za društvena pitanja,* Nos. 7–8 (Sarajevo, July-August 1953), 71;

Vladimir Skarić, *Sarajevo i njegova okolina od najstarijih vremena do austro-ugarske okupacije* (Sarajevo: Opština grada Sarajeva, 1937), 61.

32. Evliya Efendi [Evliya Çelebi], *Narrative of Travels in Europe, Asia, and Africa in the Seventeenth Century,* trans. from the Turkish by Josef von Hammer-Purgstall (London: Oriental Transaction Fund of Great Britain and Ireland, 1834), p. 13.

33. George Kingsley Zipf, *National Disunity: The Nation as a Bio-Social Organism* (Bloomington, Ind.: Principia Press, 1941), pp. 10–11, 33, 36–37, 49. See also Rutledge Vining, "A Description of Certain Spatial Aspects of an Economic System," *Economic Development and Cultural Change,* III, 2 (January 1955), 147–195. For a critique of the precise meaning of urban rank-size distribution in a particular nation, culture, region, or economy, see Jan de Vries, *European Urbanization, 1500–1800* (Cambridge, Mass.: Harvard University Press, 1984), pp. 87–95; Paul M. Hohenberg and Lynn Hollen Lees, *The Making of Urban Europe, 1000–1950* (Cambridge, Mass.: Harvard University Press, 1985), pp. 55–73, 345–349.

34. J[ean]-B[aptiste]-G[abriel]-Amédée Chaumette des Fossés, *Voyage en Bosnie dans les années 1807 et 1808* (Paris: Impr. de J. Didot, 1822), pp. 31–45.

35. [Louis-Auguste] Félix [baron de] Beaujour, *Tableau du commerce de la Grèce d'après une année moyenne depuis 1787 jusqu'à 1797,* 2 vols. (Paris: Imprimerie de Crapelet, *an* VIII), I, 128–129, for all the mentioned places except Ambelakia. For Ambelakia, see Traian Stoianovich, "The Conquering Balkan Orthodox Merchant," *Journal of Economic History,* XX, 2 (June 1960), 257.

36. On the existence of two sets of central-place hierarchies, see G. William Skinner, "Marketing and Social Structure in Rural China," *Journal of Asian Studies,* XXIV (1964–1965), 3–43, 195–228, 363–399; G. William Skinner, "The Structure of Chinese History," *Journal of Asian Studies,* XLIV, 2 (February 1985), 280–281; Charles Tilly, *Coercion, Capital, and European States,* rev. ed. (Oxford: Blackwell, 1992), Chapter 4.

37. These crude estimates as well as the identification of cities at the 10,000 level are my own responsibility, based on a critical reading of the following items: Archives Nationales (Paris), cited hereafter as AN, B^3 242, "Mémoire sur la situation topographique de l'Albanie, floréal an VIII," where the population of Arta is estimated at 5,000 to 6,000 in 1731, at 8,000 in 1800 (of whom there were 2,000 Jews, 2,000 Muslims, and 4,000 persons of the Greek Orthodox faith), and at more than 8,000 several years earlier; Ömer Lûtfi Barkan, "Quelques observations sur l'organisation économique et sociale des villes ottomanes, des XVIe et XVIIe siècles," in *Recueils de la Société Jean Bodin,* VII, *La Ville,* 2e partie: *Institutions économiques et sociales* (Bruxelles, 1955), pp. 289–310; Ömer Lûtfi Barkan, "Essai sur les données statistiques des registres de recensement dans l'Empire ottoman aux XVe et XVIe siècles," *Journal of Economic and Social History of the Orient,* I, part 1 (August 1957), 9–36; M[etodija] Sokolski, "Aperçu sur l'évolution de certaines villes plus importantes de la partie méridionale des Balkans au XVe et au XVIe siècles," in Association Internationale d'Etudes du Sud-Est Européen, *Istanbul à la jonction des cultures balkaniques, méditerranéennes, slaves et orientales, aux XVIe–XIXe siècles,* Actes du Colloque international organisé par l'AIESEE, en collaboration avec les Commissions internationales d'histoire maritime et des études sur la Méditerranée et les Comités internationaux de l'Asie Centrale et des études slaves, Istanbul, October 15–20, 1973 (Bucharest: AIESEE, 1977), 81–89; Lorenzo Bernardo, "Viaggio a Constantinopoli di

sier Lorenzo Bernardo per l'arresto del bailo sier Girolamo Lippomano, cav., 1591 aprile," in R. Deputazione Veneta sopra gli Studi di Storia Patria, *Monumenti Storici,* ser. 4 (Venice: R. Deputazione Veneta, 1886), 30; Frank Edgar Bailey, *British Policy and the Turkish Reform Movement: A Study in Anglo-Turkish Relations, 1826–1853* (Cambridge, Mass.: Harvard University Press, 1942), pp. 101, 110; Félex [de] Beaujour, *Tableau du commerce de la Grèce,* I, 128; [Antoine] Juchereau de Saint-Denys, *Histoire de l'Empire ottoman depuis 1792 jusqu'en 1844,* 4 vols. (Paris: au comptoir des Imprimeurs-Unis, 1844), I, 53–59, 78–80, 94–95, 107–109, and II, 19; John MacGregor, *Commercial Statistics: A Digest of the Productive Resources, Commercial Legislation, Customs, Tariffs [etc.] of All Nations* (London: Whittaker, 1850), p. 57, where the population of Galata in 1834 is estimated at 12,000; Robert Mantran, "Règlements fiscaux ottomans: La Police des marchés de Stamboul au début du XVIe siècle," *Les Cahiers de Tunisie,* IV, 2 (1956), 238; Nicolas V. Michoff [Mikhov], *Beiträge zur Handelsgeschichte Bulgariens,* II, *Österreichische Konsularberichte,* erster Band (Sofia, 1943), pp. 45–50, 81, 109–132, 141–150, 216–217, 254–262, 265–270, 313–315, 327–340, 344–364, 368–428; Nicolas V. Michoff [Mikhov], *La Population de la Turquie et de la Bulgarie au XVIIIe et au XIXe s.: Recherches bibliographiques avec données statistiques et ethnographiques,* Vol. IV (Sofia: Imprimerie de la Cour, 1935), p. 171; William Miller, *The Latins in the Levant: A History of Frankish Greece (1204–1566)* (London: John Murray, 1908), pp. 500–501; William Miller, "Greece Under the Turks, 1571–1684," *English Historical Review,* XIX (1904), 665, for Chalkis; G[uillaume] A[ntoine] Olivier, *Voyage dans l'Empire othoman, l'Egypte et la Perse, fait par ordre du gouvernement, pendant les six premières années de la République,* Vol. II (Paris: H. Agasse, *an* IX), pp. 155, 164, 255, 269, 279, 286; Dušan Popović, "Beograd za vreme Karadjordjeva ustanka," in *Geografski lik Srbije u doba Prvog ustanka,* Editions spéciales de la Société Serbe de Géographie, 32 (Belgrade, 1954), 90–102; V. Radovanović, "Priština," in St. Stanojević, ed., *Narodna enciklopedija srpsko-hrvatsko-slovenačka,* III (Zagreb, 1928), 694–696; V. Radovanović, "Prizren," in ibid., pp. 697–699; Joshua Starr, *Romania: The Jewries of the Levant After the Fourth Crusade* (Paris: Editions du Centre, 1949), pp. 75–76; Stoianovich, "The Conquering Balkan Orthodox Merchant," passim; Nikolai Todorov, *Balkanskiiat grad XV–XIX vek: Sotsialno-ikonomichesko i demografsko razvitie* (Sofia: Nauka i Izkustvo, 1972), passim.

38. For the view that dependent cities may, in fact, sometimes serve such a function, see de Vries, *European Urbanization,* p. 10. For the concept of "generative cities," see Bert F. Hoselitz, "Generative and Parasitic Cities," *Economic Development and Cultural Change,* III (April 1955), 278–294.

39. Adrien [Adriano] Balbi, *Tableau politico-statistique de l'Europe en 1820* (Lisbon: Typographie Royale, 1820), a single, large page of data.

40. The estimates for the sixteenth century are based on but vary from Ömer Lûtfi Barkan, "La 'Méditerranée' de Fernand Braudel vue d'Istamboul," *Annales: Economies, Sociétés, Civilisations,* IX, 2 (April-June 1954), 191–193; Barkan, "Essai sur les données statistiques," pp. 9–21. The estimates for the eighteenth century are based on Traian Stoianovich, "L'Economie balkanique aux XVIIe et XVIIIe siècles (principalement d'après les archives consulaires françaises)," Ph.D. diss., University of Paris, 1952, pp. 1–64. In his *Ottoman Population, 1830–1914: Demographic and Social Characteristics* (Madison: University of Wisconsin Press, 1985), p. 23, Kemal H.

Karpat accepts a population estimate for the territory south of the Sava and Danube, without Serbia, of 7,990,000 at some moment between 1800 and 1830. Estimates for the seventeenth century are yet more difficult. I have made them inferentially.

41. Spyros Asdrachas, "Histoire de la Grèce post-byzantine," extrait des rapports sur les conférences, Ecole Pratique des Hautes Etudes, IVe Section: Sciences historiques et philologiques, *Annuaire 1975/1976* (Paris: EPHE), 477–499; Spyros Asdrachas, "Problems of Economic History of the Period of Ottoman Domination in Greece," trans. from the Greek by Yiorgos Chouliaras, in *Journal of the Hellenic Diaspora,* VI, 2 (Summer 1979), 12–17; Spyros Asdrachas, "Quelques aspects des économies villageoises au début du XIXe siècle: Fiscalité et rentes foncièes," *Epitheorisi Koinonikon Ereunon,* 1981, pp. 158–179.

42. Louis-Auguste Félix-Beaujour (Félix de Beaujour), *Tableau du commerce de la Grèce, formé d'après une année moyenne, depuis 1787 jusqu'en 1797,* 2 vols. (Paris: Imprimerie de Crapelet, an VIII), I, 118–119; Nicolas G. Svoronos, *Le Commerce de Salonique au XVIIIe siècle* (Paris: Presses Universitaires de France, 1956), pp. 49, 272, 380, 398–399.

43. Vladislav Milenković, *Ekonomska istorija Beograda do Svetskog rata* (Belgrade: Za Narodnu Stampariju Mirko Drobac, 1932), pp. 32–34; Dragiša Lapčević, *Istorija socijalizma u Srbiji* (Belgrade: Geca Kon, 1922), p. 10; Dragoslav Janković, *O političkim strankama u Srbiji XIX veka* (Belgrade: Prosveta, 1951), p. 149.

44. Eton, *Survey of the Turkish Empire,* p. 253, for consumption in Istanbul.

45. On the "social cost of urban production," see Serafina Cernuschi-Salkoff, "L'Historicité du concept de ville," *Cahiers internationaux de sociologie,* L (1971), 84–87.

46. Fernand Braudel, *Civilization and Capitalism, 15th–18th Century,* trans. from the French by Siân Reynolds, 3 vols. (New York: Harper & Row, 1984), III, *The Perspective of the World,* pp. 76–80.

47. Halil Inalcik, "Capital Formation in the Ottoman Empire," *Journal of Economic History,* XXIX, 1 (March 1969), 104–105.

48. William H. McNeill, "The Ottoman Empire in World History," in *Meletemata ste mneme Basileiou Laourda: Essays in Memory of Basil Laourdas* (Thessaloniki, 1975), pp. 374–385. On protection production, see Frederic C. Lane, "Economic Consequences of Organized Violence," *Journal of Economic History,* XVIII, 4 (December 1958), 401–417; Frederic C. Lane, "The Role of Governments in Economic Growth in Early Modern Times," *Journal of Economic History,* XXXV, 1 (March 1975), 8–17.

49. Hicks, *A Theory of Economic History,* pp. 14–16.

50. Traian Stoianovich, "Balkan Peasants and Landlords and the Ottoman State: Familial Economy, Market Economy, and Modernization," in Nikolay [Nikolai] Todorov, Alexander Valtchev, and Maria Todorova, eds., *La Révolution industrielle dans le sud-est européen—XIXe s.,* rapports présentés au Colloque International de la Commission de l'AIESEE sur l'histoire sociale et économique, Hambourg, March 23–26, 1976 (Sofia: Institut d'Etudes Balkaniques, Musée National Polytechnique, 1977), pp. 172–177.

51. Deena Sadat, "Urban Notables in the Ottoman Empire: The *Ayan,*" Ph.D. diss., Rutgers University, 1969; Deena Sadat, "Rumeli Ayanlari: The Eighteenth Century," *Journal of Modern History,* XLIV, 3 (September 1972), 346–363; Avdo Sućeska, "Bedeutung und Entwicklung des Begriffes A'yân im Osmanischen Reich," *Südost-*

Forschungen, XXV (1966), 3–26; Avdo Sućeska, "Vilayetski ajani," *Godišnjak Društva Istoričara Bosne i Hercegovine,* XIII (1962), 167–198; Halil Inalcik, "Centralization and Decentralization in Ottoman Administration," in Thomas Naff and Roger Owen, eds., *Studies in Eighteenth Century Islamic History* (Carbondale and Edwardsville: Southern Illinois University Press, 1977), pp. 27–52; Stanford J. Shaw, *Between Old and New: The Ottoman Empire Under Sultan Selim III, 1789–1807* (Cambridge, Mass.: Harvard University Press, 1971), pp. 167–179, 211–246, 283–327; review of Shaw's book by Allan Cunningham, in *Journal of Modern History,* XLIV, 3 (September 1972), 414–419; Gibb and Bowen, *Islamic Society,* Vol. I, part 1, 198, 256–257, 303; Mouradgea d'Ohsson, *Tableau général,* VII, 286, 336–338. For the ayan in Anatolia, see Gilles Veinstein, "*Ayân* de la région d'Izmir et commerce du Levant (deuxième moitié du XVIIIe siècle)," *Etudes balkaniques,* XII, 3 (Sofia, 1976), 71–83.

52. Serif Mardin and I. William Zartman, "Ottoman Turkey and the Maghreb in the Nineteenth and Twentieth Centuries," Social Science Research Council, *Items,* XXX, 4 (December 1976), 63.

53. J. [Etienne-Ignace] Raicevich, *Osservazioni storiche naturali, e politiche intorno: La Valachie, e Moldavia* (Napoli, 1788), pp. 120–126; Mouradgea d'Ohsson, *Tableau général,* IV, part 1, 222–225; Walter Hahn, *Die Verpflegung Konstantinopels durch staatliche Zwangswirtschaft nach türkischen Urkunden aus dem 16. Jahrhundert* (Stuttgart: Verlag von W. Kohlhammer, 1926), pp. 48–58, on the forced sales of sheep at fixed prices; Lûtfi Gücer, "Le Problème d'approvisionnement d'Istanbul en céréales vers le milieu du XVIIIe siècle," *Revue de la Faculté des sciences économiques de l'Université d'Istanbul,* XI (1950), 153–162; Lûtfi Gücer, "Le Commerce intérieur des céréales dans l'Empire ottoman pendant la seconde moitié du XVIe siècle," ibid., pp. 163–188; Bistra Cvetkova [Tsvetkova], "Le Service des 'Celep' et le ravitaillement en bétail dans l'Empire ottoman (XVe–XVIIIe s.)," *Etudes historiques,* III (1966), 145–172; Bistra Cvetkova, "Les Celep et leur rôle dans la vie économique des Balkans à l'époque ottomane (XVe–XVIIIe s.)," in M. A. Cook, ed., *Studies in the Economic History of the Middle East from the Rise of Islam to the Present Day* (London: Oxford University Press, 1970), pp. 172–192; Nicolas G. Svoronis, *Le Commerce de Salonique au XVIIIe siècle* (Paris: Presses Universitaires de France, 1956), pp. 45–52, 379, 398–399; Marie M. Alexandrescu-Dersca, "Contribution à l'étude de l'approvisionnement en blé de Constantinople au XVIIIe siècle," *Studia et Acta Orientalia,* I (1957), 13–37; Mehmet Genç, "A Comparative Study of the Life Term Tax Farming Data and Volume of Commercial and Industrial Activities in the Ottoman Empire during the Second Half of the Eighteenth Century," in Todorov, Valtchev, and Todorova, eds., *La Révolution industrielle dans le sud-est européen,* pp. 245–248; Immanuel Wallerstein, Hale Decadeli, and Reşat Kasaba, "The Incorporation of the Ottoman Empire into the World-Economy," paper presented at the International Conference on Turkish Studies, University of Wisconsin, Madison, May 25–27, 1979; Reşat Kasaba, *The Ottoman Empire and the World Economy* (Albany: State University of New York Press, 1988); Robert Mantran, *Istanbul dans la seconde moitié du XVIIe siècle: Essai d'histoire institutionnelle, économique et sociale* (Paris: Librairie d'Adrien Maisonneuve, 1962), pp. 216–217, 461–463; Robert Mantran, "Centralisation administrative et financière, problème du ravitaillement d'Istanbul aux XVIIe–XVIIIe siècles," in Association Internationale

d'Etudes du Sud-Est Européen, *Bulletin,* XII, 1 (Bucharest, 1974), 59–68; Mantran, *La Vie quotidienne à Constantinople,* pp. 178–179; Sugar, *Southeastern Europe,* pp. 124–126; Todorov, *Balkanskiiat grad,* pp. 80–99.

54. François de Tott, *Memoirs of Baron de Tott, Containing the State of the Turkish Empire and the Crimea, During the Late War with Russia,* trans. from the French, 2 vols. in 4 parts (London, 1785), Vol. I, part 1, 32–33.

55. Inalcik, "Centralization and Decentralization in Ottoman Administration," pp. 27–52; Sugar, *Southeastern Europe,* pp. 38–42.

56. Herbert Wilhelmy, *Hochbulgarien,* a volume in a series entitled *Schriften des Geographischen Instituts der Universität Kiel,* edited by O. Schmieder and H. Wenzel (Kiel, 1935–1936), I, 283.

57. Vance, *The Merchant's World,* pp. 82, 85, 95.

58. Halil Inalcik, "The Foundations of the Economico-Social System in Cities," *Studia Balcanica,* III (1970), 17–24.

59. G. E. Brătianu, "Etudes sur l'approvisionnement de Constantinople et le monopole du blé à l'époque byzantine et ottomane," *Etudes byzantines d'histoire économique et sociale* (Paris: Librairie Orientaliste Paul Geuthner, 1938), p. 169.

60. On the Muslim-Ottoman ideology of permanent war with the alien world of nonbelievers, see John F. Guilmartin, Jr., "Ideology and Conflict: The Wars of the Ottoman Empire, 1453–1606," *Journal of Interdisciplinary History,* XVIII, 4 (Spring 1988), 721–747.

61. Clarence Dana Rouillard, *The Turk in French History, Thought, and Literature (1520–1660)* (Paris: Boivin, foreword dated 1938 [pub. 1940?]), pp. 112–113.

62. Ibid., p. 140.

63. Traian Stoianovich, "Russian Domination in the Balkans," in Taras Hunczak, ed., *Russian Imperialism from Ivan the Great to the Revolution* (New Brunswick, N.J.: Rutgers University Press, 1974), pp. 208–210.

64. John A. Armstrong, "Mobilized and Proletarian Diasporas," *American Political Science Review,* LXX (1976), 393–408; John A. Armstrong, *Nations Before Nationalism* (Chapel Hill: University of North Carolina Press, 1982), pp. 118–120, 206–213; Fernand Braudel, *Civilisation matérielle, économie et capitalisme, XVe–XVIIIe siècle,* 3 vols. (Paris: Armand Colin, 1979), III, *Le Temps du monde,* pp. 42–43.

65. Samir Amin, *Le Développement inégal: Essai sur les formations du capitalisme périphérique* (Paris: Les Editions de Minuit, 1973), p. 12. On the Jewish network of correspondence, see Werner Sombart, *The Jews and Modern Capitalism,* trans. by M. Epstein, with an introduction to the U.S. edition by Bert F. Hoselitz (Glencoe, Ill.: Free Press, 1951), pp. 169–175. The German title of the work is *Die Juden und das Wirtschaftsleben* (Leipzig: Duncker und Humblot, 1911).

66. Fernand Braudel, *La Méditerranée et le monde méditerranéen à l'époque de Philippe II,* rev. ed., 2 vols. (Paris: Armand Colin, 1966), II, 135–155.

67. For further details on the Jewish mobilized diaspora, see Stoianovich, "The Conquering Balkan Orthodox Merchant," pp. 244–248, 271–272, 299.

68. AN, B^3 239, doc. no. 18, on the "caractère des gens du pays, leur commerce," 1751–1753; Stoianovich, "L'Economie balkanique," pp. 185–192.

69. AN, B^3 239, doc. no. 1, Constantinople, 1751; Stoianovich, "The Conquering Balkan Orthodox Merchant," pp. 234–313.

70. "D. A.—S. P.," "Shipping and Commerce Through Travellers' Eyes," in Stelios A. Papadopoulos, ed., *The Greek Merchant Marine (1453–1850)* (Athens: National Bank of Greece, 1972), p. 314, citing [Julia] Pardoe, *The City of the Sultan, and Domestic Manners, in 1836,* 2 vols. (London: H. Colburn, 1837), I, 36–38.

71. Constantin François, comte de Volney, *Voyage en Egypte et en Syrie,* Jean Gaulmier, ed. (Paris and The Hague: Mouton, 1959), p. 385.

72. [Louis-François] comte de Ferrières-Sauveboeuf, *Mémoires historiques, politiques et géographiques des voyages faits en Turquie,* 2 vols. (Paris: chez Buisson, 1790), II, 151; H.A.R. Gibb and Harold Bowen, *Islamic Society and the West: A Study of the Impact of Western Civilization on Moslem Culture in the Near East,* I, *Islamic Society in the Eighteenth Century,* part 1 (London: Oxford University Press, 1950), pp. 310–311; Thomas Naff, "Ottoman Diplomatic Relations with Europe in the Eighteenth Century: Patterns and Trends," in Naff and Owen, eds., *Studies,* pp. 102–103.

73. AN, B[3] 237, memoir on the commerce of Salonika (Thessaloniki), August 1736; Félix [de] Beaujour, *Tableau du commerce,* I, 150–153; Louis-Auguste Félix Beaujour [Félix, baron de Beaujour], *A View of the Commerce of Greece, Formed After an Annual Average, from 1787 to 1797,* trans. from the French by Thomas Hartwell Horne (London: printed by H. L. Galabin for James Wallace, 1800), pp. 100–103; Svoronos, *Le Commerce de Salonique,* pp. 188–189, 240–242.

74. Yolande Triantafillidou, "L'Industrie du savon en Crète au XVIIIe siècle: Aspects économiques et sociaux," *Etudes balkaniques,* XI, 4 (Sofia, 1975), 85–86.

75. Süraiya Faroqhi, "The Early History of the Balkan Fairs," *Südost-Forschungen,* XXXVII (1978), 67.

76. Stoianovich, "The Conquering Balkan Orthodox Merchant," p. 257.

77. Ibid., pp. 254–258; Traian Stoianovich, "Pour un modèle du commerce du Levant: Economie concurrentielle et économie de bazar," in Association Internationale d'Etudes du Sud-Est Européen, *Bulletin,* XII, 2 (Bucharest, 1974), 109–112; Svoronos, *Le Commerce de Salonique,* pp. 240–241. For a similar proposal to reduce the Ottoman Empire to a supplier of raw materials (cotton and grains) and buyer of British manufactures, see David Urquhart, *Turkey and Its Resources: Its Municipal Organization and Free Trade* (London: Saunders and Otley, 1833), pp. 142–143.

78. Triantafillidou, "L'Industrie du savon en Crète," pp. 75–87.

79. P[eter] S[imon] Pallas, *Travels Through the Southern Provinces of the Russian Empire in the Years 1793 and 1794,* trans. from the German, 2d ed., 2 vols. (London: printed for J. Stockdale, 1812), II, 480, 484–485.

80. Viron Karidis, "A Greek Mercantile Paroikia: Odessa, 1774–1829," in Richard Clogg, ed., *Balkan Society in the Age of Greek Independence* (Totowa, N.J.: Barnes & Noble Books, 1981), pp. 125–128.

81. Stoianovich, "The Conquering Balkan Orthodox Merchant," pp. 269–270.

82. G. G. Gervinus, *Insurrection et régénération de la Grèce,* trans. J. F. Minssen, and Léonidas Sgouta (1863), p. 99.

83. Svoronos, *Le Commerce de Salonique,* pp. 391–392.

84. AN, B[3] 415, "Réflexions sur la situation politique et commerciale de la France dans les états du Grand Seigneur," copy of a memoir presented to the duc de Richelieu by the student vice consul Mareescheau(?), November 13, 1820; Stoianovich, "The Conquering Balkan Orthodox Merchant," pp. 302–303.

85. F[rançois]-C[harles]-H[ugues]-L[aurent] Pouqueville, *Voyage en Morée, à Constantinople, en Albanie, et dans plusieurs autres parties de l'Empire othoman, pendant les années 1798, 1799, 1800 et 1801,* 3 vols. (Paris: Gabon et Cie, 1805), I, 518, 520, and II, 265–266.

86. HHSA, St A. Türkei I/230, undated and unsigned memoir in Italian on the import and export trade of Austria with the Levant; Stoianovich, "The Conquering Balkan Orthodox Merchant," pp. 296–297.

87. D. J. Popović, *O Cincarima: Prilozi pitanju postanka našeg gradjanskog društva,* 2d ed. (Belgrade: Drag. Gregorić, 1937), pp. 149–156.

88. Stoianovich, "The Conquering Balkan Orthodox Merchant," pp. 301–302.

89. Charles Tilly, "Flows of Capital and Forms of Industry in Europe, 1500–1900," *Theory and Society,* XII, 2 (March 1983), 123–142; Tilly, "States, Coercion, and Capital," especially chapter 1.

90. Gustav Friedrich Hertzberg, *Geschichte Griechenlands,* 4 vols. (Gotha: Friedrich Andreas Perthes, 1876–1879), III, 378–379; G. Chassiotis, *L'Instruction publique chez les Grecs depuis la prise de Constantinople par les Turcs jusqu'à nos jours* (Paris: Ernest Leroux, 1881), p. 69; [Ambroise Firmin Didot], *Notes d'un voyage fait dans le Levant en 1816 et 1817* (Paris: Typographie de Firmin Didot, 1826), p. 139. Hertzberg estimates the population of Kydoniai in 1820 at 30,000 to 40,000.

91. Georges B. Dertilis, "Réseaux de crédit et stratégies du capital," in Georges B. Dertilis, ed., *Banquiers, usuriers et paysans: Réseaux de crédit et stratégies du capital en Grèce (1780–1930)* (Paris: Fondation des Treilles, Editions de la Découverte, 1988), pp. 42–43.

92. Popović, *O Cincarima,* pp. 99–103.

93. Huri Islamoğlu and Süraiya Faroqhi, "Crop Patterns and Agricultural Production Trends in Sixteenth-Century Anatolia," *Review: A Journal of the Fernand Braudel Center for the Study of Economies, Historical Systems, and Civilizations,* II, 3 (Winter 1979), 401–436.

94. My use of the term *peripheral economy* differs from the common usage, which in many respects is Eurocentric, making a periphery of whatever is not western Europe or the North Atlantic. Europe and the North Atlantic world, in fact, were the periphery, and the Ottoman Empire was a core or world system within the larger core or complex of world systems of the world continent. By being peripheralized, the Ottoman Empire became dependent on what had been the periphery. Only by peripheralizing other cores or world systems did the periphery become a core. The term *peripheral economy* probably originated among German or central European scholars. It seems to have reached Latin America before it made an impact elsewhere. Among early post-1945 users of the term were Raúl Prebisch and Roberto T. Alemann. See, in particular, Roberto T. Alemann, "Die Theorie der peripherischen Wirtschaft," *Weltwirtschaftliches Archiv,* LXXIV (1955), 7–44. On peripheralization in general, I need not cite Immanuel Wallerstein's well-known and influential works. But for Wallerstein on the peripheralization of the Ottoman Empire, see his "Ottoman Empire and the Capitalist World-Economy: Some Questions of Research," *Review: A Journal of the Fernand Braudel Center for the Study of Economies, Historical Systems, and Civilizations,* II, 3 (Winter 1979), 389–398.

95. Stoianovich, "The Conquering Balkan Orthodox Merchant," pp. 259–260, 274–275, 282–283; Stoianovich, "Russian Domination in the Balkans," pp. 212–213; Stoianovich, "Pour un modèle du commerce du Levant," pp. 66–68, 70–71, 76–83, 100–102.

96. Braudel, *Civilisation matérielle, économie et capitalisme,* III, 413.

5

Cities and Citizenry as Factors of State Formation in the Roman-German Empire of the Late Middle Ages

PETER MORAW

IF WE APPLY QUESTIONS formulated from the perspectives of Southern or Western Europe to early German history[1] or to experience in northern and eastern regions more generally, we soon discover the variability of European history. That is certainly the case if we ask about the contribution of citizens and city-dwellers to European state formation from the thirteenth to eighteenth centuries. Even within the Empire, we must answer the question differently for each region.[2] Even if urbanization[3] occurred everywhere, it occurred in different contexts as a result of different conditions. Before the main question can be raised, we must discuss both groups of determinants.

THE GERMAN PROCESS OF STATE FORMATION

There are reasons why the older German process of state formation has been and still is only partly understood elsewhere. It obviously was more complicated than elsewhere in Europe. It is therefore of utmost importance to state immediately that the evolution went fundamentally in the same direction as elsewhere, even as in the often discussed example of the French monarchy. The starting point was different, however, and so were the further circumstances; as a consequence, the results likewise diverged.

The two major structures in the post-Roman history of western Christian Europe—what would be France and Germany—emerged at nearly the same time from the Carolingian empire.[4] Their structures differed in two major aspects, however:

1. The more highly developed heritage, resting on a more intensive urbanization during Roman antiquity, appeared almost exclusively in the future French West. The segments of "Older Europe" belonging to the later German Empire were located in narrow strips on the Rhine's left bank, also south of the Danube. The new German history unfolded in the less-developed "Younger Europe" where practically no towns existed; it had to hope for lasting and complicated adjustments.[5]

2. On the other hand, the "feudal" strength of central authority in the Eastern Empire in the tenth century, and the corresponding weakness of the Western part, brought the ancient-Carolingian imperial heritage into the hands of the Ottonian dynasty in the East, in the shape of a new Roman Empire. Paradoxically, a structure with a weak urban culture took the name of the city *kat exochen,* whose empire many people saw as a part of Salvation history, "*Heilsgeschichte.*" Then and later this offered the finest thinkable legitimation for the "state," to which one remained firmly committed. For a long period, no need was felt therefore for a "German" concept, which would have better suited realities. The Western community had to do with the next best legitimation available in Europe: the Frankish one, although the Francs were no Celtic/Gallic people but a "German" one, and although Charlemagne's Aix-la-Chapelle belonged to the Eastern Empire. Thus, the names of both empires had more to do with legitimation than with reality.[6]

Differences of development and legitimacy had a real impact on state formation in relation with towns and citizens. The differences of development can be traced easily by the nature, the magnitude, and the chronology of the urbanization process, mainly from West to East.[7] In a first stage, the Elbe and Saale marked relevant differences; later, from 1300 onward, the Silesian-Polish border became the dividing line. Within the Empire, real shifts took place reducing the differences substantially without eliminating them, however. As an indication, we can point to the fact that the first reversal in the trend in the late Middle Ages took three generations to pass through the Empire from West to East (before 1300 to 1370/1400). The next major reversal took only one generation (1450/60–1480). Nevertheless Germany touched Europe's periphery and even spanned parts of it—e.g. Livonia—while at the lower Rhine it participated in one of the two European centers of modernization. If we may use this term with respect to such a wide variety of extremes, the average German development was of middle rank, never attaining the level of Northern Italy. No medieval German town reached the size Trier had reached in the ancient Roman Empire. This indicates that the fundamental development directions of the older European history, from South to North and from West to East, were accentuated by the medieval and early modern Empire, but did not change significantly.

Legitimacy meant that changes in imperial structures had to be fashioned in accordance with traditional ways of thought. From the fourteenth century onward, Italian *signori,* often of very low origins, paid the Emperor huge sums just to obtain a legitimation. Legitimation also meant that new things were called by new names rather late and rarely, while not being immediately recognized as such; many innovations were introduced as by-products while people thought they were keeping old things. This was done with respect and sympathy rather generally until the eighteenth century; the Enlightenment finally brought about symptoms of decomposition which could no longer be repaired. Birth and privilege constituted the most important proofs of legitimate existence. Consequently, it was impossible to reduce the traditional social disadvantage of burgher descent in the noble *Reichstag,* whatever legal arguments may have been produced. Therefore it was necessary to introduce wanted novelties or to obstruct unwanted ones by the means of established privileges, which for these purposes could be extended to great lengths or unscrupulously reinterpreted.

From the twelfth and thirteenth centuries onward, old German state formation took place dualistically on two levels: the King's or Emperor's[8] and that of the whole Empire on the one hand, and on the territorial level of the princes and cities, on the other.[9] The processes were legally complementary but practically at odds, undergoing many crises and setbacks. Only from a great distance do they seem really consequential. The two levels were bound to each other not only by the necessity to be or at least to seem legitimate, but also by the fact that during these centuries, political culture was primarily characterized by the high aristocracy. In this milieu, different life-styles were not accepted or not taken seriously. Value orientations in the upper class in the first place were directed to the dynasty and only in the second place to the "state" or the "nation." This constitutional dualism between the Empire and the territories remained intact mainly for three reasons:

1. the great size of a continental Empire that could not be crossed in less than one month;[10]
2. a comparatively insufficient level of modernization, because the degrees of urbanization, monetarization, the formation of elites, and bureaucratization did not allow for an adequate accumulation and stabilization of centralized means of power;
3. numerous misfortunes or "accidents" of event-oriented history hardly allowed a dynastic continuity and lasting successes to occur for the central power during the decisive centuries (the thirteenth to fifteenth) when state structures were still weak.

Consequently, the principalities of the Empire grew up to a strength without peer in Europe. The territories of the princes likewise won the competition for state formation, because their proximity enabled a much higher concentration of energies than was possible on the level of the Empire.

The Empire as a whole thus remained at a disadvantage. Kingship, itself being merely based on traditional seignorial rights, would have been desperately overburdened. But being the head of a major dynasty, the ruler became the most important territorial lord in the Empire. Royalty and great dynasty became symbiotic. The great dynasts were the Hohenstaufens (until 1250), then the Luxemburgs, and to a lesser degree the Wittelsbachs, and most of all the Habsburgs. After their huge acquisitions around 1500 the Habsburgs were in a position to take up the challenge of the Valois and to enter in a conflict over predominance in Europe. In the century between 1250 and 1350, however, no full-fledged major dynasty came to the fore, which brought about serious delays in the development of a central power. The more successful dynastic royalty became, the more it provoked a new dualism within the Empire, one that now became visible on the map: the lands belonging to the ruler's heritage were distinctly opposed to the rest of the Empire. When the *Reichstag* came into being, for example, the royal territories were not represented except by the ruler himself.

These problems were exacerbated by the fact that, by its specific evolution and as a consequence of the weak continuity and accumulative powers of its dynasties, the Empire did not develop a central region with a great residential capital. Such a capital would also have become the economic and cultural center as well as the traffic junction of Germany. This truly is the heaviest mortgage of older German history, a fundamental difference with the evolutions of France and England. In the late fourteenth century, a relatively advantageous alternative developed along the axis from Frankfurt am Main through Nuremberg and Prague to Breslau, with Prague and Nuremberg as centers, but this did not last. The later imperial city, Vienna, was far too eccentric, and it took a long time before it became of sufficient importance as an urban center to play any role.[11]

Seen in chronological sequence, the evolution of the territorial states went rather regularly from the twelfth and thirteenth to the eighteenth century— leaving aside fluctuations from the general trends. For the Empire as a whole, it went differently; its state formation seems to have been determined by "challenges" and "responses." Apart from the short period of the Hussite movements (1419–1434), challenges that may be compared with that of the Hundred Years' War for France and England occurred only from about 1470 onward. At that time, Turks and Hungarians, Burgundians, and Frenchmen were threatening the Empire. Until then, the Empire had existed without challenges in the form of an "open constitution" with a minimum of institutions and obligations; it could neglect the impulses toward modernization that had been going on elsewhere. A general, basic understanding as to the Empire's continuity, its unity and indivisibility, and its superior legitimacy helped to forge stability. Finally, different "fundamental processes" in the social, economic, technical, and cultural fields, which contemporaries could hardly notice and even less consciously influence, worked in the same direction. Examples of this are the growth of intellectual, especially juridical, elites, the extension of supra-regional linkages of capital, the generalization of printing, the reception of Roman law, and rapidly spreading national consciousness.

As a consequence of such changes, a new period of German constitutional history started about 1470: it can be described as the phase of "densification." As the relatively small and bureaucratically weak imperial court was insufficient as a center, a second scene grew in the form of the *Reichstag,* the expression of the now convergent dualistic powers, which was to become the largest assembly of estates in Europe. Now, princes, counts, and prelates were called to the sides of the Electors, who until then had been the active core of the dualism and to the sides of the imperial cities that had taken up most of the burden. It is a matter of discussion how far this was the result of intentional acts by reformers or an unintended effect of short-term incremental decisions; our inclination is toward the last explanation. The institutionalization of dualism took place painfully, hesitantly, and incompletely. It concerned a very large space indeed and a number of political forces unknown elsewhere, which could not be compelled but had to be convinced over and over again. Not only feudal or municipal dependency, but mere membership now required achievements for the empire. The king acquired a new mobility in external and military affairs by means of considerable concessions in internal politics. On the whole, the most urgent imperatives of defense could be met, and soon even the heavy crisis of the Reformation could be mastered. Unlike the French case, where the ruler was the architect of the growing state unity, subordinating at his will princes and towns one after the other, the imperial dynasty and the other members of the Empire, constituting the dualism of the estates, had to find their way in collaboration and antagonism.[12]

CITIES OF THE ROMAN-GERMAN EMPIRE

The number of cities in the late medieval–early modern Empire can be estimated at 3,000 to 4,000 or even more.[13] The bishop's cities west of the Rhine and south of the Danube, situated in "Old Europe," were at the origin of German urbanization. They referred more or less clearly to Roman precedents and began to display an urban way of life when German history started in the tenth century. But qualitatively and quantitatively larger differences are to be noted from the situation in Northern Italy, the most modern of that time.[14] Regardless of their sizes, the southern cities can be characterized as power centers, with an urban nobility or a nobility linked to the city, with a mobile and differentiated social structure and important economic activity. The world North of the Alps still was generally traditional and rural. The vast majority of older German cities developed between the late eleventh century and about 1450, partly from non-agrarian precedents, partly without such roots; the evolution was gradual in time and quantity, mostly displaying a West-East direction.

But the South-North axis also showed relevant differences. At the end of the Hohenstaufen era (1250), one counted one city per 400 square kilometers in today's Baden-Württemberg, while in Schleswig-Holstein it was only one per 1000 square kilometers.[15] Non-Mediterranean Europe remained a principally agrarian and aristocratic environment. Recently, the level of urbanization around 1500 has been calculated as about 20 percent in central Europe; in a few progressive regions it reached 25 percent, and only in the Flemish-Brabantine area—with which we are not dealing—it was about one-third.

Fundamental for our problem is the fact that the vast majority of German cities were relatively small and that even its few larger ones remained far behind the metropoles of "older Europe." Leaving aside Brabant and Liège, the largest cities in the fourteenth century, Cologne and Prague, with nearly 40,000 inhabitants, were of comparable size with London, which was then the center of a rather small realm. Paris, Milan, and Venice had double that population or more: Florence, Bruges, and Ghent were also larger. Considerably smaller than Cologne were Lübeck, Danzig, Metz, Strasbourg, Nuremberg, Vienna, and Breslau, and even farther behind were Hamburg, Frankfurt am Main, Braunschweig, Augsburg, Erfurt, Magdeburg, Rostock, and others. Although Nuremberg, Augsburg, and Vienna saw their populations increase up to the early sixteenth century, they did not pass the 50,000 mark. Not only did the Empire lack a large central residential capital, it even lacked a city with metropolitan attraction. In relation to the 15 to 20 million inhabitants of the Empire before and after the great waves of plague, such a city would have been incomparable in a continental location: something like an addition of Milan and Venice, or more than a second Paris.

Another equally important fact is that the largest German cities were generally situated at great distances from each other, in most cases more than a hundred kilometers and thus several days' journey. At best, large, middle, and small communes formed urban chains along the important trade routes. A city network of really powerful towns, comparable to Flemish conditions, was nowhere to be found. The normal configuration in the Empire was the subordination of several smaller towns to a greater one, leaving almost no political power to the smaller. While the small towns enter into the scope of legal and regional history, the problem of state formation is to be explained solely by the role of the great communes. Noticeable economic achievements helped the buildup of political weight, too.[16] In this field, German cities did perform rather well in relation to their agrarian and feudal environment and in comparison with the better situated parts of Europe. This phase ran until about 1550 and started mainly in the fourteenth but partly in the thirteenth or even twelfth century.

There was no united German economic area. It is possible to discern economic spaces along the Rhine, in the Hanseatic area, and in the South. At the end of the Middle Ages a central-eastern district perhaps can be additionally distinguished. The centers were Cologne, Lübeck, and consecutively Regensburg, Nuremberg, and Augsburg, and in the end Leipzig as well. The Hanseatic and the Southern economic spaces expanded far beyond the Empire's borders toward the North, the East, and the Southeast.

The "commercial revolution" of the twelfth century had started in Italy and penetrated Western Europe up to the Rhine in the next century; again it demonstrated the difference between the "older" and the "younger Europe." During the fourteenth century, an interior financial system developed on the right bank of the Rhine, mainly under the impetus of merchants from Nuremberg. Before 1400 it was still closely linked to the Western Italian system and tended to catch up with the Mediterranean advance during the fifteenth century. The Frankfurt fairs distributed the goods for central Europe. Germany became central in the European trade routes. At the moment in 1500 when Augsburg took the place of Nuremberg as the leader of the South German economy, the imperial city on the Lech was already a great European center of political finance. The sources show more long-distance trade than nearby market functions. Nevertheless, the economically most successful German cities were those with an export industry and long-distance trade, as well as the seaports. So we have to name first Cologne, Nuremberg, Augsburg, Braunschweig, and others, and second Lübeck, Danzig, Hamburg, and others. From about 1450, the expansion of mining and smelting in southern and central German regions, which played the critical part in imperial politics, speeded up the process and opened up previously inconceivable opportunities for individuals and firms. According to a rough estimate, the production of silver in the Empire in 1530 reached the quintuple of that in 1460. Taxed wealth in Augsburg multiplied thirteenfold between 1470 and 1550. In 1473 Jakob Fugger took the lead in his firm and before 1500 became the greatest banker of his time.

Cities large and small took their first steps from economics to politics by controlling their adjacent countrysides.[17] That control concerned the security of supplies with foodstuffs and raw materials, the furtherance of sales in the area, and finally the production of goods in a division of labor with the countryside. In light of the multiplicity of seignorial rights, which were especially common in the Western parts of the Empire, cities strove to exploit this mixed position and to obtain seignorial rights themselves; in the same vein, they sought indirect economic and financial influence. Outside the Netherlands, nowhere did the sphere of political interest of one city reach that of one or more others; a fully city-dominated large countryside thus remained out of sight. A number of imperial cities acquired more or less extensive territories. Examples are Bern and Zürich, with their cantons existing until recently or even to the present day; Nuremberg controlled 1,500 square kilometers, encompassing six towns and many villages; Ulm, Rothenburg, and Schwäbisch Hall likewise controlled their own hinterlands.[18] This did not lead to the expansion of the cities' statecraft beyond their own narrow area; nor did it originate a model of domination in competition with the monarchial style of ruling. On the contrary, cities ruled "feudally," as if they were territorial princes. Representation of estates only developed in the "Territorium" of the imperial city Eger, which had been mortgaged to the king of Bohemia in the fourteenth century.

Such powerful cities as Cologne or Frankfurt am Main did not acquire a territory of any significance and nevertheless flourished economically. More important than territorial domination was open access to economic resources in the immediate or more distant hinterlands. Territorial acquisition could not solve this problem. It was rather a matter of urban "foreign policy" and of ongoing, long-term changes in the characteristics of the state. Notwithstanding all complaints about instability and insecurity, late medieval towns striving for autonomy and independence found their opportunities in the same conditions that created these dangers: the multiplicity and lack of clarity of seignorial rights enabled the intrusion of urban interests.

In the early modern period, the more or less autonomous city faced an increasingly legalistic Empire and better organized territories. Except for the very mightiest, the alternatives now became stagnation or subordination—in an economic and hegemonic sense—to the most powerful neighbor.

Participation in an industrial district was another form of late medieval economic dynamism beyond city walls. The creation and flourishing of such districts occurred independently from the territorial history of the cities; rather they were dependent on the goodwill or the help of the king; politically splintered landscapes might well offer the best opportunities. Towns with similar production (and, whenever possible, collective exports) collaborated in industrial districts from the fourteenth century onward. These agreements offered advantages to all participants, resulting in remarkable successes in exports. The most important examples are the linen region near the Lake of Constance, the bombazine areas in Swabia and Oberfranken, and the mountain district in Oberpfalz, dominated by Nuremberg.[19]

A fundamental problem for the older urban communities in continental Europe was that, although they were hardly vulnerable within their walls, they found it extremely difficult to protect the vital trade routes beyond a certain distance from these walls. Notwithstanding all problems of maritime transport, coastal cities found themselves in a much better position in this respect: they could realize a much higher degree of political and economic independence and self-protection. Further we still have to discuss the German Hanse. The best illustration of this situation is to be found in the extraordinary efforts made by the harbor city Hamburg, located far from the sea, to control the lower Elbe effectively. High costs, violence, and judicial manipulation were invested. The first position was acquired in 1299 on the Wattenmeer island of Neuwerk; it was militarily protected in 1310. An imperial privilege from 1359, interpreted in the broadest sense, offered the legal foundation for control of the lower Elbe. In 1450, the 135-kilometer-long waterway down to the coast was marked by floating barrels. Everyone knew to whom the river belonged.[20]

The connection of economy and politics in German urban life raises the question of the relation between the self-maintenance of the communes and their interior organization. This question surely makes sense in a perspective of European comparison; the German answer, however, throws less light than one could have hoped. In the thirteenth century the constitutions providing councils were generally introduced; later on, numerous specific differences from one city ordinance to another can hardly lead to a general interpretation of the parallels with economic success or failure. More relevant is the question of whether differences in the social base of a city government had economic consequences. In many cases that was true; nevertheless, in the full breadth of late medieval urban life, other factors were really more relevant. To these belonged the relations to the city overlord and still more general changes connected with the evolution from "open constitution" to "densification," on the one hand, and with the secular economic trends, on the other. In any case, in a large city long dominated by craftsmen such as Augsburg, "social acceptability" pushed toward external relations fitted to an aristocratic political culture and represented by patricians.

The last question to be raised in this context concerns the successes or failures of urban interests in larger German politics. While greatly expanded long-distance trade was among the evident manifestations of urban success, spatial and material parallels with royal policy were hardly avoidable in Southern Germany, which was the rulers' main operational base. The impact of royal intervention was still unclear in Hohenstaufen times but increasingly visible from the fourteenth century onward. Some important cases display a remarkable "pair of scissors." The constitutional successes and the statecraft of the cities in the old Empire were rather weak; in particular political questions, however, as well as in the personal policies at court, they scored some noticeable successes. A classical example for this is the symbiosis with the ruler's activity, grown from the interests of the imperial city Nuremberg, which lay close to the king and fulfilled the functions of a capital during generations.[21] Royal needs for finance, credit, and experts were exchanged for commercial privileges and protection against impediments of trade. Truly "modern" behavior is to be observed here as early as the fourteenth century; German policies toward Italy or Hungary cannot be understood without considering urban and particularly Nuremberg economic interests. No less a success of metropolitan policy was the victory of the large cities led by Danzig over the Teutonic Order in Prussia.[22] In a quantitative sense, however, both examples surely were exceptions that the greatest number of cities never could hope to attain.

EFFECTS OF COMMUNAL LIFE
ON THE STATE'S FORMATION IN THE EMPIRE

After the sketch of "statal" and basic urban data for our theme, we have to consider the effects of the main types of communal life on the formation of a state. The distinctions drawn by constitutional history can help us best in this respect. In the late Middle Ages, it distinguishes three categories of towns: free cities, imperial cities, and territorial cities. All three had unclear borders, were subdivided in different subcategories, and underwent substantial changes over time.

The smallest group, the *free cities*,[23] included especially the bishop's cities along the Rhine (Cologne, Mainz until 1462, Worms, Speyer, Strasbourg, Basel) and Regensburg at the Danube (until 1486). In political practice, they had freed themselves from their clerical overlords and therefore claimed a free status; its recognition, however, was far from secured.

Imperial cities,[24] which numbered at some times up to a hundred and more, found, in their classical form, their origins in the royal cities of the Hohenstaufen. This core group was enlarged up to the fifteenth century by other cities that became free from territorial overlords under different conditions. At the same time and later in the early modern period their number was reduced by mortgaging to territorial princes, by the transition to the inherited lands of the ruler, and later also by territorial losses of the Empire. Most of the imperial cities were located in the Southwest and in Southern Germany; in the North only a few cities enjoyed imperial status (Lübeck, Dortmund, Goslar, etc.). The main traditional revenues the late medieval kingship extracted from the Empire outside the heritage lands consisted of annual taxes from the imperial cities, different particular payments, and sums extorted from local Jewish communities. It is impossible to describe in a general way the position of imperial cities. As for the free cities, particular fortunes were crucial. Their evolution followed the path of emancipation from rigid royal overlordship in the high Middle Ages toward more or less far-reaching factual autonomy in the fourteenth century. The highest possible number of particular royal privileges secured this evolution. The link to the ruler might be loosened but not broken, otherwise the status as imperial city would have been lost. Consequently, interventions in the city's constitution could still occur at any time. Some imperial cities were close to royal influence, others far away, just as happened with free cities; the situation could change from one decade to another as a function of fluctuating interests.

By far the largest group were the *territorial cities*,[25] which consequently were highly differentiated. Small communities formed the vast majority of the thousands of territorial cities. In many cases, the territorial lord had been the city's founder, following other than economic motives, which explains why many of them could not really develop. Some of the territorial cities, such as the residences Prague, Vienna, and Munich, had quite large populations. All over the Empire, numerous larger territorial cities displayed tendencies to autonomy similar to those of the free and imperial cities; many of them even succeeded over the centuries (especially in the fourteenth to sixteenth centuries) in a practical, if not also juridical, way. The only really successful cases were Hamburg (in 1618, then 1786) and Bremen (in 1646, then 1741): they indeed became free imperial cities in the sense usual in the early modern period (see below). In the time of "densification," between 1470 and 1550, people didn't know this yet; so some territorial cities (Braunschweig, Lüneburg, Rostock, Göttingen, Magdeburg, Erfurt, and others) are to be found in the early imperial taxation lists (*Reichsmatrikel*) and among the invitations to the *Reichstag*, which formally ought to have been reserved to the imperial cities, and for a few matters to the free cities.

Under these conditions, we shall further consider free, imperial, and half-autonomous territorial cities as one group. They, and they only, maintained relations with the Empire as a whole; one can thus get an insight into their contribution to state formation of the entire Empire. It is essential to notice the parallelism, both in time and in form, between the emancipatory tendency of the cities and that of the territorial lords; even with that of the kings or emperors as territorial lords, facing an Empire in which estates had developed. This emancipation or (positively formulated) this strengthening of princely power was not only or not necessarily in the first place directed against the King or Emperor; at least in theory one remained loyal to him. Such behavior rather was a consequence of the extension of organizational tasks and a response to the growing complexity of a modernizing society. These things simply could not be regulated centrally under the conditions of the older German history. Towns and territories took advantage of these tasks in favor of particular state formation, and found in them new legitimations when the new tasks were pursued successfully. So, the elected bourgeois city councils gradually became real authorities similar to the princes.

The individual city thus was left with little space for territorial expansion. Two encompassing phenomena however are still to be considered: the urban leagues[26] and participation in the *Reichstag*. The first small regional leagues of neighboring communes developed in 1226 or just before in the Rhine valley, then also in Swabia and on the coast. The Rhenish urban league of 1254 constituted the first important case. Northern Italy had offered the example, as it had for the importation of councils. A negative incentive was found in the heavy crisis of monarchy after the catastrophe of the Hohenstaufen, while the cities' increase in economic potential had a positive impact. They took the responsibility of taking care of peace and justice in the absence of a King competent to do it and did so in the name of a Christian, not national legitimation. The Empire provided a base, but they did not seek to take its lead or even to represent it. Collective action was hampered by the rapid extension of the league. So it broke down about the election of two kings in 1257, without leaving noteworthy traces in constitutional structures. The later leagues of imperial and free cities in southern Germany underwent the same fate, notwithstanding their important role in political events and in the monarchy. As long as there was no great dynasty, the rulers badly needed the support of the communes; that secured them many particular advantages but did not provide competitive advantages to the cities as a whole.

The Swabian urban league, led by Ulm from 1376 and this time directed against the King, constituted the culminating point. It successfully opposed payment orders seen as unequal—which they really were—and even elaborated a legitimation against the ruler on the basis of an abstract conception of the Empire. The precise notion of "imperial city, *Reichsstadt*" was in the first place derived from this context. But even the dualism apparent here— beside the more important one of the electors—did not develop into constitutional practice. If such a thing had been wanted, which is most doubtful, the opposition from the princes was too strong; the King equally disliked purely communal coalitions. He rightly considered polarization on the basis of estates as conflict generating and therefore furthered regional peace leagues encompassing several estates. The Golden Bull of 1356, in which the electors' core of dualism was fixed, forbade autonomous urban leagues, albeit with little effect. During the periods of weakness of King Wenceslaus, the Swabian urban league, soon extended as the Swabian-Rhenish league (1381), made a major conflict with the princes unavoidable. The first urban war, 1388–89, saw the defeat of the communes.

This meant the end of the heyday of urban leagues. The communes did not allow King Sigismund to use them on any larger scale as a substitute force against the princes; their regional connections were already too intensive. A last upswing led to the second urban war in 1449–51, in the same region as sixty years earlier, and with the same result. The "Imperial League in Swabia" (1488–1533/34) was the most successful of all unions in southern Germany, but it then united cities as well as nobles and some princes under the emperor's lead. In this respect it belonged to the "densification" of the Empire, which it furthered in its turn.

Although the phenomenon of the urban leagues was partially successful in securing peace, one might not ascribe to it real state-building power. It did not become a structuring principle in the imperial constitution, in which the quality of the city's overlord remained determinative. The most divergent particular interests of the cities were predominant, most of all their economic links with a particular region. Added to this was their self-perception as being socially inferior subjects who could therefore not be held responsible for the whole and their short-term defensive evaluation of economic and financial matters in terms of their immediate advantage. Evidently, all participants in the political strife had in mind their own profit, but only a few German cities had interests large enough to impress other competitors so strongly that they outweighed social differences. The cities displayed with good reason a notable distrust toward the princes. For all these reasons, elaboration of the urban network had a large impact on the lives of individual communes.

From 1470 onward, military pressure on the Empire forced the emperor to raise considerably higher monetary claims than ever before. Beginning in 1471, the free and the imperial cities responded by urban meetings[27] which had to elaborate common attitudes. Princes and electors required in return for their payments that the king authorize them to maintain more sharply the territorial peace; further they claimed a resident high court, distinct from the mobile royal court, in whose personal composition the estates would have a say; both innovations also touched the communes. Cities feared the easily imaginable by-products of this "densification" provoked by the princes and legitimized by the king, as much as they feared high taxes. Nevertheless, neither innovation could be held back. Since the *"Reformreichstag"* at Worms in 1495, the cities were regularly called to meetings of the new *Reichstag*.[28] They did not come to take part in the decision making, however, but to hear the claims and to accept them after some opposition won them time and reduced the amount.

Contemporaries saw the long-term consequences of the evolution which has been summarized here much less consciously than does the later historian. The fluidity of terminology shows as much. It concerned a pragmatic dualism, legitimated only afterwards, legally open and combined with monistic requirements of the emperor. The cities seemed to slide into the new situation. For several decades, their policy shifted between attempts at codetermination and efforts to ward off the innovations. Both were equally in vain as a consequence of the above-mentioned facts, which were already established irrevocably before 1495. It was the definitive stabilization of the dualistic monarchial state in Germany, institutionalized at that moment—an event with wide consequences. It was likewise one of the most notable peace-imposing systems of large states in early history, albeit one at the costs of the cities, installed for the next three centuries without military force but supported by an uncontroversial fundamental consensus.

That is how we see things today. In those days, the whole evolution took place without any preconceived plan aiming at the "exploitation" of the cities or even less at the contrary, the elimination of a less "feudal" alternative to the imperial constitution. The actual behavior of contemporaries was highly determined by by-products of immediate decisions. The best proof for this view is the fact that two fundamental changes in the role of the cities occurred without being really noticed:

1. In a relatively short time, definitively around the middle of the sixteenth century, free cities lost their position as the best-off within the Empire, and were pushed down to the weaker status of the imperial cities. Although they had loudly claimed that their "free" status meant freedom from taxes, only one category of free imperial cities remained. They had to face excessive taxation, which they were unable to avoid and could but slowly reduce to supportable proportions.

2. Within the institutionalized dualism between King or Emperor and Empire, the cities changed sides. They stepped from the side of the ruler, whose subjects they had been in the royal cities, to that of the electors and princes. But the latter did not accept them as equals in social status at all. This shift was far from being unequivocal or complete. The traditional legitimacy of the imperial constitution and the purely factual introduction of innovations created a situation hardly tolerable in modern systematic thought: at the same time cities held the old and the new positions. For the king it did not matter in consequence of which mechanism they paid, as long as they did pay. Within the *Reichstag* around 1500 neither the cities nor the princes displayed a clearly delimited "modern" voting behavior or polarization. Nor should we anachronistically think of the king as renouncing his claim of monistic rulership, which was at first actually strengthened by the reception of Roman law.

The opposition of particular imperial and free cities to the new developments was inspired by two mutually linked models of thought, which held some legitimacy and could have some success if the geographical and military position was favorable. First, there was the reference to the legitimate "open constitution" of before 1470; those cities that had been able to defend themselves had found this situation, with its minimal obligations, quite suitable. Second, we have already mentioned the extreme and even abusive interpretation of old privileges, insofar as these could not be falsified on geographical and military grounds. Both positions might be accentuated by a weakening of the fundamental consensus, especially in marginal locations. Except for some imperial cities in the periphery, such as Metz, enjoying semi-free conditions, the Swiss, directed by the imperial Bern and Zürich (and from 1501 joined by the free city Basel) were most successful in taking this hold. Their military achievements and those of their allies were the main cause of their success. In the neighboring and closely linked free cities Basel

and Strasbourg, mentalities tended to diverge: the southern one stubbornly
stuck to its "freedom" in a retrospective meaning, while the northern one became the forum of the new German "nationalism." In this way, the fate of
the Confederation was gradually decided.[29] It did not leave the Empire; it
wanted on the contrary to remain as a member of the old Empire, that of the
"open constitution," not the new Empire with its manifold obligations. At
the same time, the Confederates had some reasons to fear the neighboring
great Habsburg dynasty. Until the seventeenth century any other Swiss legitimacy is hard to find; the historians' search for republican and democratic
thoughts will be anachronistic. It thus was a traditional, not a modern, position: the Empire underwent a further evolution, the Confederation did not.

Other peripheries displayed similar problems, even when they were less
marked by urbanization. The loosening and final break from the Empire of
the highly urbanized northern Netherlands, on the other hand, rested on a
different set of facts: together with the other Habsburg territories, they
shifted toward the ruler's side of the new dualism and turned away from the
"Empire" of the estates. Their fate was not fundamentally determined by
proceedings of the *Reichstag,* but by dynastic decisions and failures. A similar situation occurred in Bohemia. The "densification" of the Empire after
1470 had no effects there as a belated consequence of the Hussite movements. It thus remained in the "open constitution" Empire until the Habsburgs could force it into the heritage territories' side of the dualism and durably domesticate the region (1526, then 1620).

The "densified," more modern Empire was thus smaller than that of the
"open constitution," but in a better position to survive. The residual districts
of the "open constitution" separated themselves gradually (Switzerland) or
were torn off (Livonia); others were finally incorporated at one or the other
side of the institutionalized dualism of the new "densification" (Friesland,
Bohemia). For the free imperial cities remaining within the smaller Empire,
freedom of action had already been limited.

Until 1803/1806 nothing essential was altered in the series of orientations
taken or initiated around 1500. So a short view on a few fundamental facts
of the early modern period may be sufficient.[30] Notwithstanding the considerable economic and cultural role of many cities, reformation brought about
a further strengthening of princes. During these turbulent decades, it was
hard to take a united attitude in the free imperial cities which became predominantly Protestant. Protestant princes did not display a more favorable
view on Protestant cities than that of their Catholic forerunners. The minimum of political and military power necessary for autonomous development
increased; the cities felt this painfully in the Schmalkaldic war. The imperial
constitution, traditional power relations, and old legitimacy withstood the
innovations introduced by the Reformation.

These conclusions as well as the whole of our endeavor do not confirm the opinion that concrete possibilities for a fundamentally new constitution of the Empire would have existed mainly between 1450 and 1550. These possibilities, which remained unrealized, would have consisted of a coalition of the King and the imperial cities against the princes, with a modern centralized monarchy as the goal.[31] Only a brief review of the main facts forbidding such an interpretation will be sufficient here.

1. The king was part of a high aristocratic and great dynastic society that was in itself already clearly at a distance from the cities and that could hardly let political opportunity prevail above social prejudices.

2. The urban society did not produce constructive views of a larger state structure. These were just as unusual as were longer-term ideas about the reformation of the Empire on the side of the princes, as recent research has shown. In any case, the imperial cities were skeptical about far-reaching plans of the king concerning regional peace treaties (*Landfrieden*) and economic and fiscal matters. Conscious of the huge differences in interests among the cities, the great communes looked for separate arrangements. The plans would in any event have meant high costs for the cities and conflicts with neighboring princes, which they tried to avoid entirely.

3. The example of the Swiss Confederation, which effectively emancipated itself from the principality, should not be generalized or idealized. Its evolution took place under circumstances impossible to repeat. From a viewpoint of "state theory" it was backward rather than forward oriented.[32]

4. The conditions in southwestern Germany, where many imperial cities coexisted with few principalities, were not representative for the whole Empire. Medieval Swabia was only one of fourteen greater regions;[33] in nearly any other region, the conditions were much more unfavorable for autonomous cities. The political core of the Empire had long since shifted toward the east, where the possibilities for autonomous cities were the smallest.

5. It is hard to believe that the princes would have been easy to control, because their ever-growing power and their solidarity even crossed religious boundaries. On the other hand, solidarity and coherence of the cities were not so impressive as is often believed. The word "Hanse," for example, was hardly known in the South or was roughly misunderstood as "cities near the sea" (*Hansestädte* = *An-See-Städte*).

6. Any alternative would have had to break through a number of traditional legitimations and values upon which rested the essential self-perception and basic consensus of the Germans. Even the Confederates never considered themselves to be revolutionaries;

instead they thought they were defending the old privileges against unjustified innovations.

The continued existence of the Empire as a modernized princely state with an imperial summit was thus really consequential. Institutionalized dualism was a rectilinear, realistic solution while it was legitimized with old law, which could contain many new elements just because it was not recognized as really new. The early modern constitutional development of the Empire was no diversion; nor was it simply a special case. It was the consequential evolution from European and German preconditions under the almost unconscious influence of fundamental standardization processes of economic, social, and cultural change and of the historical events.

The catastrophic Thirty Years' War meant further weakening of the autonomous cities, whose number radically diminished within each territory. The princes won again; soon they were to be called absolutist and mercantilist. The legalization of the Empire that ensued did secure the survival of legitimate political structures, but did not prevent economic decay or social and cultural stagnation. The basic attitude of even the greatest communes now really became defensive. In practice, the electors and princes did not recognize the "votum decisivum" in the *Reichstag,* by which the Peace of Westphalia (1648) had formally accorded an equal rank to the free imperial cities. Even more than before, the great powers developed hegemonies to which the smaller had to submit, with or without protecting treaties. The economic linkage of most imperial cities to a neighboring power became a matter of survival since the greater territories tended to control economic life. Some of the great communes specialized in wider essential functions. Frankfurt am Main, for example, became the commercial and banking center of the middle West. Only a few large autonomous cities such as Hamburg, Bremen, and Frankfurt am Main saw a clear increase in the number of their inhabitants during the seventeenth and eighteenth centuries. Some tendencies toward political modernization did occur in this environment during the Enlightenment, but they did not reach a wider audience beyond their walls. Around 1800, fifty-one free imperial cities were left, thirty-one of which belonged to the Swabian Circle.

ESSENTIALS OF STATE FORMATION
IN THE TERRITORIES

The development of the territorial cities,[34] either constantly dependent on the territorial prince or temporarily emancipated, evidently differs considerably from one region to the other. Only the historian sees them as a whole, for these communes never created common organizational structures. The essentials of state formation are here reviewed briefly.

The position of the prince as the city's overlord often went back to the foundation act. From the beginning onward, town foundation was a form of development and intensification of territorial lordship. When the town remained small, the dependency then established remained unchanged. Different factors determined the level of urbanization of a territory, first of all the general level of development of the region. In the interior of the Empire, there were no urban regions of neighboring great and "modern" communes. In Germany, real state formation initiated by cities, taking over from the territorial princes the decision power and the partial or total determination of the social and economic life, occurred in few cases and for short periods. But the fact that middle-sized and large communes developed earlier than the principalities—in the fourteenth and fifteenth centuries—had constitutional consequences. Similarly to the practice in the sphere of the imperial cities, the most successful bought independence from their lords or simply exchanged large numbers of particular rights. Frequent crises of princely power offered them opportunities for gain. In this way, the town council could emerge as an authority in its town. The general European reversal of the development started in Germany in the fifteenth century and reached its goal at last in the early eighteenth century. The reduction of the political power of the communes was not identical to the economic or social deterioration of the oligarchical elites. Economic crises may well have overpowered the political will of the participants. Within the new territorial economic system, the particular city became constrained in its economic system, in its economic movements, and in its economic decisions in a way that cannot be explained solely by the market position of the commune.

The representative assemblies of the German territories,[35] however diversified in their concrete shape, generally featured participation of the cities in the *Landtag.* As was the case in the *Reichstag,* their place was then distinctly behind the noble and clergy estates, and where it existed, before that of the rural representatives. Generally, cities had only a small part in political decisions. There and in territorial assemblies, their inferior social position remained an incurable drawback. From the beginning, the nobility was the real political estate, solely and unquestionably linked to the court by feudal structures. Personal relations only smoothed the constitutional dualism for the nobility. In this confrontation, the cities' normally considerable fiscal achievement was the main instrument at their disposal. The dualism of the representative assemblies was after all an absolutely ambivalent phenomenon: real or apparent participation in the decision making came close to integration in the territories and facilitated the way toward a relatively uniform category of subjects. The shift in the position through which the imperial cities drove toward dualism and away from the king around and after 1500 was reinforced within the territories by the opening up of the domains (*Kammergut*).

In the fourteenth and fifteenth centuries urban leagues within the territories had over and again anticipated the attitude of the cities as an estate. Most of these unions were directed against the prince; they normally had short lifetimes and little effect. They concerned less the form of the state as a matter of principle than fiscal affairs and dynastic crises. Some exceptions existed. The cases of a territorial prince taking the initiative for such an urban league, or the typologically similar leading role of a sole greater city, are rather rare. Particular problems concerning the prince were more important in these cases than the cities' own grievances. In both cases indeed, a neighboring country (*"Nebenland"*) far away from the prince's residence had to be pacified more or less in his interest.

A classical example for the first case is the union of the six Oberlausitz cities from 1346 onwards;[36] for the second case, the example is the princely position of Breslau city within the principality of the same name, likewise during the Luxemburg period. The council's oligarchies of Görlitz, Bautzen, and similar places, facing a relatively weak nobility, could handle the nearly 150,000 inhabitants of Oberlausitz. The *"Hauptmannschaft"* taken up by the city of Breslau since 1357[37] included the acceptance of the homage of nobles and prelates. In both cases, however, the land did not become urban, but it was ruled by a city under the enduring conditions of "feudal" structures. No new Flanders emerged this way. The situation always led to princely rule.

Another form of symbiosis between city and principality appeared in the royal residential towns.[38] What never could be realized satisfactorily for the Empire as a whole was a reality in most territories. The examples of Prague, Vienna, Munich, Coblenz, Mannheim, or Berlin-Cölln can be extended by many others. The demographic growth and often the economic success and architectural development of the residence cities were far beyond average, especially in the early modern period. This expansion corresponded to the imposition of an especially intensive political discipline from the fifteenth or sixteenth century onward. At the same time, the urban bourgeoisie saw the influx of a larger number of other types of inhabitants about whom we will have to say more elsewhere. They pushed aside the traditional representatives of urban life in numbers, landed property, and influence; the social and economic weight of the princes provoked a new value orientation of the bourgeois toward the new urban population.

The general circumstances of the old Empire meant that the large population of a capital or residence could only carry on social and political agitation leading to state reform in the style of Paris in the French Revolution, within its own territorial space. The only historically significant (albeit short-lived) example was the "revolutionary" agitation in Prague, which became Hussite in and directly after 1419. The old order remained intact until just before the death of King Wenceslaus, who had long been unable to govern effectively. The old city of Prague claimed and up to a certain level temporarily acquired a leading role in Bohemia, which was left *de facto* without a king. It did so by leading a town league until the restoration of the old establishment's formal structure in 1436. Over the long term absolutely nothing remained; at the end of political Hussitism, the high aristocracy appeared to be the main victor.

At the end of this theme, we have to mention the largest and most durable union of territorial cities in older Europe, the Hanse.[39] It embraced a huge space in lower Germany, from the left Rhine bank in the West to Livonia in the Northeast. For centuries, it dominated (at least economically) the Northeastern quarter of Europe. We cannot characterize in a few lines a phenomenon to which an enormous amount of research has been devoted and which nevertheless does not yet seem to have been unequivocally and completely described and understood. We thus can only offer a sketch.

The king and the Empire had only limited contacts with the roughly 70 active and 100 to 130 passive Hanse towns, widely scattered over the north third of the Empire. Most enterprising in this respect were Charles IV and Sigismund. Incompatibilities of institutions and life-styles separated Hanse and Empire more than sheer distance did. What they had in common was the often-mentioned fundamental consensus. Members of the Hanse knew very well that they were "homines imperatoris," the emperor's men, or "cities of the German Hanse."

As far as state formation is concerned, we have to turn to the territorial cities. It therefore does not concern the very few imperial cities such as Lübeck or Dortmund or the free city Cologne but Hamburg, Rostock, Danzig, Lüneburg, or Soest. It is necessary to look at the origins of cities, taking into account wide differences in the periodization and especially a certain time lag of the North as compared to Southern Germany. Research has overestimated the institutional coherence and solidarity at the level of the overall Hanse space, even for the so-called Hanse of the cities from the fourteenth century onwards (we leave aside here the smaller town groups within the general Hanse). The huge West-East distance and the differences between coastal and landbound cities proved to be impossible to overcome. Reactive measures, concentrated on a concrete item, remained possible, but long-term constructive actions were not. Only a general consensus could be attained.

It rested on common territorial or even kinship backgrounds of the elites who had been migrating from West to East. They also had a community of interests in the disposition of public authority in cities and the shared profit from privileges for aliens. This consensus in principle, spanning a very extended space, could only be activated in the face of concrete challenges, as long as the crisis lasted and usually only among those directly involved. The common institutions should not be overestimated. On the other hand, one can notice that Lübeck formed the central nexus of the Hanse; its concrete effects on the cities of the union differed from one case to another. The organizational consolidation taking place in the fifteenth and sixteenth centuries was a reaction to movements on the side of the opponents of the Hanse and its privileges.

Although the Hanse often forced kings and princes to capitulate, no one had the idea of founding a "modern" city-state, as a common empire somewhat comparable to the monarchies and principalities of the Hanseatic space. The Empire with its "open constitution" offered enough legitimacy for the cities and at the same time the space wanted by the strongest. Constitutional history of the Hanse as a whole is therefore the history of the hegemony of some cities over others. The West and the East, Rhineland-Westphalia, and the Baltic region, including the leading cities Cologne and Lübeck, converged because Lübeck's leadership was ever more recognized. According to recent research, the *Hansetag* existed since 1356 as a relatively clearcut but modest institution. It is not to be compared with the *Reichstag* or with some *Landtag* and its urban estate, but rather with the assemblies of imperial and free cities that reacted to the *Reichstag* from 1471 onward.

Under such conditions, it seems most convenient to consider smaller spaces within the global Hanse area. The core of the Hanse association formed in the Wendic urban region, where the capital Lübeck was regularly surrounded by Hamburg, Lüneburg, Wismar, Rostock, and Stralsund. It displays the kind of regionalism typical for any part of the Hanse. For example the territorial organization of the communes in the bishopric of Münster, which was to become an urban estate of the *Landtag*, can equally be understood as a fundamental structure of the Hanse. Similarly the urban league of Lower Saxony, formed at the end of the fourteenth century around Braunschweig and Magdeburg as a response to the problems of semi-autonomous cities with their territorial prince; it provided the basis for the participation of its members in the Hanse.[40] More global actions resulted from the temporal collaboration of two or more urban groups. In some circumstances, this might be the basis for opposition against Lübeck as well.

The densification of the territories, which generally began in the North during the fifteenth century, threatened to restrict the fundaments of encompassing economic interests of the Hanse. As a first response, the association developed better organizational structures and more decisive military action. Then, however, weakening and decay occurred, especially in the seventeenth century. The economy of commercial privileges had become outdated and was overruled by the princely state that now included economic interests. Thus princes in the area of the Saxon urban league eliminated the conditions and privileges sustaining the semi-autonomous position of the communes before the end of the fifteenth century.

In two cases, however, the greater cities in the Hanse area had significant successes in state formation: the case of Hamburg and Bremen that has already been mentioned and that of the Prussian cities. What did succeed here and what did not seems relevant for the opportunities and limits of the older German cities in general.

1. The fixing of the status of imperial cities in both North Sea harbors[41] in the seventeenth and eighteenth century did not contradict the general expansion of princely power. It rather ran parallel to it, albeit at a certain distance from the normal development. From the viewpoint of the cities, indeed, those acts have to be seen as concessions that had become unavoidable under threats from the environment. Until then, a much more favorable, undefined floating situation had existed, dating back to the distant period of the "open constitution." It could best be compared to the position of the Swiss confederation in the sixteenth century, as we described it above. Because of their successful military self-defense, nobody was able to sanction their interpretation of old privileges, which objectively was abusive. Similarly, Hamburg and Bremen did not pay taxes to the territorial prince or to the emperor and Empire, except with delays and reductions; they had not been disciplined for their delinquency. Only when no possibility for escape remained did they submit themselves to the most distant and mildest lord.

2. The greater Prussian Hanse cities,[42] led by Danzig and Elbing, revolted against their territorial lord, the Teutonic Order. The rebellion's end in the second peace of Thorn (1466) was only a partial success for the communes. The self-produced legitimacy of *de jure* autonomy was hardly conceivable, let alone realized. The Teutonic Order was a threatening competitor in the economically decisive grain trade, as it was a territorial lord with a Hanse membership of its own. Furthermore, it had to raise high taxes from the estates to resist Polish pressure. So, nobility and towns formed a joint opposition to the Order. Military success was not sufficient in the revolt against the Grand Master or against the Emperor and the Pope as protectors of the Order. The new situation needed legitimation by a new territorial lord, a weak and generous one, if possible. Only the king of Poland was disposed to this role. The cities submitted themselves to him, hoping for a future full of privileges, which were indeed enacted. National feelings were not at stake for the cities; they took for granted that they remained members of the Hanse in a Baltic area stamped with German influences. This is the best testimony to the evidently general fact that medieval "state" theory, based upon legitimacy as we described it, is to be taken absolutely seriously in Germany during the fifteenth century and even beyond. This thought provided no opportunities to the cities that came from "below," even when they were equal or superior militarily. A modern, self-produced, ideological legitimation of power could

emerge only when they could effectively stay intact until the time of the *raison d'état* and the accomplished European state system, as did the Swiss.

CONCLUSIONS

The fundamental characteristics of older German constitutional history were not determined by the urban-bourgeois element but by that of the princely state and nobility; the King/Emperor in this respect was equally a prince. This situation appeared at a very early stage, with respect to some conditions even before the beginnings of German history in the tenth century. An average level of urbanization comparable to that in Flanders or Northern Italy, which may have created a "modern" urban atmosphere, was simply excluded in the context of the development of the Empire. Nevertheless, the urbanization process, starting mainly in the twelfth century and bringing major changes in the fields of demography, economy, and social and cultural phenomena, did have consequences with respect to the "state." Its many effects occurred in close interaction with the leading aristocracy. This interaction stabilized the social and political aristocratic structure in the short and middle term, and only in the middle and longer term did restructuring occur. The "feudal" Empire and its princely states were for a very long period not less adequate within the European context than were other imaginable social structures.

Regional histories, however, included interesting particular cases of cities intruding in state-building processes. Normally the result was a mixture of "feudal" and urban elements. When one takes into consideration the many communal leagues, the conclusion must be that in most cases the "feudal" world won.

The elites playing a role in all these circumstances were not only those closely linked to the communes; persons and groups with looser connections to particular cities often placed themselves into the service of the king or princes. When these groups formed social networks, then they adapted themselves easily to the prevailing "state" context. The main occupations in the bureaucracy, the economic life, the Church, and education existing in the eighteenth century existed already in principle in the Middle Ages.

With respect to periodization and breaks, some time lags are to be observed in the general directions West-East and South-North. Under this remark, we can distinguish until 1800 a primary phase (from around 1250 to 1450/1470), a core phase (1450/1470 to 1650), a phase of continuation (from 1650 to after 1750), and finally a phase of transition (second half of the eighteenth century). This global situation surely can be considered to be backward in comparison to Western Europe.

When one is looking forward to bourgeois freedom in industrial society, our endeavor urges caution for all-too-hasty overviews of pre-modern history; the particular phenomena have to be placed prudently in the context of their time. In this respect, the search for a modern bourgeois alternative to the traditional constitution of the estates around 1500 tends to be anachronistic. Freedom of particular cities and the citizenry in Germany were movements within the whole of the "feudal" world, which in its turn was modified by them. As the assemblies of estates preluded parliamentarism, the urban movement prepared the modernity in Central Europe, without being its direct and exclusive cause.

Notes

1. Peter Moraw, *Von offener Verfassung zu gestalteter Verdichtung: Das Reich im späten Mittelalter 1250 bis 1490, Propyläen Geschichte Deutschlands 3* (Berlin: Propyläen, 1985); Heinrich Lutz, *Das Ringen um deutsche Einheit und kirchliche Erneuerung: Von Maximilian I. bis zum Westfälischen Frieden 1490 bis 1648, Propyläen Geschichte Deutschlands 4* (Berlin: Propyläen, 1983); Rudolf Vierhaus, *Staaten und Stände: Vom Westfälischen bis zum Hubertusburger Frieden 1648 bis 1763, Propyläen Geschichte Deutschlands 5* (Berlin: Propyläen, 1984).

2. Otto Brunner, *Neue Wege der Verfassungs- und Sozialgeschichte* (Göttingen: Vandenhoeck & Ruprecht, 1968); Ernst Schubert, *König und Reich* (Göttingen: Vandenhoeck & Ruprecht, 1979); *Deutsche Verwaltungsgeschichte*, ed. Kurt G.A. Jeserich et al., Vol. 1 (Stuttgart: Deutsche Verlagsanstalt, 1983); Peter Moraw, Reich I–III, in *Geschichtliche Grundbegriffe*, ed. Otto Brunner et al., Vol. 5 (Stuttgart: Klett-Cotta, 1984), S. 423–456; Heinz Angermeier, *Die Reichsreform 1410–1555* (Munich: Beck, 1984).

3. *Bibliographie zur deutschen historischen Städteforschung*, ed. Brigitte Schröder and Heinz Stoob, Vol. 1 (Cologne: Böhlau, 1986), for the North; for the South: *Bibliographie zur Städtegeschichte Deutschlands*, ed. Erich Keyser (Cologne: Böhlau, 1969); *Bibliographie zur Geschichte der Städte Oesterreichs*, ed. Wilhelm Rausch (Linz: Österreichischer Arbeitskreis für Stadtgeschichtsforschung, 1984); *Deutsches Städtebuch*, ed. Erich Keyser and Heinz Stoob, Vol. 2, parts 1–5 (Stuttgart and Berlin: Kohlhammer, 1939–1974); *Österreichisches Städtebuch*, ed. Alfred Hofmann, Vol. 1, parts 1–5 (Vienna: Hollinek, 1968–1980); *Deutscher Städteatlas*, ed. Heinz Stoob (Dortmund: Grösschen, 1973 ff.); *Stadt und Stadtherr im 14. Jahrhundert*, ed. Wilhelm Rausch (Linz: Österreichischer Arbeitskreis für Stadtgeschichtsforschung, 1972); *Die Stadt am Ausgang des Mittelalters*, ed. Rausch (Linz: Österreichischer Arbeitskreis für Stadtgeschichtsforschung, 1974); *Stadt und Städtebürgertum in der deutschen Geschichte des 13. Jahrhunderts*, ed. Bernhard Töpfer (Berlin: Akademie, 1976); *Die Stadt des Mittelalters*, ed. Carl Haase, 3 vols. (Darmstadt: Wissenschaftliche Buchgesellschaft, 1976–1984); *Guide international d'histoire urbain, l. Europe*, ed. Philippe Wolff (Paris: Klincksieck, 1977), 40 ff., 90 ff., 466 ff.; *Städtische Führungsgruppen und Gemeinde in der werdenden Neuzeit*, ed. Wilfried Ehbrecht (Cologne: Böhlau, 1979); *Deutsche Führungsschichten in der Neuzeit*, ed. Hanns Hubert Hofmann and Günther Franz (Boppard: Boldt, 1980); *Die Stadt an der Schwelle der Neuzeit*, ed. Wilhelm Rausch (Linz: Österreichischer Arbeitskreis für Stadtgeschichtsforschung, 1980); Eckhard Müller-Mertens, "Bürgerlich-städtische

Autonomie in der Feudalgesellschaft," *Zs. f. Geschichtswiss.* 29 (1981), 205–225; *Beiträge zum spätmittelalterlichen Städtewesen,* ed. Bernhard Diestelkamp (Cologne: Böhlau, 1982); *Civitatum communitas, Festschrift f. Heinz Stoob,* 2 vols. (Cologne: Böhlau, 1984); *Bürgerliche Eliten in den Niederlanden und in Nordwestdeutschland,* ed. Heinz Schilling and Hermann Diederiks (Cologne: Böhlau, 1985); *Österreichs Städte und Märkte in der Geschichte,* ed. Erich Zöllner (Österreichischer Bundesverlag, 1985); *Stadt im Wandel,* 3 vols. (Stuttgart: Cantz, 1985).

4. Karl Ferdinand Werner, *Les origines* (Paris: Fayard, 1984), Histoire de France, Vol. 1.

5. Peter Moraw, "Über Entwicklungsunterschiede und Entwicklungsausgleich im deutschen und europäischen Mittelalter," in *Hochfinanz, Wirtschaftsräume, Innovationen, Festschrift f. Wolfgang v. Stromer,* Vol. 2 (Trier: Auenthal, 1987), 583–622.

6. Karl Ferdinand Werner, "Deutsch-französische Nachbarschaft," in *Frankreich und Deutschland* (Hannover, Bonn: Schlüter, 1986), 9–32.

7. Heinz Stoob, *Forschungen zum Städtewesen in Europa,* vol. 1 (Cologne: Böhlau, 1970); *Die Stadt,* Stoob, editor (Cologne: Böhlau, 1979); *East-Central Europe in Transition,* ed. Antoni Maczak et al. (Cambridge: Cambridge University Press, 1985). See also note 5.

8. The core of state formation was the Kingship. During the Middle Ages, the title of Emperor could only be acquired with a trip to Rome and papal coronation; after 1500, the title of Emperor was used directly after the coronation as King even without papal sanction; thus did the emperorship outweigh the position of King.

9. *Der deutsche Territorialstaat im 14. Jahrhundert,* ed. Hans Patze, 2 vols. (Sigmaringen: Thorbecke, 1970/71); Dietmar Willoweit, *Rechtsgrundlagen der Territorialgewalt* (Cologne: Böhlau); *Deutsche Verwaltungsgeschichte,* Vol. 1, as in note 2; Peter Moraw, "Die Entfaltung der deutschen Territorien im 14. und 15. Jahrhundert," in *Landesherrliche Kanzleien im Spätmittelalter,* Vol. 1 (Munich: Arbeo-Gesellschaft, 1984), 61–108.

10. Moraw, *Verfassung* (see note 1), 47 f. For the development of post offices from the late fifteenth century onward, see 390 f.

11. Peter Moraw, "Zur Mittelpunktsfunktion Prags im Zeitalter Karls IV," in *Europa slavica—Europa orientalis, Festschrift f. Herbert Ludat* (Berlin: Duncker u. Humblot, 1980), 445–489.

12. In addition to references in note 1, see *Das Römisch-deutsche Reich im politischen System Karls V,* ed. Heinrich Lutz (Munich: Oldenbourg, 1982).

13. Exact figures are unavailable. The most recent estimates appear in H. Stoob, in *Die Stadt,* see note 7.

14. Alfred Haverkamp, "Die Städte im Herrschafts- und Sozialgefüge Reichsitaliens," *Historische Zeitschrift,* N.S., Beiheft 7, n.d., 149–245; Bernhard Diestelkamp, "Königtum und Städte in salischer und staufischer Zeit," in ibid., 247–297; Ferdinand Opll, *Stadt und Reich im 12. Jahrhundert (1125–1190)* (Cologne: Böhlau, 1986).

15. Erich Maschke, "Die deutschen Städte der Stauferzeit," in *Die Zeit der Staufer,* Vol. 3 (Stuttgart: Württembergisches Landesmuseum, 1977), 59–73, esp. 69.

16. Franz Irsigler, "Deutschland: Städtische Sozial- und Wirtschaftsgeschichte," in *Lexikon des Mittelalters,* Vol. 3 (Munich: Artemis, 1986), 893–909. As a particular

example, see his *Die wirtschaftliche Stellung der Stadt Köln im 14. und 15. Jahrhundert* (Wiesbaden: Steiner, 1979). See also note 21.

17. Rolf Kießling, "Stadt-Land-Beziehungen im Spätmittelalter," *Zs. f. bayer. Landesgesch* 40, 1977, S. 829–867; *Städtisches Um- und Hinterland in vorindustrieller Zeit,* ed. Hans K. Schulze (Cologne: Böhlau, 1985).

18. Manfred Wilmanns, *Die Landgebietspolitik der Stadt Bremen um 1400* (Hildesheim: August Lax, 1973); Wolfgang Leiser, "Territorien süddeutscher Reichsstädte," *Zs. f. bayer. Landesgesch* 38, 1975, 967–981; Gerd Wunder, "Reichsstädte als Landesherren," in *Zentralität als Problem der mittelalterlichen Stadtgeschichtsforschung,* ed. Emil Meynen (Cologne: Böhlau, 1979), 79–91; Bernd Schneidmüller, "Städtische Territorialpolitik und spätmittelalterliche Feudalgesellschaft am Beispiel von Frankfurt am Main," *Bll, f. dt. Landesgesch* 118, 1982, 115–136.

19. Wolfgang v. Stromer, *Die Gründung der Baumwollindustrie in Mitteleuropa* (Stuttgart: Hiersemann, 1979); Stromer, "Gewerbereviere und Protoindustrien in Spätmittelalter und Frühneuzeit," in *Gewerbe- und Industrielandschaften vom Spätmittelalter bis ins 20. Jahrhundert,* ed. Hans Pohl (Stuttgart: Steiner, 1986), 39–111.

20. Moraw, *Verfassung* (see note 1), 115.

21. Wolfgang v. Stromer, *Oberdeutsche Hochfinanz 1350–1450, Part 3* (Wiesbaden: Steiner, 1970); Hektor Ammann, *Nürnbergs wirtschaftliche Stellung im Spätmittelalter* (Nuremberg: Verein für Geschichte der Stadt Nürnberg, 1970); *Nürnberg: Geschichte einer europäischen Stadt,* ed. Gerhard Pfeiffer (Munich: Beck, 1971); Eva-Maria Engel, "Finanzielle Beziehungen zwischen deutschen Königen und Städtebürgern von 1250 bis 1314," *Jb. f. Wirtschaftsgesch* 1975/IV, 95–113.

22. See note 42.

23. Hugo Stehkämper, "Über die rechtliche Absicherung der Stadt Köln gegen eine erzbischöfliche landesherrschaft vor 1288," in *Die Stadt in der europäischen Geschichte, Festschrift Edith Ennen* (Bonn: Röhrscheid, 1972), 343–377; *Bischofsund Kathedralstädte des Mittelalters und der frühen Neuzeit,* ed. Franz Petri (Cologne: Böhlau, 1976). See also note 24.

24. Götz Landwehr, *Die Verpfändung der deutschen Reichsstädte im Mittelalter* (Cologne: Böhlau, 1967); Eberhard Isenmann, "Reichsstadt und Reich an der Wende vom späten Mittelalter zur frühen Neuzeit," in *Mittel und Wege früher Verfassungspolitik,* ed. Josef Engel (Stuttgart: Klett-Cotta, 1979), 9–223; Peter Moraw, "Reichsstadt, Reich und Königtum im späten Mittelalter," *Zs. f. hist. Forschung* 6, 1979, 385–424; Georg Schmidt, "Reichsstadt und Territorialstaat," *Esslinger Studien* 21, 1982, 71–104; *Deutsche Verwaltungsgeschichte* 1 (see note 2); Paul-Joachim Heinig, *Reichsstädte, Freie Städte und Königtum 1389–1450* (Wiesbaden: Stiner, 1983); Eberhard Isenmann, "Reichsrecht und Reichsverfassung in Konsilien reichsstädtischer Juristen (15.–17. Jahrhundert)," in *Die Rolle der Juristen bei der Entstehung des modernen Staates,* ed. Roman Schnur (Berlin: Duncker & Humblot, 1986), 545–628; *Reichsstädte in Franken,* ed. Rainer A. Müller, 3 vols. (Munich: Haus der Bayerischen Geschichte, 1987); Volker Press, "Die Reichstädte in der altständischen Gesellschaft," in *Neue Studien zur frühneuzeitlichen Reichsgeschichte,* ed. Johannes Kunisch (Berlin: Duncker & Humblot, 1987), 9–42 (Beih. 3 of *Zs. f. hist. Forschung*).

25. See notes 34, 36–38, and 40.

26. *Die Urkunden und Akten der oberdeutschen Städtebünde vom 13. Jahrhundert bis 1549,* ed. Konrad Ruser, Vol. 1 (Göttingen: Vandenhoeck u. Ruprecht, 1979); Brigitte Berthold, "Überregionale Städtebundprojekte in der ersten Hälfte des 15. Jahrhunderts," *Jb. f. Gesch. d. Feudalismus* 3, 1979, S. 141–179; Karl Schnith, "Reichsgewalt—Schwäbischer Städtebund—Augsburg," *Zs. d. hist. Vereins f. Schwaben* 74, 1980, 104–119; *Der Rheinische Städtebund von 1254/56* (Koblenz: Landeshauptarchiv, 1986); *Kommunale Bündnisse Oberitaliens und Oberdeutschlands im Vergleich,* ed. Helmut Maurer (*Vorträge und Forschungen* 33) (Sigmaringen: Thorbecke, 1987).

27. Martin Brecht, "Die gemeinsame Politik der Reichsstädte und die Reformation," *Zs. d. Savigny-Stiftung f. Rechtsgesch* 94, Kanon. Abt. 63, 1977, 180–263; Georg Schmidt, *Der Städtetag in der Reichsverfassung* (Wiesbaden: Steiner, 1984); Schmidt, "Die Freien und Reichsstädte im Schmalkaldischen Bund," in *Martin Luther: Probleme seiner Zeit,* ed. Volker Press and Dieter Stievermann (Stuttgart: Klett-Cotta, 1986), 177–218.

28. Eberhard Isenmann, "Zur Frage der Reichsstandschaft der Frei- und Reichstädte," in *Stadtverfassung, Verfassungsstaat, Pressepolitik: Festschrift f. Eberhard Naujoks* (Sigmaringen: Thorbecke, 1980), S. 91–110; Peter Moraw, "Versuch über die Entstehung des Reichstags," in *Politische Ordnungen und soziale Kräfte im Alten Reich,* ed. Hermann Weber (Wiesbaden: Steiner, 1980), 1–36.

29. Hans Conrad Peer, *Verfassungsgeschichte der alten Schweiz* (Zürich: Schulthess, 1978); *Geschichte der Schwetz und der Schweizer,* Vol. 1 (Basel, Frankfurt M.: Helbing u. Lichtenhahn, 1983); Peter Moraw, "Reich, König und Eidgenossen im späten Mittelalter," *Jb. d. Hist. Ges. Luzern* 4, 1986, 15–33; Helmut G. Walther, "Basel: Reichsbewußtsein und Reichsferne am Oberrhein in der zweiten Hälfte des 15. Jahrhunderts," in *Europa 1500,* ed. Winfried Eberhard and Ferdinand Seibt (Stuttgart: Klett-Cotta, 1987), 227–246.

30. In addition to notes 3, 23, 24, 26, and 27, see *Stadtbürgertum und Adel in der Reformation,* ed. Wolfgang J. Mommsen (Stuttgart: Klett-Cotta, 1979); *Städtische Gesellschaft und Reformation,* ed. Ingrid Batori (Stuttgart: Klett-Cotta, 1980); *Schichtung und Entwicklung der Gesellschaft in Polen und Deutschland im 16. und 17. Jahrhundert,* ed. Marian Biskup and Klaus Zernack (Wiesbaden: Steiner, 1983).

31. Thomas A. Brady, Jr., *Turning Swiss: Cities and Empire 1450–1550* (Cambridge: Cambridge University Press, 1985).

32. See note 29.

33. Moraw, *Verfassung,* 175 f.

34. Arbitrary choice from a huge literature: Werner Mägdefrau, *Der Thüringer Städtebund im Mittelalter* (Weimar: Böhlau, 1976); Wilhelm Janssen, "Stadt und Stadtherr am Niederrhein im späten Mittelalter," *Rhein. Vierteljahrsbll.* 42, 1978, S. 185–208; Franz-Josef Verscharen, *Gesellschaft und Verfassung der Stadt Marburg beim Übergang vom Mittelalter zur Neuzeit* (Marburg: Elwert, 1985); Peter Czendes, "Des riches houptstat in Osterrich," *Jb. f. Landeskunde v. Niederösterreich* NF 53, 1987, 47–58.

35. Herbert Helbig, *Der wettinische Ständestaat* (Münster and Cologne: Böhlau, 1955); F. L. Carsten, *Princes and Parliaments in Germany from the Fifteenth to the Eighteenth Century* (Oxford: Oxford University Press, 1959); *Ständische*

Vertretungen in Europa im 17. und 18. Jahrhundert, ed. Dietrich Gerhard (Göttingen: Vandenhoeck u. Ruprecht, 1974); Rudolf Vierhaus, "Land, Staat, und Reich in der politischen Vorstellungswelt deutscher Landstände im 18. Jahrhundert," *Hist. Zs.* 223, 1976, S. 40–60; *Die geschichtlichen Grundlagen der modernen Volksvertretung,* ed. Heinz Rausch, 2 vols. (Darmstadt: Wissenschaftliche Buchgesellschaft, 1974–80); *Der moderne Parlamentarismus und seine Grundlagen in der ständischen Repräsentation,* ed. Karl Bosl (Berlin: Duncker u. Humblot, 1977); Franz Quarthal, *Landstände und landständisches Steuerwesen in Schwäbisch Österreich* (Stuttgart: Müller and Gräff, 1980); *Städte und Ständestaat,* ed. Bernhard Töpfer (Berlin: Akademie, 1980); Horst Wernicke, "Städtehanse und Stände im Norden des Deutschen Reiches zum Ausgang des Spätmittelalters," in *Der Ost- und Nordseeraum* (Weimar: Böhlau, 1986), 190–208.

36. Karl Czok, "Zur Entwicklung der Oberlausitzer Sechsstädte vom 13. Jahrhundert bis zur Gründung des Sechsstädtebundes 1346," in *Beiträge zum spätmittelalterlichen Städtewesen,* ed. Bernhard Diestelkamp (Cologne: Böhlau, 1982), 103–118.

37. *Schleslen,* ed. Hugo Weczerka (Stuttgart: Kröner, 1977), 43 (*Handbuch der historischen Stätten*).

38. Hans Patze and Gerhard Streich, "Die landesherrlichen Residenzen im spätmittelalterlichen Deutschen Reich," *Bll. f. dt. Landesgesch* 118, 1982, 204–220; Etienne Francois, *Koblenz im 18. Jahrhundert* (Göttingen: Vandenhoeck u. Ruprecht, 1982).

39. Philippe Dollinger, *Die Hanse* (Stuttgart: Kröner, 1976); *Lübeck, Hanse, Nordeuropa, Gedächtnisschrift f. Ahasver v. Brandt* (Cologne-Vienna: Böhlau, 1979); Volker Henn, "Die Hanse: Interessengemeinschaft oder Städtebund?" *Hans. Geschichtsblätter* 102, 1984, 119–126; Detlev Ellmers, "Die Entstehung der Hanse," in ibid., 103, 1985, 3–40; *Der Ost- und Nordseeraum* (Weimar: Böhlau, 1986).

40. Matthias Puhle, *Die Politik der Stadt Braunschweig innerhalb des Sächsischen Städtebundes* (Braunschweig: Waisenhaus, 1985); Puhle, "Der Sächsische Städtebund und die Hanse im späten Mittelalter," *Hans. Geschichtsbll.* 104, 1986, 21–34; Friedrich Bernward Fahlbusch, "Zur Hansischen Organisation im Hochstift Münster im 15. und 16. Jahrhundert," *Westfäl. Forsch.* 35, 1985, 60–72.

41. Heinrich Reincke, "Hamburgs Aufstieg zur Reichsfreiheit," *Zs. d. Vereins f. Hamburg. Gesch.* 41, 1961, 17–34; *Hamburg: Geschichte der Stadt und ihrer Bewohner,* Vol. 1 (Hamburg: Hoffmann u. Campe, 1982); Karin Newman, "Hamburg in the European Economy, 1660–1750," *Journal of European Economic History* 14, 1985, 57–93.

42. Hartmut Boockmann, *Der Deutsche Orden* (München: Beck, 1983); Ernst Manfred Wermter, "Die Bildung des Danziger Stadtterritoriums in den politischen Zielvorstellungen des Rates der Stadt Danzig im späten Mittelalter und in der frühen Neuzeit," in *Ordensherrschaft, Städte und Stadtpolitik,* ed. Udo Arnold (Lüneburg: Nordostdeutsches Kulturwerk, 1985), 81–123.

◀ 6 ▶

State and Towns
in the Middle Ages:
The Scandinavian Experience

ANDERS ANDRÉN

IN THE THREE SCANDINAVIAN countries, Denmark,[1] Sweden, and Norway, there existed, in the Middle Ages, approximately 175 places which could be called towns.[2] My aim in this chapter is to study the relation between these places and the State, a task involving several issues. They have to do with the function of towns in society, with the position of towns in a hierarchy of power, and with the concepts "State" and "town," i.e., with concepts that do not appear in a very clear-cut way in medieval Scandinavia.

For a discussion on the relation between "state" and "towns" in the Middle Ages, these concepts must be comprehended in a very general sense. It is important, though, not to disregard totally the specific designations of the concepts in the medieval period.[3] One way of attempting to combine general and specific features of these concepts is to set up periods within whose limits a more abstract "contemporaneity" can be analyzed.

Urbanization in Scandinavia has frequently been periodized; but the periods have not always been given a methodological function, as urbanization has often been viewed in an immutably ahistorical manner. Towns have been traditionally regarded as being connected with market-economic commerce and crafts. This approach is conditioned by academic traditions (cf., for instance, Pirenne and Weber) as well as by influences from outside the academic world (projection of present-day urbanization). Beside this customary view of towns and urbanization, though, the last ten years have witnessed the emergence of lines of thought where discontinuity is stressed instead. The present study proceeds from a similarly discontinuous point of view, and the division into periods is based on the shifting relation between state and towns.[4]

128

In an investigation of the connection between state and towns in medieval Scandinavia one must pay attention to the empirical situation, too. The region is characterized by few written sources, especially from the period between 1000 and 1300. To obtain a more complete picture it is necessary to take the physical remains in towns into consideration. In the present study some very evident remains come up for discussion, namely, town churches, friaries, town defenses, and guildhalls. It stands out clearly from the following lines that these "manifest traces" have much to tell us about the size and the structure of the town.

MEDIEVAL SCANDINAVIA: A PRIMARY SURVEY

From different points of view Scandinavia can be regarded as the margin of medieval Europe. It was here that the agrarian settlement was replaced by the non-Christian saami-culture of hunters and fishermen. It was here that many features of medieval European society had their northern limits. Outside this framework nature did not allow a countryside that was sufficiently populated for the existence of monasteries, castles, and towns. The restriction of nature is very obvious if you compare the location of medieval towns with the ecological zones of potential vegetation (see Figure [6.]1).[5] Most towns were situated in the southern and most fertile region (the nemoral zone), whereas there were less numerous towns in the transition area (the boreonemoral zone), and practically no towns at all in the northern and least fertile region (the boreal zone). Though there were extensive agrarian settlements on the boreal zone, it is significant that three out of four towns in this area were connected with mining.

Another feature due to the marginal position of Scandinavia was that the heritage of Antiquity was lacking, as a background to society and its organization. Instead, the establishment of Kingship and Church in the Middle Ages was the first tendency toward a centralized power in this region. The medieval kingdom does not appear as a disintegration of the political power, but rather as a step toward the territorial state.[6]

In a wide social and economic sense Scandinavian society can be regarded as feudal. For instance, the different forms of feudal lordship, defined by Georges Duby,[7] can be traced in the area. The medieval "state" was above all expressed by the sovereignty that was exercised in a diffuse zone between the public and the private, as in the rest of Europe. An important feature in the character of the Scandinavian State was the permanent exemption from taxes granted the Church and the lay aristocracy. However, no heritable fief of continental pattern was established, apart from the duchy of Slesvig in the southernmost part of Denmark.

The continuous royal control over some parts of the sovereignty meant that most towns were subordinate to the king, and usually were founded by

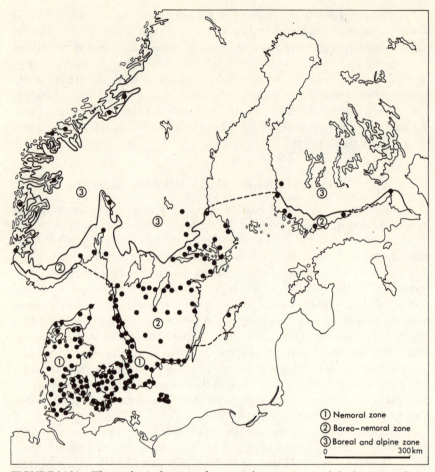

FIGURE [6.]1   The ecological zones of potential vegetation and the location of medieval towns (1000–1500) in Scandinavia.

the king, too. Exceptions from this rule were twenty-one minor towns (12 percent of all towns), belonging to different bishoprics and monasteries. In several cases, though, these places were only secondarily granted by the king to the new lords. In fact, it is only in a very few cases that we know bishops were actually founding towns. Irrespectively of whom the power over the towns belonged to, though, the same forms of feudal lordship can be traced in towns, as elsewhere in society. The most important change in the dominion over the town was that the power was shifted from the individual inhabitants to the town as a whole. With this change the urban regime emerged as a typically feudal medium between the town and the lord of the town. The urban regime represented the town versus the lord, but at the same time it became a participant in the lord's supremacy over the town, because fines, tolls, and other duties were partly at the disposal of the town council. Though this tendency to independence never went as far as in other European regions, Scandinavian towns partly held the same special position as other towns in feudal society. These unique features can be best summarized in John Merrington's words, "the internal externality."[8]

This very short and general survey of Scandinavia and its towns can be varied in several ways. The relation between state and towns changed in the Middle Ages, and there were also several important regional differences in the area. These regional contrasts can illuminate, in an interesting way, the complicated relation between state and towns.

THE CONGESTED COUNTRYSIDE (1000–1150)

The period from about 1000 to the middle of the twelfth century corresponds to the establishment of the three Scandinavian realms. The previous, external exploitation, in the form of Viking raids, was gradually replaced by internal exploitation, based on personal duties from the peasants. In connection with this kind of new exploitation the Kingship and the Church created a new form of sovereignty and political organization. The formation of a Christian State is discernible from the end of the tenth century in Denmark and from about 1000 in Norway. There were signs of a state in Sweden about the year 1000, but a more permanent political unit was not created until the beginning of the twelfth century.

The contemporary towns can be, in many ways, regarded as *points d'appui* for the new political order. It was in these places that several central functions of the Kingship and the Church were located. According to the Icelandic sagas the Norwegian kings expressly founded towns to get control over different parts of the country. In this way Trondheim was founded about the year 1000 in direct opposition to the heathen chieftains in Trøndelag.[9]

The connection between state formation and urbanization is also evident from the appearance of the urban profile of the period (see Figure [6.]2). Most of the towns arose in Denmark, where state formation can be traced at an earlier stage and was more pronounced than in the rest of Scandinavia. In Norway the towns were less numerous, and in Sweden, which experienced a much later political unification, the towns were extremely few. The relation between state and towns can also be illustrated by the sizes of the towns. It is possible to make a rough ranking of the towns, by counting the number of churches in each place.[10] As figure [6.]2 shows, the largest towns were situated in Norway and above all in Denmark.

The size of a town seems to have been dependent, to a high degree, on the structure of the political power. And it was important how many functions

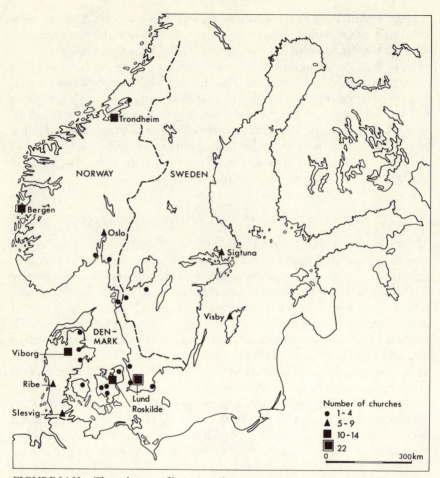

FIGURE [6.]2   The urban profile in Scandinavia, 1000–1150. The ranking of towns according to the number of churches in each town.

were located in each place. An illustrative example is Lund, which, with its twenty-two churches, was the largest city in Scandinavia. Lund was situated in eastern Denmark, where the Kingship exercised a more extensive royal power than in the rest of the realm. The city was the largest mint in the country, a royal residence, a legal center, a bishopric for eastern Denmark, and the archbishop's see for Scandinavia as a whole, including Iceland and Greenland. Similar multifunctional conditions can be traced in other large cities of the period, such as Roskilde, Viborg, and Trondheim.

The close connection between state and towns must have also influenced the character of the urban economy. The economic life of towns should probably be viewed as a kind of consuming economy, closely connected with those institutions and persons that exercised the new sovereignty. For instance, it is told in Icelandic sagas how, in the 1060s, the Norwegian King sent out his men from Oslo to collect taxes, rents, and fines in the surroundings.

Trade and handicrafts were found in towns, even if on a small scale. These activities should probably be regarded as an expression of the royal and ecclesiastical need of "necessary articles," which were mandatory in order to maintain and justify the new supremacy. Thus, it is clear from Icelandic sources that in the 1060s Norwegian coins were used as pay to royal housecarls.

The internal urban organization is unsatisfactorily known. According to the few contemporary sources, however, a close connection between state and towns can also be traced in respect to urban organization. The town was governed by a royal sheriff or "gälkare" (literally, "geld exactor"), who exercised the primary supremacy over the town inhabitants. This power was expressed by particular town taxes, which were exacted from each household or "hearth." The earliest known evidence of such a town tax is the "midsummer geld" that is referred to in three Danish towns in 1085. The population was dependent on the lord of the town in other ways as well. One example is the situation of the inhabitants of Schleswig. Before the middle of the twelfth century they were forced to have royal permission to invite foreign merchants to their city.

The urban character can be illustrated by the ecclesiastical structure, too. The ecclesiastical organization was distinguished by many churches in towns and by diffuse boundaries between town and countryside. Many parishes comprised rural as well as urban settlements, although the churches were situated in the towns. The numerous churches and the "open" relationship to the countryside show that towns were functioning in a more or less "rural" manner. Thus, towns can be principally designated as "congested countryside." This concept helps us to understand many of the precommunal features of urban organization. Special denominations for town inhabitants were lacking, and there was no clear legal distinction between town and country. Slavery still existed in Scandinavian towns about 1200, and this fact discloses that the principle *"Stadtluft macht frei"* was not yet valid.

There was no town regime except for the royal sheriff. The only known expressions for urban organization were the guilds, and in the current period they are known from Sigtuna, Trondheim, and Schleswig. The character of these guilds, however, is uncertain. "The Frisian Guild" in Sigtuna might have been a merchant organization, whereas "The Great Guild" ("Miklagillet") in Trondheim and "The Sworn Guild" ("Edslaget") in Schleswig probably had more general features. It is characteristic, though, that these guilds cannot be directly interpreted as expressions for urban independence.

In Trondheim the guild was founded by the king, and in Schleswig the Danish duke seems to have played an important role in the guild.

The concept of "the congested countryside" can, in several ways, summarize the position of towns in this period. The towns were closely connected with the political power, and this meant that they were lacking an urban independence that would have made it possible to distinguish them from the countryside.

THE MUNICIPAL TRANSITION (1150–1350)

From the middle of the twelfth century to the middle of the fourteenth century the Scandinavian states developed more distinctive feudal features than earlier. The system of enfeoffment became an element of growing importance in the exercise of power. This change in the character of the State took place at different times in the three countries but followed the same political pattern: First disruptive civil wars, then external expansions, and lastly major or minor conflicts between the Kingship and the aristocracy. The external expansion resulted in a more or less permanent political control from the Scandinavian countries over surrounding regions, such as the Atlantic islands and the southern shores of the Baltic, Estonia, and above all Finland.[11]

The character of the State changed at the same time that the social position of many people was redefined. The last remnants of slavery disappeared, and the personal duties of the peasants were converted into regular taxes. These taxes laid the foundation of a new administration, which was based on castles and professional warriors. Gradually the warriors, like the Church, obtained more or less considerable exemptions from taxes. Accordingly, the aristocracy began to collect royal taxes from their tenants, which meant that sovereignty was exercised by many people and institutions.

Regular taxes can be traced in Denmark and Norway from the latter part of the twelfth century but in Sweden not until the thirteenth century. In Sweden and above all in Denmark taxes were high and the exemptions from taxes were extensive. In Norway, on the other hand, taxes were low and the exemptions from taxes were less extensive. Instead, the military role of the peasantry was partially preserved, beside the military service of the aristocracy. These regional differences in the execution of power were reflected in the relations between the Kingship and the aristocracy, too. In Norway the privileged classes were tied to the king, while the Swedish and the Danish aristocracies had a much more independent position. The conflicts between the Kingship and the privileged classes were especially pronounced in Denmark, where this antagonism ended in a political disintegration (1332–1340), when the realm was lacking a sovereign.

The rise of these more typical feudal states in Scandinavia had several consequences for the towns and their inhabitants. Larger and more mobile resources were created when the supremacy was exercised by different author-ities and when the exploitation was transferred from personal duties to products and taxes. These new resources can be viewed as the economic background to many of the new towns in the current period. The connection between the exercise of power and urbanization is apparent from the re-gional differences. In Norway, where the privileges of the aristocracy were least extensive, the new towns were few and built on a small scale. In Den-mark and Sweden, where the fiscal pressure was as heavy as the exemptions of taxes were extensive, more towns were established than in any other period in the Middle Ages. Especially in the thirteenth century many new towns arose along the Danish and Swedish coasts. And in the first part of the fourteenth century there existed several towns in the Swedish "Eastern Counties" that correspond to present-day Finland.

Through this new structure of power towns obtained a more intermediary role than before. It was in the town that the aristocracy could find a market for their products and acquire "necessary articles," in order to maintain and justify their lordship. Very important articles seem to have been horses, weapons, cloth, and goldsmiths' work, which are mentioned in several Dan-ish borough customs. Accordingly, trade and handicrafts became more ex-tensive in the towns, which meant that the towns gradually became more vi-tal as sources of fiscal revenues. The growing fiscal interest in towns is noticeable in a whole range of new charges connected with urban economic life, for instance, charges of markets, shops, and different crafts. By the mid-dle of the thirteenth century it was also noted in Denmark that the founding of towns was a "profitable pursuit." And like any other source of income, Danish and Norwegian towns were granted to bishop sees and monasteries by the middle and latter part of the twelfth century.

The growing importance of urban trade and handicrafts had conse-quences for the practitioners, too. The crafts became gradually more special-ized and independent in this period. Many craftsmen seem to have been bound in feudal relations as "urban tenants" ("coloni") in the twelfth cen-tury and the first part of the thirteenth century. However, from the middle of the thirteenth century several groups of artisans succeeded in gaining bur-gher status. The growth of independence can primarily be traced among those specialists who took care of the urban maintenance, for instance, butchers, bakers, and brewers.

Trade was still partially carried on by the aristocracy, but from the middle of the twelfth century more independent merchants are mentioned. In Den-mark a national merchant's guild ("The Guild of St. Canute") was instituted under royal patronage around 1170, and as early as 1177 it was represented in several towns of the realm. Scandinavian merchants are known from many parts of the Baltic and North Sea areas throughout the period. In the thirteenth century commerce expanded considerably, and consequently the fiscal interest shifted from the merchant himself (personal toll) to his commodities (duties on goods). At the same time as commerce expanded, an accumulation of capital can be traced in Scandinavian towns. It is known that from the end of the thirteenth century Danish and Swedish burghers lent money to kings and bishops in financial difficulty.

Foreign, especially German, merchants began to appear in Scandinavia in this period. The German influence became most important after the middle of the thirteenth century, when some of the important cities in northern Germany, like Lübeck, began to organize a town league: an organization that later developed into the Hanseatic League. As mediators of articles in demand, the Germans were favored in their activities by privileges and treaties. However, the German merchants not only covered the needs of the Scandinavian authorities but also mediated Scandinavian raw materials to the rest of Europe. Important commodities in the increasing Scandinavian export were hides, butter, fish, wood products, iron, and copper. The Germans gradually reached a dominating position in this international commerce. In Norway the German cities and their merchants gained more or less of a monopoly of foreign trade, after a victorious commercial blockade in the 1280s. And, in Scandinavia as a whole, their influence became even more evident in the following period.[12]

In many respects the urban profile of this period can be viewed in relation to the political structure as well as international trade. It is possible to make a rough ranking of the towns by counting the number of mendicant friaries in each town.[13] As figure [6.]3 shows, the structure of the earlier urban profile is still visible, but there are signs of changes.

In Norway, the relation between the large towns was unchanged. Trondheim became the archbishopric of the country, whereas Bergen became the center of the Norwegian fish market and functioned as a sort of economic and political "capital" of the realm. In Denmark the urban ranking had remained fairly unaltered since the previous period. The international trade, however, was concentrated here to the Scanian fairs that arose outside the major cities. In Sweden the situation was different, as it was only in this period that this country was thoroughly urbanized. In the western part of the realm, Skara, which was a city from the previous period, became the leader. In the eastern part of the country, on the other hand, Sigtuna lost its earlier central position. Instead Stockholm, founded in the middle of the thirteenth century, became the dominant city. Within a few decades this place was already one of the leading cities of the realm and a significant port for the Swedish export of iron and copper. Visby, which can be regarded more as a Gotlandic city than as a Swedish one, had been an important place already in the previous period. In the thirteenth century, though, Visby became the most important commercial city in Scandinavia. The city was gradually dominated by German merchants and functioned more or less as the center

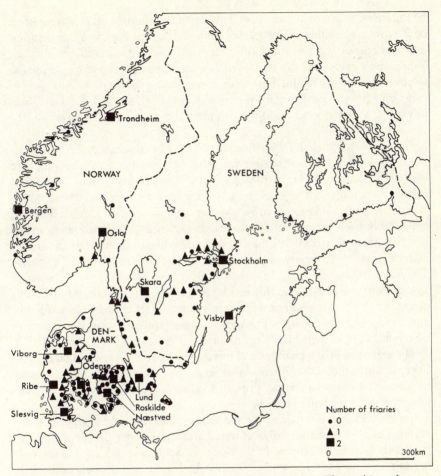

FIGURE [6.]3   The urban profile in Scandinavia, 1150–1350. The ranking of towns according to the number of friaries in each town.

of Baltic trade. The enormous significance of Visby is most evident from the approximately 600 to 800 masonry warehouses that were built in the city in the thirteenth and early fourteenth centuries.

The altered character of the state had consequences for urban activity and also for urban organization and the power over towns. The aristocracy was made responsible for different social functions (religious organization and military service) in exchange for participation in political control, and accordingly towns became partly responsible for urban activities, in return for similar privileges and enfeoffments. The towns became more or less clearly delimited from the countryside when they obtained their own borough customs and jurisdiction. At the same time the lordship over the town came to be exercised by a town council, consisting of the sheriff and representatives of the town inhabitants. The council obtained part of fines and other duties, and sometimes the members of the council were exempted from taxes. When, in this way, the urban supremacy was partly exercised by persons in the town, new class distinctions were created in the urban unit. This fact became especially evident when the councils were "self-supplying." Occasionally in the years around 1300 we also hear about internal conflicts in some Danish towns.

This growth of urban independence can only be observed in its main outlines. The earliest known charters and other benefits date from the middle of the twelfth century and refer to some of the major Danish towns. The oldest borough customs in Denmark and Norway can be dated to about 1200, whereas the earliest lawsuits in Sweden are later. The oldest Danish borough seals imply the existence of "town guilds" conducted by aldermen, in the first half of the thirteenth century. From the middle of the thirteenth century Danish towns were governed by councils, according to continental patterns. The office of councillor is also found in the major Norwegian and Swedish towns from the end of the thirteenth century. It is uncertain whether this growing urban independence was a result of actual struggle by town inhabitants as was the case in many European towns. However, occasional notices on conflicts are known from Copenhagen in the 1290s.

The extent of urban charters and privileges varied in Scandinavia, according to that of other enfeoffments in society. The independence of the aristocracy and that of the towns can thus, in an abstract sense, be viewed as parallel expressions for feudal society.

In Denmark, the towns, like the aristocracy, had the most independent position. The towns were legally delimited and were under the jurisdiction of particular borough customs. In the duchy of Schleswig, which was the only heritable fief in Scandinavia, each town had its own borough custom. In other parts of Denmark the borough customs were in force for several towns in the same area. In Norway urban autonomy was less distinct, just as the aristocratic independence was minor. The towns were under the jurisdiction of local variants of two succeeding borough customs, first "Bjärköarätten" and then the common urban code. The legal delimitation of the towns, however, was not unambiguous, as every person was free to choose court of justice, either in a town or in the countryside.

In Sweden the urban and aristocratic autonomies appeared at a later stage than in Denmark. Even around 1300 local variants of the Swedish "Bjärköarätt" functioned as "auxiliary laws," when the common provincial laws were insufficient. Only after 1300 did the Swedish towns become clearly distinguished from the countryside, especially when the common urban code was introduced about 1350. A special Swedish case, however, was Visby. This city was situated in Gotland, and the island was only loosely connected with Sweden. Without any extensive political control from the Swedish Crown, Visby obtained a very autonomous position as early as the thirteenth century. The city was an important member of the German town league, which later became the Hanseatic League.

The growth of urban independence can also be proved by physical remnants, such as churches, town defenses, and guildhalls. Many of the new towns of the current period received an ecclesiastical organization that was totally different from that of earlier towns. Often one single church was erected, for the purpose of the town only. This "closed unity" can be traced in many Danish towns that arose after 1200 and in several Swedish towns from the period after 1250. On the other hand, this form of ecclesiastical organization did not exist in Norway.

The urban delimitation from the countryside was also expressed in town defenses. In Denmark the earliest urban defenses were built by the middle of the twelfth century around some of the most important cities. In the thirteenth and fourteenth centuries several other Danish towns were fortified, often with earthen walls and masonry gates. Except for two vague traces, there are no statements or remnants of defenses around Norwegian towns in the Middle Ages. In Sweden most towns remained undefended, too, in this period. Three important exceptions, however, were Visby, Stockholm, and Kalmar, which were all defended by strong stone walls. The town wall of Visby was expressly erected against the hostile countryside in the 1280s.

Though councils were introduced in Scandinavia, no guildhalls are mentioned in this period. Again, one exception was Visby, where the largest medieval guildhall in Scandinavia was erected, probably at the beginning of the fourteenth century.

In summary, I want to point out that the metaphor "the municipal transition" is an attempt to catch the changing position and function of the town in this period. Through the changing character of the state, towns obtained a different economic base, and simultaneously they participated in the supremacy. Accordingly, urban units were created that were functionally and organizationally more delimited from the countryside than towns were earlier. This urban delimitation and autonomy, however, developed over a long time and with large regional variations, which were closely tied to the execution of power in society as a whole.

THE MERCANTILE SUPREMACY (1350–1550)

The late Middle Ages correspond to a crisis in feudal lordship, in Scandinavia as well as in the rest of Europe[14]—a crisis that manifested itself in decreasing population, desertion, and political disruption. The most acute and evident part of the Scandinavian crisis occurred in the second half of the fourteenth century. In this period the bases of the situation of later times were formed.

The so-called agrarian crisis can be traced in Denmark from about 1320 onwards and in the two other countries from about 1350. The devastation and the decrease in population seem to have been most permanent in Norway, less extensive in Denmark, and of least significance in Sweden and Finland.[15] Not only the countryside was hit by the crisis but the towns and their economy too. No new towns were founded in Scandinavia in the second half of the fourteenth century. Instead some minor Norwegian and Danish towns disappeared, whereas other towns were partially deserted.

In connection with this acute crisis in the latter part of the fourteenth century German merchants and the Hanseatic League (instituted in 1356) succeeded in gaining the most far-reaching influence ever in Scandinavia. The German influence was of varied character, according to the different relations between the Germans and the three countries.

In Norway, the German merchants gained a very extensive influence, as they dominated international trade and participated in domestic exchange. The Hanseatic trading-station ("kontor") that was established in Bergen in the 1360s was of specific significance. This organization made it possible for the Germans to live segregated from the Norwegian town inhabitants for centuries. In some of the other Norwegian towns, German commercial associations ("kompani") were founded, as well. In Denmark, the Hanseatic League gained direct control over Scania and the Scanian fairs, in the period 1370–85, after a victorious commercial war. Besides, German commercial associations were established in many Danish towns. The German merchants had their most extensive privileges at the Scanian fairs, whereas their activities were always restricted by "the Guest Code" in ordinary towns.

In Sweden, the German influence resulted in a much more integrated settlement than in the other two countries. This situation was probably partly due to the German interests in the Swedish mining and export of iron and copper. The integration of the Germans became especially evident about 1350, when the new common urban code prescribed that councils should be divided into Swedish and German sections. The German influence is also very clear from the fact that two of the most important Swedish towns were attached to the Hanseatic League in the second half of the fourteenth century, namely, Stockholm and probably Kalmar. Gotland came under Danish political control in 1361, but Visby retained much of its independence in the fourteenth century. The city was a member of the Hanseatic League until the middle of the fifteenth century.

The fourteenth century also witnessed a political crisis in Scandinavia, including disruptive tendencies and conflicts between the countries. Out of these political conflicts a Scandinavian Union was created in 1397, with one sovereign for the three countries. The Union was formally in existence until

1523, but from the middle of the fifteenth century onward, there were permanent conflicts between the King and the Swedish part of the Union.

The formation of the Union can be seen as a response to the feudal crisis of the previous half-century. The Union was a political alliance against the Hanseatic League and a new kind of state, trying to reestablish its supremacy over the population. This state was organized in a more formal way than previously. The aristocracy was prohibited from erecting their own castles, and the sheriff became a kind of official, with obligations of keeping accounts. This new political order was also characterized by a protectionist legislation, directed against the peasants and the foreign (German) merchants. Another feature was the new extra taxes (for military purposes) that were imposed on the peasantry as well as the aristocracy and the towns. The extra taxes were charged in ready money, and this fact enforced a kind of market economy that was controlled by mercantile leaders.

The protectionist legislation can be traced as far back as the end of the thirteenth century in Norway and Sweden and the middle of the fourteenth century in Denmark. It was not until the formation of the Union about 1400, though, that this legislation was implemented. The principle was that all trading activity should go by way of town burghers and that all crafts should be practiced in towns. Peasants and foreign merchants were prohibited from trading with each other, except in the case of annual fairs. General prohibitions against "rural purchase" were imposed everywhere. In western Denmark specific "circumferences" were established around the towns, and in these zones the burghers demanded a complete monopoly of trade and crafts. The activity of the German merchants was gradually reduced in other ways, too. In the 1470s their commercial associations were prohibited in Denmark, and at the same time they were expelled from the councils of the Swedish towns. The state also tried to encourage foreign competition with the Germans, with the help of privileges and treaties with English and Dutch merchants.

The principle of the legislation was to concentrate mercantile activity in towns, where the state could exercise fiscal control. Besides, the charters supported the activity of the burghers and their accumulation of capital. This urban accumulation of capital became a potential source of credits for the state. Consequently, this legislation meant that a mercantile supremacy had been established, in which the towns and the state were mutually dependent on each other.

The mutual dependence between state and city was especially evident in the case of Stockholm,[16] which about 1350 obtained the monopoly on foreign trade with commodities from the Bothnian Gulf and the Gulf of Finland. The city gave very important financial support to the Swedish Crown, but the state did not allow it to become too important. Sometimes, Stockholm got very extensive charters, for instance, in 1461 after a major loan to the state. In other cases the activity of the city was reduced when surrounding towns obtained more comprehensive privileges or when totally new towns were founded within the economic sphere of Stockholm.

The most overt expression of concentrated mercantile supremacy was the never-realized plan for a Scandinavian commercial association, after 1520. According to the drafts, all foreign trade with Scandinavia should have been carried out by the association and its merchants. The company should have been in charge of Swedish mining, and offices should have been situated in Copenhagen, Stockholm, probably Antwerp, and a Finnish town (maybe Viborg, on the Russian border).

The late medieval urban profile (see figure [6.]4) reflects, to a high degree, the mercantile supremacy and the market economy that the state tried to control by legislation. In the fifteenth century and at the beginning of the sixteenth century many new towns were founded in Denmark and Sweden. Usually, they were small towns, established in regions that had not been much urbanized in previous periods. In other words, these foundations can be viewed as consistent attempts to uphold the mercantile supremacy even in regions with little experience of earlier towns.

The towns can be roughly ranked by means of written sources from the beginning of the sixteenth century, for instance, using lists of burghers, as well as of taxes and other assessments.[17] An estimation of the sizes of the towns, based on written sources, is well in accordance with the testimony of the physical remnants of the towns. In the major cities of the current period, town churches were gradually rebuilt to cathedral-like monuments. In several major places new mendicant friaries and hospitals were founded, too.

The ranking of the towns was fairly unchanged in Norway and Sweden, though there were important differences in the character of the leading cities. In Norway, Bergen was the most important city, and this place possessed the monopoly of the Norwegian fish market. However, German merchants and the Hanseatic trading station dominated the fish market, so that the domestic accumulation of capital was insignificant.

In Sweden, Stockholm, Åbo, and Kalmar were the leading cities. As has previously been said, Stockholm was especially favored by the Swedish legislation, and besides the city was very well situated in respect to trade routes. Stockholm was Sweden's most significant port for the export of iron and copper, and the city came to be regarded as the economic and political "capital" of the country. The accumulation of capital among the burghers was large, a fact that is clear from the big loans to the Swedish Crown and from the approximately 250 brick houses that were built in the city in the fifteenth and sixteenth centuries.

In Denmark, the urban profile was radically changed. The previously leading cities lost their dominant roles, and the Scanian fairs lost much of their importance when international trade became more "urbanized." In-

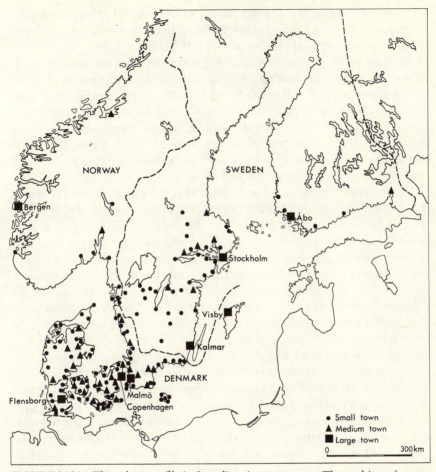

FIGURE [6.]4   The urban profile in Scandinavia, 1350–1550. The ranking of towns is an "educated guess," based on different written sources.

stead the area around the Sound emerged as the urban center of the realm. Some of the richest agricultural districts in Denmark were situated along the shores of the Sound, and this strait was also a central commercial link between Eastern and Western Europe. The most significant cities in this region were now Malmö and Copenhagen. The latter began to function as an economic and political "capital" in the fifteenth century and was often used as a legal model in Danish urban legislation.

In the almost independent duchy of Schleswig-Holstein, Flensborg became the leading Danish town. Many of its merchants participated in the extensive ox trade in Jutland. The island of Gotland was conquered by Denmark in 1361, but it was only in the fifteenth century that the Danish Crown had control of the island. The significance of Visby was, by then, already declining, and it lost its unique role in the fifteenth century, when there was no longer need for a special meeting place for Baltic trade.

The mercantile supremacy meant that urban organization and the sovereignty over towns changed, too. By means of legislation the towns obtained a growing responsibility that reached outside the towns, and included peasants and foreign merchants. As a service in return for this responsibility still larger portions of the sovereignty over the towns were conferred on the councils. The regime that was previously divided between the sheriff and the councillors disappeared when the sheriff was submitted to the council, and the charge was taken over by the lord mayor.

The increased urban autonomy meant that the lordship over the towns was shifted from the individual inhabitants to the council, which consequently had the immediate power over the town population. This shift in power is directly discernible in the fiscal relationship between state and towns. Previously, the representatives of the urban lords had exacted the different charges and taxes from each town inhabitant. From about 1400, though, many of these different duties were replaced by a fixed urban tax ("pactus"), which was imposed on the town as a whole. And it became the responsibility of the town council to divide the burden of this tax among the town inhabitants, according to property and income. The new situation is also apparent in respect to the artisans, who were forced to submit their crafts and guilds to the control of the council. In most towns craftsmen were prohibited from becoming councillors, which meant that the urban regime became closely tied to the trading capital. The supremacy of the council gave rise to increasing internal opposition. Open conflicts between the town regime and the urban population are reported from several Danish towns. The conflicts led to compromises in the field of financial administration, and special "committees of 24 men" were appointed from the 1480s onward.

The late-medieval autonomy varied, according to time and space, like the previous growth of independence. In Norway the undeveloped autonomy was fairly unchanged. The Kingship preserved the control over the towns, through royal judges who were in charge of the councils and had the legal responsibility in towns as well as in rural districts. In as important a city as Bergen the first lord mayor is mentioned only in the 1530s.

In Denmark the office of lord mayor is mentioned from the middle of the fourteenth century in several important cities, and the office seems to have been represented in most towns in the fifteenth century. The autonomy became especially pronounced in Malmö and Copenhagen, in the 1520s and the 1530s, when their lord mayors were appointed without royal consent. These two cities also played an important political role in the civil war of 1533–1536, but later they were again submitted to the Danish Crown.

The office of lord mayor is mentioned in some important Swedish towns as early as the 1320s, but the office became more widespread at a later stage. Stockholm had an especially independent position and followed its own political line in the late-medieval struggle for power among Sweden, the Union, and the Hanseatic League. The political role of the city was complicated by the fact that the three opposing parties had their supporters in different fractions of the city population. The vital significance of Stockholm is maybe most conspicuous in the "Massacre of Stockholm." When the Danish King had reconquered Sweden in 1521 he had eighty-two of his political opponents executed; thirty-two of these persons were leading burghers in Stockholm.

The urban autonomy was also expressed by the erection of guildhalls in the late Middle Ages. Guildhalls are mentioned in some Danish and Swedish towns about the middle of the fourteenth century, but the preserved buildings seem to have been erected only in the fifteenth century. Major guildhalls were, above all, built in the most important cities, such as Flensborg, Copenhagen, Stockholm, and Åbo. In respect to the urban autonomy it is also interesting that notices on real guildhalls are lacking in Norway, except for Bergen.

The concept "mercantile supremacy" can in many respects be seen as a summing up of the urban role in late-medieval Scandinavia. Mercantile supremacy meant that the towns and the state were mutually dependent on each other. This dependence favored the power of the trading capital and the urban regime over the towns and their rural surroundings.

CONCLUSION

The relationship between state and towns in medieval Scandinavia was a close and a complicated one. Towns were part of the political power, but they were also something else "outside" the state.

From an "internal" perspective the towns can be regarded as forming part of the power-cum-control system of the state. In medieval Scandinavia this meant that towns should, above all, be considered against the background of the extent and possession of the supremacy right. During the 1000–1150 stage, towns formed political and religious *points d'appui* for the new feudal sovereignty. In the course of the 1150–1350 stage, they also became vital centers for that exchange of goods that was instigated by the people who were in possession of feudal supremacy. Finally, from 1350 to 1550, the towns became the original bases for the new, mercantile supremacy, in a mutual relation with the emerging territorial state. In feudal society, it was of decisive importance from the beginning to be in control of production; as time went by, however, it turned out to be just as essential to control distribution as well.

From an "external" perspective the medieval towns of Europe had specific features which set them apart from towns in other epochs and in other places. This "externality" is best regarded as a part of the structure of feudal society, which was founded on the exercise of power by means of enfeoffments. The towns were subservient to feudal supremacies, but groups in the towns gradually came to exercise lordship within as well as outside the towns. In medieval Scandinavia this "externality" can be conceived as a gradual process of liberation from the state: first a period in 1000–1150, when towns were totally subordinate to the political power; then a stage in 1150–1350, when the external delimitation and the internal partial autonomy were developed; and lastly a period from 1350 to 1550, when towns obtained internal independence and external influence as well. This external influence was, in a few instances, directed against the state, too.

Though the main lines of the internal and external development of the towns can be traced in Scandinavia as a whole, there were important regional differences between the countries. The formation of a state and the urbanization were most evident in Norway and above all in Denmark, at an early stage. The Danish urban profile kept its structure for a long time and was radically changed only in the late Middle Ages. In Norway minor adjustments were made in the urban profile at an earlier stage, but during the late-medieval agrarian crisis both the state and the towns stagnated. In Sweden the formation of a state and the urbanization were of a later date, which meant that the urban profile became more adjusted to international trade at an earlier stage. The importance of mining also meant that several towns were connected with a partly different kind of economy than Danish and Norwegian towns. Besides, the most far-reaching autonomy can be traced in Swedish cities, such as Visby, Stockholm, and Kalmar.

In connection with the formal dissolution of the Union in 1523 and with the Reformation in Sweden (in 1527) and in Denmark-Norway (in 1536), the bases of new "bureaucratic" states were laid in Scandinavia. As before, it is possible to trace evident differences in the character of the two states. In Denmark an aristocratic state was organized, where the burghers had less influence than before. In Sweden the position of the aristocracy was dominant, too, but the state was more consistently organized in a bureaucratic way and the burghers maintained some of their influence. An expression for the new Swedish administration was the national land registers that were set up in the 1540s. Similar surveys did not occur in Denmark until the end of the seventeenth century.

The development of the "bureaucratic" state, above all in Sweden, meant that a new form of politically controlled exploitation was created. This new political order opened up economic and social possibilities for urban settlements in new areas. At the end of the sixteenth century and in the seventeenth century the previous ecological limit of urbanization was exceeded,

FIGURE [6.]5   The ecological zones of potential vegetation and the location of new towns from 1550 to 1700 in Scandinavia.

and many new towns were founded in the boreal zone, along the shores of the Bothnian Gulf (see figure [6.]5).[18] This urban burst of the ecological setting of previous periods can be regarded as one of the conditions for the Swedish empire in the Baltic in the seventeenth century.

Notes

1. This article is based on my 1985 thesis on the towns of medieval Denmark. It has been possible, however, to expand the Danish perspective into a Scandinavian survey, thanks to other studies. The most important works consulted are Authén Blom 1977 and the summary of the "Medieval Town Project" in Sweden and Finland (Andersson, in print). It must be noted, however, that in some cases I have made other interpreta-

tions of the age and the structure of towns, in accordance with the principles of my thesis. Other important earlier surveys of Scandinavian towns are Schück 1926, Jørgensen, *Dansk Retshistorie,* 1947, and various entries in *Kulturhistoriskt lexikon för nordisk medeltid,* 1956–1976. In addition, most towns have been discussed in special monographs. The most important recent monographs are Blomkvist 1979 and Helle, *Bergen bys historie,* 1982. References to older works can be found in the previously mentioned surveys and in *Bibliography of Urban History,* 1960. I refer here only to the above-mentioned works. No further specific references will be made, since practically all works on Scandinavian towns are written in Scandinavian languages.

2. Besides the early-medieval towns, there already were another three or four towns in Scandinavia in the "Viking Age" (750–1000). Two of these places disappeared in the tenth and eleventh centuries, and only in one or two cases does there seem to have been continuity in the settlement.

3. Further issues on the definition and the function of towns can be found in Sjoberg, *The Preindustrial City,* 1960, Haase 1965, Schledermann, *The Idea of the Town,* 1970, Wheatly 1972, Hilton, *The Transition from Feudalism to Capitalism,* 1976, and Abrams, *Towns in Societies,* 1978.

4. The periodization has been somewhat modified from Andrén 1985. This modification is due to later criticism of my work and to adjustments to the Scandinavian situation.

5. The division into ecological zones was presented in *Naturgeografisk regionindelning,* 1984. The nemoral zone corresponds to a potential vegetation of deciduous forests. The boreonemoral zone corresponds to a potential vegetation of mixed deciduous and coniferous forests. The boreal zone corresponds to a potential vegetation of coniferous forests.

6. General historical surveys of medieval Scandinavia are found in Christensen et al., *Danmarks historia,* 1977–1980, Sveaas Andersen 1977, Helle, *Norge blir en stat,* 1974, Rosén, *Svensk historie I,* 1962, and Lindkvist and Ågren, *Sveriges medeltid,* 1985. This reference serves as a general note in respect to historical facts in this article.

7. Duby, *Rural Economy and Country Life in the Medieval West,* 1968, 196ff.

8. Merrington in Hilton, *The Transition from Feudalism to Capitalism,* 1976.

9. Icelandic notices on Norwegian towns have been collected in Nilsen 1976.

10. The method of ranking towns according to the number of churches was presented in Andrén 1985, 50ff. The major cities of the period might have had approximately 2,000 to 3,000 inhabitants.

11. The Scandinavian expansion in the Baltic area was described by Christiansen, *The Northern Crusades,* 1980.

12. The role of the German merchants in Scandinavia has been debated for a long time. An earlier summary of the discussion can be found in *Det nordiske syn,* 1957.

13. The method of ranking towns according to the number of mendicant friaries was presented by Le Goff, *Ordres mendiants et urbanisation dans la France médiévale,* 1970.

14. See Bois, *The Crisis of Feudalism,* 1984.

15. A modern survey of the late-medieval desertion in Scandinavia can be found in Gissel et al., *Desertion and Land Colonization in the Nordic Countries 1300–1600,* 1981.

16. The particular position of Stockholm in the late Middle Ages has been considered by Sjödén 1950 and Friberg 1983.

17. The ranking of the towns is an "educated guess," based on many different sources. First of all the common urban tax ("pactus") from the fifteenth century has been used to rank the towns of each country (Mackeprang 1900–1902, Forssell 1875, Sønderjyske Skatte- og Jordebøger). Secondly, the ranking has been adjusted according to lists of burghers, taxes, and other assessments from the first half of the sixteenth century (published and unpublished notices, sometimes in the town monographs). Thirdly, the ranking has been compared to the evidence of physical remnants, above all the sizes of town churches (cf. Andrén 1985, 53ff.). Lastly, the ranking in each country has been compared to the ranking in the other countries, in order to obtain a uniform picture. The major cities, like Stockholm, Copenhagen, and Bergen, might have had 6,000 to 8,000 inhabitants.

18. Information on the new towns from the 1550–1700 period can be found in Authén Blom, *Urbaniseringsprosessen: Norden,* part 2, 1977.

7

Power and Towns in the Polish Gentry Commonwealth: The Polish-Lithuanian State in the Sixteenth and Seventeenth Centuries

ANDRZEJ WYROBISZ

WHEN STUDYING THE relation between the state and towns in the Polish Commonwealth of the sixteenth and seventeenth centuries, one should consider certain characteristics of the Polish-Lithuanian state: the dominance of villages over towns, the strength of the gentry and great nobles, and the absence of anything resembling an absolute monarchy.

Within the European economic system of that era, Poland and Lithuania were, above all, producers of agricultural goods and raw materials. The Polish economy was based almost exclusively on extensive exploitation of natural resources and on equally extensive agriculture and livestock breeding.[1] As a result, Poland's villages predominated over towns. The economic weakness of towns was apparent in the underdevelopment of industry and the lack of capital in the hands of burghers.

In the first half of the seventeenth century, the commonwealth was one of the largest countries in Europe, covering an area of some 990,000 square kilometers and containing approximately 10 million people; there were about 2,200 towns, with their townspeople accounting for 20 to 25 percent of the population. Only nine of these towns, however, had more than 10,000 inhabitants. In contrast to the rapid growth of population in the great urban centers of western Europe in the sixteenth and seventeenth centuries, Polish towns grew very slowly or did not grow at all. The exceptions are Danzig, Warsaw, Cracow, and Lublin, which flourished because of their economic, political, and cultural roles. But only in Danzig did the population exceed 40,000 in the seventeenth century. About 150 Polish towns had 2,000 to 10,000 inhabitants, and nearly half had less than 600. Moreover, urban density in the commonwealth was very uneven, ranging from one town per 245 square kilometers in Little Poland (the southern sector) to one town per 586 square kilometers in the eastern part of the Grand Duchy of Lithuania. But at the same time, Royal Prussia, with one town per 546 square kilometers, contained the three biggest and wealthiest Polish towns (Danzig, Elbing, and Thorn), so that region must be considered intensively urbanized.[2]

The gentry and the great nobles held a monopoly of power in the Polish state. The middle class took no part in state authority or political life, and no burgher had access to any office higher than those in municipal government. Burgher representation in the *Sejm* (parliament) was composed of delegates from only a few cities (Cracow, Vilna, Poznań, Lublin), and their role was mostly symbolic. These city deputies had to ask the gentry deputies, senators, and the king to address the particular affairs of their towns, for only the gentry could settle urban matters.[3] Burgher representatives had no voice in national or regional issues.

Danzig was of great importance because of its economic role as the only Polish port exporting corn and wood, the main articles exported by the Polish nobility. Therefore, it was the base of prosperity for Poland's nobility in the sixteenth and seventeenth centuries. Danzig was also important as a source of capital. The city was given many charters by the Polish kings from the fifteenth century on, and thus it could play an important political role. But Danzig citizens represented their own economic interests exclusively; they did not fight for the interests of other Polish towns. Cracow, the old medieval capital of Poland, had lost its role as a commercial center, and by the end of the sixteenth century, it was no longer the residence of Polish monarchs. It kept its historical tradition and its prestige as the coronation place for Poland's kings, but it became a rather weak city: It had too many churches and cloisters and lacked economic, political, or military significance. Warsaw, Vilna, Lublin, and a few other cities housed the royal court and/or other central institutions that lacked economic importance. But the citizens of these cities did not derive any profits from this and did not gain political influence; even tax collection was carried out by noblemen deputies appointed by the Sejm, rather than local merchants or other citizens.

In addition, there was not even a hint of absolute monarchy in Poland. The king's position—despite his many important prerogatives—was very weak. To a large degree, he was dependent on the gentry and important nobles for he had neither a financial system that would provide him with an adequate and permanent income nor a standing army. And he was always enmeshed in the rivalry between the gentry, the magnates, and their organizations. The position of the king was additionally weakened by the fact that he was an elected monarch—a situation that was also responsible for the hesitant and changing domestic policy of successive rulers.[4] The Polish kings of the sixteenth and seventeenth centuries did not seek support from the middle class, which, after all, was too weak politically and economically to help the monarchy in any significant way. Neither did the kings pursue any definite urban policy nor make any practical decisions of importance to the towns. In 1578, the gentry even deprived the king of the right to ennoble burghers, transferring the decisionmaking in these matters to the gentry Sejm. Until the end of the commonwealth, the king retained the exclusive right to found new towns, grant charters, and issue permits for markets and fairs, but these royal prerogatives were mostly formalities and were executed by the royal chancery as privileges; the real initiatives were taken by the gentry and magnates. In the Grand Duchy of Lithuania, the Third Lithuanian Statute of 1588 permitted even the gentry to found new private towns without requesting royal agreement. Consequently, of the 186 new towns established in the central territories during the sixteenth and seventeenth centuries, only 19 were founded by kings; the rest (167, or 90 percent) were private towns founded by the gentry, the clergy, and important nobles. By the end of the seventeenth century, private towns accounted for 64 percent of the total number of towns in Poland and 75 percent of those in Lithuania. It must be noted that part of those towns belonging to the crown estates (provided to *starosts* [elders] as their endowment) resembled private towns in that the latter were dependent on their private owners, just as crown estate towns were dependent on the starosts (whose offices were often hereditary).[5]

Private towns were sometimes important trade centers but only on a regional scale (primarily benefiting the landowners' private estates). They were also deprived of any political significance. Indeed, their economic isolation from the country market and economy and their dependence on private landowners has led some scholars to consider them as factors in the disintegration of the Polish townspeople as a social group.

In this context, the relation between political power and the towns in the Polish-Lithuanian state of the sixteenth and seventeenth centuries was fundamentally a relationship between the gentry and the towns. Members of the gentry were not only the ruling group, they also made all vital state and local decisions in municipal matters, either as individual owners of private towns, as officials charged with handling municipal affairs (*voivodes*), or through their representatives in the Sejm. The gentry-town relationship can be studied both in terms of the programs, policy ideas, and opinions formulated by the gentry and in terms of practical activities—for example, founding new towns, granting statutes, passing laws concerning townspeople, and assessing taxes or ordering their relief.

The Polish and Lithuanian gentry of this period did not devise any general social and economic doctrine. The gentry's economic culture was undeveloped, and its economic notions were very primitive. Except for Frycz Modrzewski, whose work was not well known in his homeland, Polish noble writers, journalists, and speakers primarily addressed local social and economic concerns. Among the gentry's economic ideas, only certain early elements of bullionism (or early mercantilism) can be discerned; there was no full theoretical or practical acceptance of the principles of the mercantilist and protectionist schools. One of the characteristics of the Polish gentry was a notable pragmatism, driven by current politics and the economic and practical problems of life. The gentry spoke only of looking for solutions for such matters. Hence, although Polish writers of the time offered no coherent system of ideas on towns, urban economy, or government, their works do contain many opinions on various particular questions.[6]

Marcin Bielski, chronicler and poet, believed that towns existed for the comfort and benefit of the gentry. An advocate of the country's economic self-sufficiency, he encouraged the development of native crafts using local raw materials in order to further Poland's independence from imports. To restrict the activity of alien merchants and reduce their excessive profits (which caused high prices in the home market), he believed that trade and craft production should be conducted in the suburbs and that the towns themselves should be inhabited by the gentry, who would move there both for their own comfort and for a more efficient defense of the country.[7] Bielski's ideas are fairly typical of the mentality of sixteenth-century nobles. On the one hand, the nobles protested the dearth of industrial goods and wanted to entirely subordinate the middle classes to the interests of the gentry; on the other hand, they understood the need for crafts and trading in the country's economic structure.

Perhaps Bielski's idea of moving the nobles to towns and the traders and artisans to the suburbs is not as naive and absurd as it first appears. His observation was based on the reality of changes taking place in his time. The number of nobles shifting their residences temporarily or permanently from country to city grew gradually in the sixteenth and seventeenth centuries;[8] contrary to Bielski's plan, however, most of them located in suburbs rather than the center. At the same time, the suburbs were expanding, and many artisans and merchants moved there from the town center because the suburbs were a more suitable area for economic activity for many reasons.[9]

Interestingly, Bielski's notion of the economic functions of towns also addressed the issue of feudal rent. If members of the gentry resided in the towns, they would not only live more comfortably and enjoy a privileged social status but also spend their incomes there. Thus, there was both a social and an economic aspect to this arrangement. The towns would benefit on a large scale from the influx of feudal rents. But, in turn, they would have to develop services and certain branches of production and trade. Bielski did not, however, pursue this subject and, as we know, the evolution of Polish towns did not proceed very far in that direction: Villagers did not know how to take advantage of the possibilities offered by the presence of gentry inhabitants or of the nobles attending fairs, court sessions, tribunals, regional assemblies, sejms, and elections of kings.

The idea of settling the gentry in towns was also expounded by Łukasz Górnicki in his "Rozmowa Polaka z Włochem o wolnościach i prawach polskich" (Conversation Between a Pole and an Italian About Polish Freedoms and Rights). In this essay, the Italian character probably expresses the views of the author himself.[10] Górnicki came from the middle class, but his career brought him into the noble estate; indeed, he identified so thoroughly with nobility that his views may be considered those of the gentry.[11] In "Conversation," the Polish character states that "towns bring more bad than good things"; he sees them as the seats of harlotry, luxury, and dissipation and recalls the examples of Spartans and Tartars who spurned towns. His Italian opponent, by contrast, considers the lack of towns as evidence of primitivism and barbarism and paints a broad picture of the benefits accruing from towns:

> Where would you crown your king if there were no city? Where would you convene Sejms? Where would you sell what you had bred at home? From where would you supply the demands of your homes? Believe me, Poland would be much richer if she had more towns. ... Now your riches come only from Gdańsk, but not all may succeed in getting to Gdańsk. But if there were many towns, not one, then they would provide a place for the landowner to sell grain, cattle, wool, hemp, linen, mead, hides, tallow, and wax, as well as various dairy products, straw, hay, even kindling and cane. Well, a landed gentleman would not breed a cow near Gdańsk if it did not bring him thirty zlotys a year. How? Because he sends milk and whatever is made of milk to Gdańsk. And what better if you would build towns and strongholds on the borders ... not only for defense against the Tartars, but also in order to be able to chase them out of their lands some day.[12]

Thus, the Italian pointed to the economic as well as the cultural and military profits that could be derived from towns. According to him, towns would revive the entire Polish economy, including the countryside. Characteristically, he thinks that only a city can fulfill the functions of a capital; only there can a king be crowned and sejms convened. The Italian, coming from the second most urbanized country in Europe, considered that Poland had only one real city—Gdańsk—and Górnicki, educated in Padua and thus personally familiar with Italy, reflected this view. (Another Pole educated in Italy, Krzysztof Warszewicki, had similar notions about towns.[13]) The concept presented by Górnicki in the words of an Italian was a gentry concept. According to this view, towns were, above all, to serve the nobles. They were to pour fresh blood into the rural economy and bring income to landowners; create markets for the gentry's farming, breeding, and forest products; and provide the manors with the necessary craft goods.

We know "Conversation Between a Pole and an Italian" only from the 1616 edition, though it was not the first. But Górnicki's work was most certainly preceded by that of Anzelm Gostomski, author of *Gospodarstwo* (Farming), published in 1588 but written much earlier (probably 1560–1570). "In towns the economy and income of artisans are the greatest,"[14] Gostomski wrote, having in mind towns belonging to the gentry—that is, either private property or property in the hands of starosts and therefore part of crown lands. Such towns were to be the prime source of the gentry's income. Gostomski, an "ideologue with a wolf's appetite for surplus product," as he was called by Professor Edward Lipiński, was little concerned with the development of towns as such and did not ponder their place in the country's economy. Rather, he was interested solely in the profits they could generate and in their development insofar as it was necessary for obtaining such profits. He also advised the town's master to give municipal authorities a sum of money for lending at no or little interest, in order to stimulate the burghers' economic activity.[15]

According to Gostomski, an important purpose of a private town (and a source of income to its owner) was to organize the purchase and "floating" of grain, not only from the owner's farms but also from elsewhere in the countryside. Gostomski recommended only moderate exploitation to avoid impoverishing peasants and townspeople by extreme oppression. However, he was more ruthless with respect to eliminating competitors: He warned that no outside beer or bread should be brought to "landowner's townships" and complained that rural fairs held by churches drained towns financially.[16]

Some nobles expressed their ideas simply through their day-to-day activities or through legal acts. For example, Jan Zamoyski gave a speech at the elective Sejm of 1575 that became famous. The future founder of Zamość, the most magnificent town of the Polish Renaissance, described his ideas regarding towns in the following words:

> Everything is different with the foreigners. ... Their villages and towns are flourishing because the townspeople enjoy many rights. But because this magnificence is accompanied by wrong done to gentry freedom, I would rather not have it at all than have it at such a price. People's happiness cannot be measured with artisans' goods, with walls and spacious buildings, which we do not lack: but with their freedom, virtue and good manners. I hope that in this respect we are at par with everybody.[17]

But this was a political and demagogic statement, pandering to the multitude of the gentry and expressing the concept of gentry freedom as a foundation of the commonwealth and the order prevailing there—all of which was characteristic of Zamoyski's entire political activity. In his speech, he probably referred to Sejm acts passed earlier (e.g., in 1539 and 1543) that described craftsmen's guilds and their privileges as an insult and injury to gentry freedoms, accusing Gdańsk burghers of oppressing the nobles.[18] Similar statements were made in the mid-1600s by Adam Kazanowski, the presumed author of *Dyskurs* (Discourse), which was published in 1638; in it, he attacked the residents of Gdańsk: "If the people of Gdańsk have privileges, who gave them privileges so contrary to our liberty? We are free in our Commonwealth, so how is it possible that only the city of Gdańsk should boast of privileges which might threaten our freedom?"[19]

Several years later while drawing up the charter of Zamość, Zamoyski expressed his ideas on municipal affairs in a different way. He wrote in the preface to that document that he had decided to build a town "with a view to the safety and benefit not only to myself and my friends but to all the neighborhood and the serfs from my neighboring villages." Further on, he declared that the inhabitants of Zamość should pursue the trades and businesses for whose establishment the town's chief officer had received funds, leaving farming to peasants. Other paragraphs of the charter concerned the dates of fairs and showed that the founder of Zamość was well versed in the mechanism of urban economic life and the organization of trade, for the dates of the city's fairs coincided with trade conventions in Chełm, Jarosław, Lublin, and Lwów.[20] Another time, while addressing the Sejm of 1605, Zamoyski touched upon the matter of urban economy, protested luxury, and spoke about the presence of foreign artisans; he also explained the lack of success in the production of morocco leather in Zamość, blaming foreign merchants who sold their imported goods at low prices and thereby made local manufacture unprofitable.[21] In expressing such ideas, Zamoyski set himself against the concept of "closing the frontiers," which was then popular among the gentry. His opinions and his activity in Zamość show that the chancellor and grand hetman was fairly well informed about the urban economy and held reasonable views on related matters but sometimes had to give in to political considerations.

The demand to close the frontiers was first formulated in writing by Andrzej Ciesielski, whose pamphlet *Ad equites legatos ad conventionem Varsoviensem publice designatos et declaratos ... oratorio* (oration to the Knights delegated, selected, and reorganized for the Warsaw meeting) was printed in Cracow in 1572. Ciesielski wanted to prevent Polish merchants from going abroad in order to compel foreign merchants to "come to our towns for commercial purposes, where they could buy without restrictions from our traders whatever they needed, and not only bear all the troubles but also all the costs."[22] Ciesielski imagined that this would cause an inflow of foreign capital to Poland, that foreign merchants would settle in Polish towns and "build more imposing houses," and that the money paid for Polish goods and customs duties would remain in the country and become a source of its wealth. These and other of his views were naive and typical of a gentleman who thought primarily about his own profits. He believed, for example, that if towns flourished and there was an abundance of money, the burghers would pay the gentry "a just price" for agricultural produce. Another benefit would be an increase in the towns' ability to pay taxes and other public expenses, which would free the gentry from such obligations. Consequently, Ciesielski said, the gentry ought to make certain concessions and even certain sacrifices regarding towns—for instance, they should stop maintaining craftsmen, brewers, and innkeepers on their farms, for these individuals competed with urban artisans and caused the "obvious poverty" of small towns. Ciesielski was acquainted with Marcin Bielski and probably on friendly terms with him, and he knew Bielski's views on the country's internal circumstances, which must have influenced his own ideas.[23]

The question of the harm caused by the gentry who organized artisanry in the villages and thereby competed with urban merchants and artisans was tackled by many writers in the first half of the seventeenth century. These included Sebastian Petrycy of Pilzno, Krzysztof Falibogowski, Wojciech Gostkowski, and Szymon Starowolski, all writing at a time when the crisis in Poland's urban economy was becoming increasingly apparent.[24] On the other hand, Stanisław Cikowski, in his pamphlet W sprawach celnych odpis (On Customs Matters), drew attention to the connection between the impoverishment of Polish towns and the crisis in the gentry economy: "The impoverished towns destroyed the artisans and thus devastated the gentry estate and all the Crown citizens because of the high prices of goods; they bought so many villages that in the Proszowice, Cracow and Wiślica districts there are hardly twenty landed gentlemen in their fathers' villages." Cikowski understood the connection between the prosperity of the towns and the economic conditions of the gentry, and he saw the role of towns in the context of the whole economy. He did not treat towns exclusively as an addition to the gentry rural economy, although he, like the majority of the writers then addressing the problem, considered towns primarily as a source of income for the gentry and the state.[25]

Another writer, Stanisław Zaremba, emphasized the development of industry as a condition of Polish prosperity in his book Okulary na rozchody w Koronie i z Korony (A Look at Expenditure in the Crown and from the Crown), published in 1623. He advocated, among other things, the support of native artisanry and the need to bring in foreign specialists; thus, although he was by no means favorably inclined toward the townspeople, he understood the economic role of towns.[26]

In a more penetrating and mature way, the matters of urban economy were discussed by Jan Grodwagner in his Dyskurs o cenie pieniądza teraźniejszej (Discourse on the Present Price of Money), published in 1632.

He saw the connections among the various areas of the economy: the circulation of money, customs and tax systems, trade, crafts, farms and breeding, and raw materials and resources, and he came close to understanding the economic role of towns in light of the country's economy as a whole.[27] He advocated restricting exports of primary materials from Poland and importing industrial goods and thought that native crafts should be developed, for thereby "the Commonwealth would be enriched and the burden of taxes alleviated."[28] This last sentence reveals Grodwagner's gentry point of view: He wanted to relieve the gentry of some of its tax burdens by developing towns, crafts, and trade. He also identified the interests of Polish merchants with those of the state. Grodwagner qualified his critical remarks about merchants, noting that "no one should think that the merchant body is being rebuked. Because there are in it, as in every other body, many pious people, honestly pursuing their trade according to their vocation." (A marginal note adds, "The merchant body is good in itself and numbers many pious people").[29] He also emphasized the usefulness of bankers.

But to the authors quoted here, the chief indicator of the country's wealth was its store of precious metals. Towns and their economy (crafts or trade) interested them only insofar as they led to the augmentation of that wealth; the writers therefore placed trade ahead of everything else in that pursuit and treated industrial production as an auxiliary branch that provided the merchants with goods and helped obtain a favorable trade balance. None of them took a comprehensive look at the role of towns in the commonwealth's gentry economy. In fact, this was done only by the anonymous author of *Dyszkurs o pomnożeniu miast w Polszcze* (Discourse on the Multiplication of Towns in Poland), published in Cracow in 1648 (or possibly for the first time in 1617). His opinions were repeated almost verbatim by Krzysztof Opaliński in his satire *O sposobach pomnożenia miast i na nierzd w nich* (On the Means of Multiplying Towns and Their Bad Government), printed together with other works by that author in 1650.[30]

The anonymous author of *Dyszkurs* and Opaliński borrowed some ideas from Giovanni Botero's Italian treatise *Della ragion di stato libri dieci con tre libri delle cause della grandezza delle città* (Ten Books on State Interests with Three Books on Causes of the Greatness of Cities) (published in Venice in 1589 and reprinted many times). But most of their opinions were based on an observation of Polish reality. They were concerned with the problems of private towns and considered them to be one of the main sources of income to the landlords. Therefore, they followed and further developed Gostomski's views. Both authors devoted much space to crafts and suggested that the situation of home crafts could be improved in three ways: by bringing foreign craftsmen to Poland and settling them there, by using domestic raw materials, and by fixing prices for domestic articles lower than those of imports. But the main source of income to the towns and their landlords—

according to the *Dyszkurs* and Opaliński's satire—was trade. They recommended settling towns on the banks of rivers for the easy floating of grain from noblemen's farms, wood from the forests, and other natural resources. They also advocated building granaries in riverine boroughs and argued that a busy land route crossing the town would also be desirable. Opaliński favored the settlement of craftsmen and opposed the settlement of foreign merchants in Polish towns because they might compete with the gentry, but he did recommend help in the development of fairs because the landlords could derive a considerable part of their income from market fees if the number of trade assemblies was increased. The efforts of private town owners in the sixteenth and seventeenth centuries to secure royal privileges concerning markets and fairs were a good illustration of this tendency.[31]

Opaliński was in favor of urban privileges and against both the jurisdiction exercised by noblemen and the clergy "when they break municipal laws" and the breaching of municipal laws by starosts. He considered improvement in the town council and the administration of justice indispensable. Moreover, he thought that towns should have the right to hold landed estates and even to send deputies to the Sejm. But these prerogatives of the nobility should, in his opinion, be granted only to urban communes, not to particular burghers. Opaliński explained that he sought to protect the gentry privileges, not diminish them or share them with the middle class. Further, he felt that if the burghers' rights were respected, the elite of the middle class would no longer hope to enter the gentry class—a prospect that caused much anxiety to the nobility in the first half of the seventeenth century. Opaliński also underlined the advantages a town received as the residence of a landlord or a king's court, the sessions of tribunals and the Sejm, and the role of schools and academies in urban life.[32]

Did those economic publications by nobles in the sixteenth and seventeenth centuries have any practical significance? Did they shape the gentry's policy toward the towns? Did they have any impact on the resolutions passed at regional assemblies or on laws passed by the Sejm of that time? Some of the writers and economic treatises—such as Ciesielski's pamphlet—were directly linked with parliamentary activity and with political and economic discussions. They must have influenced the course and results of Sejm debates, thus shaping the legislation expressing the gentry's policy on towns. Indeed, many of the demands presented by the authors of the works quoted earlier were reflected in resolutions passed by regional assemblies, in acts voted by the Sejm, and in speeches made in both forums.

These very speeches sometimes contained more than specific propositions to settle current, concrete matters. Some featured concise conceptions relating to the whole of urban affairs and determining the place that the towns should occupy, according to the nobility, in the commonwealth. At the Piotrków Sejm in 1562, one speaker noted that "towns are not lesser parts of the Polish Commonwealth, and the stronger they become, the more the Commonwealth might use them with respect and profit ... so it would be greatly damaging if this treasure be destroyed for these and other needs of the Polish Commonwealth."[33]

But it is not always clear whether the economic writings actually inspired Sejm deputies and led to suitable resolutions or whether, on the contrary, the literature repeated and developed subjects already being considered in sejms and justified the acts passed there. After all, the 1565 Sejm resolutions on closing the frontiers preceded Ciesielski's pamphlet and the work of other supporters.[34] A. Popioł-Szymańska was right when she remarked that Polish normative acts dealing with urban matters in the sixteenth century were marked by great conservatism resulting from a stiff economic model and were frequently repetitive, which points to the difficulties of carrying out economic decisions.[35]

The urban matters dealt with by regional assemblies and sejms centered on the three main problems in which the gentry were most interested. One was the taxing of towns and the shifting of the greatest burdens to the burghers in order to free the nobles and their subjects from them. Yet at the same time, there was a genuine concern not to destroy this source of revenue—not to impoverish the towns through excessive taxing that would lead to their depopulation and general decline. In 1658, the nobles of Zator fairly requested that Cracow merchants be granted partial tax relief because they could not meet their tax obligations due to the burdensome billeting of troops.[36] Additionally, the gentry took into consideration the fact that, in the sixteenth and seventeenth centuries, an increasing percentage of towns in the commonwealth were private or quasi-private, that is, they belonged to the Crown but in practice remained under the rule of starosts-for-life or hereditary starosts. Thus, when taxing such towns, the nobles indirectly taxed themselves, giving the state treasury a part of the burghers' income that would otherwise be used in a different way for the benefit of the town owner.

In the times of King Stefan Batory (1576–1586), taxes paid by towns accounted for approximately 30 percent of all state revenue, including some 20 percent from taxes on the sale of spirits; direct urban taxation of some 12 percent, including the *schoss* (a basic tax on property paid by the towns), accounted for only 5 percent of state revenue; the tax on crafts and trade about 3 percent; and the tax on fiefs paid by towns a little over 1 percent. The structure of public revenue was similar at the time of King Sigismund III Vasa (1587–1632).[37] Obviously, only the tax on the sale of drinks accounted for any substantial part of the revenue; the schoss and other municipal taxes played only a minor part. So exemptions from taxes, though they were a big relief to the exempted towns, actually had only a small impact on state revenue and could be distributed fairly freely and frequently during this period.

The exemptions lowered total state revenues on the average by only 0.2 percent a year. Even when exemptions were most frequent (1589, 1616, 1635), they did not exceed 1 percent of the total revenue. They had, first and foremost, a propaganda value, creating the appearance of the gentry's involvement in the affairs of towns.

Regional assemblies often tabled motions on tax exemptions for towns, passing them in generous measure.[38] The motions listed causes that devastated towns, such as floods, epidemics, and war destructions. The Sejm act of 1635, for example, reminded the tax collectors that "in accordance with old laws, victims of fires and of the Crown's enemies were entitled to exemptions lasting four years."[39] Of course, there were also shorter exemptions (of one, two, or three years) and longer ones (of up to eight years). Characteristically, the gentry sometimes demanded that "the clergy and people from other estates [presumably including the gentry] who evade paying schoss from many properties under the urban administration ... all bore *onera aequaliter* [equal burdens]."[40] This was not just a propaganda gimmick. But, on the other hand, the nobility also began to limit the taxation autonomy of the towns as early as the fifteenth century in order to exercise full control over that source of state revenue.[41]

Another problem attracting the attention of the regional assemblies in the sphere of urban matters involved prices. The gentry wanted to obtain a privileged position in their internal market, that is, to maintain the highest possible prices for the products of farms, stock-raising, and forests and the lowest possible (or at least controlled) prices for industrial products, goods manufactured by local artisans, and imported goods. This end was achieved by various steps and a whole series of acts passed by the sejms concerning: warehousing policy,[42] closing of the frontiers,[43] drawing up price lists and the principles of their keeping,[44] the standardization of weights and measures,[45] exemptions from customs duties granted to the gentry,[46] laws on luxury (another frequent demand voiced in economic literature),[47] and elimination of monopolies, which primarily but not exclusively meant a demand to abolish or at least restrict the activity of craft guilds.[48] (The goal was not so much to abolish the guilds as organizations of producers but to make it impossible for them to impose high prices on craft goods; the gentry defended the guilds when their ability to pay their share of taxes was threatened.)[49]

The third problem, not exclusively economic but with some economic aspects, was that of the towns' defensive role—their fortifications and their use as the country's points of defense. This was particularly important in the eastern and southeastern borderlands, which were constantly troubled by enemies in the sixteenth and seventeenth centuries, especially by Tartar raids. Because the commonwealth did not have any state defense system for the country, the treasury was incapable of financing such fortifications, and because the gentry did not want to pay for them, some other means had to be devised. One was to fortify the towns most threatened by enemies using funds provided by the inhabitants; when this was impossible or insufficient, the gentry would also contribute. The nobles of the Ruthenian voivodship demanded that the border towns have good defenses suitably manned by soldiers, and they even provided money for this purpose.[50] But the nobles of the Cracow voivodship, less threatened than those of the Ruthenian voivodship, adopted a different attitude in such matters. When the Cracow burghers asked for permission to use one tax collection for the repair of municipal walls in 1573, the gentry at the regional assembly at Proszowice refused, maintaining that "their walls need little or nothing at all, for their defence would be very weak should the enemy be allowed to come as far into the country as to stop by them."[51] Yet in 1602, 1606, and 1662, the regional assembly at Środa evinced interest in the way the city of Poznań had used the sums destined for the town's defense, gathered from the tax on the sale of spirits for the previous ten years.[52]

In summary, then, there were vital differences between the gentry and the townspeople—even conflicts of interest resulting from the different places they occupied in the country's economic structures, for each group derived income from different sources and had a different share of the authority that determined that income. Hence, the attitude of the nobles toward the urban economy was neither identical to nor always favorable toward that of the burghers. But the two groups nonetheless shared many common interests, as well. As a result, the attitude of the gentry toward the towns cannot be described in simple terms. In looking for the causes of the weak development and the later deep crisis of the old Polish towns, one should not limit research to the internal relations of the commonwealth. Rather, it is necessary to look at world economic relations, which were definitively unfavorable to the progress of urbanization of the Polish, Lithuanian, and Ruthenian lands in the sixteenth and seventeenth centuries.[53]

Notes

1. Cf. M. Małowist, *Wschód a Zachód Europy w XIII–XVI wieku: Konfrontacja struktur społeczno-gospodarczych* [The East and West of Europe in the Thirteenth to Sixteenth Centuries: Confrontation of Socioeconomic Structures] (Warsaw, 1973); A. Wyrobisz, "Economic Landscapes: Poland from the Fourteenth to the Seventeenth Century," in Antoni Maczak, Henry K. Samsonowicz, and Peter Burke, eds., *East Central Europe in Transition from the Fourteenth to the Seventeenth Century* (Cambridge: Cambridge University Press, 1985), 36–46.

2. S. Alexandrowicz, "Zaludnienie miasteczek Litwy i Białorusi w XVI i pierwszej połowie XVII wieku" [Population of Small Towns in Lithuania and Byelorussia in the Sixteenth and First Half of the Seventeenth Century], *Roczniki Dziejów Społecznych i Gospodarczych* XXVII (1965), 38; A. Wyrobisz, "Townships in the Grand Duchy of

Lithuania During the Agrarian and Urban Reform Called *pomera na voloki* [second half of the sixteenth and first half of the seventeenth century]," in *Gründung und Bedeutung kleinerer Städte in nördlichen Europa der frühen Neuzeit* (Wiesbaden, 1991), 195–197; M. Bogucka, "The Network and Functions of Small Towns in Poland in Early Modern Times [sixteenth to first half of seventeenth centuries]," ibid., 222–224, 230.

3. J. Maciszewski, *Szlachta polska i jej państwo* [The Polish Gentry and Its State] (Warsaw, 1969); A. Mączak, "The Structure of Power in the Commonwealth of the Sixteenth and Seventeenth Centuries," in J. K. Fedorowicz, *A Republic of Nobles: Studies in Polish History to 1864* (Cambridge, 1982), 113–134; A. Wyczański, "The System of Power in Poland, 1370–1648," in Maczak, Samsonowicz, and Burke, eds., *East Central Europe in Transition*, 140–159.

4. Wyczański, "System of Power."

5. M. Bogucka, "The Towns of Central Europe from the Fourteenth to the Seventeenth Century," in Maczak, Samsonowicz, and Burke, eds., *East Central Europe in Transition*, 97–108; idem, "Polish Towns Between the Sixteenth and Eighteenth Centuries," in *A Republic of Nobles*, 138–152; A.Wyrobisz, "Rola miast prywatnych w Polsce w XVI i XVII wieku" [The Role of Private Towns in Poland in the Sixteenth and Seventeenth Centuries], *Przeglad Historyczny* LXV (1974), 19–45; idem, "Townships in the Grand Duchy of Lithuania," 196–197; H. Samsonowicz, "Sviluppo e declino delle città in Polonia dal tardo Medio Evo all'inizio dell'Età Moderna," *Cheiron* VI (1989–1990), 133–146.

6. E. Lipiński, *Studia nad historią polskiej myśli ekonomicznej* [Studies in the History of Polish Economic Thought] (Warsaw, 1956), passim; A. Wyrobisz, "Mieszczanie w opinii staropolskich literatów" [Townsmen in the Opinion of Old-Polish Writers], *Przegląd Historyczny* LXXXII (1991).

7. W. Wisłocki, ed., *Marcina Bielskiego Satyry* [Marcin Bielski's Satires] (Cracow, 1889), 74.

8. Cf. W. Dworzaczek, "Przenikanie szlachty do stanu mieszczańskiego w Wielkopolsce w XVI i XVII w." [Infiltration of Gentry into the Middle Class in Great Poland in the Sixteenth and Seventeenth Century], *Przegląd Historyczny* XLVII (1956), 656–684; J. Zimińska, "Andrzej Humiecki: Zycie i działalność gospodarcza kupca warszawskiego przełomu XVI i XVII w." [Andrzej Humiecki: Life and Economic Activity of a Warsaw Merchant at the Turn of the Sixteenth Century], *Rocznik Warszawski* III (1962), 5–22; J. Maroszek, "Osadnictwo drobnoszlacheckie w miastach podlaskich w XVI–XVIII wieku: Problem konkurencji gospodarczej" [Petty Gentlemen Settlers in Podlasie Towns in the Sixteenth to Eighteenth Centuries: The Problem of Economic Competition], *Zeszyty Naukowe,* Warsaw University branch in Białystok, XIX, Humanistyka IV, Section H—historical works (1977), 201–217; F. Kiryk, "Szlachta w Bochni: Ze studiów nad społeczeń XVII 'stulecia" [Bochnia Nobles: From Studies on the Community of Mining Towns in Little Poland in the Sixteenth and First Half of the Seventeenth Century], *Społeczeństwo staropolskie* II (1979), 71–124.

9. H. Samsonowicz, *Sviluppo e declino della città in Polonia,* 140.

10. Łukasz Górnicki, *Pisma* [Writings], vol. II, ed. R. Pollak (Warsaw, 1961), 459.

11. Concerning the biography of Łukasz Górnicki, see the introduction by R. Pollak to the edition of his works and J. Kozielewski, *Łukasz Górnicki: Studium*

historyczno-literackie [Łukasz Górnicki: Historical and Literary Study] (Lwów, 1929).

12. Łukasz Górnicki, *Pisma*, vol. II, 458–459.

13. K. Warszewicki, *De optimo statu libertatis libri duo* [Two Books on the Best Condition of Freedom] (Cracow, 1598), 30. Cf. A. Popioł-Szymańska, "Poglądy szlachty i mieszczan na handel wewnętrzny w Polsce od końca XV wieku do połowy XVII wieku" [Views of the Gentry and the Middle Classes on Home Trade in Poland from the End of the Fifteenth Century to the Mid-seventeenth Century], *Roczniki Historyczne* XXXVII (1971).

14. A. Gostomski, *Gospodarstwo* [Farming], ed. S. Inglot (Wrocław, 1951), 100. About Gostomski, see E. Lipiński, *Studia,* 142–148.

15. A. Gostomski, *Gospodarstwo,* 102. This advice forms part of Gostomski's theory of money; he said that money was "fertile." See E. Lipiński, *Studia,* 144–145.

Gostomski was not the only one interested in granting small and cheap credits to townspeople. The same matter was taken up by the Jesuit Marcin Śmiglecki, who published the treatise *O lichwie* (On Usury) in 1596; this must have been written on public demand, so to speak, because it had numerous editions, and Śmiglecki himself often referred to the many questions asked him concerning this topic. It also aroused the interest of Jan Zamoyski, a great statesman who founded Zamość at the same time that Jesuit Piotr Skarga organized the first *montes pietatis* (pawnshops) in Poland (in 1597 at Vilna, 1598 at Cracow).

M. Śmiglecki, *O lichwie i trzech przedniejszych kontraktach: Wyderkowym, czynzowym i towarzystwa kupieckiego* [On Usury and Three Prime Contracts Dealing with Repurchase, Rent and Merchant Associations] (Vilna, 1596, two later editions of the same year, and seven in the first half of the seventeenth century). Cf. A. Szelągowski, *Pieniądz i przewrót cen w XVI i XVII wieku w Polsce* [Money and the Price Revolution in Sixteenth- and Seventeenth-Century Poland] (Lwów, 1902), 26; E. Lipiński, *Studia,* 155–169.

A. Tarnawski, *Działalność gospodarcza Jana Zamoyskiego* [Jan Zamoyski's Economic Activity] (Lwów, 1935), 397–399; J. Warężak, "Mons pietatis w Łowiczu" [Mons Pietatis at Łowiczu], in *Studia z historii społecznej i gospodarczej poświęcone Prof. dr. Franciszkowi Bujakowi* (Lwów, 1931), 288.

16. A. Gostomski, *Gospodarstwo,* 100–101.

17. Wybór mów staropolskich świeckich, sejmowych i innych [Selected Old-Polish Lay, Sejm and Other Speeches], ed. A. Małecki (Cracow, 1860), 76–77.

18. *Volumina legum,* vol. I, folios 549, 568.

19. Ł. Kurdybacha, "Polemika o prawach Polski do morza (1638–1640)" [Discussion on Poland's Right to the Sea, 1638–1640], *Rocznik Gdański,* vol. IX–X (1937), 284–285.

20. *Archiwum Jana Zamoyskiego* [Jan Zamoyski's Archives], vol. II, ed. J. Siemieński (Warsaw, 1902), 392–393. Cf. R. Szczygieł, "Zamość w czasach staropolskich: Zagadneinia gospodarczo-społeczne" [Zamość in Old-Polish Times: Socioeconomic Questions], in *Czterysta lat Zamościa,* ed. J. Kowalczyk (Wrocław, 1983), 99–100.

21. *Pisma polityczne z czasów rokoszu Zebrzydowskiego, 1606–1608* [Political Writings at the Time of Zebrzydowski's Revolt, 1606–1608], vol. II, ed. J. Czubek (Cracow, 1918), 91. Cf. R. Szczygieł, "Zamość," 108.

22. *Pisma polityczne z czasów pierwszego bezkrólewia* [Political Writings from the First Interregnum), ed. J. Czubek (Cracow, 1906), 121–122. About Ciesielski, see S. Krzyżanowski, *Andrzej Ciesielski: Studium z literatury politycznej XVI w* [Andrzej Ciesielski: Study on Political Literature of the Sixteenth Century] (Cracow, 1886); A. Szelągowski, *Pieniądz,* 18–22; E. Lipiński, *Studia,* 213–214; J. Górski, *Poglądy merkantylistyczne w polskiej myśli ekonomicznej XVI i XVII wieku* [Mercantilistic Ideas in Polish Economic Thought of the Sixteenth and Seventeenth Centuries] (Wrocław, 1958); A. Popioł-Szymańska, "Poglądy szlachty," 58.

23. S. Krzyżanowski, *Andrzej Ciesielski,* 6–8.

24. A. Popioł-Szymańska, "Poglądy szlachty," 68–69.

25. Stanisław Cikowski, *Merkantylistyczna myśl ekonomiczna w Polsce XVI i XVII wieku: Wybor pism* [Mercantilistic Economic Thought in Sixteenth- and Seventeenth-Century Poland: Selected Works], ed. J. Górski and E. Lipiński (Warsaw, 1958), 117–118, 123–124. Cf. E. Lipiński, *Studia,* 243–246; idem, "Rozkwit polskiej myśli ekonomicznej w pierwszej połowie XVII wieku" [The Blooming of Polish Economic Thought in the First Half of the Seventeenth Century], *Nauka Polska* II (1954), 232–234.

26. Cikowski, *Merkantylistyczna myśl ekonomiczna,* 300–306. Cf. E. Lipiński, *Studia,* 269–273; idem, "Rozkwit," 236–238.

27. Cikowski, *Merkantylistyczna myśl ekonomiczna,* 333–347. Cf. A. Popioł-Szymańska, "Poglądy szlachty," 78; E. Lipiński, *Studia,* 274–276; idem, "Rozkwit," 248–249; Z. Sadowski, *Pieniądz a początek upadku Rzeczypospolitej w XVII wieku* [Money and the Beginning of the Decline of the Commonwealth in the Seventeenth Century] (Warsaw, 1964), 277–302.

28. *Rozprawy o pieniądzu w Polsce pierwszej połwy XVII wieku* [Writings on Money in Poland in the First Half of the Seventeenth Century], ed. Z. Sadowski (Warsaw, 1959), 300.

29. Ibid., 279.

30. I have discussed the problem of the authorship of the *Dyszkurs* in the article "Attitude of the Polish Nobility Towards Towns in the First Half of the Seventeenth Century," *Acta Poloniae Historica* XLVIII (1983), 80.

31. Cf. A. Wyrobisz, "Polityka Firlejów wobec miast w XVI wieku i założenie Janowca nad Wisłą" [The Firlejs' Policy Toward Towns in the Sixteenth Century and the Founding of Janowiéc on the Vistula], *Przegląd Historyczny* LXI (1970), 595.

32. The text of the *Dyszkurs* and of Opaliński's satire are republished in Cikowski, *Merkantylistyczna myśl ekonomiczna,* 351–367, 371–384. An extended bibliography concerning these treatises can be found in A. Wyrobisz, "Attitude of the Polish Nobility."

33. *Źródłopisma do dziejów unii Korony Polskiej i W.X. Litewskiego* [Sources Concerning the Union of the Polish Crown and the Grand Duchy of Lithuania], part 2, section I, ed. T. Działyński (Poznań, 1861), 120.

34. *Volumina legum,* vol. II, folios 683–686.

35. A. Popioł-Szymańska, "Problematyka handlowa w polityce 'miejskiej' szlachty w Polsce centralnej w XV i XVI wieku" [Commercial Questions in the Urban Policies of Nobles in Central Poland in the Fifteenth and Sixteenth Centuries], *Roczniki Dziejów Społecznych i Gospodarczych* XXXI (1970), 47.

36. *Akta sejmikowe województwa krakowskiego* [Records of Regional Assemblies of Cracow Voivodship], vol. II, ed. A. Przyboś (Wrocław/Cracow, 1955), 595.

37. A. Pawiński, *Skarbowość w Polsce i jej dzieje za Stefana Batorego* [Treasury in Poland and Its History Under King Stefan Batory] (Warsaw, 1881), 15–177, 203–206; A. Filipczak-Kocur, *Skarb koronny za Zygmunta III Wazy* [Crown Treasury Under King Sigismund III Vasa] (Opole, 1985), 45ff.

38. See, e.g., *Records of Regional Assemblies of Cracow Voivodship*, vol. II, 271, 427, 674–675; vol. III (Wrocław/Cracow, 1959), 58, 109, 299, 352; *Volumina legum*, vol. II, folios 1242, 1287–1290; vol. III, folios 25–26, 181, 191, 287, 299–303, 380, 580–581, 616, 825, 826–828.

39. *Volumina legum*, vol. III, folio 870.

40. *Records of Regional Assemblies of Cracow Voivodship*, vol. II, 271.

41. See A. Popioł-Szymańska, "Problematyka," 52–53.

42. *Volumina legum*, vol. II, folio 683, 686, 700–709.

43. *Akta sejmikowe województw poznańskiego i kiliskiego* [Records of Regional Assemblies of Poznań and Kalisz Voivodships], vol. I, part 1, ed. W. Dworzaczek (Poznań, 1962), 78, 223; part 2, 104, 165, 256; *Volumina legum*, vol. II, folio 683, 686; vol. III, folio 426.

44. Legal acts concerning the establishment of prices were compiled and discussed by B. Ulanowski, "Kilka zabytków ustawodawstwa królewskiego i wojewodzińskiego w przedmiocie handlu i ustanawiania cen" [Some Old Royal and Voivode Legislation Concerning Trade and Prices], *Archiwum Komisji Prawwiczej*, vol. I (1895), 37–79. See, e.g., *Lauda sejmików ziemi dobrzyńskiej* [Resolutions Passed by Regional Assemblies of Dobrzyń Region], ed. F. Kluczycki (Cracow, 1887), 29–31; *Records of Regional Assemblies of Cracow Voivodship*, vol. III, 232; *Corpus Iuris Polonici*, vol. III (Cracoviae, 1906), no. 7, 36–38; no. 51, 106–107; *Volumina legum*, vol. I, folios 81–82, 158, 254, 293, 305, 362, 400, 504, 523–524; vol. II, folios 688, 978, 1018; vol. III, folios 370–371, 425, 807; vol. IV, folio 75.

45. Legal acts concerning weights and measures in Poland were compiled and discussed by W. Kula, *Miary i ludzie* [Measures and People] (Warsaw, 1970), 276–334. See, e.g., *Records of Regional Assemblies of Cracow Voivodship*, vol. III, 232; *Corpus Iuris Polonici*, vol. III (Cracow, 1906), no. 7, 36–38; no. 51, 106–107; *Volumina legum*, vol. I, folios 81–82, 158, 254, 293, 305, 362, 400, 504, 523–524; vol. II, folios 688, 978, 1018; vol. III, folios 370–371, 425, 807; vol. IV, folio 75.

46. *Volumina legum*, vol. I, folios 152–153, 261–262, 298, 375, 517.

47. *Volumina legum*, vol. III, folios 183, 371, 619; vol. V, folio 659; vol. VII, folio 83; vol. VIII, folios 893, 980. The economic aspects of *legum sumptuarium* as regulator of prices were tackled by, foremost, A. Szelągowski, *Pieniądz*, 98–99; A. Popioł-Szymańska, "Poglądy," 75–76; J. Górski, "Poglądy," 110–112; S. Estreicher, "Ustawy przeciwko zbytkowi w dawnym Krakowie" [Laws Against Luxury in Old Cracow], *Rocznik Krakowski* I (1898), 118–124; S. Grodziski, "Uwagi o prawach przeciwko zbytkowi w dawnej Polsce" [Remarks on Laws Against Luxury in Old Poland], *Zeszyty Naukowe UJ* 20, Prawo vol. V (1958), 67–86.

48. *Akta grodzkie i ziemskie* [Acts of the Courts of Nobility] IX (1883, 24), 35; *Volumina legum*, vol. I, folios 81–82, 253, 535, 568; vol. II, folios 598, 921.

49. *Records of Regional Assemblies of Cracow Voivodship*, vol. III, 248–249, 310.

50. Acts of the Courts of Nobility, vol. XX, no. 59, 101–102; no. 114, 167; no. 168, 291; vol. XXI, no. 32, 57; no. 62, 124, 126; no. 208, 384; vol. XXII, no. 30, 67; vol. XXIV, no. 205, 392.

51. *Records of Regional Assemblies of Cracow Voivodship*, vol. I, 30.

52. *Records of Regional Assemblies of Poznań and Kalisz Voivodships*, vol. I, part 1, 258, 280; part 2, 145.

53. Here I agree with the view sometimes expressed by A. Szelągowski, *Pieniądz*, 278–279.

8

Cities and the State in Spain

PABLO FERNÁNDEZ ALBALADEJO

ANY DISCUSSION OF relations between city systems and state formation in Spain should start with the obvious: during the modern era Spain did not exist as a state.[1] Up to 1700 the territories that later constituted the Spanish state always formed a larger entity: an empire or a Catholic monarchy.[2] Even the term *kingdom of Spain,* which sometimes appears in sixteenth- and seventeenth-century texts, ought to be considered a proxy. Invariably the kingdom in question consisted of several crowns that maintained their own organization and whose lands stretched beyond the territory that would later be Spain.

Under the Catholic monarchs (1474–1517) the crowns of Castile and Aragon fell into the hands of a royal couple, but (as is well known) that union did not lead to political integration or institutional homogenization.[3] Both rulers consolidated authoritarian monarchies and wrought a remarkable concentration of power. But their intervention did not build anything like a modern state. The special feature of their action and that of their successors was the incorporation of new territories into the monarchy while maintaining their particular institutional structures.

Until the arrival of the Bourbons at the beginning of the eighteenth century the Spanish state was a vast but conglomerate monarchy. From 1474 it included the crowns of Castile and Aragon. The former incorporated the Muslim realm of Granada (1492) and, shortly after, the kingdom of Navarre (1512), while the kingdom of Naples, conquered in 1503, remained more closely tied to the dynasty than to the Aragonese crown. In spite of its condition as a realm outside of Christendom, Granada entered the monarchy with a series of treaties recognizing specific Muslim rights, part of a policy of assimilation that finally ended catastrophically. Navarre joined the kingdom with its own institutional order, and Naples received the same treatment.

The crown of Castile, although formed by the kingdoms of Castile and Leon, constituted a single political organization. The crown of Aragon, on the other hand, was an aggregate of diverse territories (the principality of Catalonia and the kingdoms of Aragon, Valencia, Mallorca, Sicily, Cerdeña, and Naples) linked in very different fashions to the monarch. The advent of Charles V (1517–1554) did not modify that constitutional system. Indeed, his position as emperor served to reinforce it. Despite the division of the empire fashioned by Charles V, his son, Philip II, continued to work with an imperial conception called the Catholic monarchy. In its general lines, that organization persisted until 1700. Any attempt to clarify the relations between cities and state formation in Spain ought to begin with recognition of that peculiarity, so much so that we should proceed by analyzing the principal crowns individually.

ARAGON

The existence of the two great crowns of Castile and Aragon (not to mention Portugal) reflected divisions in the Iberian peninsula's evolution that were as deep as they were decisive. The crucial moment for those differences came in the thirteenth century when through a series of circumstances the Aragonese crown, frustrated in its effort to absorb Southern France, also saw its chances to continue its expansion southward blocked.[4] In that situation, its monarchs chose to direct its internal forces into maritime activity. That option had the decisive result of turning a program of reconquest by land forces into an unprecedented effort to conquer and organize a maritime region: a part of the Mediterranean extending to Greece and including important bases along the African coast. In that seaward expansion commercial and imperial interests typically intertwined. As a result a commercial and dynastic empire formed; the power of its ruling family depended narrowly on the support given it by the commercial sector. Within that sector, the city of Barcelona turned out to be the strongest defender of the crown's interests.

Yet the change of direction instituted by Jaime I (1213–1276) and Pedro III (1276–1285) caused major problems of balance for the crown's general policy. That is especially true of those members of the monarchy (for example, the landed nobility of the kingdom of Aragon) whose interior locations left them neglected. The weakened finances and international relations that intermittently beset the monarchy gave those interior interests the chance to impose certain constitutional conditions regarding their new position. For the monarchy the price of compromise was the recognition of the bulk of their privileges and a series of guarantees that the Cortes would deliberate important decisions. These concessions gave a decisive push to the establishment of parliamentary institutions, although the interests involved were quite different: clearly dominated by the landed nobility in the kingdom of Aragon but strongly representing cities around the periphery.

Between 1240 and 1270 Jaime I conceded to Barcelona, Mallorca, Valencia, and Perpignan a series of rights with respect to internal organization, allowing for a wide margin of autonomy. These concessions reached their peak in 1283, when an act of the Catalan Cortes extended the regime to all Catalan municipalities. In that assembly Barcelona enjoyed a special position as a result of a broad expansion of its municipal autonomy. The city acquired one of its crucial advantages in 1265 when the monarchy authorized the creation of the *Consell de Cent*, the chief institution of municipal power; its deputies were elected from the most important members of the urban patriciate. A parallel withdrawal of royal representatives accompanied that process.

For present purposes, the most salient outcome of the alliance between monarchy and urban interests was the appearance of the consulates (*consulados*), institutions designed specifically to protect commercial interests and to facilitate their activity. In domestic affairs, the consulates had their own courts where merchants could resolve their differences. In foreign affairs, the monarchy granted them wide privileges that facilitated their activity, more so than did other monarchs. Between 1258 and 1282 an early version of these institutions operated in Barcelona. Thenceforth and more officially, consulates appeared in Valencia (1283) and (between 1343 and 1385) in the other principal cities. At the same time external consulates sprang up in foreign places with which the empire maintained substantial trade. Again Barcelona received a special status: the monarchy delegated to Barcelona's *Consell* the election of consuls for all places outside the empire.

During the 150 years of the Catalan-Aragonese empire's greatest prosperity (1250–1400), relations between the urban system and state formation were characterized by cohabitation between commercial expansion and growth of the monarchy, without it being possible to say that the action of the state diluted the urban system. The singularity—and in some respects the weakness—of the system lay in the fact that it was composed of a single city.

Barcelona was not one of those cities that (in the terms used by thirteenth-century jurists) "recognizes no superior," but it was by no means completely subordinated to royal power. Its autonomy was visible in concrete powers and actions: the city had its own fleets (of which its counselors were the admirals), its own militias (of which the first counselor was colonel), and its own fiscal apparatus. With those attributes in mind, Pierre Vilar concluded that if one could not call Barcelona a city-state, one could say that the crown of Aragon had the marks of a state-city. The peculiar position of the city exerted a decisive influence, impeding the possible movement of the system toward a higher political stage.

The economic crisis of the late Middle Ages revealed the limited possibilities of growth within that system. Caught between a dynastic desire for grandeur and the decline of economic activity, the alliance between monarchy and city cracked. Committed to the maintenance of the empire at any price, the monarchy resorted to a massive expansion of public debt as its principal means of coping. In a crisis setting, that decision exerted a decisive influence on the behavior of the urban patriciate: the issuing of paper for public debt transformed a society of entrepreneurs into a society of rentiers, and the previous economic dynamism dissipated into a strategy of territorialization[5] organized around the city itself.

The situation became especially bad from the moment the city became involved in a series of social conflicts that accompanied the economic crisis. The civil war that raged between 1462 and 1472 capped that series of contradictions. By then, Barcelona had lost the important commercial position in Mediterranean trade it had retained until the beginning of the fifteenth century. The lack of an alternative city then became obvious: Valencia tried to play the role but lacked sufficient weight. It had only the modest activity of a peripheralized economy, dominated by the presence of other more active Mediterranean urban economies, notably that of Genoa.[6]

Using Castile as his base, Ferdinand the Catholic did not have enormous trouble in restoring order in the cities and developing an effective administration of municipal finances. But his recovery plan served more to stop further decline than to regain the positions the cities had lost. The displacement of trade toward the Atlantic gave the final blow to the cities of Aragon, especially those on the coast. The monarchy's evolution during the modern period was marked by that fundamental economic change. Aragon's peripheral position in relation to the political nucleus of the court—Madrid—forced it to play an increasingly secondary role. Often the chief political activity of the cities shrank to the jealous defense of previously conceded privileges, a defense that they engineered through judicious financial aid to the crown.[7] The tenacity with which they defended their own political identities, nevertheless, saved them in large measure from the catastrophe that struck Castilian cities in the seventeenth century.

CASTILE

As in Aragon, the process of reconquest shaped the evolution of cities in Castile. The turning point there likewise occurred in the thirteenth century; after the victory of Las Navas de Tolosa (1212) Castilian monarchs conquered (between 1224 and 1264) the large territory of western Andalusia (around 60,000 square kilometers). But differences between Aragon and Castile appeared at the same time. In Castile they were not dealing with the sea, and there were hardly any specifically urban interests that could affect the effort. Castile had a monarchy and a community especially prepared for war that had developed in the midst of what we can reasonably call a "war economy."[8]

In the division of lands (*repartimento*) that followed the conquest, the monarchy repaid the nobility for its participation by granting it important concessions of land and jurisdiction. These concessions were largely compensated for by the augmentation of the crown's resources (especially fiscal resources), which allowed favored treatment for the oligarchies of the principal Castilian cities in return for their unconditional support. To be sure, such precautions did not prevent a period of social instability led by a segment of the nobility opposing the authoritarian apparatus that the crown was trying to put into place. The conflict ended its first phase with the civil war of 1366–1369, after the rebel nobility named its own candidate to the throne.

Over the period as a whole the improved situation of the cities reinforced the monarchy's position. They continued to support the crown once the new monarchs felt obliged to reinstate authoritarian control over the same people they had previously favored. In return for their unconditional support, the cities persuaded the monarchy to sanction a distinctly oligarchical type of municipal power, the *regimiento*: it placed the chief towns in control of the urban gentry (*caballeros villanos*).[9]

At the same time, the urban centers gained their own place in the constitution of the realm. The procedure used was the acquisition of a corporate identity—*universitas* or *communitas*[10]—that made its property inalienable, thus erecting a formidable defense against seignorial powers and against any concession the crown made to those powers. In the middle of the fifteenth century through the so-called Treaty-Law of 1442, the crown officially recognized the position of the cities. By means of these actions, the oligarchy of urban gentry managed to transform itself into a true patriciate; while retaining some of the knightly traits of its previous stage, it made room for those who had prospered through commercial activity.

The anti-Jewish pogroms of 1391 played a fundamental part in reinforcing the patriciate: after the burst of forced conversions that followed the massacres, segments of the Jewish community entered the ranks of the Christian patriciate. By the mid-fifteenth century the integration of the two elites was quite clear. The series of municipal ordinances that the chief municipalities then enacted established full recognition and constitutionalization of patrician power. The urban disturbances that followed in 1449 only serve to demonstrate the resistance from below to the patriciate's consolidation;[11] the resistance frequently came from places brought under the cities' feudal jurisdiction.

Once the Castilian civil war of 1475–1479 had ended, the Catholic monarchs definitively recognized the positions their cities had acquired during the previous century. During their reign relations between crown and cities became more than satisfactory: the cities collaborated decisively in the conquest of Granada. As a reward, the monarchy ordered a reduction, to the extent possible, in the excesses committed by the nobility within territories under urban jurisdiction. Urban oligarchies accepted the representation when they realized that the presence of the king's representatives in the cities did not diminish their own power.

The most spectacular proof of mutual goodwill appears in the cession to the cities of the royal administration's largest block of revenue, the *alcabalas*. The administration of that revenue source operated by means of a procedure—the *encabezamiento*—that was extraordinarily beneficial for urban centers and that generalized rapidly between 1495 and 1538.[12]

The gains realized likewise reflected the good economic situation the cities and the crown experienced, in sharp contrast to the Aragonese case. Over the fifteenth century as a whole and especially after 1450, Castile enjoyed strong economic growth, aided by the feeble impact of the Black Death, the orientation of its trade toward the Atlantic, and the opportunities afforded by a territory having an excellent balance between people and resources. The principal characteristics of Castilian growth[13] were these: (a) within rural areas diverse forms of production could coexist without entering into conflict, even when they competed with each other (mixed cultivation and cattle-raising joining with transhumant herding); (b) dynamic patterns of rural-urban articulation (notably in the textile sector) grew up; (c) if the origin of growth lay in the rural world, the peculiarity of the Castilian case was the participation of the cities (more than 6 percent of the population in 1500) in the process; (d) in spatial terms growth concentrated around the cities of Old Castile, so that the commercial centers of the periphery became subordinated to them.

The integration of Castilian economic space into international economic circuits, which occurred at the end of the fifteenth century, demonstrates the maturity and growing importance of the whole process. It was responsible for the creation of the *Consulate* of Burgos (1494) and the appearance of the settlement fairs of Medina del Campo. The principal cities of Old Castile came under the jurisdiction of the *Consulate,* which adjudicated the various disputes growing out of mercantile activity, especially the wool trade and sea transport. At first the institution was entirely controlled by the crown. The development of the settlement fairs of Medina del Campo resulted from the necessity of having a center for the liquidation of balances resulting from commercial exchanges. Starting with the sixteenth century, as internationalization proceeded, the fairs of Medina abandoned the sale of goods to serve chiefly for the clearing of accounts.

The rapport between cities and the monarchy produced the economic bonanza that Castile enjoyed between roughly 1480 and 1570. The available quantitative information indicates so: between 1530 and 1590 the Castilian population grew 64% annually, exceeding the other kingdom's average growth.[14] It was—as said before—a growth characterized by an important increase in the urban population, which grew at a 62% average rate during that period, while the kingdom of Castile's average growth was 48%. Hence, the 20 urban centers with over 10,000 inhabitants in Spain by 1500 were practically doubled a century later. The majority of them were in Castile, whose urban network (36 nuclei of over 10,000 inhabitants) appeared better balanced than that of the kingdoms of Aragon, dominated by the demographic weight of their respective capitals. Thus, the Spanish urbanization rate (11.4%) was one of the highest of the continent.

Nonetheless toward midcentury the good feeling between the crown and cities decreased as a result of the excessive maintenance costs of the empire, which in 1557 forced Philip II to declare the first suspension of payments. In addition to casting doubt on the imperial structure, bankruptcy signaled the need to recast the cities' role in the Empire's sustenance. The good relations maintained under Charles V were at bottom somewhat fictitious: they depended on a blatantly pro-urban fiscal system, based on the freezing of the *alcabala* and on the shifting of the fiscal burden to the rural world. The scheme remained operable through royal recourse to international bankers who took the crown's ordinary income as security for their loans. Tributes from the Indies completed the system. In 1538 the emperor tried to break the vicious circle, but the Cortes vigorously opposed the reform.

This state of affairs set a time bomb that exploded in Philip II's hands. Overwhelmed by the size and the interest of the existing debt, the king tried to change the approach his father had followed. For that purpose, he undertook a systematic alteration of the main lines of his father's policy, a decision that directly affected the cities. Philip II started by increasing his own fiscal resources, both by broadening (new taxes) and by deepening (increasing existing taxes). Simultaneously, with the intention of reducing the debt, the monarch declared that the realm (constituted by the eighteen cities that voted in the Cortes) would take charge of indebtedness, and he undertook discussions with the realm about technical proposals, which all finally failed for lack of agreement.[15]

The same program included the substitution of Castilian bankers for the powerful foreign syndicates, especially those of Genoa. As it happened, the plan came to naught. Philip II found no other remedy than continuing to accept the presence of Genoese bankers, the only ones who could assure the regular payment of his troops in cash wherever they were.[16] Philip II also tripled the level of the *alcabala*, bringing it to its legal maximum.

The new fiscal policy meant the end of the favorable fiscal conditions Castilian cities had enjoyed. It also damaged economic development. The enlarged tax burden was often transferred to manufactured goods or financed through procedures that aggravated the plight of the popular classes. The transfer of taxes occurred, furthermore, at a particularly difficult moment: exactly when, because of the price revolution in Spain, the country's manufactured products were facing difficulty in international markets. The activities of the most dynamic urban centers were thus seriously damaged, and in the 1570s the economic nucleus of Old Castile began to decline.

Cities such as Medina del Campo, which had specialized in the clearing of accounts, likewise felt the negative effects of royal policy and not only with regard to taxation. The fact that since the beginning of the sixteenth century the royal administration had been carrying out ever-larger credit operations in the fair itself became visible as a destructive influence. Increasingly, the fairs came to depend on the crown's own settlement of its accounts, and when in straits the crown delayed the fair until the fleet's arrival allowed it to pay its debts. The repetition of these delays—the *largas de ferias*—blackened the reputation of Medina, which finally slipped to the edge of the international circuit of fairs.

Independently of the clearly negative effects that resulted from these royal actions, the needy monarchy adopted an expedient that had even more serious consequences for the cities' immediate future. Although Charles V had resorted to the issuance of claims on the public debt (*juros*), Philip II used that device beyond any reasonable measure. Despite declining interest rates, the debt financed by that procedure sextupled between 1550 and 1598. Interest on the state's debt often exceeded the total amount of ordinary fiscal receipts. The monarchy's responsibility for the situation was clearly visible: given the growing difficulty of economic enterprise, important segments of the urban population abandoned trade to become rentiers. As Felipe Ruiz Martin has indicated, the surer interest of the *juros*, of public credit, acted like a magnet on private credit, keeping it from being channeled into productive activity. Castilian economic growth suffered acutely from that orientation. From 1570 a frenetic *juromania* spread across Castile, so that Castilian cities began to turn into financial cemeteries, veritable *pensionopolises*, in Weber's term.[17]

Leaving aside details and qualifications, the major turning point in relations between cities and the monarchy occurred during the second half of the sixteenth century. The cities paid a very high price for their initial support of the crown. The more the logic of imperial power took over, the less cities had any chance of developing on their own. Nonetheless, they never became simple toys in royal hands. At the beginning of the seventeenth century, as the power of Genoese financiers declined, the monarchy tried again to obtain the support of cities, which finally gave in—at a price. The most crucial price of all was the imposition on the crown of a fiscal system (the *servicios de millones*) that was even more favorable than the *alcabala* to the cities having votes in the Cortes.

During the reign of Philip III (1598–1621) the *millones*, initially conceived as a temporary loan to the monarchy by the cities, became a regular revenue of the exchequer. Gradually they would even exceed the amount of the *alcabalas;* thus the fiscal history of the Castilian seventeenth century would be focused on them.[18] The *millones* also meant an important novelty: they were a tax voted in Cortes and whose funds were strictly controlled—in principle—by the Cortes. Certainly it was neither the only nor the first tax which enjoyed such conditions, but this was the first time that cities decided to keep a firm control over it against the crown's controlling attempts. In such a way and versus the royal treasury, the *millones* became the basis of the early organization of a treasury of the kingdom.[19] In order to limit the monarch's margin of action, the new tax was formalized in a public document, a contract that contained a series of conditions (*condiciones de millones*) which left its control totally to the cities. Because this was a contract, the monarch was placed in an awkward situation each time he sought to act independently or against those conditions.[20]

Objectively, the *millones* somehow reformulated, on a new basis, the advantages previously obtained by the cities. This agreement was decisively influential in the period of a certain political peace enjoyed by Castile during the seventeenth century,[21] though this does not mean that the process was costless. The main cost, as said before, affected the urban dynamism enjoyed by Castile during the sixteenth century. Therefore, during the seventeenth century, that laboriously built urban system would be totally disbanded.

In the light of the data [given in Table 8.1],[22] specialists understand the seventeenth century as a period of de-urbanization, whose significance would reach well into the nineteenth century.[23] The recovery and later demographic growth of the eighteenth century would be based on a substantially different model: small and medium-sized rural nuclei would be the base of such growth.[24] In any case, the urban decadence of the seventeenth century was a complex phenomenon, whose development should be further specified. In a first period, between 1580 and 1630, the industrial and service sectors—as said before—were badly damaged by the tax burden and by the urban oligarchies' rentier tendencies. That period coincided with an important recession in the rural world, affected by a series of poor harvests in the earliest years and mainly by the double action of royal taxation and the increase of land rents.[25] In addition, this recession was deepened by sales of the villages' community properties by the monarchy.[26] Therefore, the collapse of rural demand and simultaneously the urban recession destroyed the process of formation of a domestic market; the basic city-country connection began to crack, and its effects were noticed in a different and selective way. For those villages with a certain degree of industrial specialization, the blow was decisive, while those villages that specialized in farming or cattle surmounted the crisis somehow.[27] The cities had fewer possibilities: some of them (Burgos, Medina del Campo) rapidly suffered the consequences of imperial policy, while those with long-range trading connections and less affected areas could postpone the crisis. But they, too, would succumb to it.[28]

[TABLE 8.1]   Evolution of the Population of the Main Cities of Castile

Cities	circa 1600	circa 1700
Avila	12,700	4,340
Burgos	12,000	8,500
Segovia	25,000	7,300
Toledo	50,000	22,500
Valladolid	38,000	16,400
Medina del Campo	25,000	6,500
Ocaña	12,010	5,120
Alcaraz	7,660	6,885
Alcázar San Juan	7,766	5,670
Ciudad Real	7,798	5,555
Totals	197,934	78,770

In such a way between 1580 and 1630 the majority of the main centers of the urban network were affected by the crisis. Nevertheless, Madrid was a notable exception, registering a spectacular growth.[29] However, Madrid's growth should not be understood as a positive element per se within that context. As suggested by Ringrose, Madrid was at the beginning a minor place in such a system. Its growth was due to strictly political reasons (the decision to establish the capital of the monarchy there from 1561),[30] far from a natural process of economic selection. Given the traditional and enforced priority accorded to the good order of the capital, Madrid's growth was produced at the expense of a constant drain of men, food, and materials from its environments. Prices and wages were affected immediately, but this cost could be borne by the high incomes of bureaucrats and courtiers. The problem was that these politically captured resources were vital for the continuity of the old system, so Madrid finally gave it the coup de grâce. The hierarchical, interconnected network of cities, hitherto playing an active role, was replaced by a new system ruled solely by Madrid. Toledo, which had played the role of coordinator within the old system, became the main victim of the process. In addition to this, the most disturbing aspect of this change derived from the fact that a political capital[31] took the lead in directing the economy of an urban system. Therefore, the monarchy's political defeat in the second half of the seventeenth century halted any possibility of evolution for the system.

Ruralization is the most adequate term to summarize what happened in the urban world from 1630 on. However, the cities did not disappear. They certainly lost those functions used by geographers and economists to define them, but their legal personality subsisted—their condition of *universitas* which defined them in a more meaningful way. In such a way the urban system functioned simultaneously as a political system. Within it, the cities of first rank enjoyed the privilege of having a vote in the Cortes. Thus, in representing the kingdom, they had the possibility of dealing with the monarch, a contact normally used by the cities to obtain particular grants. Besides, there were corporations which controlled, to a greater or lesser extent, the jurisdiction or the taxation of a rural district (*la tierra*), holding the title of *señoras*. Altogether the system had to deal with two types of conflict: on the one hand, a conflict among the cities without a vote, hoping to reach the highest rank; on the other hand, that of a great deal of *aldeas* and *lugares* which were part of each of the *tierras,* trying to be released from their controlling cities. Both types of conflict had had a long history.[32] Up to 1623 the cities with a vote managed to keep closed the access to their exclusive group; new entries were few.[33] By far, the system's main conflict was the fight for the condition of *villa de por sí.* This term defines the frontier of the urban political power in Castile. In the *escritura de millones* the cities tried to obtain guarantees from the monarch not to alter the political map.[34]

Nonetheless, the reign of Philip IV (1621–1665) registered a spectacular increase in that type of transaction by the exchequer,[35] a decision taken because of the low performance of the *servicios de millones* from 1630–1635 on. There is little doubt that the internal crisis of Castile had to do with that situation, but the main reason for low performance was the corruption of the cities' fiscal management system. This explains why, simultaneously, the monarchy enforced a policy whose consequences would be decisive in the long run: facing the inability of the Cortes to ensure a sound taxation, the monarch turned increasingly to particular negotiations with the cities—whether they had a vote in the Cortes or not—in order to increase revenues (donations, loans) to compensate for the low performance of ordinary taxation. Paradoxically the cities with a vote in the Cortes accepted the new situation without any great objection: by that time the Cortes had become a less useful mechanism for the cities, which had already lost confidence in the institution.[36] For different reasons, the monarchy would reach the same conclusion. Therefore, nobody regretted that they were not summoned again during the reign of Charles II.[37]

Thus during the second half of the seventeenth century the rapport between monarchy and urban political system came to be established in a different way. Contrary to the evolution of the urban network, the political network experienced a process of decentralization: the Cortes did not become a center of direction and coordination for the system, nor did they monopolize the political scene of the kingdom. Favored by the monarchy, the number of participants in the system had grown, and each of them negotiated separately. Because of this disintegrated system, negotiations could be relatively more comfortable for the monarch. However, given his delicate financial situation, the result of those negotiations played again into the consolidation of a more powerful monarchy. The outcome of this dynamic was the gradual and firm establishment of a political "localism" under a superior monarchical power more fictitious than effective.[38] Unlike the French case, the Spanish experience, as seen from Castile, did not end with the complete submission of cities to the monarchy's expansive centralization.[39] There was no state on the political horizon.

IMPLICATIONS AND CONCLUSIONS

Madrid's parasitical role and the cities' deep-rooted political localism were two of the crucial questions that the newly arrived Bourbon dynasty had to face.[40] Throughout the eighteenth century Madrid again grew spectacularly (from 125,000 to 200,000 inhabitants), far exceeding the growth of the inland cities. But what seems more important is that the eighteenth century's growth model lost the self-centered and articulated character that had developed during the fifteenth and sixteenth centuries.[41] The growth of Madrid dominated the interior's economic activity while some trading peripheral nuclei were integrated, to a varied extent, in the Atlantic international trade market in a subordinated position and always meeting elite demands of Madrid's market. This evolution brought about some differences between the interior and some peripheral areas but not to the point of shaping a dual Spain. It was not the birth—as happened in France—of a *société marchande* different or opposed to the *monarchie administrative:*[42] the monarchy had nationalized the business with a mercantilist order and was usually behind the periphery's commercial stimulus. Something similar might be said about the economic reform projects so typical of the eighteenth century: their raison d'être derived from the dynastic and patrimonial absolutism, not from any interest in an urban system. Certainly, trade and, in general, those activities usually linked to the urban bourgeoisie could be favored, but the global logic of those activities was not bourgeois at all. Anyway, as happened with the continental absolutisms, the rearrangement of the rural economies appeared to be the primary objective in efforts to strengthen the system.[43]

Besides, the relative dynastic victory reached in Utrecht allowed the deployment of a power's technology of administration—a deployment which, in addition to a political-institutional simplification, also meant the beginning of more effective control over the urban corporations.[44] Therefore, the cities finally lost the political standing that they earlier had enjoyed, through the Cortes or particular negotiations. For better or for worse, the monarchy finally consolidated a more stable and regularized fiscal system, which operated without urban consent. Gradually, the cities were trapped within the kingdom's administrative network, without any privilege or special recognition. Thus, the situation turned out to be completely different from that of two centuries earlier. It is significant that when the monarchy, by the end of the century, was again in financial difficulties, rural wealth and not the cities rescued the royal treasury.[45] The cities had not died, but politically they were not a problem anymore. At the beginning of the liberal-bourgeois revolution and in more democratic moments, Madrid and Charles IV's centralism were to be blamed, not without reason, for most of that urban liquidation.[46] But such an accusation would be useless; the moderate regime of 1845[47] would demonstrate the importance of such territorial and administrative interests in the political and constitutional transformation of Spain.

Notes

In its first version this chapter was translated from Spanish by Charles Tilly; this enlarged version was translated by Javier Rambaud.

1. About this question, from a theoretical perspective, see B. Clavero, *Tantas personas como estados: Por una antropología política de las historia europea* (Madrid: Tecnos, 1986), and lastly, idem, "Anatomía de España," *Quaderni Fiorentini*, n. 34/35 (Milan: Giuffrè, 1990), 47–86.

2. J. Lalinde Abadia, "España y la Monarquía Universal," *Quaderni Fiorentini*, n. 15 (Milano: Giuffrè, 1986), 109–166; idem, "La dominición española en Europa," *Diccionario de Historia de España*, M. Artola, ed. (Madrid: Alianza, 1988), 421–494.

3. P. Fernández Albaladejo, "Los Austrias Mayores," *Historia de España* (Barcelona: Planeta, 1988), vol. V, 54–171.

4. For a general survey, P. Vilar, *La Catalogne dans l'Espagne Moderne* (Paris: SEVPEN, 1962), vol. I; J. M. Salrach, *Historia dels Països Catalans* (Barcelona: Edhasa, 1981); T. N. Bisson, *The Medieval Crown of Aragon* (Oxford: Clarendon Press, 1986).

5. About this term, Y. Barel, *La ville médiévale: Système social, système urbain* (Paris: Presses Universitaires Grenoble, 1977), 304–336, containing very interesting considerations.

6. M. Perez Picazo, G. Lemeunier, P. Segura, eds., *Desigualdad y dependencia en el Mediterráneo* (Murcia: Editorial Regional, 1986).

7. J. M. Torras, *Els municipis catalans de l'Antic Régim* (Barcelona: Curial, 1983); J. Amelang, *Honored Citizens of Barcelona* (Princeton: Princeton University Press, 1986); J. Casey, *The Kingdom of Valencia in the Seventeenth Century* (Cambridge: Cambridge University Press, 1979).

8. A. MacKay, *Spain in the Middle Ages* (London: Macmillan Press, 1977); T. Ruiz, *Sociedad y poder real en Castilla* (Barcelona: Ariel, 1981); P. Iradiel Murugarren, "La crisis medieval," *Historia de España* (Barcelona: Planeta, 1988), vol. IV, 9–295.

9. M. A. Ladero Quesada, "El poder central en España del siglo XIV al final del Antiguo Régimen," *Revista de derecho administrativo*, n. 94, 1981, 173–198; idem, "Corona y ciudades en la Castilla del siglo XV," *Estudios en memoria de C. Sánchez Albornoz* (Madrid: Universidad Complutense, 1986), vol. I, 551–574.

10. J. Pardos, "Comunidad, *persona invisibilis*," *Revista de las Cortes Generales*, n. 15, 1988, 143–180.

11. P. Fernández Albaladejo, "Monarquía y reino en Castilla, 1538–1623," paper presented to the XIV Settimana di Studio, Istituto Francesco Datini, Pratto, 1982.

12. M. A. Ladero Quesada, *La Hacienda real de Castilla en el siglo XV* (La Laguna: Universidad, 1973), 61–93; R. Carande, *Carlos V y sus banqueros* (Madrid: Sociedad de estudios, 1949), vol. II, 222–257.

13. For a general survey, F. Ruiz Martin, *Pequeño capitalismo, gran capitalismo* (Barcelona: Grijalbo, 1990); P. Iradiel Murugarren, *Evolución de la industria textil castellana en los siglos XIII–XVI* (Salamanca: Universidad, 1974); idem, "Estructuras agrarias y modelos de organización, precapitalista en Castilla," *Studia Historica,* Salamanca, vol. II, 1983, 87–112.

14. V. Perez Moreda, "El crecimineto demográfico español en el siglo XVI," *Jerónimo Zurita: Su época y su escuela: Congreso* (Zaragoza: Diputación Provincial, 1986), 55–71; J. E. Gelabert, "Il declino della rete urbana nella Castiglia dei secoli XVI–XVII," *Cheiron,* n. 11, 1989–1990, 9–39, for the urban data following.

15. The last analysis is from J. I. Fortea Perez, *Monarquía y Cortes en la Corona de Castilla: Las ciudades ante la política fiscal de Felipe II* (Salamanca: Cortes de Castilla y León, 1990).

16. F. Ruiz Martin, "La banca en España hasta 1782," *El Banco de España: Una historia económica* (Madrid: Banco de España, 1970), 3–196.

17. Fernández Albaladejo, "Monarquía y reino."

18. C. Jago, "Habsburg Absolutism and the Cortes of Castile," *American Historical Review,* n. 86, 1981, 307–326; I.A.A. Thompson, "Crown and Cortes in Castile, 1590–1665," *Parliaments, Estates and Representation,* n. 2, 1982, 29–45; P. Fernández Albaladejo, "Monarquía, Cortes y 'cuestión constitucional' en Castilla," *Revista de las Cortes Generales,* n. 1, 1984, 11–34.

19. On this point, M. Artola, *La Hacienda del Antiguo Régimen* (Madrid: Alianza, 1982), 141–143.

20. P. Fernández Albaladejo, "La resistencia en las Cortes," *La España del Conde Duque de Olivares,* J. H. Elliott and A. García Sanz, eds. (Valladolid: Universidad, 1987), 317–337.

21. Jago, "Habsburg Absolutism," 325–326.

22. References in J. M. Perez Garcia, "La crisis socioeconómica," *Historia de España* (Barcelona: Planeta, 1988), vol. VI, 209; with similar criterion, V. Perez Moreda, "La población española," *Enciclopedia de Historia de España,* M. Artola, ed. (Madrid: Alianza, 1988), vol. I, 369–384.

23. M. Artola, *La burguesía revolucionaria:* Historia de España Alfaguara, vol. V (Madrid: Alianza, 1973), 75–77.

24. A. Garcia Sanz, *Desarrollo y crisis del antiguo régimen en Castilla la Vieja* (Madrid: Akal, 1977), 44–50, 84–89; Gelabert, "Il declino," 28–29; B. Yun Casalilla, "Estado y estructuras sociales en Castilla: Reflexiones para el estudio de la crisis del siglo XVII en el valle del Duero (1550–1630)," *Revista de Historia Económica,* n. 3, 1990, 567–568.

25. A. Garcia Sanz, "La crisis del siglo XVII," *Historia del España Menéndez Pidal,* (Madrid: Espasa-Calpe, 1989), vol. XXIII, 197–201, 207–214; B. Yun Casalilla, *Sobre la transición al capitalismo en Castilla: Economía y sociedad en Tierra de Campos (1500–1830)* (Valladolid: Junta de Castilla y León, 1987), 276–305.

26. D. Vassberg, *La venta de tierras baldías* (Madrid: Ministerio de Agricultura, 1983); idem, *Land and Society in Golden Age Castile* (Cambridge: Cambridge University Press, 1984).

27. Garcia Sanz, *Desarrollo y crisis,* 56–74.

28. M. Weisser, "The Decline of Castile Revisited: The Case of Toledo," *Journal of European Economic History,* n. 3, 1973, 614–640; retarded in relation with Castile and with less intensity, the crisis touched the Andalusian cities, too.

29. D. R. Ringrose, *Madrid and the Spanish Economy* (Berkeley: University of California Press, 1983); idem, "El desarrollo urbano y la decadencia española," *Revista de Historia Económica,* n. 1, 1983, 37–57, whom I am following in this paragraph.

30. A. Alvar Ezquerra, *Felipe II, la Corte y Madrid en 1561* (Madrid: CSIC, 1991).

31. About this point see the comments of J. Brown and J. H. Elliott, *Un palacio para el rey* (Madrid: Alianza, 1981), 40 (English original version in Yale University Press, 1980).

32. Fernández Albaladejo, "Monarquía y reino."

33. In 1623 the region of Galicia obtained the vote, as did Extremadura and the city of Palencia in 1656 and 1666, respectively; the total number of privileged towns grew to 21.

34. This was something the king could always accomplish constitutionally if there was a situation of *necesidad,* and that was done through the selling of titles of *villazgos,* or the municipal offices.

35. A. Dominguez Ortiz, "Ventas y exenciones de lugares durante el reinado de Felipe IV," *Anuario historia del derecho Español,* 1964, 163–207, and the recent study by H. Nader, *Liberty in Absolutist Spain* (Baltimore: Johns Hopkins University Press, 1990), 99–129.

36. For the causes of this attitude, see I.A.A. Thompson, "Cortes y ciudades: Tipología de los procuradores," *Las Cortes de Castilla y León en la edad moderna* (Valladolid: Cortes de Castilla y León, 1989), 193–248.

37. I.A.A. Thompson, "The End of the Cortes of Castile," *Parliaments, Estates and Representation,* vol. IV, n. 2, 1984, 125–133; Fernández Albaladejo, *Resistencia en las Cortes,* 335–337.

38. See especially I.A.A. Thompson, "Castile," *Absolutism in Seventeenth Century Europe,* John Miller, ed. (London: Macmillan, 1990), 69–98.

39. Nevertheless, the same process of centralization and submission in the French cities' case now seems questionable (Gail Bossenga, "City and State: An Urban Perspective on the Origins of the French Revolution," *The Political Culture of the Old Regime,* K. M. Baker, ed. [New York: Pergamon Press, 1987], 114–140).

40. About this process see P. Fernández Albaladejo, "La Monarquía," *Actas del Congreso Internacional sobre "Carlos III y la Ilustración"* (Madrid: Ministerio de Cultura, 1989), vol. I, 1–89.

41. E. Fernández de Pinedo, "Coyuntura y política económicas," *Historia de España,* M. Tuñón de Lara Dirigidores (Barcelona: Labor, 1980), 122–160.

42. About this question, in extenso, see E. W. Fox, *L'Autre France* (Paris: Flanmarion, 1973), 57–86.

43. P. Fernández Albaladejo, "El decreto de suspensión de pagos de 1739," *Moneda y Crédito,* n. 142, 1977, 51–85.

44. Not without problems, Fernández Albaladejo, *"La Monarquía,"* chapters II and III.

45. R. Herr, *Rural Change and Royal Finances in Spain* (Berkeley: University of California Press), 79–158, 713–754.

46. See the very significant pamphlet *España y Madrid: Discurso político sobre el origen de la monarquía española, y único medio de evitar su total ruina y destrucción* (Cádiz: 1836).

47. M. Artola, *Burguesía revolucionaria*, 211–222; B. Clavero, *Manual de Historia Constitucional de España* (Madrid: Alianza, 1989), 71–83.

◄ 9 ►

Cities and the State in Portugal

ANTONIO MANUEL HESPANHA

ONE OF THE REMARKABLE characteristics of Portuguese demography from the Middle Ages to the modern era is the virtual absence of cities[1] (Godinho 1971, Silva 1972). Lisbon has always been the major exception, especially after the start of overseas expansion.

At the end of the thirteenth century, Lisbon had 23,000 inhabitants, a middle level in the European urban scale. A century later, its population was 35,000 people, which brought it to the level of such middling cities as Salamanca, Dijon, Siena, and Danzig. For Portugal, however, Lisbon was enormous, at least twice the size of the next in line (Évora, Santarém). At a lower level stood a set of small urban centers, dominated by the interior cities that lived from stock-raising, agriculture, or trade with Castile.

Later (especially starting in the fifteenth century) cities formed in the grain-growing southern plains (Alentejo) and among the ports of the west and south coasts, the latter engaging in long-distance shipping or the coastal trade. Among the ports was Oporto,[2] whose growth was spectacular, making it the kingdom's second-largest city by the middle of the sixteenth century.[3] Each of the two categories had a different social structure. Artisans and merchants predominated in the coastal cities, while in those of the southern interior the dominant classes were political officials, holders of ecclesiastical benefices, and more or less ennobled landlords.

Toward 1527, at the time of the kingdom's first general cadastre, Lisbon had 13,000 households, or about 65,000 inhabitants. It was a great city, larger than such centers as London, Cologne, or Madrid. Its growth continued, furthermore, reaching 100,000 people in 1551.[4] As for the rest of the country, it contained 33 urban agglomerations with more than 500 households; the most important cities on the coast were Oporto (about 15,000 inhabitants), Lagos (6,500), and Tavira (7,500); in the southern interior, the chief cities were Santarém (about 10,000 inhabitants), Évora (14,000), and Elvas (9,500).

184

As is well known, the sixteenth century marked the apogee of Lisbon, where the East Indiamen (operated directly by the crown) set out and returned.[5] Lisbon's physical, commercial, financial, and political rise followed the rhythms of the Indies trade. The importance of other urban centers depended on different activities. The coastal leaders—such as the towns of the North Atlantic shore (Porto, Viana, and Aveiro) and those of the southern coast (Lagos, Faro, and Tavira)—were tied to the Atlantic trade, which was less expensive and therefore more private than commerce with the Indies; the Atlantic trade linked the continent, the Atlantic islands (which had some important urban centers, such as Ponta Delgada in the Azores, designated a city in 1546), the African coast, and, increasingly after the seventeenth century, Brazil.

Finally, the cities of the southern interior lived on agricultural or pastoral production and trade—domestic or with Castile's Extremadura and Andalusia. In those places, changes in social structure clashed less with the traditional social and ideological foundations of authority. Early sixteenth-century proposals to move the kingdom's capital there stemmed from the discrepancy between ruling-class ideas of caste or nobility and the social ferment of a city like Lisbon, which a foreigner described as a "receptacle of Jews, shelters of Indians, chain gang of Mohamedans, shop of merchants, hotbed of usurers, pigsty of luxury, chaos of greed, mountain of pride, refuge of criminals" (Claude de Bronseval, *Peregrinatio hispanica*, 1531–1533). But Lisbon had finally become the very base of royal power—the place where the crown collected its revenues, its courts sat, and its military power rested on the fleets that anchored in the Tagus estuary. Written, quantitative, and protobureaucratic culture, the base of the new royal administration, sprang from the warehouses and shops that ran overseas trade.

These differences in the social and economic foundations of the three types of cities (Lisbon, the Atlantic ports, and the interior centers) explain their changing places in the kingdom's regional balance from the sixteenth to eighteenth centuries. Up to 1550 the predominance of the Indies trade, by comparison with which the Atlantic trade was secondary,[6] assured the preeminence of Lisbon. Significantly, the classic descriptions of the capital written to celebrate its greatness appeared then, in a style dominated by quantitative and statistical discussion: inventories of the population, revenues, food supply, trade, officials, salaries, and occupations.[7]

In these accounts, Lisbon is a great city—"the largest in Europe," if not the world. And its greatness is different: not the magnificence of a venerable history (which the authors hardly discuss) or of its buildings (the architect Francisco de Holanda felt, indeed, that the character of its public buildings was one of the city's weaknesses) but of its teeming population, its extensive trade and revenues, its splendid political and administrative apparatus.

A purely demographic criterion, however, will not suffice to define a city. As the basis for a certain type of social organization, a city is above all a community where commercial and industrial activities predominate, where people do not produce their own means of subsistence. Beyond minimum population levels that vary from one era to another, the economic functions of cities define them as such. The same applies to political definitions of cities.[8] In this regard urban functions are not the commercialization and transformation of raw materials but the structures of control over territories larger than those of primary communities that, employing adequate technologies of political communication, are capable of overcoming distance and of mastering the complexity and scale of urban life.

One might be tempted to use a purely administrative criterion for cities, singling out settlements having major political and administrative functions, such as the capitals of Portuguese *correições* and *comarcas*. But if one wants to isolate a characteristic type of community political life, it is probably necessary to adopt less linear standards, such as those formulated by medieval common-law jurists. They depend on the presence of various attributes of authority including the presence of a bishop, the number of physicians, lawyers, teachers, and professors, the grandness of palaces, and the jurisdiction of judges.[9] From this point of view, Lisbon was clearly a great city by the standards of the time.

In fact, it hosted an administrative structure far more extensive than that of many of Europe's largest cities. Toward 1552, the royal service absorbed almost 1,350 people, of whom 73 percent worked in the administration of finances and royal trade, 18 percent in the administration of justice, and 9 percent in different sorts of "police" activity[10] (see Table [9.]1 for details). That distribution represented a radical overturning of the traditional balance of political and administrative activity, previously dominated by the administration of justice. Furthermore, public service constituted some 5 percent of the labor force (which was around 26,000 people altogether) and 1.3 percent of the total population: roughly 74 people per official. For a big city like Lisbon, the bulk of officialdom is remarkable; it confirms not only the intensification of the Portuguese crown's central administration but also the weight of overseas affairs, of which Lisbon was the center, in the overall activity of the crown.

A century later, toward 1640, Lisbon's political and administrative apparatus was still expanding. New institutions had appeared. Justice and police were still growing. But the administration of overseas trade was in decline in response to the crisis of that trade, especially with the Indies. Around 1640, the number of permanent officials of the *Casa da India* and the *armazens* (royal storehouses for overseas trade) seems to have been cut in half.

Indeed with the second half of the sixteenth century the India trade, which was run by the crown and based in the capital, suffered from competition by

TABLE [9.]1   Lisbon's Labor Force Around 1552

Officials		1,338
Justice	242	
Finances and administration of trade	978	
Civil government	118	
Independent professions		355
Merchants		1,202
Artisans and shopkeepers		20,839
Female domestic servants		2,000
Poor and widows		2,419
Total		28,153
Total population		c. 100,000

Source: Oliveira 1554; Serrão 1977: 224.

the Atlantic trade, which was accessible to private merchants who worked from the seaports.[11] This inversion of the scenarios of Portugal's foreign trade caused the demographic, social, and economic development of cities such as Viana do Castelo (which became the seat of a *correição* during the second half of the sixteenth century), Oporto (seat of a *correição* and location of the realm's second high court of justice, the *Casa do civel,* from the end of the sixteenth century), Aveiro (seat of the chief duchy of the central region), Setubal (integrated into the crown and made capital of a *correição* during the second half of the sixteenth century), Lagos, and Tavira (headquarters of the *correições* of the Algarve). The rise of the Atlantic ports brought an expansion of their political apparatus. In 1640, the 31 cities having middle-sized administrative structures (more than 30 officials) included not only almost all seats of *correições* but also all the important ports (Faro, Vila do Conde, Peniche, Aveiro). Within those structures, customs services occupied an important place.[12]

Finally, we have the hinterland, with its more traditional urban centers, whose importance resulted from agriculture, stock-raising, trade attached to them, or traditional positions in political administration. Among the cities specializing in domestic trade were Leiria, Santarém, Évora, Estremoz, and Beja. For trade with Spain, Castelo Branco, Castelo de Vide, Portalegre, and Elvas stood out. Political centers included Viseu, Guarda, Leiria, and Lamego. There were also ecclesiastical seats such as Braga or Miranda and cultural centers such as Coimbra.

The three categories of city—Lisbon, the Atlantic ports, and the centers of the interior—played unequal roles in the development of royal power and of characteristic modern political structures. Let us consider those roles.

First, there is the place of cities in royal finances. During the modern period (sixteenth to eighteenth centuries) the crown had two major sources of income. First came revenues collected in European Portugal, which were generally different forms of taxes, especially excise and customs (at first chiefly on imports, later extended to exports as well). Rents from the royal domain and income from royal patronage of churches and military orders were insignificant (less than 5 percent of total revenue).[13]

As for revenues from outside the kingdom, little came from taxes. Although overseas customs did generate some income, profits from foreign trade (notably of the East Indies, run as a royal monopoly) dominated the crown's foreign revenues. Around the end of the sixteenth century, overseas income was equal to that from the kingdom; in 1627 the value of pepper carried by the three annual ships of the Indies fleet equaled the excise taxes of the entire kingdom outside of Lisbon. During the following years, however, the amount of this overseas income dropped steadily.

When it came to expenditures, revenues from inside the kingdom were supposed to cover "ordinary" expenses: administrative costs, official salaries, and royal gifts (cash prestations, pensions, and annuities). On the other hand, overseas income went chiefly into the organization of armies and the defense of conquered territory; occasional surpluses took care of extraordinary expenditures, covered deficits in the regular budget, or guaranteed loans drawn from financial markets.

The typical feature of Portuguese crown revenues, then, was their great dependence on the kingdom's foreign trade. The ports, especially Lisbon, therefore played a primary role. Among the crown's domestic revenues, income from foreign trade or from Lisbon's commercial activity increased from 23 percent in 1527 to 53 percent in 1607 (see Table [9.]2). During the following years, the crisis of seaborne trade brought about by the war with the English and the Dutch produced a drop in the proportion. After war's end, maritime revenues rose, but the creation of new domestic taxes (the *décimas*) reduced their relative importance. Lisbon weighed heavily among all the cities yielding revenues. The customs and excise houses of Lisbon produced the bulk of total income despite the growing importance of the kingdom's other maritime customs. The place of Lisbon takes on even greater importance when we recognize that overseas income entered through its port—from the Atlantic islands, from Brazil, and from India; around the beginning of the seventeenth century, these places supplied half the king's revenues.

In addition to its place in the ordinary budget, Lisbon was the chief source of extraordinary revenues. The city supplied financial services for exceptional or urgent expenses such as royal visitations and the organization of armadas to defend Brazil or India. It also sold notes (*padrões de juros*) secured by royal revenues. Lisbon's market constituted the king's surest source of financial aid.

No one has studied Lisbon's activity as the royal bank adequately. A preliminary survey of the sources nevertheless makes possible an estimate of the volume and character of the municipality's (usually coerced) involvement as

TABLE [9.]2   Income of the Portuguese Crown, 1527–1680

	1527	1593	1607	1627	1680
Total income	197,949	1,018,391	1,672,270	733,882	2,636,025
From kingdom	156,949	492,671	679,228	546,688	2,026,788
Maritime customs	8%	34%	39%	25%	21%
Customs on trade with Spain	3%	–	6%	6%	–
Lisbon excise	15%	10%	14%	18%	10%
Other excise	55%	45%	29%	37%	20%
Other revenue	19%	11%	12%	14%	49%
Atlantic islands	19,500	54,877	61,400	46,244	55,237
Other (mainly overseas)	21,500	47,083	931,642	140,950	554,000

the crown's banker under the Portuguese kings of the House of Austria (1580–1640). Beset in their dynastic lands by financial troubles and cut off from important revenues by the decline of trade during the Atlantic war, the Habsburgs had to raise money for the defense of Portugal's colonies, as well as (at a far lower level) for the financing of European military campaigns, on Portuguese financial markets. The sale of notes (*juros*) guaranteed by royal taxes (especially customs) or commercial revenues (especially Indian pepper) had become difficult because of previous commitments—some of them dating to the beginning of the sixteenth century, and most from the time of the tragic Moroccan expedition of Portugal's King Sebastian in 1580—that still weighed on the treasury. The *Senado* (municipality) of Lisbon sold notes secured by its own revenues, especially the municipal excise on wine and meat, the *reais d'agua*, while taking from the crown notes against royal revenues.

That transaction was less a business deal than a payment of tribute. Sometimes a gap opened between the interest paid by the city, which matched the prevailing rates in the market for annuities, and the rate fixed by the king. In 1615, the crown announced a reduction of its interest from 6.25 to 5 percent. That reduction was badly received; Lisbon's municipality could only sell its notes at the old interest rate and even then with difficulty: it sold mainly to ecclesiastical institutions or noble rentiers and only rarely to true financiers. On the other hand, it was not always easy to convince the crown to pay more than the interest it had set. The result was a loss on the operation.

The loss became worse when the crown, beset by increasing financial difficulties, suspended payment of part of the interest (1637–1639). Equally harmful was another form of municipal financial intervention, the forced sale of pepper, which occurred in 1615 and 1616. In fact, the sale price could be lower than its purchase price, especially when the city competed with the royal storehouse (the *Casa da India*), which sometimes sold at a discount to meet its pressing need for cash; these circumstances forced the *Senado* to buy the remainder of the pepper that was in storage.[14]

If Lisbon's municipal notes were unpopular, they could still be a lesser evil as compared with such alternatives as forced loans or gifts. Starting especially in the 1620s the crown resorted to general taxes (*fintas, serviços*) on the kingdom. Since the nobility and clergy were exempted in principle (at least until the middle of the 1630s), merchants in the ports, especially Lisbon, paid a major share of the taxes.

Between 1580 and 1640, the kingdom's extraordinary taxes amounted to almost 100 million réis, which as an annual average remained relatively modest by comparison with the ordinary budget (16 percent). But during the 1630s, the critical period for royal finances, the annual amount came to around 300 million réis; that was a large amount, almost equal to two-thirds the ordinary income from excise taxes collected in all the kingdom and to half the revenues of the ordinary budget.[15]

All in all, for this period, annual average extraordinary revenues from the kingdom (which means, to a large degree, the urban mercantile classes, especially in Lisbon) amounted to about a sixth of ordinary revenues. Because the growth of royal expenditure resulted chiefly from the crown's (eventually unsuccessful) effort to build the apparatus of a great power, an effort that created a statist political system, the cities (especially Lisbon) became crucial economic bases for that transformation.

The capital also served as the seat of the crown's military power. The fleets on which Portuguese power depended were built in Lisbon's port. From 1618, the city also housed the army's only permanent mercenary unit, the *corpo de guardas marinhas*. The city's payment for troops (for example 500 out of 2,000 in 1636 and 200 out of 6,000—or perhaps 1,600—in 1639) were likewise decisive.[16] As for the rest of the kingdom, its military organization depended on communal militias whose organization had been prescribed by an ordinance of 1569; it is hard to judge their effective strength over the country as a whole.[17]

From the early seventeenth century, all these circumstances led Lisbon to play an exceptional role as intermediary between the king and the rest of the kingdom. Especially in the 1620s and 1630s Lisbon became the (Austrian or Braganza) kings' privileged interlocutor when the time came to gain the kingdom's assent to new revenues; that position resulted in part from the city's symbolic role as *caput regni* but especially from its financial position as commercial center and seat of the country's richest merchants. The municipality (*câmara*) of Lisbon conducted the entire negotiation over the increase in excise taxes, over the extension to the whole kingdom of the *real d'agua* (around 1631) or of the *renda fixa* (1632–1635), and (under the Braganza dynasty) over the creation of the royal tithe (*décimas:* 1641–1642). The city itself authored plans to collect the required sums and negotiated them with the other cities that were represented in the Cortes.[18] With the less frequent Cortes meetings of the seventeenth century but sometimes as a complement to negotiations begun in the Cortes (e.g., in 1641), the capital gained an eminent new position; to some degree, it took the place of the Cortes in the creation of taxes.

The political role of the other urban centers became correspondingly less important. From the Middle Ages onward, municipalities took part in the Cortes. During the sixteenth and seventeenth centuries about ninety communes sat with equal rights, although the benches on which their representatives sat marked their traditional rank. In the first row sat four cities (Lisbon, Porto, Évora, and Coimbra) and one town (Santarém). From the sixteenth century onward the communes in the front rows, which included the chief cities and towns, actually dominated the deliberations, especially when it came to fiscal matters. During the Habsburg period, the concentration of power to represent the kingdom in the capitals for *comarcas* increased; for example, the negotiation of the 1609 subvention or a royal visitation involved the king and the twenty-seven cities that were *comarca* capitals, with Lisbon playing the part of intermediary. But they never created as oligarchic a structure as the Cortes of Castile, where a score of cities committed the entire kingdom.

In any case, prerogatives of participation in the Cortes are not the final measure of the balance between crown and other powers in the Portuguese political system of the seventeenth and eighteenth centuries. Other mechanisms also mattered.[19] Space forbids any more than a sketch of that broad topic.

The Portuguese political system of that era was marked by particularism, by relatively weak concentration of power. Multiple factors explain the situation. On the judicial level, law and (especially) judicial doctrine and practice gave extensive protection to peripheral political bodies, particularly to communes (election of judges and officials, recognition of local laws, barriers to central intervention in their areas of self-government) but also to religious institutions (recognition of legal and judicial autonomy, exemption from taxes and other financial obligations). The law also gave individuals effective judicial protection against royal action.

In regard to finances and personnel, here is the situation: Because royal financial means stabilized in nominal value and declined in real value between 1540 and 1640, the government lacked financial means to establish political and administrative control of the periphery by the center. As a result, royal officials constituted only a small share of all officials. Of the roughly 12,000 officials in the kingdom, communes employed 85 percent, while the crown's provincial administration employed only 10 percent.[20]

When it comes to government policy, two facts stand out. First, many people held an idea of the monarch as a passive instrument for maintaining political balance rather than as a source of discipline or a center of command; the learned discussions of the time used the phrase *justitiam facere.* Second, because unlike a number of other Central and Western European monarchies the crown did not rely heavily on domestic taxes, it had few incentives to install daily, practical, effective surveillance of the kingdom. The guarantee of formal subordination of peripheral powers to the crown's hegemony sufficed. One might even say that delegation of the practical work of government and surveillance was an essential condition of the system's balance, given the inability of the royal political and administrative apparatus to take up those tasks.

For these reasons, the Portuguese political system remained largely decentralized until the second half of the eighteenth century. The lack of important cities and the swarming of about 950 small communes, furthermore, impeded the information of political poles substantial enough to check royal action. Of course Lisbon existed. But it was a court city, attached in many ways to the crown's destiny and therefore unable to keep its distance from the crown.

The larger towns fostered the development of new techniques of political communication. First and foremost was political communication based on the existence of a paid staff who regarded their administrative responsibilities as the center of their lives; who increasingly followed criteria of professional competence; who handed posts from father to son under the protection of a judicial order that recognized in principle the right of children to the offices of their parents; who assumed and reproduced the proper social and political values; who cultivated professional identity, an attachment to technique (often coupled with studied hermeticism), *esprit de corps,* a cult of the written as record, proof, demand, or claim; who cherished the separation from traditional elites and, as a complement, an increasing attachment to administrative authorities and high-ranking protobureaucratic circles such as the *corregador,* national judicial bodies, and the court. All these characteristics were more pronounced among the lettered administrative elite that was led by jurists with university educations, as were the *corregedores* (itinerant judges charged with the surveillance of local administration and justice) and the *juízes de fora* (career magistrates, named by the king to serve in the largest communes) from 1539 onward.

Still Portugal of the seventeenth and eighteenth centuries was a rural country. Around 1640, career magistrates only served in some 10 percent of all municipalities, including the seats of *correições.* In the rest, judges were unlettered, often illiterate. The breakdown of communes by number of nonhonorary officials is shown in Table [9.]3.

Case studies make reasonable an estimate of 40 regular officials as the minimum for a true city. By that standard, only 2 percent of Portugal's communes qualified as cities. In that regard, Lisbon occupied a unique position,

TABLE [9.]3   Communes by Number of Non-Honorary Officials

Less than 11 officials	721	84%
11–20	94	11%
21–40	28	3%
41–100	17	2%
100–150	2	
More than 150 officials	1	
Total	863	100%

alone in the top category. However, the magnificence of Lisbon's proto-bureaucratic apparatus did not give it the means to govern the rest of the country. The central administrative structure had two handicaps:

> *First,* its lack of internal unity, which stemmed from the absence of structures linking the all-powerful highest tribunals; it was the "monarchy without a brain" that figures in historians' discussions of the administrative model made famous by the House of Austria.
>
> *Second,* the near absence of peripheral extensions of the central administration and a relation of guardianship rather than true hierarchy between the rare royal representatives (e.g. the corregedores) and the political units, especially the communes, that they were supposed to supervise.

As for the spread of written culture, estimates based on the receipts of notaries and scribes show that the population reached by written legal culture—those who used notaries and writs—included around 260,000 people.[21] Considering that the total population of the time was about 500,000 households and that ordinarily only the parents in those households had independent juridical lives, we can conclude that about a quarter of the population made regular use of written judicial administration.

While the use of written administrative communication, especially in judicial affairs, was fairly widespread, the bureaucratic apparatus of communes remained thin. The new frameworks of political and administrative life, which were pervasive in the large cities and formed the basis of political relationships in the modern era (as Max Weber saw), lacked great influence over the country as a whole. In general, historians' and demographers' characterizations of early modern Portugal as a country without cities (or, rather, a country with just one city) seem to apply equally to the history of political power and administration. In this regard, Lisbon played a decisive role.

First, the city supplied the bulk of the financial and material means of a crown whose power depended on mastery of seas rather than on control of a small, poor mainland. It thereby helped free the crown of constraints that elsewhere in Europe made its counterparts prisoners of various estates. Second, Lisbon was the seat of a well-developed royal administration oriented (especially during the sixteenth century) to mercantile and logistical activity and therefore soon adept in quantitative techniques.

During the seventeenth century, the crown's administrative structure weakened. The change occurred especially in political and judicial administration, whose center was no longer the commercial world of Lisbon but the world of jurists educated at the University of Coimbra. A heavy cultural burden weighed down the dominant segments of administrative life; it did not lighten until Enlightenment political and social culture gave new value to *politia,* economic activity, and technical knowledge.

Still the new economic surge of the early eighteenth century, which was due to the exploitation of Brazil's wealth and to the political and cultural strength of the courts of Dom Joao V (1707–1750) and Dom José (1750–1777), maintained the decisive importance of Lisbon as an economic arena, as a center of symbolic and cultural diffusion, and as a political base for royal policies aiming, with the reforms begun in the late eighteenth century, at the more effective control of the kingdom's interior.

The resource-poor monarchy maintained only symbolic ties with the rest of the country. Nevertheless, the absence of important cities prevented any strong centrifugal movement. If the expansion of Lisbon served as the foundation of the crown's power, the rurality of the provinces gave it the handicap of a fragmented and spineless political periphery that enjoyed dissimulated *de facto* autonomy but lacked its formal and visible trappings.

Notes

1. Vitorino Magalhães Godinho, *A estrutura na antiga sociedade portuguesa* (Lisbon: 1971); José-Gentil da Silva, "Vida urbana e desenvolvimento: Portugal, país sem cidades," *Arquivos do Centro Cultural Portugues* 5 (1972): 734–746.

2. The Portuguese name *"Porto"* has an English version, "Oporto."

3. A. H. de Oliveira Marques, *Portugal na crise dos séculos XIV e XV* (Lisbon: Ed. Presença, 1987), 1982.

4. Joaquim Veríssimo Serrão, *História de Portugal* (Lisbon: Verbo, 1977), III, 224.

5. Jaime Cortesão, *Teoria geral dos descobrimentos portugueses: A geografia e a economia da restauração* (Lisbon, 1948); Frédéric Mauro, *Le Portugal, le Brésil et l'Atlantique au XVIIe siècle (1570–1670)* (Paris: Fundação Calouste Gulbenkian, 1983); Aurélio de Oliveira, "A sociedade portuguesa no Antigo Regime—aspectos económicos e sociais (em busca das constantes e inovações estruturais—sécs XV—XVIII," in Maria Emília Cordeiro Ferreira, editor, *Reflexões sobre a história e cultural portuguesa* (Lisbon: INED, 1985).

6. F. Mauro, *Le Portugal.*

7. Joao Brandão, Anselmo Brancaamp Freira, & Gomes de Brito, editors, *Tratado da magestade, grandeza e abastança da cidade de Lisboa, na 2^d metade do sec. XVI* [1552] (Lisbon: 1923); Cristóvao Rodrigues de Oliveira, *Sumário em que brevemente se contém algumas cousas (assim eclesiasticas domo seculares) que há na cidade de Lisboa* (Lisbon: Biblion, 1555, used 1938 edition).

8. See V. Godinho, *A estrutura,* 18.

9. António Manuel Hespanha, *As vésperas do Leviathan: Instituições e poder politico: Portugal—séc. XVIII* (Lisbon: author's edition, 1986, 2 vols.) I, 142.

10. C. Oliveira, *Sumário.*

11. Jaime Cortesão, *Teoria geral;* F. Mauro, *Le Portugal.*

12. A. M. Hespanha, *As vésperas,* I, 320, II.

13. Ibid., I, 163.

14. A. M. Hespanha, "Portugal e a política de Olivares," paper presented to Simposio Internacional Sobre la España del Conde Duque de Olivaress, Toro, 1987; now published in *Penélope* 2 (1989).

15. Ibid.

16. Ibid.

17. A. M. Hespanha, *As vésperas,* I, 262.

18. J. V. Serrão, *História de Portugal,* 44.

19. A. M. Hespanha, *As vésperas.*

20. Ibid., I, 312.

21. A. M. Hespanha, "Centro e periferia nas estruturas administrativas do Antigo Regime," *Ler História* 8 (1986): 35–60.

10

Intercity Rivalries and the Making of the Dutch State

MARJOLEIN 'T HART

> In this city of Amsterdam is the famous Bank, which is the greatest Treasure either real or imaginary, that is known any where in the World. [The] security of the Bank lies not only in the effects that are in it, but in the Credit of the whole Town or State of Amsterdam, whose Stock and Revenue is equal to that of some Kingdoms.[1]

SO WROTE SIR WILLIAM TEMPLE, a former ambassador of England in the United Provinces, in his *Observations* of 1668. No wonder the burgomasters of Amsterdam regarded themselves as kings during the glory period of the northern Netherlands.[2] Amsterdam, with its extensive power resources, was situated in Holland, which was, in turn, superior among the other northern Netherland provinces.

However, Amsterdam was not the center of a kingdom, and the city itself actually held little institutional power within the republic. The Dutch state of the seventeenth and eighteenth centuries was a federation with little centralization. It was sometimes even threatened with disintegration, its main divisive elements being provincial separatism, rivalry among urban oligarchies, competition among the government colleges of the central bureaucracy in The Hague, and the dualist position of the stadtholder. The latter was the former governor for the king in the provinces, yet after the revolt he had become an official in the service of the provinces. The stadtholder was the head of the republican military forces, and this office came to be dominated by the princes of Orange, who displayed, at certain intervals, monarchical pretentions.

In this chapter, I will discuss the ways in which the character and density of urban organization affected the course of state formation in the Dutch Republic. What matters above all are the supralocal power structures that were created by the ruling classes of the major trading cities in the first decades of

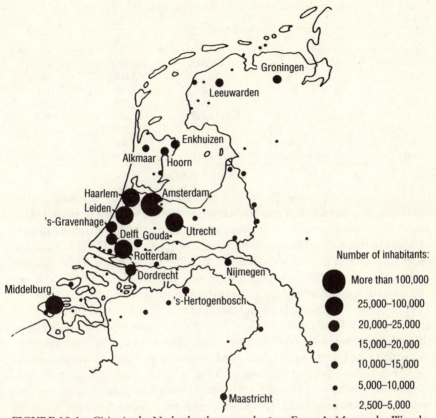

FIGURE 10.1   Cities in the Netherlands, around 1675. From A. M. van der Woude, "De demografische ontwikkeling," 137.

the revolt against Spain. The development of some key institutions will be analyzed: specifically, the navy and war-making and fiscal organizations—institutions that were used by other state-makers as levers of central power but that, in the Dutch Republic, served in the balancing of power due to the dispersed structure of the resources of the urban ruling classes. Finally, in the third part, I will discuss how the organization of the public debt was of crucial importance in maintaining the republic during the wars and how it created direct links between members of the bourgeoisie and the state.

THE URBAN ENVIRONMENT

One of the main characteristics of the provinces in the northwestern Low Countries was the high level of urbanization. In 1514, more than half of Holland's population lived in cities.[3] However, these cities had been compara-

TABLE 10.1   Approximate Number of Inhabitants of Eight Major Cities in Holland, 1514–1795

	1514	*1622*	*1675*	*1795*
Amsterdam	13,500	104,900	200,000	217,000
Leiden	14,300	44,800	65,000	31,000
Haarlem	13,500	39,500	37,000	21,200
Rotterdam	5,200	19,500	45,000	53,200
Delft	11,700	22,800	22,500	13,700
The Hague	5,500	15,800	22,500	38,400
Dordrecht	10,900	18,300	22,500	18,000
Gouda	14,200	14,600	17,500	11,700

tive latecomers in Europe. In the eastern part of the Low Countries and to the south, towns had been established much earlier, stimulated by the Hanseatic and Mediterranean trade. As sea trade gradually became more important, the maritime regions were offered rich opportunities. Holland's advantages were that it owned an extensive fleet due to the tradition of fisheries and that it had a well-developed, prosperous hinterland that provided models of technology, institutions, and capital accumulation.[4]

The countryside of Holland and Zeeland was characterized by broad rivers, islands, and extensive marshes. Serfdom was rare, and the influence of the nobility was small. Towns gained control by buying land and seigneuries, reclaiming lakes and marshes, and acquiring privileges from the sovereign. Agriculture became commercialized, and its productivity increased. Meanwhile, the town industries were stimulated as great peat resources provided them with cheap and easily obtainable fuel. A canal system provided the region with a high degree of physical mobility. And as maritime trade expanded, the major ports assumed functions that served much of Europe and allowed them to draw agricultural resources from distant areas. This made it possible for Holland to maintain a high level of urbanization in proportion to its "natural" resources.[5]

This high level of urbanization persisted as the population increased rapidly after 1550. The development of the major cities is traced in Table 10.1.[6]

Amsterdam became the entrepôt for the Baltic trade and held first place in the trade with the Mediterranean, but it had to yield a similar position in the trade with England and France to Rotterdam and Middelburg. The Northern Quarter towns of Hoorn and Enkhuizen concentrated on fisheries and northern trade; Leiden, housing the first Dutch university (founded in 1575), and Haarlem were the main industrial cities; Dordrecht, the oldest city, was the main river trade entrepôt; Gouda was the major inland market; The Hague became the bureaucratic center; Rotterdam was primarily a fisheries center but took up river and sea trade as well; Delft was an important dairy market and beer producer; Utrecht was a religious and cultural center; and

Middelburg had a strong connection with the French trade. Each city could more or less count on their textile and brewing industries, on trade and some bureaucracy, on schools and local markets. But taken together, the cities of the northwestern Low Countries constituted a mosaic, each having its own dominant color, its own history, and its own main produce.

The actual governing of the Dutch cities was performed by two, three, or four burgomasters with seven or more aldermen, elected by the *vroed-schap*—a council whose members were chosen for life by co-optation. Guilds had little influence. Only in Dordrecht did some guild representatives participate in a kind of council (*de Achten*). In Amsterdam, Leiden, and Brielle, the vroedschap had only indirect influence in the election of burgo-masters, which enhanced the aristocratic character of their governments.[7] The urban middle classes had an institutionalized voice through the burgher militias (*schutterijen*). The latter played a considerable role during the begin-ning of the revolt and in times of war, yet they were usually adequately con-trolled by the magistrates.[8] In the seventeenth century, the polities became more and more oligarchic. The number of *vroedschappen* was reduced, and so, too, were the number of families admitted to city government. Those holding municipal office became the real ruling class in the republic: They were commonly known as the regents.[9]

A STATE OF FIFTY-EIGHT CITIES

During the sixteenth century, a period of rapid growth, the province of Hol-land would even experience a "financial revolution" in its provincial govern-ment.[10] Yet the country's economic heart was still situated in the southern Netherlands, around Antwerp. It would be two decades before the north had taken over the position of the south or before an immigrant from Ant-werp would say: "*Hier is Antwerpen selve in Amsterdam verandert*" (Ant-werp has turned into Amsterdam).[11] The *renten* (loans) that were issued by Holland during 1515–1534 were subscribed in a much larger amount outside the province. Despite considerable capitalist development, individual cities experienced great financial difficulties. Indeed, Leiden was not solvent for almost the whole century, and the financial burden for Delft proved ex-tremely onerous.[12]

Again, the period of 1570 to 1590 was dominated by a general shortage of money in the north. The newborn state started out with a near bankruptcy: In 1581, it had to suspend the payment of interest. Many thought that after the fall of Antwerp in 1576—regarded as the center of the revolt—the north-ern provinces could not hold out on their own. In several cities, emergency coins were issued, and the right of minting, a privilege of Dordrecht alone in the provinces of Holland and Zeeland, was extended to Middelburg, Am-sterdam, Hoorn, Enkhuizen, and Medemblik. Measures violating the stability of the currency were adopted, much in contrast to the careful mint policy of the Burgundians a century before. A new coin—the *leeuwendaalder*—was issued at a higher rate than its intrinsic silver value, yielding about 1 million guilders as pure profit. And in 1573, the Estates of Holland and Zeeland ordered that all coins in use had to be validated by a special stamp, which increased the nominal value by 15 percent, paid to the estates as a loan.[13]

Those conditions determined the formation of the Dutch state. With virtually no funds for the war against Spain, it was necessary to obtain the active support of all cities and provinces in order to mobilize all available resources. The result was a federation with a states general, in which the provinces remained sovereign and had autonomous financial institutions. On all important issues, such as war and peace or taxation, unanimity was required. The revolt, in which traditional and local privileges of oligarchic rule were revived, was very much a war against the Spanish centralization policy. In all, fifty-eight cities obtained voting rights within the seven provinces. In the provincial estates of the inland and northeastern regions, the rural-noble votes balanced or slightly outweighed the cities, but in the west, the cities dominated. In the Provincial Estates of Holland, eighteen cities had a right to vote, whereas the nobility retained its single compounded vote. In Zeeland, the proportion was six city votes to one vote for the nobility.[14]

Although Holland and Zeeland were preponderant among the northern provinces, there was no clear-cut center that could take the lead in the new state. Stadtholder William of Orange assumed a leading position, yet there was no Dutch nobility to support his claims, and decisionmaking was largely left to the cities. Dordrecht still had the reputation of being Holland's first city, yet it failed to obtain a dominant position in the recent maritime trade. Moreover, it had created a great deal of resentment among the other cities because it had been the favorite of the Burgundians and the Habsburgs, who had supported its claims to important staple privileges on the river trade. Its credit base was still very strong, although its capital was more passive and engaged in intermediary roles by comparison with Amsterdam.[15]

Amsterdam was probably not much larger than Leiden and Haarlem, yet it had the largest capital resources and the strongest credit base of all cities, drawing much profit from the Baltic trade. Its financial resources were already extensive in the first half of the sixteenth century, which was reflected in the fact that Amsterdam issued renten independently of the five other great cities.[16] But Amsterdam did not participate in the first formative meetings of the new state, which began in 1572; rather, it continued to support the Spanish king until 1578. In addition, trade suffered a heavy blow because of blockades by the Sea Beggars; the Baltic shipments went to Rotterdam. Other cities, like Dordrecht, Hoorn, and Enkhuizen, also took over parts of the Amsterdam trade. Ultimately, although Amsterdam quickly recuperated after 1578, the city would suffer seriously from its disloyal image.

The other cities were still important, but none of them had sufficient power to be an independent center. Leiden was the second largest city, and its textile industry would become Europe's largest in 1650. It did not, however, have many financial resources. Production was just recovering from a sluggish period because of foreign competition. With few maritime trade relations, it was an atypical Holland city, like Haarlem. Both had suffered seriously under the Spanish siege, and Haarlem was also hit by a fire in 1576. Delft, previously the third city because of its credit and the strongest candidate after The Hague to become the bureaucratic center, had experienced a period of decline in its brewing and textile industries. Gouda, which had been, in turn, the strongest candidate after Leiden for housing the new university, saw its industry on the decline, too. Meanwhile, the growth of Rotterdam was only recent, and the city was still too dependent upon Dordrecht for its capital.

Cities outside Holland had few chances to become centers at all. Utrecht, though not a bad candidate, was too closely associated with its governor Leicester's policies, which had become very unpopular in Holland, and its trade had declined because of competition from Amsterdam and Dordrecht.[17] And Middelburg, though a strong city, was too closely associated with the province of Zeeland as a rival to Holland.

The Hague was chosen as the seat of the States General and the Estates of Holland and eventually of the other central colleges (Council of State, Chamber of Accounts, Court of Holland, Council of Brabant, and Court of the Stadtholder). This was a curious choice, for the place was not fortified, had no city rights, and had no voting rights in the Provincial Estates. It had also been impoverished during the sixteenth century: Grass now grew in the formerly paved streets, and a lot of rebuilding was needed. Nevertheless, there was a certain bureaucratic tradition in The Hague. The Provincial Estates had convened there regularly. It had housed the tax-gathering bureaucracy of the sovereign lords, and the Court of Holland had had its seat there, which gave The Hague a certain stylish character. The Englishman Sir William Brereton, who visited the country in 1634–1635, described it as follows: "It is but a *Dorpe* [small town or village], but the finest in all the land."[18] The Hague was chosen because it was acceptable to the eighteen constituent cities: "*omme alle jalousies te verhoeden*" ("to avoid all rivalry"), as the 1578 decision expressed it.[19]

The Court of the Stadtholder added a noble stature to The Hague. The stadtholder, who was at once an official of the States General and of each of the estates of several provinces, had some "sovereign" appointment rights; he could, for example, appoint magistrates from a list of nominations drawn up by city councils. As the head of the army and navy, he also had considerable powers of patronage. Patronage was, for that matter, strong in the governments of the provinces and cities too, and as such, it was often a source of factionalism. The prince was generally supported by the nobility in the inland provinces. He could also count on Zeeland, where he controlled three out of the seven votes, and on the Holland cities of Leiden, Haarlem, and Enkhuizen. But problems often arose with the major trading cities. They had no interests in the dynastic policies of Orange, and the stadtholder did not have nomination rights in Amsterdam.

Moreover, The Hague was internally divided. The relation between the States General (the federative sovereign body with representatives of the seven sovereign provinces) and the Council of State (made up of provincial delegates and the stadtholder, the executive power) was characterized by many disputes over the powers of various participants. Instructions to delegates from their provinces were vague and subject to several interpretations. The Estates of Holland, also convening at the "Binnenhof" in The Hague, had an overall influence upon policymaking.

Other cities would also prevent The Hague from asserting more power. The government of the city was financially and juridically subordinated to the *Societeit* (association), in which the Court of Holland, the High Court, and the Chamber of Accounts were represented next to the two burgomasters. Some parts of the city were even fully under control of the Court of Holland and the Chamber of Accounts. Attempts by The Hague magistrates to act outside the Societeit were defeated, and all requests to obtain the right to vote in the estates were denied. Delft, which feared its neighbor The Hague, played a leading role in this regard, opposing the appointment of a The Hague receiver of taxes and preventing the construction of a wall around the city. In 1575, Delft had even proposed to the estates to burn The Hague down, alleging that it was a potential base for the enemy: Unfortified, it could easily be turned into quarters for the Spanish army.[20]

As a result, The Hague itself did not act as a centralizing power, though it would become one of the major urban centers. The stadtholder, in turn, was checked by coalitions of cities that often included Amsterdam. But Amsterdam was not always opposed to the stadtholder. At times, he was needed to outweigh the influence of the Estates of Holland, represented by the grand pensionary. In 1616–1617, for example, when the pensionary Jan Van Oldenbarnevelt relied on the eight cities of Haarlem, Leiden, Gouda, Alkmaar, Rotterdam, Brielle, Schoonhoven, and Hoorn, Amsterdam sided with the faction that supported the stadtholder. And although it was mainly due to the influence of Amsterdam that no stadtholder was appointed after the coup d'état of William II (in 1650), the city supported the aspirations of William III in 1672 to curb the power of the pensionary Jan De Witt, who was generally backed by Dordrecht, Rotterdam, and Delft.[21]

The outcome of the formative period was a state in which the smallest province had the same rights and powers as Holland; furthermore, in the sovereign province of Holland, the thriving city of Amsterdam had no more power than any of the other seventeen cities. This had much to do with the fact that economic hierarchies were not as clear as they would be later in the seventeenth century. Rather, these hierarchies were subject to change because of the war and the rapid development in trade. When Amsterdam was reluctant to join the revolt, Rotterdam was regarded by immigrants from the south as the first place to go, mainly because of new links with the Baltic trade (although many went also to Middelburg). In fact, Rotterdam might well have taken the top position instead of Amsterdam. Moreover, the traditional power of Dordrecht was still strong. And threats from outside the region remained: Antwerp, if recovered from Spain, would change the whole urban hierarchy in Holland. That in itself was an important factor in the war policy of the republic.

ADMIRALTIES AND WAR: CONFLICT
AND CONTROVERSY IN THE EARLY REPUBLIC

The rivalry between the several potential centers of the new state was clearly reflected in the institutionalization of the admiralties. Rotterdam was preeminently fit for housing an admiralty because of its role in fisheries and shipping and its central position near the sea and the main rivers. The traditionally strong city of Dordrecht, collecting about the same amount of customs as Rotterdam, claimed the Holland seat, but Rotterdam won, and a general admiralty was effectively established there. Significantly, however, this admiralty was not named after the city but after the river Maze.[22] The Amsterdam harbor, on the other hand, was not easily accessible, and the disloyal attitude of Amsterdam during the revolt played a role, too, in the decisions on where to locate the admiralties. Meanwhile, the Province of Zeeland refused to submit itself to a Holland admiralty in Rotterdam. Consequently, a general admiralty was set up in Veere, which had housed one in 1488. Then, however, the Northern Quarter towns would not agree to having two admiralties in the south, so one was established at Hoorn. After this initial distribution, it was impossible to return to any central command over the admiralties. When the Stadtholder Frederick Henry proposed, in the 1640s, to reduce the number of admiralties to one, to install it at Hellevoetsluis (with the seat in The Hague), and to have all customs collected by tax farmers, there was no way to make this project feasible.[23]

Disputes continued. Middelburg, having the largest capital resources and engaged in a centuries-long rivalry with Veere and Flushing, managed to obtain the seat of the admiralty of Zeeland. In the Northern Quarter of Holland, where no city stood clearly above the others, strife arose, and the seat moved temporarily to Amsterdam. But when Amsterdam subsequently refused to return it, all seven Northern Quarter towns, fearing the domination

TABLE 10.2   Percentage Distribution of Customs Revenue of Dutch Admiralties, 1586–1671

	1586–1600	1621–1630	1641–1650	1660–1671
Amsterdam	31.3	47.9	47.9	53.8
Rotterdam	26.4	21.0	20.7	20.0
Hoorn-Enkhuizen	5.8	7.7	6.5	7.2
Middelburg	30.0	19.4	22.6	16.6
Dokkum-Harlingen	6.2	4.1	2.3	2.4
	100.0	100.0	100.0	100.0

of Amsterdam, were furious. In the end, a fourth admiralty was established, which was to move every three months between Hoorn and Enkhuizen. Friesland, protesting that it would come under the command of the north Holland cities, finally obtained the fifth admiralty.[24]

The power of the admiralties, who were in charge of the navy, was vested in the collection of customs. The more funds they collected, the greater the admiralties' independence from the States General. The shift in the economic hierarchy of the admiralties is illustrated in Table 10.2.[25]

The position of Zeeland between 1586 and 1600 was almost comparable to that of Amsterdam, and it explains the claim for a separate admiralty. But by the end of the seventeenth century, even Rotterdam outstripped Middelburg in terms of customs revenues collected. Friesland's admiralty (with a seat in Dokkum, later in Harlingen) was originally not much weaker than those of the Northern Quarter towns Hoorn and Enkhuizen, but it ended up as an institution that could barely collect its own maintenance costs. By the 1660s, Amsterdam alone collected as much revenue as all the other admiralties combined, which reflects the economic hierarchy of the major trading cities in the republic.[26]

Disputes between admiralties and custom offices over the collection of duties were frequent and would continue for years, for there were several "authorities" claiming supremacy: the province, the admiralty, the city, the Council of State, the States General or Chamber of Accounts, and even the custom tax farmers who were appointed between 1625 and 1640. In the 1580s, a near war broke out between Holland and Zeeland because Middelburg imposed customs on all ships passing its waters, even when they were bound for Holland. And when the States General decided to farm out the collection of the customs (a measure designed to raise the revenue and reduce local influences), the admiralty of Amsterdam proved extremely obstinate, hindering the tax farmers as much as possible. The result was that the collection of the customs was returned to the hands of the receivers of the admiralties in 1640. And in general, the Chamber of Accounts faced difficulty in controlling the finances. For example, until 1635, the admiralty of Middelburg continued to use Flemish pounds instead of the standard Dutch pound, and its accounts started in October instead of January.[27]

Decisionmaking over issues of war and peace was, like the institutionalization of the navy, a highly complicated matter as well. When the interests of the various provinces conflicted, those of Holland and Amsterdam tended to prevail, provided they were in agreement. Yet that was not always the case. In the 1630s and 1640s, a serious dispute arose on whether the Dutch should engage in peace negotiations with Spain. It dragged on for years; in the end, no decision was made at all because Holland itself was seriously divided over this matter.[28] The three "war provinces" (Zeeland, Groningen, and Friesland) stood against the three "peace provinces" (Gelderland, Overijssel, and Utrecht [excluding the city of Utrecht]). In Holland, the "war cities" included Leiden, Haarlem, Gouda, Hoorn, and Enkhuizen (supported by Utrecht), whereas the "peace cities" were Amsterdam, Rotterdam, Dordrecht, Alkmaar, Delft, and some smaller ones. The nobility supported peace initiatives, too, and the stadtholder ultimately shifted from a slightly prowar position to a propeace standpoint.

In large part, the dilemma could be explained by the different interests of the urban elites. The textile industry feared competition from the southern Netherlands, whose products' high wartime customs rates were excluded from the North. Leiden (cloth industry) and Haarlem (renowned for its finishing and bleaching of textiles) were at the core of the antipeace party, directed against Amsterdam.

Amsterdam, together with other cities primarily interested in trade, generally regarded war as harmful. But the opposition was not simply a matter of trade versus industry, and some trade cities joined the antipeace party as well. There was a contradiction between the European carrying trade and river trade, on the one hand, and the colonial trade, on the other. Carrying and river trade suffered heavily from trade restrictions imposed by Spain, Portugal, and the republic, and the raids of privateers at sea (Dunkirkers) were particularly damaging for ships traveling between England and France. (The Dutch Republic lost approximately 3,000 ships with an estimated value of 20 to 25 million guilders to the Dunkirk privateers betwen 1621 and 1646.) The colonial trade, however, gained from the opportunity to attack Spanish and Portuguese possessions in the Far East and in the Americas.

In Amsterdam, the factions representing the European carrying trade came to dominate municipal policy. They were also stronger in Rotterdam and Dordrecht; the wealth of the latter was based upon the river trade and its connections with the German and southern Netherlands cities. But in Hoorn and Enkhuizen, as well as in Middelburg, the colonial interests overcame the influence of the factions promoting the European carrying trade, which explains the cities' support for the antipeace party.

Antwerp was also a factor to be reckoned with, for if a peace were negotiated at this stage, this formerly glorious city would remain outside the northern Netherlands. Stadtholder Frederick Henry and cities such as Utrecht and Middelburg would have welcomed a city with enough financial power to outweigh Amsterdam. But it was very much in Amsterdam's interests, on the other hand, to keep this possible rival out of the country.[29] Finally, in the Peace of Westphalia (1648), Antwerp agreed to stay out of the republic, but the north still had the power to hinder access to its harbor.[30]

Generally, in naval matters (more so than in army matters), Amsterdam was able to exert a direct influence on the war-making policy. Stadtholder Henry, who had dynastic interests in England—his son William had married Mary Stuart in 1641—tried to organize a fleet to help his son's in-laws during the Spanish Revolution (1640–1660), but he could not get the support of the admiralties. But in 1645, Amsterdam (against the will of the stadtholder) launched a Dutch intervention in the war between Sweden and Denmark, sending a fleet of warships to the sound in order to force the king of Denmark to lower the sound tolls, which had been increased greatly some years earlier. In 1655, the republic sent warships to the Baltic, as demanded by Amsterdam, to prevent Charles Gustavus of Sweden from taking Danzig. And in 1658, Amsterdam pleaded for military assistance for the Danes, who were facing a Swedish attack—a very risky proposition since France and England might intervene. Ultimately, Amsterdam succeeded in obtaining the support of "The Hague."[31]

With local interests playing such an important role, there were continuous negotiations. Indeed, provinces and cities seemed to be allies rather than fellow members of a union. For example, Zeeland, having a great interest in the West India Company, tried to convince the others to send massive amounts of money to support the company in coping with the Pernambuco rebellion in Brazil. Holland and Amsterdam finally agreed to do so, in exchange for Zeeland's consent to establishing a peace with Spain. Similar negotiations were necessary in the following years: Zeeland would sign the treaty with Denmark that was so important for the Amsterdam Baltic trade, and Holland (Amsterdam) would continue to support the West India Company.[32]

Clearly, then, there was a continuous shifting of coalitions in the republic. The efficacy of the republic was seriously limited because conflicting local and particularist interests played such a large role in decisionmaking. At the same time, the state's revenues—which enabled the republic to maintain its position vis-à-vis foreign competitors—were heavily dependent on the trade and wealth of cities.

FISCAL RESOURCES AND MUNICIPAL POWER

Although The Hague and the stadtholder, two major potential nuclei of central power, scarcely acquired any new institutional resources after the establishment of the republic, Amsterdam gathered economic and financial strength. As Sir William Brereton wrote: "[In Amsterdam] the customs and excise [are] very great, but I could never attain to an exact knowledge thereof, though I applied myself to enquire; but this I heard, that this town affords as great revenues, to maintain the wars to the States, as four provinces—Zeland, Utrech, OverIsell, and Friseland."[33]

How could the position of Amsterdam versus that of Holland and the republic be characterized in financial terms? Was Amsterdam really that dominant over other cities? One measure of this involved the costs of warfare, which had increased considerably during the war with Spain. In fact, sums voted for warfare in the States General rose from 2.9 million in 1586 to 18.3 million in 1640.[34] These sums were divided over the provinces in a quota system, with Holland paying about 58 percent in all; Friesland 12 percent; Zeeland 9 percent; Utrecht, Groningen, and Gelderland 6 percent each; and Overijssel 4 percent.[35]

Though Amsterdam could not profit from the spin-off wealth of the high bureaucracy, its financial power was based on the fact that the merchants of the southern Netherlands had come to the city to establish commercial houses and financial institutions. Amsterdam was the site of the most important chamber of the statelike East India Company, whose dividends averaged 37.5 percent annually from 1605 to 1612. In addition, a chamber of assurance was founded there in 1598, a new bourse in 1608, and a bank of exchange in 1609—all of which were controlled by the city magistrates. Amsterdam itself, profiting from the steady growth of trade and the conquests in the Far East and the west from which the city could draw taxes, tripled its own revenue from 1620 to 1679.[36]

The other cities had their own financial institutions, though not as extensive as those in Amsterdam. Most had their own Bank van Leening (loan office) and a receiver of taxes who functioned as a banker, too. The East and West India Companies had several chambers, and there were banks of exchange in Delft (1623–1635), Middelburg (dating from 1616), and Rotterdam (from 1635 on, established after the English Merchant Adventurers had moved there). Rotterdam also had a bourse of its own.[37] Yet Amsterdam remained the dominant financial and economic center.

In relation to the annual ordinary revenue of the state, Amsterdam contributed almost 3 million guilders. This was about 26 percent of Holland's total, which was, in turn, about 15 percent of the whole *Staat van Oorlog*

TABLE 10.3   Average Ordinary Revenue in Holland, 1671–1677

	Amount (in guilders)	Percentage of Total State Revenue
Taxes on lands and houses	3,488,479	30.9
Indirect taxes (mainly excises)	6,410,985	56.8
Stamp duties	1,391,967	12.3
Total	11,291,432	100.0

("war budget").[38] Amsterdam's wealth and its considerable role in state finances brought the city fame, as expressed by Sir William Brereton in the previous quote. However, though significant, the city's share of the state's revenues was actually less than is assumed usually. Amsterdam, too, needed the cooperation of other urban elites, and it could be checked by a coalition of the stadtholder and other cities in Holland.

The mesolevel of government (the provinces) came to dominate the other cities in the republic. The provinces levied taxes to provide for their quotas (the original shares of the state's revenues), to which the city excises had to be subordinated. The representatives in the Provincial Estates could dispose of a wide range of excises, tolls, stamp duties, office taxes, land taxes, and "extraordinary" taxes on property in which houses, lands, and obligations were assessed in times of emergency. The makeup of the average annual ordinary revenue of Holland is shown in Table 10.3.[39]

Revenue-raising emphasized indirect taxes, a feasible strategy because of extensive urbanization and commercialization. Most excises were farmed out, and bonds were sold to the highest bidders. And because the leases were short—three months, half a year, or one year only—the tax farmers could not enrich themselves at the expense of the state. Apart from provincial revenue, cities had their own revenue from excise taxes (particularly on beer and wine) and from duties levied on their markets, ferries, bridges, roads, and streets.

In Holland, most revenue came from the cities, particularly the "traditional" six large cities (Amsterdam, Leiden, Haarlem, Delft, Dordrecht, and Gouda) and the rising centers of Rotterdam and The Hague. Table 10.4 shows the revenue derived from the capitation tax (reflecting the population distribution), the tax on property (houses, lands, and offices), the indirect taxes, and the tax on obligations. The table also reveals that 45.5 percent of the population lived in the smaller cities and in the countryside and contributed relatively little to the whole.[40]

The burden on the countryside was fairly light. This was an advantage to the republic, for direct taxes on agricultural production are rather inelastic; indirect taxes are more easily increased and administered. This is not to say that Dutch agriculture was in a poor condition. But since the bourgeoisie

TABLE 10.4   Percent Distribution of Several Items of Revenue in Holland (Southern Quarter)

	Population (1622)	Property Taxes (1654)	Indirect Taxes (1682)	Obligations Taxes (1673)
Amsterdam	20.8	38.5	28.3	29.0
Leiden	8.9	6.0	14.9	5.4
Haarlem	7.8	4.9	10.4	5.3
Rotterdam	3.9	7.3	9.0	6.0
Delft	4.5	4.6	7.5	7.6
The Hague	3.1	11.4	7.6	32.0
Dordrecht	3.6	2.6	6.7	5.1
Gouda	2.9	1.6	3.8	3.3
Remainder of the urban areas and rural southern Holland	45.5	23.1	11.9	6.2
Total	100.0	100.0	100.0	100.0

had invested heavily in land, increases in the burden on lands were not at all welcomed by city-dwellers. Costs of drainage were high, too, so it was hard to impose additional taxes there. And because of interurban rivalry, control over rural areas was scattered and decentralized.[41]

As reflected in the property tax levels, wealth was concentrated in the larger cities, especially in Amsterdam and in The Hague, the city with the wealthiest households in the republic on average. With scarcely any significant trade or industry, the bureaucratic families were still able to develop considerable private properties there.[42] As could be expected, the indirect taxes had a clear urban base as well; the smaller towns and rural regions contributed a mere 12 percent of such taxes. Cities, of course, competed with each other for control over these financial resources. Because the beer excise, in particular, was very profitable (making up the largest single item in the revenue) and because cities controlled part of the countryside as well, there inevitably were many disputes.[43] Yet all in all, the cities of Holland provided the Dutch state with a varied and broad commercial base for its revenue-raising.

RENTIERS AND THE DUTCH STATE

The broad tax base was not the only factor that sustained the fragmented institutions of the republic. The loan policy also involved many centers of wealth and drew in a large group of regents, who thereby had a personal financial interest in the success of the state. In the taxes on obligations in particular, the influence of the cities is obvious: Only 6 percent of the revenue came from the villages and smaller towns (see the fourth column in Table 10.4).

The republic's long-term debt originated in the Eighty Years' War and stood at 4.9 million guilders in 1617. At the end of the war in 1648, it came to 13.2 million, with a debt service of 557,384 guilders.[44] In the meantime, the Estates of Holland had contracted a much larger public debt than the Generality (the federal state in its executive capacity) to fulfill its quota in the repartition system. Holland also undertook loans upon request for other provinces, for the admiralties, and for the States General. In 1621, Holland's debt stood at 1.5 million guilders, but in 1650, it amounted to 130 to 140 million and carried a debt service of 6 to 8 million.[45]

Every loan of the Estates of Holland had to be approved by all the cities. The debt was contracted by the receiver general of Holland (with an office in The Hague) and by the local receivers (who had their offices in the constituent cities). The successful floating of a loan depended largely upon the receivers themselves. With their private wealth, they were responsible for the sums in their *Kantoren,* and they were, for the most part, well acquainted with the leading merchants and bankers of their cities.[46]

This policy worked well most of the time, and related troubles were only minor. In the end, all loans were subscribed by a few large and many small rentiers. The number and geographic distribution of sales offices, the number of receivers involved, and their private and local contacts fostered a loan policy that drew a very large number of Dutch burghers into state finances. The Dutch also developed a habit of providing for their old age and for their families by buying annuities. At the same time, the opportunity to invest money without assuming the risks of commerce appealed to many. For example, when Louis de Geer, a famous Amsterdam merchant, died in 1648, he left 142,999 guilders in debentures and short-term notes of the Province of Holland, 9,000 in obligations, and 5,852 in redeemable annuities from various cities.[47] Such confidence in the issuing body was unequaled by other seventeenth-century states (except Genoa) and secured by the broad base of taxation. For the city-based loans, the excise on beer was of supreme importance in this regard.[48]

Unlike most other states, the Netherlands did not need to ask for funds from foreign bankers, and its rate of interest was low, declining to a mere 3 or 4 percent in the last quarter of the seventeenth century. Individual bankers at Amsterdam, such as de Geer, Trip, and Deutz, are mentioned frequently in the files of the States General, asked to stand bail for loans or to intermediate, reselling state obligations. But Amsterdam was not the only place for such activities. In Rotterdam, one leading person in this field was Johan Van der Veken.[49]

Given the roles they played, merchants had an overriding impact upon state policies. Louis de Geer, who had numerous interests in the Swedish metallurgical industry (many regents had invested in Sweden, too), even financed and organized a fleet for the Swedish king in the autumn of 1643.[50]

And many officials and civil servants in The Hague, which accounted for such an important share of the tax on obligations payments (see Table 10.4), were buying the state's loans as well.

In Holland, the distribution of wealth checked individual acts by cities: A coalition of the other cities was always possible. There were, of course, problems if one city did not agree to a loan. In 1626, when Gouda refused to furnish more than 400,000 guilders for a loan and The Hague, too, murmured that its part was high, those cities had to be "persuaded." In 1640, Delft complained, in turn, that its debt was much higher than that of other cities—a complaint that was resolved by raising an extra loan to pay off Delft's debt.[51]

More serious were the problems that arose when Amsterdam did not agree to a loan. In 1683, for instance, it willfully delayed William III's war against France by refusing to vote for the funds necessary to raise troops. No resolution for recruitment could be issued because "outvoting" in financial matters had never been allowed: Article 6 of the constitution of the Estates of Holland (1574) stated that "nobody shall be outvoted against their will in question of consent to petitions and subsidies, or in making any contributions to the other members." In the end, troops were raised without the financial support of Amsterdam.[52]

CONCLUSION

The republic became a state in which the bureaucratic center (The Hague) was separate from the economic and financial center (Amsterdam). There was also a distinct traditional center (Dordrecht or Utrecht) and cultural center (Leiden, site of the state's first university).

One of the republic's weakest places was chosen to house the central government. And though there was some bureaucratization at The Hague, it was prevented from asserting more power by several means. Some institutions and functions—such as the navy, minting, and taxation—were even more decentralized as compared to the period before the revolt. Police, civil, and criminal justice likewise fragmented. Urban oligarchies obviously suffered very little constraint from above.

Merchants dominated not only local but also national and international politics, and cities had an overarching impact on the Dutch state. Above all, the state's success originated from the fact that its institutions could deploy extensive financial resources. The Dutch Republic was a typical example of state-making in a capital-intensive region.[53]

But its constitution also prevented the possibility of change and adaptation to new international balances of power, which eventually was an important cause of the Dutch decline in the eighteenth century. It was extremely hard to meet the requirement of unanimity, and consequently, factions of the regents could prevent policies by holding back their money for new loans and by forming coalitions. The result was a continually changing bargaining for power in the Dutch Republic. Amsterdam was influential, but its interests did not always coincide with other powerful factions of the ruling class. And even when the stadtholders' power was critically high (as in 1618, 1650, and 1672), this was only because the stadtholders were part of coalitions with the urban oligarchies.

Amsterdam built a very impressive city hall, described by one visitor to the republic as the "Wonder of the World, the Pride of Amsterdam and the Glory of the Seven Provinces."[54] It even came to be called *Paleis* (the Palace). But it did not make the burgomasters kings. The state built by the cities did not institutionalize hierarchies. To chart the various interests of the ruling class in order to understand the constraints on aspiring state-makers,[55] one would need a very detailed map indeed. Cities overwhelmingly shaped the destiny of the Dutch state, for they both contained and distributed the capital necessary to maintain the republic's integrity in the face of foreign incursions. But contradictions were, at times, so strong that one could hardly speak of *one* ruling class. In a region where power resources were so dispersed among a variety of potential centers, the result was a state and a ruling class that reflected those divisions in economic, financial, institutional, and political respects.

Notes

1. Sir William Temple, *Observations upon the United Provinces of the Netherlands* (London: Edward Gellibrand, 1676), 99–100.

2. H. Brugmans, *Opkomst en bloei van Amsterdam* (Amsterdam: Meulenhoff, 1911), 152.

3. Jan de Vries, *European Urbanization 1500–1800* (Cambridge, Mass.: Harvard University Press, 1984), 81. See also Walter Prevenier and Wim Blockmans, *The Burgundian Netherlands* (Cambridge, Mass.: Harvard University Press, 1986), 29.

4. To use Stein Rokkan's term, the region belonged to Europe's *central trading belt*, which stretched from northern Italy to the Low Countries. See also Hans Daalder, "Consociationalism, Center and Periphery in the Netherlands," in Per Torsvik, *Mobilization, Centre-Periphery, Structures and Nation-Building* (Bergen: Universitetsforlaget, 1981), 181–240.

5. Jonathan I. Israel, *Dutch Primacy in World Trade, 1585–1740* (Oxford: Clarendon Press, 1989); Jan de Vries, *The Dutch Rural Economy in the Golden Age, 1500–1700* (New Haven: Yale University Press, 1974), 25, 48, 81; J. W. de Zeeuw, "Peat and the Dutch Golden Age: The Historical Meaning of Energy-Attainability," A.A.G. Bijdragen 21 (Landbouwhogeschool Wageningen: Afdeling Agrarische Geschiedenis, 1978), 23; T. S. Jansma, *Tekst en uitleg* (The Hague: Nijhoff, 1974), 34–43.

6. Utrecht in 1514: 30,000, in 1675: 25,000; Middelburg in 1514: 7,500, in 1675: 26,000. A. M. van der Woude, "Demografische ontwikkeling van de Noordelijke

Nederlanden 1500–1800," *Algemene Geschiedenis der Nederlanden* V (1980), 102–168. For the Holland cities in 1514: J. C. Naber, *Een terugblik: Statistische bewerking van de resultaten van de informatie van 1514* (Haarlem: Stichting Contactcentrum voor regionale en plaatselijke geschiedbeoefening in Noord-en Zuid Holland, 1970 [1885]), the number of "communicanten" times 1,5; for 1622, Gemeente Archief Amsterdam 5030, 137, "Quoyer van 't hoofdgeld"; for 1675 estimations, Van der Woude; for 1796, Gemeente Archief Amsterdam 5059, 101a, "Rapport van de commissie. ..."

7. Maarten Prak, "Sociale geschiedschrijving van het Nederlands Ancien Régime," in *Tijdschrift voor Sociale Geschiedenis* 14 (1988), 152; A.C.J.M. Gabriëls, *De heren als dienaren en de dienaren als heer* (The Hague: Hollandse Historische Reeks, 1990), 15.

8. Militias were even officially banned in 1581 by the Estates of Holland. They remained in existence, however, and were revived in times of emergency, but on everyday policies they had little to say. J. C. Grayson, "The Civic Militia in the County of Holland, 1560–81: Politics and Public Order in the Dutch Revolt," *Bijdragen en mededelingen betreffende de Geschiedenis der Nederlanden* 95 (1980), 58. At times, the *schutterijen* posed a threat to the magistrates: Paul Knevel, "Onrust onder schutters: De politieke invloed van de Hollandse schutterijen in de eerste helft van de zeventiende eeuw," in *Holland* 20 (1988), 158–174; A. F. Salomons, "De rol van de Amsterdamse burgerbeweging in de wetsverzetting van 1672," in *Bijdragen en Mededelingen betreffende de Geschiedenis der Nederlanden* 106 (1991), 198–219.

9. D. J. Roorda, "The Ruling Class in the Seventeenth Century," in *Britain and the Netherlands* II (1964); R. Fruin, "Bijdrage tot de geschiedenis van het burgemeesterschap van Amsterdam tijdens de Republiek," in R. Fruin, *Verspreide Geschriften* IV (1901), 306.

10. Important in this respect was the development of long-term arrangements and the involvement of a large group of rentiers with a public body issuing loans against the revenue of excises. It preceded the so-called financial revolution in England. James D. Tracy, *A Financial Revolution in the Habsburg Netherlands* (Berkeley: University of California Press, 1985), 3, 123, 138. See for a recent revision of Tracy's work, the dissertation of Yvonne Bos-Rops, "De financiën van de Graaf van Holland van 1386 tot 1433" (Leiden, 1992), which predates the financial revolution of Holland.

11. Literally, "Here Antwerp itself is transformed into Amsterdam." J. H. Kernkamp, *Johan van der Veken en zijn tijd* (The Hague: Nijhoff, 1952), 9.

12. Izak Prins, *Het faillissement der Hollandsche steden: Amsterdam, Dordrecht, Leiden en Haarlem in het jaar 1494; uit de wordingsgeschiedenis van den Nederlandschen staat toegelicht* (Amsterdam: S. van Loog, 1922), 30; J. C. Boogman, "De overgang van Gouda, Dordrecht, Leiden en Delft in de zomer van het jaar 1572," *Tijdschrift voor Geschiedenis* 57 (1942), 91; J. H. van Dijk, "De geldelijke druk op de Delftsche burgerij in de jaren 1572–1576," *Bijdragen voor Vaderlandsche Geschiedenis en Oudheidkunde*, VII, part 5 (1935), 184. On the city finances and the "central government" in the fourteenth to sixteenth centuries, see Wim Blockmans, "Finances publiques et inégalite sociale dans les Pays-Bas aux XIVe–XVIe siècles," *Genèse de l'Etat Moderne: Prelevement et Redistribution* (Paris: Editions de CNRS, 1987).

13. This revenue (250,000 guilders) was, in fact, never reimbursed to the owners of the coins. Prins, *Het faillissement der Hollandsche steden,* 30; H. E. van Gelder, *De Nederlandse munten* (Utrecht: Aula, 1965), 78–82.

14. The eighteen cities in Holland were Amsterdam, Leiden, Haarlem, Dordrecht, Delft, Gouda, Rotterdam, Schiedam, Gorinchem, Brielle, Schoonhoven, Hoorn, Enkhuizen, Alkmaar, Medemblik, Edam, Monnikendam, and Purmerend. In Zeeland, the six voting cities were Middelburg, Tholen, Zierikzee, Veere, Flushing, and Goes. See also J. W. Koopmans, *De Staten van Holland en de Opstand* (The Hague: Hollandse Historische Reeks, 1990), 18.

15. Jansma, *Tekst en Uitleg,* 154, 164. See Gemeente Archief Amsterdam, Scheltema II, November 24, 1505, for an example of a coalition of cities (Haarlem, Amsterdam, Rotterdam, Enkhuizen, Hoorn, and others) against the staple of Dordrecht; also J. C. van Dalen, *Geschiedenis van Dordrecht* (Dordrecht: C. Morks, 1931–1933); J. P. Sigmond, *Nederlandse zeehavens tussen 1500 en 1800* (Amsterdam: Bataafsche Leeuw, 1989), 32. After the revolt, the staple was revived again: Bijlsma, *Rotterdams welvaren,* 22.

16. Much to the chagrin of the others. See Tracy, *A Financial Revolution,* 16, 58.

17. F. G. Oosterhoff, *Leicester and the Netherlands 1586–1587* (Utrecht: Hes Publishers, 1988). Leicester's governorship for England lasted only a couple of years (1585–1587), yet his centralizing policies were disliked by Holland. The subsequent 1588 settlement for the Council of State curbed any centralizing force and boosted the power of the provinces in the States General.

18. Sir William Brereton, *Travels in Holland, the United Provinces, England, Scotland and Ireland* (*Remains of the Chetham Society* I, 1844 [1634–1635]), 28. *Dorpe* = village.

19. H. E. van Gelder, *'s-Gravenhage in zeven eeuwen* (Amsterdam: Meulenhoff, 1937), 110; Koopmans, *Staten van Holland,* 32.

20. The proposal was not accepted. J. Smit, *Den Haag in den Geuzentijd* (The Hague: Meester, 1922), 286; Van Gelder, *'s-Gravenhage,* 120; Koopmans, *Staten van Holland,* 181.

21. D. J. Roorda, *Partij en factie: De oproeren van 1672 in de steden van Holland en Zeeland, een krachtmeting tussen partijen en facties* (Groningen: Wolters Noordhoff, 1978); J. L. Price, *Culture and Society in the Dutch Republic During the 17th Century* (London: Batsford, 1974), 52.

22. When Brereton visited Rotterdam in 1634, he was impressed by the harbors and declared: "An infinite number of tall and gallant ships belong to this city." Brereton, *Travels to Holland,* 6; Sigmond, *Nederlandse zeehavens,* 74.

23. See also the work by one of the opponents of the Stadtholder power: Pieter de la Court, *The True Interest and Political Maxims of the Republic of Holland* (New York: Arno Press, 1972 [1662/1746]), 186.

24. As of 1596, five admiralties were established that remained until the end of the eighteenth century. Harold E. Becht, *Statistische gegevens betreffende den handelsomzet van de Republiek der Vereenigde Nederlanden gedurende de 17e eeuw (1579–1715)* (The Hague: Boucher, 1908), 112–113; Julius F. Engelhard, *Het generaal-plakkaat van 31 juli 1725 op de convooien en licenten en het lastgeld op de schepen* (Assen: Van Gorcum, 1970), 248; Sigmond, *Nederlandse zeehavens,* 68 and 186. The province of Groningen, in turn dependent upon Friesland's admiralty, would

be one of the strongest advocates of a central admiralty, too. On Hoorn: C. Lesger, *Hoorn als stedelijk knooppunt* (Hilversum: Verloren), 1990; on Enkhuizen: R. Willemsen, *Enkhuizen tijdens de Republiek* (Hilversum: Verloren), 1988.

25. Figures have to be reviewed with care as fraud was considerable, but the table shows at least the shifts in relative position. The calculation is based on Becht, *Statistische gegevens,* 201, Appendix 1.

26. The position of Amsterdam was even more central than this table shows, as within the admiralty the customs office of Amsterdam alone collected 92 percent. By comparison, the customs office of Rotterdam did not collect much more than the customs office at Dordrecht, and the customs office of Middelburg at times yielded less than Tholen or Flushing. Algemeen Rijksarchief The Hague, States General 12561.98; Chamber of Accounts 1.01.43 954.

27. This occurred despite repeated requests to change the format of the accounts. The dispute between Holland and Zeeland was settled by allowing officers from Middelburg to collect customs in the Holland offices (half-licent, 1590); Algemeen Rijksarchief The Hague, Chamber of Accounts 1.01.43 90. On the influence of the city of Amsterdam on the admiralty, see W.F.H. Oldewelt, "De Hoeffijserse schuld (1616–1681)," in *Jaarboek Amstelodamum* 51 (1959); on the direct interference of the city in a dispute between tax farmer and receiver: Algemeen Rijksarchief The Hague, States General 12562.23, February 13 and April 30, 1638.

28. See J. I. Israel, "The Holland Towns and the Dutch-Spanish Conflict, 1621–1648," in *Bijdragen en Mededelingen betreffende de Geschiedenis der Nederlanden* 94 (1979), 41–69.

29. Pieter Geyl, *The Netherlands in the Seventeenth Century (1648–1715),* II (New York: Barnes & Noble, 1964). David Maland, *Europe at War 1600–1650* (Totowa, N.J.: Rowman and Littlefield, 1980), 177: The Amsterdam regents condemned Frederick Henry's determination to liberate Antwerp as a self-seeking ploy to provide the House of Orange with an independent principality. On the Dunkirk privateers: A. Th. van Duersen, *Het kopergeld van de Gouden Eeuw: Volk en Overheid* (Assen: Van Gorcum, 1979), 90.

30. The war-minded coalition lost, but it consented because of some specific peace conditions. J. I. Israel, *The Dutch Republic and the Hispanic World, 1606–1661* (Oxford: Clarendon Press, 1986), 374.

31. J. G. van Dillen, "Amsterdam's Role in the Seventeenth Century Dutch Politics and its Economic Background," in *Britain and the Netherlands II* (Groningen: Wolters Noordhoff, 1964), 143; Geyl, *The Netherlands in the Seventeenth Century,* 165; John J. Murray, *Amsterdam in the Age of Rembrandt* (Norman: University of Oklahoma Press, 1967), 37; De la Court, *The True Interest,* 189–191.

32. C. R. Boxer, *The Dutch Seaborne Empire 1600–1800* (New York: Alfred A. Knopf, 1965), 88–89.

33. Brereton, *Travels to Holland,* 65.

34. Algemeen Rijksarchief The Hague, Chamber of Accounts 1.01.43 90 "Staat sommier van de petitien."

35. The "repartition" was controversial. In 1609, such a disagreement arose that even French and English mediation was necessary. P. H. Engels, *De geschiedenis der belastingen in Nederland* (Rotterdam: Kramers, 1862), 22.

36. 1,109,000 in 1620, 3,348,000 guilders in 1679. H. J. Koenen, *Voorlezingen over der geschiedenis der finantien van Amsterdam* (Amsterdam: Bingen & Zn, 1855), 122, 128; Antonio Porta, Joan Corver, and Gerrit Corver, *De politieke macht van Amsterdam (1702–1748)* (Assen: Van Gorcum, 1975), 35; Gemeente Archief Amsterdam, 5028 Accounts Wisselbank; J. G. van Dillen, *Bronnen tot de geschiedenis der Wisselbanken* (The Hague: Rijksgeschiedkundige Publicatien 1925), 985. See also Lesger, *Hoorn als stedelijk knooppunt,* 121, on the centrality of Amsterdam.

37. Van Dillen, *Bronnen tot de geschiedenis der Wisselbanken;* Murk van der Bijl, *Idee en interest: Voorgeschiedenis, verloop en achtergronden van de politieke twisten in Zeeland en vooral in Middelburg tussen 1702 en 1715* (Groningen: Wolters Noordhoff, 1981).

38. In the 1670s, Amsterdam contributed 2,920,872; Gemeente Archief Amsterdam 5030, 153.

39. Gemeente Archief Amsterdam 5030, 153. Land and house tax = *verponding,* indirect taxes = *gemeene middelen,* stamp duties = *40e, 20e penning* and *zegelrecht.* In addition, there was the extraordinary revenue consisting of loans and property taxes. See for the eighteenth century: J.W.F. Fritschy, *De patriotten en de financiën van de Bataafse republiek* (The Hague: Hollandse Historische Reeks, 1988).

40. The table represents the larger part of Holland, the so-called Southern Quarter. The Northern Quarter, contributing about 11 percent in the total revenue of Holland, is left out because not all data are available. The capitation tax shows the population distribution, and was levied rarely, as a measure of emergency. The property tax of 1654 includes houses, lands, offices, and obligations; this tax was an "extraordinary" levy but repeated several times. The indirect taxes are a selection of major excise duties levied in 1682, and the obligation tax is part of the tax on property levied in 1673. Gemeente Archief Amsterdam 5030, 153, 137 (Staet wat de 1000e en de 200e penning ... ; Quoyer ...). As for the taxes on obligations, they were controversial and thought to harm the credit of the Republic: Dirk Houtzager, *Hollands lijf-en losrenteleningen voor 1672* (Schiedam: NV HAV bank, 1950), 53.

41. De Vries, *Dutch Rural Economy,* 44–48, 194, 199.

42. Wealthy bureaucrats were, for example, François van Aerssen, Clerk of the States General, whereas the Receiver General Cornelis de Jonge van Ellemeet was able to enrich himself while in office to buy three seigneuries at the end of the century. B. E. de Muinck, *Een regentenhuishouding omstreeks 1700: Gegevens uit de prive-huishouding van Mr. Cornelis de Jonge van Ellemeet, Ontvanger-Generaal der Verenigde Nederlanden (1646–1721)* (The Hague: Nijhoff, 1965), 341; H. E. van Gelder, "Haagsche Cohieren I en II," *Die Haghe Jaarboek 1913 & 1914,* 9–67, 1–117. See also J. L. van Zanden, "De economie van Holland in de periode 1650–1805: Groei of achteruitgang," in *Bijdragen en Mededelingen betreffende de Geschiedenis der Nederlanden* 102 (1987), 568.

43. For some lawsuits, see Gemeente Archief Rotterdam, Oud-Archief 3727–3728, 2180, 2181, 2184, 2185, 2186; Van Dalen, *Geschiedenis van Dordrecht,* 294; Jansma, *Tekst en Uitleg,* 43.

44. Algemeen Rijksarchief The Hague, States General 1.01.06 12548–188 (excluding a debt of 1.5 million).

45. Gemeente Archief Amsterdam 5030, 153, gives a figure of 99.8 million guilders as Holland's debt in 1647; J. J. Weeveringh, *Handleiding tot de geschiedenis der*

staatsschulden (Haarlem: J. J. Weeveringh, 1852), I, 6, gives 140 million in 1650; Engels, *Geschiedenis der belastingen*, 23, has 132 million in 1652. The differences might be explained that the life annuities are not always reckoned as long-term debt. See also E.H.M. Dormans, *Het tekort, Staatsschuld in de tijd der Republiek* (Amsterdam, NEHA, 1991), 66.

46. Cities were most eager to have a provincial tax receiver within their walls. Koopmans, *Staten van Holland*, 226–227.

47. Violet Barbour, *Capitalism in Amsterdam in the 17th Century* (Baltimore: Johns Hopkins University Press, 1950), 83.

48. Sidney Homer, *A History of Interest Rates* (New Brunswick: Rutgers University Press, 1977), 175; P. Blok, "Stadsfinancien onder de Republiek," in *Verslagen en Mededelingen van de Koninklijke Academie van Wetenschappen*, Lett. V-2 (1917), 293. Temple, *Observations*, 252, estimated that 65,500 rentiers had invested funds in the Dutch state in the 1660s.

49. De Muinck, *Een regentenhuishouding*, 22. On Johan van der Veken, see Kernkamp, "Johan van der Veken," 24; W. E. van Dam van Isselt, "De geldmiddelen onzer Republiek voor den veldtocht van 1599," in *Bijdragen voor Vaderlandsche Geschiedenis en Oudheidkunde*, V-2 (1920), 79.

50. Maland, *Europe at War*, 169, 176.

51. Houtzager, *Hollands lijf-en losrenteleningen*, 140; see also Van Dijk, "De geldelijke druk der Delftsche burgerij." As for bargaining in financial matters, the industrial cities Leiden and Haarlem were always relatively weak. See also Tracy, *A Financial Revolution*, 127. Hibben, *Gouda in Revolt*, 189, 213: Gouda had a strong tradition of particularism and had refused to contribute to loans in the 1570s and 1580s. The Estates of Holland virtually had to buy the city's loyalty.

52. Amsterdam had only Schiedam at its side, Delft joining later when the pensionary suggested that Amsterdam had to subject itself to the majority (outvoting). Geyl, *The Netherlands in the Seventeenth Century*, 165. Hibben, *Gouda in Revolt*, 142.

53. Charles Tilly, *Coercion, Capital, and European States, A.D. 990–1990* (Cambridge, Mass.: Blackwell, 1990), 17.

54. Quoted by John J. Murray, *Amsterdam in the Age of Rembrandt* (Norman: University of Oklahoma Press, 1967), 20. The costs were almost 8 million guilders: Koenen, *De geschiedenis der finantien van Amsterdam*, 24.

55. See Charles Tilly, *Big Structures, Large Processes, Huge Comparisons* (New York: Russell Sage Foundation, 1984), 141.

11

Voracious States
and Obstructing Cities:
An Aspect of State Formation
in Preindustrial Europe

WIM P. BLOCKMANS

AROUND THE MIDDLE of the fourteenth century, Emperor Charles IV developed broad views on the economic possibilities of his huge territorial possessions. His *Hausmacht* (personal domain) extended from Luxembourg to Bohemia. So he launched the idea of an alternative trade route between Venice and Bruges, between the Adriatic and the North Sea. With a clear intention to stimulate trade in his territories, he tried to persuade the Venetians to leave the perilous and lengthy sea route around Italy and Iberia and over the risky Bay of Biscay. Instead of the dangers of pirates and storms, he offered the security of imperial roads and waterways through his capital, Prague, along the Elbe to Hamburg and from there on the regular sea route to Bruges. The Venetians did not directly reject the idea: The supply of metals from Bohemia and southern Germany was of real importance to them, and for such high-value products—as well as for wool, linen, and cloth—transport by land had advantages. However, the emperor underestimated the distance from Hamburg to Bruges and seemed too optimistic about the security of the roads and the weight of tolls within his empire. Venetians continued to send their galleys through the Strait of Gibraltar.[1]

The emperor's curious proposal illustrates the tensions between trade and territory, cities and monarchs. Monarchs regularly strived for total control of a territory from their administrative center. Cities, on the other hand, reckoned with profits, cared little about borders, and preferred easy communication lines along coasts and rivers.[2] I shall try to draw some comparative lines, linking the functions of cities within economic systems to their powers

218

within states. I shall concentrate on roughly the fourteenth to sixteenth centuries, during which important shifts in the economic cores occurred while the process of state formation accelerated dramatically. (See Figure 11.1.)

First, the weight of the urban phenomenon must be established. The contributors to this volume have given population figures, numbers of cities per category, and indications about the spread of cities in territories. The best overall computation of these parameters of urbanization seems to be the *urban potential* calculated by Jan De Vries for 1500 to 1800.[3] For the 154 European cities of at least 10,000 inhabitants in 1500, his measure accounts for the population size, the proximity of other large cities, and the ease of traveling between them. Evidently, one may wish to take into account the capital flows and the per capita purchasing power as well, but since these data are not as widely available as those De Vries has used, his urban potential values seem to offer the best global parameter of urbanization. (See Maps 11.1, 11.2, and 11.3.)

The isolines—lines circumscribing zones with particular levels of urban potential—show three distinct zones of high values around 1500:

- the Po Valley, with Venice, Milan, and Genoa as the main centers;
- the southern Netherlands, with Bruges, Ghent, and Antwerp as the centers and Dordrecht and Tournai as the extremes; and
- Naples and its direct surroundings.

In these three zones, relative urban potential values are at least 80 percent of the highest value at that moment, scored by Venice. The distance to the next level is clear-cut: above 50 percent in the area around Paris and at least 50 percent in an area encompassing the Netherlands, the lower Rhineland, northern France, and southeast England, as well as in the lower Rhône Valley, the Ligurian coast, and the Rome-Naples-Palermo triangle. The 40 percent isoline includes the Catalan, Atlantic, and North Sea coasts and the city corridors of southern Germany and southern France. An urban potential lower than 30 percent is found in Castile, Portugal, Celtic Britain, Scandinavia, and eastern Europe.

At first glance, it appears that early, large consolidated states grew in areas with a low urban potential: the German Empire and England in the twelfth and thirteenth centuries and later on France, Castile, Portugal, Denmark, Poland, and Hungary. On the other hand, solid territorial states, later incorporated in larger, "national" structures, developed in highly urbanized zones: Italy; the Low Countries; the German northern, western, and southern periphery; southern France; and Catalonia. The evolution requires a more elaborate explanation, however: The empire of the fifteenth century was more urbanized but politically weaker than it was in the twelfth, yet its relatively low urban potential, as compared with Italy and western Europe,

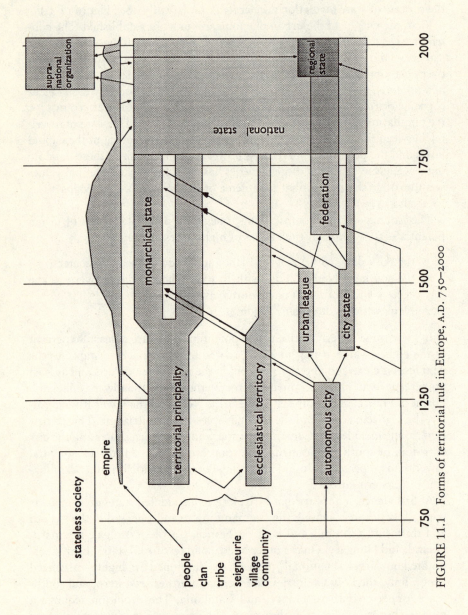

FIGURE 11.1   Forms of territorial rule in Europe, A.D. 750–2000

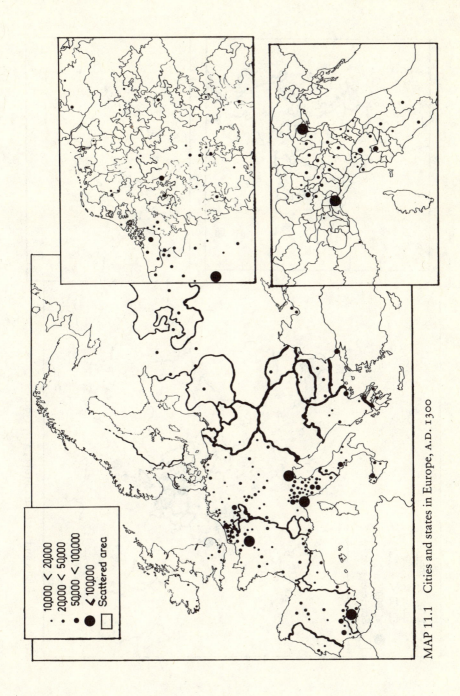

MAP 11.1   Cities and states in Europe, A.D. 1300

10,000 < 20,000
20,000 < 50,000
50,000 < 100,000
< 100,000
Scattered area

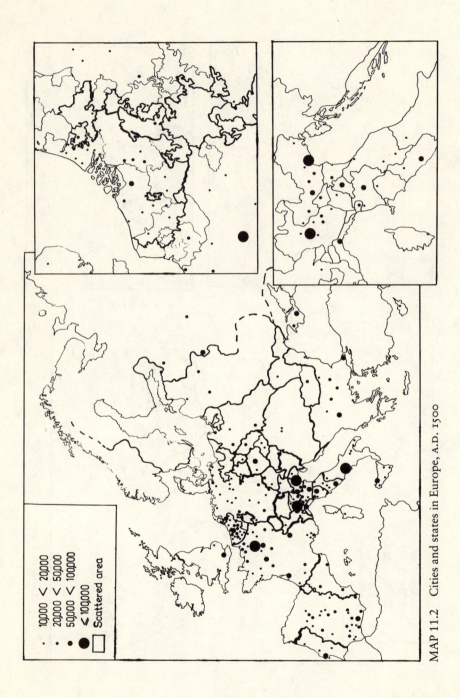

MAP 11.2   Cities and states in Europe, A.D. 1500

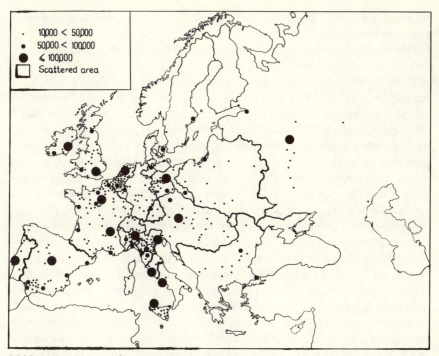

MAP 11.3   Cities and states in Europe, A.D. 1750

did not directly lead to a strong "national" state in 1500. Moreover, the Polish state virtually lost its power toward 1600 despite a very low urbanization.[4] And even the dynastic unity of Spain and France should not obscure
the relatively low levels of real integration and centralization of state functions there.[5] We therefore must look more closely at the relations between
urban potential and other power formations, including the dimension of
change.

The level of urbanization calculated for the period around 1500 does not
reflect the chronology of the development of rivaling power structures
within particular regions. One may expect that the early acquisition of a
power base continued to influence the subsequent process. Since urbanization spread over Europe from south to north and from west to east, the soci-
etal complex in which it took place differed. In northern Italy, the urban
growth from the tenth century onward was strongly influenced by the survival of late Roman power structures, by the close links to the more progressive areas in the eastern Mediterranean, and by the absence, in the long term,
of a real sovereign authority. In southern France and the southern Netherlands, urban growth arose in the eleventh century in a context of multiple
but discontinuous territorial monarchies. Both regions displayed, albeit in

different measures, favorable circumstances for the development of relatively powerful cities.

Obviously, the primary reason for this growth lay in macroeconomic conditions, including a favorable geographic site and easy communications—especially the location along coasts and navigable rivers and the connection to important markets. The expression of this demographic and economic strength in terms of political power depended on the cities' relations with the other contenders. In Italy after the thirteenth century, only economically expanding cities augmented their political power; in the Low Countries, complex temporary coalitions with territorial princes or kings enabled the cities to ward off intrusions of noble or ecclesiastical feudal lords. The status the early urban communities tended to achieve was, in fact, the same as that of the era's feudal lords: the power to exercise public rights, such as minting, rendering justice, regulating the public life, and securing peace.[6]

As long as the concentration of capital was low in a weakly urbanized society, this feudal model prevailed. The capital accumulated in the cities was welcomed by emerging territorial princes as an additional resource in their ongoing competition with other feudal lords. As long as the young cities did not challenge the prince's power in the same measure as his feudal rivals did, an objective community of interests existed between cities and princes. Their bargaining produced a privileged status on one side and resources on the other. If a city was rapidly expanding and facing a prince and a landed nobility who dispensed only limited resources, the city might well extend its privileges to a level of quasi autonomy. This meant far-reaching powers in jurisdiction, administration, foreign trade and all related regulations and protection, coinage, provisions for regional production and markets, and even military organization. The main commercial metropoles of the later Middle Ages and early modern period, in particular, attained broad privileges of this type thanks to their own human and economic resources and the limits of those at the disposal of the princes.

These first observations lead to a provisional conclusion: There were at least two stages in medieval state formation. From the eleventh to the thirteenth centuries, the driving force was purely feudal. Successful enterprises such as the Norman Conquest of England were effectuated by feudal armies that were better organized, better equipped, larger, or simply more fortunate than those of their opponents. Legitimation of a conquest was primarily based in hereditary or feudal rights, and the effectivity and consolidation of a new authority greatly depended on the pattern of vassalage bounds linking regional powers to the crown.

An alternative to English-style conquest was the centralization of feudal power, which Norbert Elias and Jan Dhondt have both described brilliantly on the basis of northern French experience.[7] Undeniably, the feudal ethic remained one of the driving forces behind the process of state formation through the centuries. Land being the main basis of feudal power and conquest the main source of honor, the European nobles believed their primary mission was to follow their suzerains to the hopefully victorious and thus rewarding wars. Warfare and conquest were, in this stage, still considered as the private prerogatives of kings and their vassals. Booty was to be redistributed among the warriors, and prisoners were to be ransomed for the private advantage of skillful knights. The land was inherited, divided, and united according to the procedures of private law. So dynastic unions arose between very distant and completely segmented territories, such as Anjou and Naples, Naples and Provence, Aragon and Naples, Bavaria and Holland, Burgundy and Flanders, Habsburg and the Low Countries, and the Low Countries and Spain. In the strategies of the rulers, any acquisition meant expansion and new resources and possibilities.

However, a second stage of state formation can be distinguished during the fourteenth to sixteenth centuries, in which more than mechanisms within the ruling class were at stake. Bottom-up movements gained their own momentum and contributed to the outcome of the struggle for power. By 1300, the overall population and that of cities in particular had grown considerably in all parts of Europe. However, cities had become a major economic and political factor only in some areas of high urban density, identified by Jan De Vries as mentioned earlier. In weakly urbanized areas, such as central and eastern Europe, central Spain, central France, Celtic Britain, and Scandinavia, feudal patterns remained vigorous. Elsewhere, the monetarization of the economy reduced, at least in relative terms, landed aristocracy's share in the "national income," and it introduced the citizens as a new power. Various possibilities were opened. Initially, population growth and the commercialization of the economy simply produced more collective wealth, of which the kings and other princes took their share in the form of rising and new income from tolls, mintage, justice, and the granting of privileges. As a further step, the princes discovered they could raise more money through new forms of taxation and by loans from foreign merchants. In this way, for example, King Edward I and King Edward III of England managed to finance their great military operations against Wales and France, respectively.[8] In other words, the commercialization of the economy, concentrated in the cities, provided new monetary means to princes of territories where these developments occurred at a significant scale.

The relations between burghers and princes were not always idyllic, however. Indeed, the two groups had fundamentally different aims. While princes dreamt of territorial expansion, of which the Hundred Years' War and the Spanish Reconquista are typical examples, burghers sought, at first, to accumulate movable capital. Both tended toward unlimited expansion, and thus, they inevitably collided over certain issues, such as the nonrefunding of loans, the blockade of trade routes, the disruption of markets, the debasement of coinage, or the overtaxation of trade. With their large concentrations of people and capital, cities were able to mobilize considerable armies that challenged the traditional predominance of the heavy cavalry. The tremendous victory of the Flemish urban and peasant militias against the French chivalry at Kortrijk in 1302 symbolized the new power relations.

Clearly, then, the impact of cities on state formation had become decisive in the most urbanized areas of Europe: Whether they strengthened princes or limited them, cities had become a factor that could not be overlooked. I shall now try to systematize the variegated and changing relations between cities and states.

AUTONOMOUS METROPOLES

The most evident and best known case of this early and highly privileged urban development is that of northern and central Italy, described in this volume by Giorgio Chittolini. The absence of really powerful territorial princes, combined with the huge size of the Italian cities, led to their unchallenged and undivided control over substantial hinterlands, measuring thousands of square kilometers. This territorial power secured the cities' absolutely vital supplies of food, water, and raw materials. All large cities lived on long-distance trade and export production. And both activities required control over roads, waterways, and production units, as well as a division of labor between town and countryside under the control of the urban entrepreneurs.[9] The huge nearby market obviously touched the rural economy as a whole quite deeply: Production had to be intensified and differentiated, and commercialization of agriculture bound the peasant to the urban market. Bourgeois investment in specific sectors like cattle-raising or simply in productive land secured the grip of the townspeople over their environment. The interests of the urban citizens were secured on a higher level by the fact that peasants were dependent on the decisions of urban judges in legal disputes. In the same way, the political decisionmaking on fiscal matters and on market and export regulations systematically favored the townsmen over the peasants.

An interesting case of an autonomous city is that of Dubrovnik, especially since its population is estimated at no more than 5,000 to 6,000 toward the end of the fifteenth century. Dubrovnik's position is all the more remarkable because northern Dalmatian cities belonged to the Venetian empire or were temporarily conquered by the Hungarian kingdom. On the other hand, the Ottoman occupation of the Balkans left Dubrovnik's independence untouched: The small city-state simply paid a tribute. Its favorable geographic location is part of the explanation for its success as an autonomous city: It was well protected at the south end of a chain of islands along the eastern coast of the Adriatic and at the outlet of main continental roads that brought products of Serbian and Bosnian mining industries to the sea.

Dubrovnik effectively belonged to Venice's colonies from 1204 until the Hungarian-Croatian occupation of the Dalmatian cities in 1358; during that time, it had thoroughly adopted Venetian institutions. The Hungarian king was satisfied with the recognition of his formal protectorate and the payment of an annual tribute. In practice, Dubrovnik developed its own pragmatic foreign policy, balancing between the competing superpowers of Venice, Genoa, Anjou, Naples, Hungary, and the Ottomans. Thanks to its good relations with the new masters of the Balkans, it managed to expand its trade in the eastern Mediterranean. Thus, the combination of its favorable geographic location, its important trade in metals, and its utility as an intermediary between rivaling powers may explain Dubrovnik's lasting independence, notwithstanding its relatively small population.[10]

On a much smaller scale, the extraordinary development during the thirteenth and fourteenth centuries of Wisby on the isle of Gotland, near Sweden's east coast, was only possible because of the weakness of territorial and feudal powers in that region. Wisby could function as an operational base for the expanding trade of the north Germans because it was free from feudal interferences. When the king of Sweden imposed his authority over the island in the fifteenth century, Wisby's central position was already lost.

In the same vein, as Anders Andrén has shown, German merchants could operate almost freely in most Scandinavian cities where they established their privileged quarters, also until the king imposed all kinds of restrictions on them. The cities of lower Germany had the advantage of being remote from the imperial power bases situated in the south, which generally reduced their dependency on the king or emperor. Until the middle of the fifteenth century, the coastal Hanse cities were fairly successful in resisting the domination of princes in small surrounding territories, and thus they attained broad autonomy. The interior cities, however, felt the weight of local overlords, such as the bishops along the Rhine and neighboring princes; these overlords proved to be much heavier impediments to urban development than those confronting the coastal cities.

One interesting autonomous metropole was Novgorod, which, by the middle of the thirteenth century, had repulsed invasions and expansionist movements by the Tatars, the Swedes, and the Teutonic Knights. It enjoyed a real independence until its annexation in 1478 by the Grand Duchy of Moscow. It had developed close links with the German Hanse, and it hosted one of the Hanse's four principal foreign establishments in its *Peterhof*. Novgorod's population may have reached a peak of 25,000 to 30,000. The urban citizenry controlled a vast rural area in the form of a true city-state, divided in five administrative territories. The city itself was equally divided in five boroughs, each with its own assembly, elders or mayor. Its political annex-

ation implied the closure of the Hanse *Kontor* (agency or store) and thus the
end of a most profitable long-distance trade.[11]

BARGAINING METROPOLES

In some regions, feudal powers played an active role vis-à-vis expanding
trading cities within their territories. A core position in the European economic system gave them such an abundance of resources that the princes and
landed aristocracy had no choice but to grant them extensive autonomy.
One such region was the territory belonging to the crown of Aragon, described in this volume by Fernández Albaladejo. In the interplay between a
vigorous nobility, an expanding monarchy, and an urban network highly involved in overseas trade, cities managed to gradually extend their prerogatives. From the middle of the thirteenth century onward, Barcelona (and
later, other cities as well) obtained self-government, exclusive judicial
powers (especially in trade affairs), monetary and fiscal authority, and even
the right to equip a war fleet. Obviously, these privileges were granted in return for gold, which the kings used for their dynastic purposes. During the
thirteenth and fourteenth centuries, bargaining between the three major
forces enabled all to realize their main goals.[12]

The second region where early and rapidly developing commercial cities
faced powerful feudal lords and princes was that of the southern Low Countries and northern France. Early in the twelfth century, the kings and counts
granted cities privileges securing the freedom and safety of trade. In 1128,
the angry townsmen wanted to dismiss a count of Flanders who violated
these privileges, especially because he had disturbed the peace of the market.
The relative weakness of the counts during the thirteenth and fourteenth
centuries meant that the cities had an opportunity to launch economic policies of their own: They negotiated and made decisions on trade relations,
both long-distance and local, and on monetary standards; they also set up
their own commercial jurisdiction, with authority over native and foreign
merchants.

In the course of the fourteenth century, the largest Flemish towns displayed a tendency to develop city-states, each of them hoping to attain public rights in a section of the county. Their efforts in this direction were
thwarted less by the counts, who had to flee from their territory more than
once, than by their sovereigns—the kings of France who repeatedly intervened with extensive military power. But even this power could not sur-
mount a coalition of the Flemish cities and their dependencies.[13]

It is noteworthy that interurban contacts—mainly concerning the safety of
trade—were organized in merchants' associations (hanses) first and in town
leagues later. Evidently, merchants controlled the city administrations, even
when some measure of participation by the artisans was allowed. The fa-

mous German Hanse was only one of these organizations, and it was, in fact, a federation of earlier regional hanses, several more of which existed in the southern Netherlands during the twelfth and thirteenth centuries. Trade protection was their general purpose. The fact that they disappeared in the Low Countries in the early fourteenth century while others survived in the empire until the seventeenth century is explained by three factors:

1. From 1302 onward, Flemish urban administrations were no longer monopolized by merchants. Newly recognized craftsmen wanted a say in economic affairs; therefore, city aldermen had to deal with artisans, instead of private Hanse associations. In the German cities, the revolts of the artisans came about one century later (1408 in Lübeck) and did not reshuffle the administrations as thoroughly as they had in Flanders. Moreover, the restructuring of the Hanse in 1356 made it an association of cities rather than merchants.

2. In comparison with less urbanized regions, Flanders had seen a steep decline in the power of the nobility, as a consequence of the decreasing traditional rent revenues. At the same time, the commercialization of agriculture was pushed by the bourgeoisie, and the lower impoverished strata of the nobility were incorporated into the local administrations. The problem of banditry on the roads therefore had become less important in Flanders than in the continental regions of the empire and France.

3. A greater density of public officers with a tendency toward creating a monopoly of violence fostered a higher degree of internal pacification in Flanders. Both the decline of the nobility and the buildup of an administrative apparatus were connected with the high level of agricultural commercialization, producing large monetarized surpluses.

Thus, in Flanders, the old protective functions of the hanses had become less urgent, and the lasting protective functions were now in the hands of other types of representative organizations, namely, those operating essentially within territorial borders.

A similar condition of de facto autonomy notwithstanding, the formal recognition of a feudal sovereign was acquired by another commercial metropolis—Danzig. It reached its peak during the sixteenth century, with more than 50,000 inhabitants and a key position in the Baltic exports of grain and wood products.[14] The Danzig town council managed to preserve its powers vis-à-vis the Polish kings, despite several attempts by the kings to dominate the city during the 1560s and 1570s. Typically, Danzig's autonomy concerned exclusive jurisdiction and administration in all maritime affairs, the imposition of its own citizens as brokers in all contacts with foreign merchants, various other economic privileges, and, naturally, self-government. The other trading cities in the lower Vistula basin—Torun and Elblag—equally profited from judicial autonomy vis-à-vis the Polish crown, and they issued their own Prussian mint. All these characteristics of metropolitan autonomy could also be detected in Barcelona and Bruges. As in Aragon and Flanders, ongoing confrontations with the nobility and the sovereign (from the late thirteenth century, the Teutonic Order and from 1466, the king of Poland) stimulated the development of an active representative system with extensive economic, fiscal, and political powers. This system rested mainly on the seven largest trading and industrial cities in the lower Vistula basin, which formed the Prussian quarter within the German Hanse.[15]

The war between the Teutonic Order and the Prussian cities from 1454 to 1466 can be seen in the same context. The ruling patrician councils objected to the economic policy of their overlords. They wanted to levy a new toll on trade the order conducted with Flanders, Holland, and England, apart from and thus in competition with the Hanse. In this conflict, the Prussian cities were not supported by Lübeck or by the Hanse league as a whole because of numerous competing interests and a fear of the reactions of the Danish king and the German princes, who sided with the Teutonic Order. On the other hand, the king of Poland took the side of the Prussians and became their new sovereign. The opposition expressed by Danzig and the other cities in the lower Vistula basin against the order proved extremely successful, for these cities could now bargain for broad privileges with the remote and relatively weak Polish kings, who also opened a large and productive hinterland. Danzig therefore had a much brighter future than Lübeck, which was hampered by neighboring territorial princes and which mainly stuck to its transit trade.[16]

The Vistula towns offer the only fifteenth-century example of a group of commercial centers successfully and durably resisting the pressure of their overlord, albeit a relatively minor one and only with the support of another, neighboring monarch. Depending on changes in the balance of power, bargaining between cities and princes sometimes resulted in near autonomy for the cities. This seems to have been the case in Danzig during the fifteenth and sixteenth centuries and in Barcelona and the Flemish cities in the fourteenth century. In the latter case, the counts simply lacked the military force to stand up to urban militias, and the kings of Aragon had to make far-reaching concessions in order to finance their expansive imperial policies. As soon as the cities became involved in a power struggle with the landed nobility and the prince, a system of negotiations was established. Thus, claims and conflicts that previously might have sparked wars could now be discussed in a legitimate forum. This, again, is an indication of a higher level of development, of civilization. In the lands of the crown of Aragon, the Cortes created the earliest large representative system based on constitutional texts and standing executive committees (*diputaciones del general*). In the Low Countries, the large cities developed quasi-permanent deputations in each of the most urbanized principalities. These shared wide powers with the princes and operated on their own behalf within and outside their borders, especially in matters concerning international trade.

A particularly interesting area is southern France. The autonomous commercial city republics flourishing there in the thirteenth century were all subjugated to the territorial princes and finally to the king of France. Although the city of Toulouse saw its communal autonomy formally broken by the so-called crusade against the Albigensians in the late thirteenth century, the kings of France down to Louis XIV nonetheless respected the administrative independence of the city's *capitoules,* the eight governors elected yearly. Moreover, the king's *taille* (property tax) was not applicable in Toulouse. This city, which counted 35,000 to 40,000 inhabitants just before the Black Death and more than 50,000 at the end of the fifteenth century, even resisted the interference in municipal elections by both the royal *sénéchal* and the *parlement.* Members of the latter court belonged to the bourgeois elite, which upheld a strong tradition of municipal republicanism through feasts, royal entries, and the ornamentation of public buildings, among other things. Only after 1560 or so did royal taxation put such heavy pressure on the city that the municipal autonomy became more and more of an empty shell.[17]

The county of Provence presents a somewhat more complicated picture. Its largest and most commercial city was Marseilles; Aix was the administrative capital. The latter had some 15,000 inhabitants by 1320, and Marseilles probably had 25,000 at the peak of its commercial activity in the late thirteenth century. This may explain the rivalry between the two cities and Marseilles's open conflict with all the other cities of Provence when these formed a *ligue* (league) in 1383 to oppose the succession to the throne by a second branch of the house of Anjou, closely related to the king of France. Marseilles was more oriented to the sea than to its hinterland and preferred a distant link with the dynasty reigning in Naples rather than the closer grasp of a native lord. The second half of the fourteenth century was marked by steady warfare in the region, in which rivaling dynasties, including that of Pope Clement VII in Avignon, and private warlords devastated the country. In response, the cities and the estates organized a defense system, financed by a special levy on property administered by officers designated by the estates. In 1359, they even nominated a council, representing the three estates, to control the government of the sénéchal.

Only when dynastic struggles grew acute did the cities manage to form a defensive union. But its effect was limited by the abstention of Marseilles and by the interference of mighty neighboring princes. Moreover, the clergy and especially the barons and nobles remained powerful, controlling many villages and strategic roads from their own strongholds. By the end of the fourteenth century, the rivalry between the dynasty and the cities over dynastic succession had confirmed the local autonomy of the cities. However, internal divisions prevented the cities from controlling the region as a whole.[18]

The case of Marseilles is typical of a flourishing commercial city that obtained its autonomy by buying off various authorities claiming overlordship during the early thirteenth century. Its development had profited greatly from the Crusades and the pilgrimages to the Holy Land. It began competing with Genoa and established a *fondouc* (entrepôt) in Acre by 1190, which became the main stronghold for its Levantine trade, and its merchants enjoyed privileges in several Sicilian and North African ports. In 1246, when he became the count of Provence, Charles of Anjou, brother of King Louis of France and future king of Naples and Sicily, met fierce opposition from Marseilles, which claimed to be depending only on the German emperor—a very distant ruler, indeed. Charles's military pressure ultimately forced the cities of Provence to surrender; Marseilles capitulated in 1257, losing all of its financial and administrative autonomy.

The union with the Kingdom of Naples and that of Sicily (1268–1282) provided some economic opportunities for Marseilles, by facilitating its grain trade with southern Italy, by securing routes, by negotiating treaties with north Italian competitors, and by employing its vast fleet. Charles even left intact Marseilles's own mint. On the other hand, he imposed his authority as an arbiter in the conflicts between Marseilles and its eternal rival, Montpellier, showing the cities' incapacity to resolve their problems themselves.

The economic advantages could not disguise the fact that Angevin policies fatally disrupted the commercial opportunities of the Angevins' ports in Provence. Steady warfare caused great commercial damages by piracy and loss of regular relations throughout the fourteenth century. This period brought absolute economic decline in Marseilles, even though its fleet and ship-building industry had found new work in the military service of their ruler. The loss of Marseilles's Levantine colony in 1291 and the decline of the Champagne fairs were serious blows for Marseilles's trade. And the loss of its autonomy hampered its citizens in their efforts to compete with northern Italy. They found their salvation in military operations, which only helped to ruin their trade. When King Louis XI became the count of Provence in 1481, he inaugurated a period in which cities were incorporated into the kingdom; consequently, no room was left for independent cities. Their demographic and commercial decline had ultimately made them incapable of any real resistance.[19]

It is precisely because mighty cities faced princes with real but not overwhelming power and because both cities and princes were threatened by a third force—the nobility in Aragon, the king of France in Flanders, surrounding princes in Provence and Brabant—that territorial representative systems could develop. All forces had to compromise since none of them outweighed the others. In northern and central Italy, however, the absence of princely power and the fusion of the landed nobility with the urban commercial and entrepreneurial elites prevented the development of similar forms of popular representation. Instead, these areas witnessed the rise of forms of domination, such as patronage, by the strongest cities. Their elites became increasingly interested in rural rents and thus lost their original commercial orientation. If the domination by a metropolis did not further the participation of weaker entities, the absence of a binding territorial element, especially a monarchy, had the effect of perpetuating loose organizations without effective means, such as regional and general meetings of the German Hanse. As a consequence, these organizations gradually lost influence, and the assemblies of estates called by territorial princes and dominated by the landed interests grew more powerful.[20]

Thus far, two paths of urban development can be distinguished: the *autonomous metropoles,* either remote from effective princely and feudal powers or incorporating them, and the *bargaining metropoles,* where the cities faced the competition of feudal and monarchical powers and developed structures of power-sharing. The early commercial cities had to provide a number of essential arrangements for their trade and industry—arrangements that the surrounding feudal society could not and would not provide. Fundamentally, that society remained hostile to the cities and their activities, which therefore needed protection.[21] The security of roads, the quick and reliable settlement of disputes between sellers and buyers, the supervision of exchange values, the freedom from tolls and arbitrary seizure—these fundamental preconditions for any regular trade had to be created by the merchants themselves since no other authority was competent and willing to do so. What later became the fields of interstate diplomatic relations—royal coinage prerogatives and monarchical jurisdictions—were primarily shaped by merchants' networks at a time when no prince had the ability or the vision to meet these typically urban needs.

In highly urbanized and commercialized regions, the private and municipal organizations therefore created networks encompassing various powers that centralizing monarchical states would later claim as part of their own exclusive rights. But since private and municipal organizations developed these networks centuries before princes and states were in a position to, those organizations had vested interests in defending them against intruders. Obviously, state agents were not always more expert in commercial and monetary techniques than townsmen; nor were they immune to influence. What they *could* offer individuals seeking justice was a greater independence vis-à-vis local interests than most aldermen could afford. This explains why high courts of justice sponsored by the state became so successful in the fifteenth and sixteenth centuries. The Great Council of Mechlin, for example, issued a yearly average of just 39 final sentences in 1500–1504 but 174 in 1546–1550.[22]

SMALLER BARGAINING NETWORKS

Comparable evolutions can also be observed in regions that had much smaller cities and a lower urban percentage in total population and that were situated inland—in other words, regions that were not equipped to become cores of economic systems. Again, all depended on the balance of power. From the thirteenth to the early fifteenth centuries, the king and the most economically and politically important cities in the southern part of the German Empire enjoyed a relationship characterized by mutual gifts and favors, each side being guided by its own direct interests. Financial elites in growing centers like Frankfurt and Nuremberg greatly profited from a direct link with the royal court, to which they evidently lent their services.[23] On the other hand, the impact of feudal elements was still very strong, urban density was relatively low, urban interests were diverse, and no one city was so much larger than the others that it naturally imposed its leadership. The repeated attempts of the cities in the south (Swabia), the Rhineland, Alsace, and Oberlausitz to form urban leagues can be compared with the earlier merchants' and cities' hanses, insofar as they tried to establish the necessary conditions for the development of their trade. Most basically, they had to fight the knightly associations known by noble names, such as the Lions, Saint George, or Saint William; some of these were, in fact, simply predatory groups, and others were antiurban leagues of princes and nobles.[24]

In periods of acute financial need, such as 1384–1388, the king made concessions to the cities, granting them, for instance, the supervision of coinage. The Rhineland and Swabian leagues tended to develop regular representative and fiscal systems and tried to set up efficient pacification mechanisms to deal with the many conflicts among cities and between cities and neighboring feudal lords. Since only Ulm and Nuremberg controlled important territories, the security of the land routes depended greatly on the lords. The repeated initiatives to unite dozens of cities resulted, for the most part, in local military successes. The leagues' organization remained weak and unstable because of divergent interests, because of the variability of possible or necessary coalitions with territorial lords, princes, or the king, and because of the long distances between cities.[25] In Swabia, for example, league members were scattered over 300 kilometers from north to south and 240 kilometers from west to east.

Although cities in the empire—apart from those belonging to the Hanse—failed to set up a lasting organization of their own and although efforts in this direction met with fierce feudal repression in 1388 and 1389 and in the late 1440s, their repeated unions nevertheless put them in a position to extract some momentous advantages from weakened princes. In Peter Blickle's words: "A reciprocal dependency of economic and political power causes the political control span of urban communities to extend when their economy is strong and their overlord politically weak."[26]

This type of power balance between the crown, the nobility, and the towns was far from exceptional in medieval Europe. Even in regions where cities were relatively small, they could still attain a substantial level of autonomy and even a real grip on state power if the monarchy was vulnerable and the coalitions between social classes were unstable. The central European monarchies all depended on election by some kind of popular representation. In Poland, for example, the largest cities participated in the king's elections from 1375 to 1506.[27] In Bohemia, this was the case during the 1420s and 1430s, and in Hungary, it was the practice from 1457 to 1508.[28] When the throne was vacant and when the regional nobility needed the support of the cities, these cities took the opportunity to share power and obtain commercial and judicial privileges in return for their political loyalty. In Poland, such a situation had already existed in the period 1285–1311 and again in the second half of the fourteenth century, which saw the marked economic growth of Cracow, Lwów and their satellites as centers of transit trade between western Europe and the Black Sea region. The crown needed the coalition and subsidies of these cities to face the virulent chivalry and external competitors. The cities therefore subscribed to international treaties and were consulted in matters of tolls and coinage.[29]

A further case of real power-sharing by a relatively small urban network is offered by Piedmont in the late fifteenth and early sixteenth centuries. The urban potential as calculated by De Vries was rather weak—30 to 40 percent in 1500—and the capital, Turin, was no more than a medium-sized city. The feudal magnates certainly held most of the wealth in the country. However, regencies and reigns of dukes who were minors or otherwise vulnerable gave the cities' elites an opportunity to impose their *capitoli*, ranging over the whole field of administration, public law, and trade regulations. Here, however, it was the increasing pressure by the mighty neighbors France, Milan, and Switzerland that weakened the monarchy so much that it could not dispense with the support of the Piedmontese upper classes, including those of the communes. Significantly, between 1515 and 1517, the Piedmontese successfully opposed the creation of a permanent army, fearing that the duke might use it against them instead of against foreign enemies. The consequence of this decision was soon felt in the French occupation of the duchy.[30]

A similar power balance between the crown, the nobility, and the cities existed in France. During the Hundred Years' War, roughly between 1340 and 1440, the crown badly needed the cities' support. The lasting disability of King Charles VI and internal wars among the great dukes of the realm further weakened the monarchy. During that period and in the following reign, which were characterized by reconstruction and great territorial expansion (especially under Louis XI), the emancipation of the cities progressed markedly. They became autonomous legal bodies that elected their own aldermen (*échevinage*) and had general assemblies of notables where fiscal and security matters were discussed. The same body also sent representatives of the city to the assemblies of estates. It was only from 1520 to 1550 onward that the fiscal pressure of the state increased so much that it pushed the cities into heavy debt. As Bernard Chevalier noted: "The requirements of the state are a major cause [of debt] because the equilibrium between the state and the cities had been disrupted."

The way to heavy urban debt had been paved since about 1450, when the "gens de robe," civil servants depending on the king, took half to three-quarters of the aldermen's seats in Paris. Unlike their Italian counterparts, the French had to keep close contact with the royal court, and only when financial matters had to be dealt with did merchants still have a prominent role to play. The chicanery of King Louis XI and King Charles VIII regarding the fairs of Lyons displayed the dangers of royal intervention in economic life. In 1462, Lyons was given a monopoly that forbade Frenchmen and foreign merchants residing in France to visit competing fairs in Geneva. However, a political alliance with the duke of Savoy caused the king to withdraw his favors to Lyons in 1466. The following year, the Lyonese bought their monopoly back by giving the king two hundred harnesses. Then, in 1471, the king forbade the importation of spices over land to Lyons, but he withdrew this order in 1476. His successor subsequently reaffirmed the exclusive rights of the ports for spice importation and simply forbade any fairs at Lyons in 1484 (though he restored two of the four fairs three years later).

Obviously, relations between the main commercial cities of the realm and the kings were vulnerable to competition and priorities posed by international relations. For the cities, the lack of security and the high price of the bargains they struck surely damaged trade.[31]

Harry Miskimin insists on the centralizing effects of the wars: "The needs of the army became more urgent as the Hundred Years' War lasted, but while the dangers and the needs increased, the quantity of the disposable minting metal diminished. … The need for funds was so urgent that it often overruled the legitimate desire to limit the arbitrary power of the crown."[32] Although this statement is surely lucid and based on solid data, one should not overrate the monetary mechanism since it was partly counterbalanced by the greater political influence the cities could acquire in a period of weakened monarchy. It is significant indeed that commercial metropoles all over Europe claimed control over coinage because it constituted the standard of exchange for their trade, which they tried to keep intact by preventing the princes from manipulating it as a simple source of revenue. The secular stability of the florin, the ducat, and the lira clearly indicates the wisdom of this policy, in contrast to the ups and downs of the franc, the ecu, and the heaume.

SUBORDINATION OF TOWNS

What caused this shift in the relationship between monarchies and towns? In the case of France, it is clear that the monarchy controlled a much larger territory in 1550 than it did in 1400. But even when the number of inhabitants increased, most French cities saw their revenues stagnating or even decreasing after 1550. Under these conditions, they found it hard to defend their autonomy by force, particularly since military techniques had given the advantage to well-trained regular armies. On the other side, state dynamics were, in the first place, determined by external warfare. Since the Italian wars and the long-lasting confrontation with the Habsburg Empire, the French state found itself in a self-perpetuating escalation of military expenditure.[33] Therefore, it had to press the cities and peasants to sharply increase taxation. This, of course, led to higher internal tensions, and the civil wars of the late sixteenth century added much to the existing financial crisis of the cities.

The result was a new relation between the crown and the cities in which the latter lost most of their autonomy and were brought under the control of royal officers and courts. Notorious demonstrations of the new monarchical presence included Emperor Charles V's ostentatious abasements of rebellious cities like Rome in 1527 and Ghent in 1540. An urban elite, however, saw the profits to be derived from playing the game under submission to the crown: The sale of offices, tax privileges, and the rents of public debts were the cornerstones of their mutual interest.

In addition to the autonomous cities and those that bargained with princes and nobility for some degree of freedom, there were also subordinated towns—a frequent outcome of the ongoing power struggle. In such cities, the monarchies inevitably proved supreme in the long run, a direct result of economies of scale that allowed them the use of superior military techniques and greater numbers of troops. The victorious monarch might have been the prince of an expanding territory or an external conqueror or heir. The presence of a high urban potential, implying a high capital concentration, facilitated the emergence of strong centralized monarchical states. I will now consider the dynamic of states as such.

As organizations, states belonged to larger systems in which competition was an essential feature. Because the ruling class still shared largely feudal ethics and perhaps even belonged to the feudal aristocracy, states were steered toward international competition by their rulers. The continuous competition provoked an unlimited need, which always tended to overexpansion, exceeding the financial capacities of the subjects of each state. The early modern kings played a role in this process. They successfully claimed the exclusive prerogative of conducting foreign relations, so their vision of the state had a real impact. That vision can rather simply be described as seeking expansion for all purposes and by all means, at least to prevent rivals from strengthening their positions. Secondarily, there was a general goal of attaining natural borders and coherent territorial units.

The simple visions of the monarchs helped shape the destiny of states, even if structural possibilities often got in the way. The monarchs' exclusive prerogatives in foreign relations, which generated the recurring pressure on state budgets, remained widely accepted or could at least be imposed successfully. Peter Moraw describes Emperor Charles IV's policy as "finally following the dynastic logic or even a familial or personal impetus; the standard of his action was profit for the dynasty."[34] Another remarkable figure is Charles the Bold, the duke of Burgundy. Milanese ambassadors observed his reactions after his terrible defeat by the Swiss in 1476: "He is outrageous because these Swiss peasants had obtained the honour of victory and were able to diminish His Excellency's honour by the cowardice of his men. He says he will regain his reputation by dying in battle or by emerging from it with an even greater power than before."[35]

Not all monarchs had the same character, but the European state system always provided some of this type, and their kind of behavior predominated. It triggered reactions even among such peaceful people as the Swiss, who felt that Charles the Bold's occupation of Alsace and Lotharingia threatened their own freedom. Evidently, representative assemblies repeatedly tried to limit the monarch's powers in declaring war, but the job was made difficult by the reciprocal faits accomplis on the field. Ultimately, subjects had little choice when the wars were legitimated as defensive, especially when the attacks could be felt. It then became difficult to refuse *post factum* the subsidies necessary to conduct war, especially when the monarchs had already contracted loans that would weigh on urban budgets in any case.[36]

The suffocating effects of monarchical warfare on the urban economy are stressed by all the authors in this volume. The kings of Aragon ruined their flourishing cities in the fifteenth century, not least of all by debasing the coinage for fiscal purposes.[37] And as Miskimin writes regarding France during the Hundred Years' War:

> The war begins by bringing into circulation precious metals and exhausts the reserves. Then it requires ever higher amounts as the supply diminishes. Looking for funds by all possible means, especially in the fifteenth century the French crown takes measures aiming to limit gifts to the papacy, to reduce and to control trade, to bring industry into the state's service and even to appropriate private mines with a view to exploiting the precious metals.[38]

The Spanish-French wars ruined the economy of both states, especially hurting Antwerp through the 1557 suspension of payments on state debts. [39]

After the middle of the sixteenth century, both Castilian and French cities were so suffocated by state taxation that their freedom of action disappeared under the pressure. Subordinated cities typically lost their autonomy and power in the areas that the state claimed, such as diplomatic relations, territorial legislation, jurisdiction, and administration. Urban elites, nominated by the crown, were bought off by personal privileges and advantages.[40]

Poland was an exception. Its skilled ruler, King Sigismund Augustus (the last of the Jagiellonians), was not able to get access to urban financiers. Furthermore, Poland's financial center, Danzig, remained beyond the king's sphere of influence, and it successfully opposed efforts toward administrative centralization.[41] This case can be generalized in the sense that the integration of territories with a tradition of urban autonomy into states with a low urban potential did not automatically lead to the abolition of all the cities' prerogatives. In some cases, their institutions were much too strong, and their capital accumulation was too important. The monarchs therefore had to proceed carefully vis-à-vis the urban peripheries. Thus, Prussia was able to keep its own coinage, taxation, trade, and judicial privileges after its incorporation into Poland in 1466. The king also considerably extended the territorial possessions of Danzig, Elblag, and Torun and opened all of Poland to Prussian merchants. Even when later kings tried to impose their rule in the 1560s and 1570s, their attempts were rebuffed.[42]

Similarly, Aragon preserved the essentials of its constitutional state organization, even under Ferdinand the Catholic.[43] The French and Spanish occupations reduced the influence of the Piedmontese parliament, but they did not eliminate it, and the local elites retained part of the advantages and revenues that accrued during the occupations. The Habsburg domination of Milan, Florence, and Naples left an even larger measure of autonomy to the former "city-states."[44] In the same vein, the Burgundy and Habsburg dynasties had to take seriously the wishes of the cities of Flanders, Brabant, and Holland to avoid paying the high price of revolt. But in any event, the cities had to accept (albeit only after repeated violence in the largest cities) severe restrictions in their administrative, judicial, and economic powers, especially insofar as they extended beyond city walls, and they had to pay steadily increasing taxes.[45]

In the second half of the fifteenth century, the cities of the German Hanse were all pushed to pay higher military and protection costs, due to the increased pressure of surrounding princes. Warfare ruined cities like Dortmund and Braunschweig, which had to resist the attacks of the duke of Braunschweig-Lüneburg. The margrave of Brandenburg forced Berlin and Frankfurt an der Oder to submit and retreat from the Hanse, a measure imposed on all towns of the Altmark in 1488.[46] The aggression of the princes put the towns along the Baltic coast in a defensive position. Much depended on the coalitions both sides were able to mobilize, but in general, the power of the cities stagnated while that of the princes increased. As an example, although the new tolls created by the duke of Mecklemburg in 1476 were abolished as a result of fierce opposition from the most concerned Hanseatic towns, Stralsund and Rostock, in 1498, the duke of Pomerania increased the toll tariffs, tried a blockade of the cities, and grabbed the so-called strand right on wrecked goods. Both princes set up an export trade to the Netherlands in grain and wood, in competition with the Hanse cities.

Urban jurisdiction, coinage, beer taxes, feudal duties on land acquired by burghers—in all these standard matters, the ambitions of state-building dukes conflicted with the long-established practices of the urban bourgeoisie. The counts of Oldenburg and Schleswig-Holstein and the related kings of Denmark had a long series of conflicts with Lübeck and Hamburg as a consequence of their rival claims on the control of land, waterways, and resources. In 1490, the king launched a blockade against the Hanse, in 1510–1512 a full-fledged war. The cities' response lacked continuity and cohesion: A series of urban leagues of widely different composition and duration offered ad hoc resistance but revealed, in the long run, the Hanse's loss of power. The lack of unity also caused the severe subjugation of Rostock by a coalition of princes in 1489. Nevertheless, the dukes of Mecklemburg and Pomerania could never treat the subjugated Hanseatic coastal cities in the same way as they did the inland ones. Although the dukes severely restricted the privileges of these cities, they had to handle them with care.[47]

The general pattern of the time, then, was one of economic sluggishness and even regression in most cities, as a consequence of the shifts in the European economic system. Growing cities in Castile, Brabant, Holland, England, and Prussia would, in their turn, clash with their monarchs later in the sixteenth and seventeenth centuries. But growing technical efficiency in public administration, jurisdiction, and warfare, as well as the expansion of their territories and resources, helped the monarchs to subordinate the major cities that their predecessors had had to respect. The instability and lack of cohesion and solidarity in the interurban organizations helped the monarchs considerably. The cities' divisiveness appears to be closely linked to their divergent interests, following from different political and economic contexts that correlate strongly with distances. It is obvious the transition from a bargaining relationship to one of submission more often than not entailed phases of physical violence, revolt, and repression.

DEPENDENT TOWNS

The very weakness of cities in eastern Europe shaped state formation by making the extraction of means for coercion and warfare more costly, as Charles Tilly points out.[48] Toward the end of the fifteenth century, Hungarian towns had to face increasing attacks on their privileges by the nobility.

Together with the degrading living conditions of the peasants, this led to a decrease in the urban population. Most of the 150 Hungarian towns were very small and belonged to the king. Their market functions were mainly interior: It took a merchant or peasant one or two days to reach the nearest marketplace.[49] In Poland during the sixteenth century, as Antoni Maczak states, "the sheer size of the country, together with its loose network of communications and low density of towns, proved advantageous to the upper and wealthier sections of the nobility."[50] In his contribution to this volume, Andrzej Wyrobisz makes it clear that most Polish towns were dominated by local nobles. Clearly, conditions in predominantly rural regions, where the most important form of capital—the land—was scattered and where communication was slow and difficult, were not suited to a lasting urban autonomy. Secondary as it was, the role the towns may have played on the political scene of these countries in earlier periods had been possible only as long as the level of organization in the nobility and the monarchy was still very low. In the sixteenth century, the magnates fully grasped the advantages of refeudalization. Since they were materially able to impose their domination directly, they did not worry about state structures. Evidently, this became a major weakness in terms of interstate competition. Under these conditions, small, dependent cities no longer wielded any influence on the process of state formation. And princes in these regions could not expect any elasticity in the fiscal returns of small cities or the countryside, which made them vulnerable competitors in the state system.

AIMS AND MEANS OF POWER

I have reviewed the evolution of the relations between cities and states as the product of changing relative power positions. For the towns, these mainly involved their population figures; their economic and financial prosperity; their communication facilities; their prerogatives in administrative, economic, fiscal, and judicial matters; and their military force. For the monarchies, the continuity and skills of the rulers mattered, and the dimensions, cohesion, and communication facilities of their territories, together with the available resources and the pressure of neighboring competitors, weighed heavily on their destiny. In a pattern of changing relations, coalitions between the weaker partners in the polity against the mightier were normal.

In most parts of Europe, urban development took place either spontaneously—outside the feudal power structure—or with the active support of princes. As long as princes and towns found a common rival in the feudal nobility, they were allies working to each other's advantage. The more a region was urbanized, the more resources the princes could get from towns by bargaining or pressure. In a sense, then, cities paid protection costs against the dangerous grip of the nobility. Where no monarch could elevate himself above the rest of the landed aristocracy, as in some areas of late medieval Germany, towns had to secure their trade routes by establishing leagues and signing treaties with feudal lords. In northern Italy, the growth and power of the cities were so overwhelming, in the absence of any real overlord, that the nobility merged with the urban elites to dominate the countryside. To a large degree, power relations reflected the shape of the hierarchy of markets. In other regions, the major trading cities reached a point in their development where their power balanced that of the monarch. In the late thirteenth and fourteenth centuries, this was true in Aragonese and Provence towns, Baltic harbors, and Flemish and Brabantine cities.

The fifteenth century was crucial for the expansion of monarchical power. While most towns stagnated economically, the monarchies could build up larger and more efficient state structures, partly by eliminating weaker competitors. "Modern" states claimed functions that had traditionally been the local and territorial prerogatives of the major cities. The list of these prerogatives is astonishingly similar from Barcelona to Danzig. "Modern" states expanded their functions in jurisdiction, coinage, economic regulation, taxation, diplomacy, and the monopoly of coercive means. Evidently, they encroached on long-established urban practices, many of them once granted as privileges by former rulers. "Modern" sovereigns, however, strove for full and direct powers and did not hesitate to use their military supremacy to eliminate all intermediary powers, thereby keeping them away from important resources.

Part of their success was derived from their capacity to introduce an overarching ideology, calling for an emotional identification by their subjects— hence, the huge efforts made by rulers since the fourteenth century to develop cults around their dynasties, national saints, and national myths. Ceremonies surrounding the royalty's entry into cities became increasingly elaborate, bolstering the image of the ideal ruler and creating a direct link between him and his people. They had a particular significance in newly acquired or subjugated regions.[51] Apparently, the fresh monarchical ideology could not simply overwhelm the strong local and regional identities, which, indeed, remained lively until the end of the eighteenth century. Nevertheless, the monarchy's ideology constituted an alternative and a challenge to the traditional sense of community. The outcome of the religious wars in the sixteenth and seventeenth centuries especially helped monarchs secure their emotional grasp on their subjects through the close collaboration between church and state, resulting in a "confessionalization."[52]

Wolfgang Reinhard recently proposed a theoretical model of the increase in state power. He noticed that the arguments of existing theories operate at different levels of abstraction without excluding each other. So he left some space for the voluntary action of individuals, situating it within the larger frameworks of political and social systems. According to his model, processes on the microlevel (personal ambitions, group egoisms reinforcing state institutions), the mesolevel (class antagonisms, tensions between rulers and the ruled, interstate competition), and the macrolevel (states versus economic and geographical systems) converge to strengthen states.[53] The studies in the present volume fully confirm this mighty vision, albeit from the perspective of cities alone; the three levels of interaction are nevertheless displayed clearly from this viewpoint.

Urban centers did not succeed, however, in creating coherent and stable power structures as an alternative to those of the monarchical states unless (1) urban potential was extremely high and thus the communications were easy and the distances short (as in northern Italy and the Low Countries in the revolt of the late sixteenth century) and (2) the feudal power was extremely weak (as in Switzerland and Holland).

In all other cases, urban leagues, federations, unions, representative organizations, and the like fell apart under the increasing pressure of the neighboring monarchical states, most of all because they were unable to consolidate their structures and restrain their internal conflicts of interests. Overwhelmingly mighty cities like Venice, Milan, and Florence created new systems in which the capitals' elites dominated the smaller cities and the countryside. In the southern Low Countries during the fifteenth and sixteenth centuries, this tendency was countered by efforts to dramatically expand monarchical power, but it came fully to the fore in the Dutch Republic. In Switzerland, both patterns of domination were avoided, and a communal federation survived. It must be observed, however, that this unique situation followed from the modest size of the Swiss cities, even in the early modern period.[54] Although solidarity, coherence, and speed in decisionmaking remained weak points in the United Provinces, they nevertheless overcame the earlier limits of urban confederations. The balance of power made it impossible for any one of the cities or territories to overrule the others, even though Amsterdam and Holland were predominant in size and capital.

My central argument is that the requirements and pressures of monarchical states suffocated the metropoles of the European economy. The competition within the state system pushed all political unities toward increasing military expenditure and more extensive bureaucratic control—developments that violated the conditions favorable to early commercial capitalism. It is striking that the core cities of the European economy were always fairly independent from monarchical pressure: At most, they bargained, like Barcelona, Prague, Augsburg, Nürnberg, and Antwerp, but never could they fulfill their metropolitan function under the rigorous control of a centralized bureaucracy. Seville, where this seemed to be a real danger in the seventeenth century, managed to circumvent state regulation by massive fraud. The chapters in this volume illustrate the reasons for this incompatibility.

Metropoles and monarchs could collaborate only as long as the latter were not yet unchallenged rulers. This was generally the case from the eleventh to the thirteenth centuries. During this period, the increasing population and expanding economy produced a growing surplus, and monetarization of the economy made life difficult for many a monastery or landlord. Thanks to their bargaining with the cities, however, most princes got an ever-increasing revenue from tolls, mintage, jurisdiction functions, and the granting of privileges. The concentration of capital in the cities made loans by merchants to princes a normal practice as early as the thirteenth century in northern Italy, the Low Countries, and England. So the commercialization of the economy strengthened the position of the princes vis-à-vis their former competitors, the landed aristocracy. Good relations with the cities were of strategic importance for these rising powers.

As soon as they began to think about consolidated, centralized, and bureaucratic "modern" states, princes had to eliminate the intermediary power structures within their territories. Major cities had lived on export industries and long-distance trade and necessarily built up such structures in their regions and even beyond. But they now became a hindrance for the trajectory toward the formation of strong states. Disturbing the preexisting regional power networks, the monarchs touched the basis of urban prosperity. The fourteenth and fifteenth centuries saw the confrontation of the old and new power structures in nearly continuous wars, in which it was hard to distinguish an external enemy from an internal one. They emanated from the momentum supported originally by the expanding commerce.

But roughly after 1300, the European economy contracted, and its population was reduced by one-third during the second half of the fourteenth century, to recover slowly only one century later. Although the states became more vigorous and more demanding in the field of taxation, the productive basis failed, especially in the cities. Meanwhile, shrinking cities with a decreasing income from their indirect taxes had to face military operations in their hinterland, as well as monetary debasements and new taxes imposed by their princes. In this confrontation, the expanding states overpowered the cities—a shift that cities indirectly contributed to by their lack of solidarity. In the long run, the increasing fiscal pressure suffocated the once-flourishing trades. The only escape was to move capital toward areas less plundered by princes.

However, even though areas with high urban potential were subjugated by monarchical states via conquest, internal war, or heritage, they did not become dependent towns like those in central Europe after 1450. Accumulated capital, existing social and political structures, and the increase in urban activity could not be annihilated by physical violence alone. There is a close correlation between the development of autonomous and active representative organizations and the urban potential. On the local scale, the turnover of town councils correlated strongly with the size and the socioeconomic differentiation of a city. In major cities, artisans had a say in the large councils, but the merchants and rentiers kept firm control and fiercely opposed popular revolts in other cities. On the supralocal scale, commercial centers necessarily developed loosely structured consultative organizations in order to regulate the material, judicial, and diplomatic aspects of trade. Intensive negotiations crossed state borders and included all kinds of partners, ranging from native or foreign monarchs to local producers.[55]

The submission of cities that were once fairly autonomous could only be accomplished by granting substantial parts of governmental revenues to local elites, who thus became rentiers. Meetings of representative institutions became less frequent and more formal, but they did not disappear. During the fifteenth century, a tendency toward a higher exclusiveness can be noticed. More conservative elites obviously were prepared to give up the political autonomy of the city for a consolidation of their personal positions.

A high level of urbanization thus fundamentally influenced the shape of consolidated monarchical states: first by facilitating their emergence and later by obstructing centralization. However, the decline in European population and production during the fourteenth and fifteenth centuries coincided with an increased propensity of the monarchical states toward continuous warfare. The resulting higher fiscal demands and destructive effects of the wars on the economy added to the downward spiral in production. Increasingly, cities found themselves in a difficult position to withstand the pressure of surrounding princes. Only the largest and still prosperous ones could maintain their previous autonomy. In the growing military competition among European states, city-states proved increasingly unable to uphold their positions. The scale of their human material resources could no longer compete with those mobilized by the larger monarchies. The weak cohesion between cities within urban networks, the little support or loyalty they could command from the subject communities, and the loss of core positions within the world economy seem to be the main factors explaining this shift.[56] Monarchies furthered the development of commercial capitalism only as long as they were unable to impose their dynastic or imperial dreams, which—unlimited as they were—necessarily exhausted even the most flourishing economy.

Notes

1. Wolfgang von Stromer, "Der kaiserliche Kaufmann: Wirtschaftspolitik unter Karl IV," in F. Seibt, ed., *Kaiser Karl IV: Staatsmann und Mäzen* (Munich: Prestel, 1978), 66–69.

2. Charles Tilly, "Space for Capital, Space for States," *Theory and Society*, 15 (1986), 301–309; Tilly, *Coercion, Capital and European States, A.D. 990–1990* (Cambridge, Mass.: Blackwell, 1990), 38–66; Paul Hohenberg and Lynn Hollen Lees,

The Making of Urban Europe, 1000–1950 (Cambridge, Mass.: Harvard University Press, 1985), 169–171.

3. Jan De Vries, *European Urbanization, 1500–1800* (Cambridge, Mass.: Harvard University Press, 1984), 158–161; his figures have been criticized by Wilfried Brulez, *Cultuur en getal: Aspecten van de relatie economie-maatschappij-cultuur in Europa tussen 1400 en 1800* (Amsterdam: NVSG, 1986), 92–99. Brulez counts 143 cities of 10,000 inhabitants, of which only 114 have been taken in account by De Vries; Montpellier, with more than 20,000, has been omitted by him. Since Brulez does not apply his data for a calculation of the urban potential, we have no alternative other than considering De Vries's results.

4. Antoni Maczak, "The Conclusive Years: The End of the Sixteenth Century as the Turning-Point of Polish History," in E. I. Kouri and T. Scott, eds., *Politics and Society in Reformation Europe* (London: Macmillan Press, 1986), 516–532.

5. Neithard Bulst, "Die französischen General- und Provinzialstände im 15. Jahrhundert: Zum Problem nationaler Integration und Desintegration," in F. Seibt and W. Eberhard, eds., *Europa 1500* (Stuttgart: Klett-Cotta, 1987), 313–329; Luis Suarez Fernandez, *Nobleza y monarquia: Puntos de vista sobre la historia politica castellana del siglo XV*, 2d. ed. (Valladolid: Universidad de Valladolid, Facultad de Filosofia y Letras, Departamento de Historia Medieval, 1975); M. A. Ladero Quesada, "Aristocratie et régime seigneurial dans l'Andalousie du XVe siècle," *Annales: Economies-Sociétés-Civilisations*, 38 (1983), 1346–1368.

6. Eckhard Müller-Mertens, "Bürgerlich-städtische Autonomie in der Feudalgesellschaft," in *Autonomie, Wirtschaft und Kultur der Hansestädte: Hansische Stdien* VI (Weimar: Hermann Böhlaus Nachfolger, 1984), 27–33.

7. Norbert Elias, *Ueber den Prozess der Zivilisation*, 2 vols. (Bern-Munich: Francke Verlag, 1969), vol. II, 123–311; Jan Dhondt, *Etude sur la naissance des principautés territoriales en France* (Bruges: De Tempel, 1942).

8. Marc Ormrod, "The Crown and English Economy in 1290–1348," in Bruce M.S. Campbell, ed., *Before the Black Death: Studies in the "Crisis" of the Early Fourteenth Century* (Manchester, England: Manchester University Press, 1991), 149–183.

9. Franz Irsigler, "Stadt und Umland im Spätmittelalter: Zur Zentralitätsfordernden Kraft von Fernhandel und Exportgewerbe," in E. Meynen, ed., *Zentralität als Problem der mittelalterlichen Stadtgeschichtsforschung* (Cologne-Vienna: Böhlau, 1979), 1–14.

10. Barisa Krekić, "Developed Autonomy: The Patricians in Dubrovnik and Dalmatian Cities," in Bariša Krekić, ed., *Urban Society of Eastern Europe in Premodern Times* (Berkeley–Los Angeles–London: University of California Press, 1987), 185–215; Krekić, *Dubrovnik, Italy and the Balkans in the Late Middle Ages* (London: Variorum Reprints, 1980); Krekić, "Four Florentine Commercial Companies in Dubrovnik (Ragusa) in the First Half of the Fourteenth Century," in H. A. Miskimin, D. Herlihy, and A. L. Udovitch, eds., *The Medieval City* (New Haven: Yale University Press, 1977) 40, 25–26; Krekić, "Quelques remarques sur la politique et l'économie de Dubrovnik (Raguse) au XVe siècle," *Mélanges en l'honneur de Fernand Braudel* (Toulouse: Privat, 1973), 313–315.

11. Henrik Birnbaum, "Kiev, Novgorod, Moscow: Three Varieties of Urban Society in East Slavic Territory," in Krekić, ed., *Urban Society of Eastern Europe*, 1–62.

12. Pablo Fernández Albaladejo, "Cities and the State in Spain," Chapter 8 in this volume; Ludwig Vones, "Finanzsystem und Herrschaftskrise: Die Kronen Kastilien und Aragon in der zweiten Hälfte des 15. Jahrhunderts," in Seibt and Eberhard, *Europa 1500*, 62–83.

13. R. Van Uytven and W. P. Blockmans, "Constitutions and Their Application in the Netherlands During the Middle Ages," *Revue belge de Philologie et d'Histoire*, 47 (1969), 399–424; W. P. Blockmans, "Alternatives to Monarchical Centralisation: The Great Tradition of Revolt in Flanders and Brabant," in H. G. Koenigsberger, ed., *Republicanism in Early Modern Europe* (Munich: Oldenbourg, 1988), 145–154; idem, "Vertretungssysteme im Niederländischen Raum im Spätmittelalter," in *Der Ost-und Nordseeraum, Hansische Studien*, VII (1986), 180–189.

14. Marian Biskup, "Polen an der Ostsee im 16. Jahrhundert," *Zeitschrift für Historische Forschung*, 5 (1978), 293–314.

15. Karol Gorski, Marian Biskup, and Irena Janosz-Biskupova, *Akta Stanow Prus Krolewskich (1479–1520)*, 7 vols. (Warsaw: Panstwowe Wydawnictwo Naukowe, 1955–1986); Marian Biskup, "Die Rolle der Städte in der Ständever-tretung des Königreiches Polen, einschliesslich des Ordensstaates Preussen im 14./15. Jahrhundert," in Bernhard Töpfer, ed., *Städte und Ständestaat: Zur Rolle der Städte bei der Entwicklung der Ständeverfassung in europäischen Staaten vom 13. bis zum 15. Jahrhundert* (Berlin: Akademie-Verlag, 1980), 177–192.

16. Stark, *Lübeck und Dantzig*, 162–182.

17. R. A. Schneider, *Public Life in Toulouse 1463–1789: From Municipal Republic to Cosmopolitan City* (Ithaca and London: Cornell University Press, 1989), 29, 59–81.

18. Noel Coulet, *Aix en Provence: Espace et relations d'une capitale (milieu XIVe s.–milieu XVe s.)* (Aix-en-Provence: Université de Provence, 1988), 59–107; Coulet, "Les Aixois dans l'Union d'Aix," in *1388: La dédition de Nice à la Savoie* (Paris: Publications de la Sorbonne, 1990), 159–173.

19. Georges Lesage, *Marseilles Angevine: Recherches sur son évolution administrative, économique et urbaine de la victoire de Charles D'Anjou à l'arrivée de Jeanne Ire (1264–1348)* (Paris: De Boccard, 1950), 91–161; Edouard Baratier, *Histoire de Marseille* (Toulouse: Privat, 1990), 80–109; Christian Bruschi, "Les aspects constitutionnels du rattachement de la Provence au Royaume de France," in *Aspects de la Provence* (Marseilles: Société de statistique, d'histoire et d'archéologie, 1983), 27–42.

20. Philippe Dollinger, *La Hanse (XIIe–XVIIe siècles)* (Paris: Aubier, 1964), 119–123, 141–144; Horst Wernicke, "Städtenhanse und Stände im Norden des Deutschen Reiches zum Ausgang des Spätmittelalters," *Der Ost- und Nordsee-raum: Hansische Studien*, VII (Weimar: Hermann Böhlaus Nachfolger, 1986), 190–208.

21. Peter Blickle, *Deutsche Untertanen: Ein Widerspruch* (Munich: Beck, 1981), 59, 71.

22. Hugo De Schepper, *"Belgium Nostrum" 1500–1650: Over integratie en desintegratie van het Nederland* (Antwerp: De Orde van den Prince, 1987), 14–16.

23. Peter Moraw, "Monarchie und Bürgertum," in Seibt, *Kaiser Karl IV*, 43–63; idem, "Deutsches Königtum und bürgerliche Geldwirtschaft um 1400," *Vierteljahrschrift für Sozial- und Wirtschaftsgeschichte*, 55 (1968), 289–328; Ulf Dirlmeier, *Mittelalterliche Hoheitsträger im wirtschaftlichen Wettbewerb*, Beihefte

der VSWG 51 (Wiesbaden: Steiner, 1966), 200–217; F. B. Fahlbusch, *Städte und Königtum im frühen 15. Jahrhundert* (Cologne-Vienna: Böhlau, 1983), 219–231.

24. Holger Kruse, Werner Paravicini, and Andreas Ranft, *Ritterorden und Adelsgesellschaften im spätmittelalterlichen Deutschland* (Frankfurt am Main: Peter Lang, 1991), 25.

25. H. Angermeier, *Königtum und Landfriede im deutschen Spätmittelalter* (Munich: C. H. Beck, 1966); W. D. Mohrmann, *Der Landfriede im Ostseeraum während des späten Mittelalters* (Kallmünz, West Germany: Lassleben, 1972); Blickle, *Deutsche Untertanen,* 55–59; Johannes Schildhauer, "Der schwäbische Städtebund— Ausdruck der Kraftentfaltung des deutschen Städtebürgertums in der zweiten Hälfte des 14. Jahrhunderts," *Jahrbuch für Geschichte des Feudalismus,* 1 (1977), 187–210; B. Berthold, "Ueberregionale Städtebundprojekte in der ersten Hälfte des 15. Jahrhunderts," in ibid., 3 (1979), 141–179.

26. Blickle, *Deutsche Untertanen,* 59.

27. Biskup, "Die Rolle," 167–175.

28. Jiri Kejr, "Zur Entstehung des städtischen Standes im Hussitischen Böhmen," in Töpfer, *Städte und Ständestaat,* 200–203; Andras Kubinyi, "Zur Frage der Vertretung der Städte im ungarischen Reichstag bis 1526," in ibid., 236–242.

29. Biskup, "Die Rolle," 164–171.

30. H. G. Koenigsberger, "The Parliament of Piedmont During the Renaissance, 1460–1560," in his *Estates and Revolutions* (Ithaca and London: Cornell University Press, 1971), 19–79, especially 42–69.

31. Bernard Chevalier, *Les bonnes villes de France du XIVe au XVIe siècle* (Paris: Aubier Montaigne, 1982), 197–217, quotation on p. 217; Jean-François Bergier, *Les foires de Genève et l'économie internationale de la Renaissance* (Paris: SEVPEN, 1963), 369–413.

32. H. A. Miskimin, "L'or, l'argent, la guerre dans la France médiévale," *Annales: Economies-Sociétés-Civilisations,* 40 (1985), 171–184, quotations on p. 184; Jean Favier, *De l'or et des épices: Naissance de l'homme d'affaires au Moyen Age* (Paris: Fayard, 1987), 367–382.

33. Charles Tilly, "War Making and State Making as Organized Crime," in P. B. Evans, D. Rueschemeyer, T. Skocpol, eds., *Bringing the State Back In* (Cambridge: Cambridge University Press, 1985), 169–191; Michael Prestwich, "War and Taxation in England in the XIIIth and XIVth centuries," in J.-Ph. Genet and M. Le Mené, eds., *Genèse de l'état moderne: Prélèvement et redistribution* (Paris: CNRS, 1987), 181–192.

34. Moraw, "Monarchie und Bürgertum," 62.

35. F. de Gingins La Sarra, *Dépêches des ambassadeurs milanais sur les campagnes de Charles-le-Hardi, duc de Bourgogne, de 1474 à 1477* (Paris-Genève, 1858), vol. I, 313–318.

36. Tilly, "War Making," 181–184; Dirlmeier, *Mittelalterliche Hoheitsträger,* 180–181.

37. Walter Prevenier and Wim Blockmans, *The Burgundian Netherlands* (Cambridge: Cambridge University Press, 1986), 214–240.

38. Vones, "Finanzsystem," 81–83.

39. Miskimin, "L'or," 184.

40. Chevalier, *Bonnes villes,* 106–112; Vones, "Finanzsystem," 72–73.

41. Maczak, "Conclusive Years," 528; Biskup, "Polen an der Ostsee," 304–311.

42. Biskup, "Die Rolle," 192–193; "Polen an der Ostsee," 311; W. Stark, *Lübeck und Dantzig in der zweiten Hälfte des 15. Jahrhunderts* (Weimar: Hermann Böhlaus Nachfolger, 1973), 181–183.

43. Vones, "Finanzsystem," 83; H. G. Koenigsberger, "Dominium Regale or Dominiun Politicum et Regale: Monarchies and Parliaments in Early Modern Europe," in his *Politicians and Virtuosi* (London and Ronceverte: Hambledon Press, 1986), 1–26.

44. Koenigsberger, "Parliament," 71–78; Giorgio Chittolini, Chapter 2 in this volume.

45. W. P. Blockmans, "La signification 'constitutionnelle' des privilèges de Marie de Bourgogne (1477)," in W. P. Blockmans, ed., *1477: Le privilège général et les privilèges régionaux de Marie de Bourgogne pour les Pays-Bas,* Standen en Landen, LXXX (Kortrijk: UGA, 1985), 495–516; Blockmans, "Alternatives to Monarchical Centralisation"; "Finances publiques et inégalité sociale dans les Pays-Bas aux XIVe–XVIe siècles," in Genet and Le Mené, eds., *Genèse de l'Etat moderne,* 79–90.

46. Dollinger, *Le Hanse,* 143–144; H. Sauer, *Hansestädte und Landesfürsten: Die wendischen Hansestädte in der Auseinandersetzung mit den Fürstenhäusern Oldenburg und Mecklenburg während der zweiten Hälfte des 15. Jahrhunderts* (Cologne-Vienna: Böhlau, 1971), 175.

47. Johannes Schildhauer, *Soziale, politische und religiöse Auseinandersetzungen in den Hansestädten Stralsund, Rostock und Wismar im ersten Drittel des 16. Jahrhunderts* (Weimar: Hermann Böhlaus Nachfolger, 1959), 1–25; Sauer, *Hansestädte,* 174–178.

48. Tilly, *Coercion.*

49. Andras Kubinyi, "Einige Fragen zur Entwicklung des Städtenetzes Ungarns im 14.–15. Jahrhundert," in Heinz Stoob, ed., *Die mittelalterliche Städtebildung im südöstlichen Europa* (Cologne-Vienna: Böhlau, 1977), 164–183, esp. 169, 173, 178, 182.

50. Maczak, "The Conclusive Years," 518.

51. Bernard Guenée and Françoise Lehoux, *Les Entrées royales françaises de 1328 à 1515* (Paris, 1978); Coulet, *Aix en Provence,* 82–83; Prevenier and Blockmans, *Burgundian Netherlands,* 214–240; J. Jacquot, ed., *Fêtes de la Renaissance:* II, *Fêtes et cérémonies au temps de Charles Quint* (Paris: Centre National de la Recherche Scientifique, 1960), 413–491.

52. Heinz Schilling, "Nation und Konfession in der frühneuzeitlichen Geschichte," in K. Garber, ed., *Nation und Literatur im Europa der frühen Neuzeit* (Tübingen: M. Niemeyer, 1989), 87–107.

53. Wolfgang Reinhard, "Croissance de la puissance de l'Etat: Un modèle théorique," in André Stegmann, ed., *Pouvoir et Institutions en Europe au XVIème siècle* (Paris: Vrin, 1987), 173–186.

54. Blickle, *Deutsche Untertanen,* 114–126.

55. Dollinger, *La Hanse,* 166–168, 352–358; Schildhauer, *Soziale, politische,* 26–40; W. P. Blockmans, "A Typology of Representative Institutions in Late Medieval

Europe," *Journal of Medieval History*, 4 (1978), 189–215; "Mobiliteit in stadsbesturen, 1400–1550," in D.E.H. De Boer and J. W. Marsilje, eds., *De Nederlanden in de late middeleeuwen* (Utrecht: Het Spectrum, 1987), 236–260.

56. Thomas A. Brady, Jr., "The Rise of Merchant Empires, 1400–1700: A European Counterpoint," in James D. Tracy, ed., *The Political Economy of Merchant Empires: State Power and World Trade, 1350–1750* (Cambridge: Cambridge University Press, 1991), 137–142.

Selected Readings

CAPITALISM, CITIES, AND URBANIZATION

Abu-Lughod, Janet (1991): *Changing Cities*. New York: Harper Collins. The most historically sophisticated and hence, no doubt the best textbook on world cities.

Aminzade, Ronald (1981): *Class, Politics, and Early Industrial Capitalism: A Study of Mid-Nineteenth-Century Toulouse, France*. Albany: State University of New York Press. Not only good history but also reflective Marxist theory.

Baechler, Jean, John A. Hall, and Michael Mann, eds. (1988): *Europe and the Rise of Capitalism*. Oxford: Blackwell. Recent thinking on a perennial subject.

Bairoch, Paul (1988): *Cities and Economic Development from the Dawn of History to the Present*. Chicago: University of Chicago Press. Sweeping but built around a statistical core.

Berend, Iván, and György Ránki (1977): *East Central Europe in the 19th and 20th Centuries*. Budapest: Akademiai Kiado. (1982): *The European Periphery and Industrialization, 1780–1914*. Budapest: Akademiai Kiado. More on industrialization than urbanization but broad in scope.

Berg, Maxine, Pat Hudson, and Michael Sonenscher, eds. (1983): *Manufacture in Town and Country Before the Factory*. Cambridge: Cambridge University Press. Protoindustrialization and related processes, skeptically observed.

Blom, Grethe Authén, ed. (1977): *Urbaniseringsprosessen i norden*. 3 vols. Oslo: Universitetsforlaget. Comprehensive survey of urbanization in the Nordic countries.

Bogucka, Maria (1982): "Polish Towns Between the Sixteenth and Eighteenth Centuries," in J. K. Fedorowicz, ed., *A Republic of Nobles: Studies in Polish History to 1864*. Cambridge: Cambridge University Press.

Braudel, Fernand (1984): *Civilization and Capitalism, 15th–18th Centuries*. 3 vols. New York: Harper & Row. Breathtaking trip across the whole of Europe-connected world history during the past half millennium.

Brower, Daniel (1977): "L'Urbanisation russe à la fin du XIXe siècle," *Annales: Economies, Sociétés, Civilisations* 32: 70–86.

Carter, F. W. (1972): *Dubrovnik (Ragusa), A Classic City State*. London: Seminar Press. How an entrepreneurial city survived.

Cattaruzza, Marina (1979): *La formazione del proletariato urbano: Immigrati, operai di mestiere, donne a Trieste dalla metà del secolo XIX alla prima guerra mondiale*. Turin: Musolini. Demographically informed social history.

Chandler, Tertius, and Gerald Fox (1974): *3000 Years of Urban Growth*. Comprehensive, if sometimes risky, compilation of urban population figures.

Chaudhuri, K. N. (1990): *Asia Before Europe: Economy and Civilisation of the Indian Ocean from the Rise of Islam to 1750*. Cambridge: Cambridge University Press. Vast Braudelian reflections on connections and distinctions among the peoples who lived on and around the Indian Ocean.

Chaunu, Pierre (1970): *La civilisation de l'Europe classique*. Paris: Arthaud. Synthesis in the grand style, emphasizing Atlantic connections.

Chaunu, Pierre, and Richard Gascon (1977): *Histoire économique et sociale de la France*. Tome I: *de 1450 à 1660*. Premier vol.: *L'Etat et la ville*. Paris: Presses Universitaires de France. City and state in the French Renaissance.

Chevalier, Bernard (1982): *Les bonnes villes de France du XIVe au XVIe siècle*. Paris: Aubier Montaigne. The place of those intermediate cities in the great system of rule.

Chirot, Daniel (1976): *Social Change in a Peripheral Society: The Creation of a Balkan Colony*. New York: Academic. Chirot, ed. (1989): *The Origins of Backwardness in Eastern Europe: Economics and Politics from the Middle Ages Until the Early Twentieth Century*. Berkeley: University of California Press. Piercing looks at eastern European politics and social organization.

Cockcroft, James D., André Gunder Frank, and Dale L. Johnson (1972): *Dependence and Under-development: Latin America's Political Economy*. Garden City, N.Y.: Doubleday Anchor. Collection of articles by the three authors plus a few collaborators, stressing dependency theories.

Corfield, P. J. (1982): *The Impact of English Towns, 1700–1800*. Oxford: Oxford University Press. Cities and national affairs in England during a period of rapid expansion for both.

Cox, Robert W. (1987): *Production, Power, and World Order: Social Forces in the Making of History*. New York: Columbia University Press. Ambitious general statement.

Curtin, Philip D. (1984): *Cross-cultural Trade in World History*. Cambridge: Cambridge University Press. Unexpected but powerful ties between the continents.

Dodgshon, Robert A. (1987): *The European Past: Social Evolution and Spatial Order*. London: Macmillan. Sweeping geographical synthesis.

Dunford, Michael, and Diane Perrons (1983): *The Arena of Capital*. New York: St. Martin's. Geographers tussle with capitalist economic organization.

Duplessis, Robert S. (1987): "The Partial Transition to World-Systems Analysis in Early Modern European History," *Radical History Review* 39: 11–27.

Finley, M. I. (1973): *The Ancient Economy*. Berkeley: University of California Press. Greek and Roman social structure viewed from the economic base; see also his posthumous *Economy and Society in Ancient Greece*. London: Chatto & Windus, 1982.

Friedman, Gerald (1990): "Capitalism, Republicanism, Socialism, and the State: France, 1871–1914," *Social Science History* 14: 151–174.

Gerhard, Dietrich (1981): *Old Europe: A Study of Continuity, 1000–1800*. New York: Academic Press. None of those catastrophic transitions for Gerhard; a compact, provocative treatment of sameness.

Gurr, Ted Robert, and Desmond S. King (1987): *The State and the City*. London: Macmillan. Politics, crime, and state authority.

Gutmann, Myron P. (1988): *Toward the Modern Economy: Early Industry in Europe, 1500–1800*. Philadelphia: Temple University Press. Well-informed, compact survey emphasizing regions of rural industry.

Hagen, William W. (1988): "Capitalism and the Countryside in Early Modern Europe: Interpretations, Models, Debates," *Agricultural History* 62: 13–47.

Hall, Peter, and Dennis Hay (1980): *Growth Centers in the European Urban System*. London: Heinemann. How urban hierarchies and regions fit together.

Hanagan, Michael P. (1980): *The Logic of Solidarity: Artisans and Industrial Workers in Three French Towns, 1871–1914*. Urbana: University of Illinois Press. (1989): *Nascent Proletarians: Class Formation in Post-revolutionary France*. Oxford: Basil Blackwell. Close comparative studies of industrial change and its social-political consequences.

Hicks, Sir John (1969): *A Theory of Economic History*. London: Oxford University Press. An outstanding institutional historian stretches himself.

Hittle, J. Michael (1979): *The Service City: State and Townsmen in Russia, 1600–1800*. Cambridge, Mass.: Harvard University Press. How the czars subordinated cities.

Hobsbawm, E. J. (1975): *The Age of Capital, 1848–1875*. London: Weidenfeld & Nicolson. Lucid, broadly Marxist synthesis. (1988): *The Age of Imperialism*. New York: Pantheon. Even anti-Marxists recognize the distinction of this synthesis.

Hohenberg, Paul M., and Lynn Hollen Lees (1985): *The Making of Urban Europe, 1000–1950*. Cambridge, Mass.: Harvard University Press. Bold synthesis of nearly a millennium.

Holton, R. J. (1986): *Cities, Capitalism and Civilization*. London: Allen & Unwin. Sustained, historically documented doubts about "urbanist" theories of social change.

Horowitz, Irving Louis (1966): *Three Worlds of Development: The Theory and Practice of International Stratification*. New York: Oxford University Press. World inequality, with sympathy for underdogs.

Jones, Eric L. (1989): *Growth Recurring: Economic Change in World History*. New York: Oxford University Press. A huge, hopeful synthesis.

Juillard, Etienne, and Henri Nonn (1976): *Espaces et régions en Europe Occidentale*. Paris: Editions du Centre National de la Recherche Scientifique. The geography of urban regions in twentieth-century Europe.

Katznelson, Ira (1992): *Marxism and the City*. Oxford: Clarendon Press. The whole literature seen critically but withal sympathetically.

Katznelson, Ira, and Aristide Zolberg (1986): *Working-Class Formation: Nineteenth-Century Patterns in Western Europe and the United States*. Princeton: Princeton University Press. Original essays, both synthetic and country-by-country.

Kellenbenz, Hermann (1976): *The Rise of the European Economy: An Economic History of Continental Europe from the Fifteenth Century*. London: Weidenfeld & Nicolson. Has the advantage not only of having been written by one of Germany's outstanding economic historians but also of being organized chiefly around types of production rather than places or time periods.

Köllmann, Wolfgang (1969): "The Process of Urbanization in Germany at the Height of the Industrialization Period," *Journal of Contemporary History* 4: 59–76.

(1977): "Zur Bevölkerungsentwicklung der Neuzeit," in Reinhart Koselleck, ed., *Studien zum Beginn der modernen Welt*. Stuttgart: Klett-Cotta.

Krekić, Barisa (1972): *Dubrovnik in the 14th and 15th Centuries: A City Between East and West*. Norman: University of Oklahoma Press. How an entrepreneurial interstitial city survived and prospered.

Kriedte, Peter (1983): *Peasants, Landlords and Merchant Capitalists: Europe and the World Economy, 1500–1800*. Cambridge: Cambridge University Press. Grand Marxist survey.

Kriedte, Peter, Hans Medick, and Jürgen Schlumbohm (1977): *Industrialisierung vor der Industrialisierung: Gewerbliche Warenproduktion auf dem Land in der Formationsperiode des Kapitalismus*. Göttingen: Vandenhoeck & Ruprecht. (English translation [1981]: *Industrialization Before Industrialization*. Paris: Maison des Sciences de l'Homme and Cambridge: Cambridge University Press.) Brash, stimulating hypotheses and observations on European rural industrialization and its demographic correlates.

Lachmann, Richard (1987): *From Manor to Market: Structural Change in England, 1536–1640*. Madison: University of Wisconsin Press. (1989): "Origins of Capitalism in Western Europe: Economic and Political Aspects," *Annual Review of Sociology* 15: 47–72. (1990): "Class Formation Without Class Struggle: An Elite Conflict Theory of the Transition to Capitalism," *American Sociological Review* 55: 398–414.

Lapidus, Ira (1973): "The Evolution of Muslim Urban Society," *Comparative Studies in Society and History* 15: 21–50.

Lees, Andrew (1985): *Cities Perceived: Urban Society in European and American Thought, 1820–1940*. New York: Columbia University Press. Perceptions of the city in the age of industry.

Lees, Lynn Hollen, and Paul M. Hohenberg (1989): "Urban Decline and Regional Economies: Brabant, Castile and Lombardy, 1550–1750," *Comparative Studies in Society and History* 31: 439–461.

Lepetit, Bernard (1988): *Les villes dans la France moderne (1740–1840)*. Paris: Albin Michel. Innovative, quantifying, dense.

Le Roy Ladurie, Emmanuel, ed. (1981): *La ville classique de la Renaissance aux Révolutions*. Tome III: *Histoire de la France urbaine*. Paris: Seuil. Adventurous, sometimes cantankerous, urban history.

Le Roy Ladurie, Emmanuel, and Michel Morineau (1977): *Histoire économique et sociale de la France*. Tome I: *de 1450 à 1660*. Second Vol.: *Paysannerie et croissance*. Paris: Presses Universitaires de France. The rural companion to Chaunu and Gascon's work.

Levine, David (1977): *Family Formation in an Age of Nascent Capitalism*. New York: Academic Press. Levine, ed. (1984): *Proletarianization and Family Life*. New York: Academic Press. Levine, (1987): *Reproducing Families*. Cambridge: Cambridge University Press. Demography, economy, and social life intertwine.

Lis, Catharina (1986): *Social Change and the Labouring Poor: Antwerp, 1770–1860*. New Haven: Yale University Press. Fine-grained and clearheaded analysis of degradation.

Lis, Catharina, and Hugo Soly (1979): *Poverty and Capitalism in Pre-Industrial Europe*. Atlantic Highlands, N.J.: Humanities Press. A remarkably systematic and well-informed brief synthesis.

Littler, Craig (1982): *The Development of the Labour Process in Capitalist Societies: A Comparative Study of the Transformation of Work Organization in Britain, Japan and the USA*. London: Heinemann. For those who like their comparisons massive.

Livet, Georges, and Bernard Vogler, eds. (1983): *Pouvoir, ville, et société en Europe, 1650–1750*. Paris: Ophrys. Cities as sites of political struggle and transformation.

Macfarlane, Alan (1986): "Socio-economic Revolution in England and the Origin of the Modern World," in Roy Porter and Mikulas Teich, eds., *Revolution in History*. Cambridge: Cambridge University Press.

Mauersberg, Hans (1960): *Wirtschafts- und Sozialgeschichte zentraleuropäischer Städte in neurer Zeit*. Göttingen: Vandenhoeck & Ruprecht. A standard synthesis of central European urban history.

McKendrick, Neil, John Brewer, and J. H. Plumb (1985): *The Birth of a Consumer Society: The Commercialization of Eighteenth-Century England*. Bloomington: Indiana University Press. (First published in 1982.) How consumerism prevailed.

McNall, Scott, Rhonda F. Levine, and Rick Fantasia, eds. (1991): *Bringing Class Back In: Contemporary and Historical Perspectives*. Boulder: Westview. Capitalist class formation and collective action.

Meyer, Jean et al. (1983): *Etudes sur les villes en Europe occidentale, milieu du XVII siècle à la veille de la Révolution française*. 2 vols. Paris: Société d'Edition d'Enseignement Supérieur. Informative country-by-country chapters on cities and urbanization.

Milward, Alan S., and S. B. Saul (1973): *The Economic Development of Continental Europe, 1780–1870*. London: George Allen & Unwin. High-level textbook dealing competently with western Europe and Scandinavia.

Moch, Leslie Page (1992): *Moving Europeans: Migration in Western Europe Since 1650*. Bloomington: Indiana University Press. Sweeping, informative synthesis.

Monnier, Alain, and Jitka Rychtarikova (1992): "Comment l'Europe s'est divisée entre l'Est et l'Ouest," *Population* 46: 1617–1650.

Mumford, Lewis (1961): *The City in History: Its Origins, Its Transformations, and Its Prospects*. New York: Harcourt, Brace & World. Masterly overview.

Nicholas, David M. (1968): "Town and Countryside: Social and Economic Tensions in Fourteenth-Century Flanders," *Comparative Studies in Society and History* 10: 458–485.

Ogilvie, Sheilagh C., ed. (1993): "Proto-Industrialization in Europe," special issue of *Continuity and Change* 8, no. 2. Informative survey and synthesis.

Pinol, Jean-Luc (1991): *Le monde des villes au XIXe siècle*. Paris: Hachette. European cities in thoughtful world perspective.

Pounds, N.J.G. (1979): *An Historical Geography of Europe 1500–1840*. Cambridge: Cambridge University Press. Much more history and economics than a narrow conception would allow.

Roseberry, William (1988): "Political Economy," *Annual Review of Anthropology* 17: 161–185.

Roy, William (1984): "Class Conflict and Social Change in Historical Perspective," *Annual Review of Sociology* 10: 483–506.

Schmal, H., ed. (1981): *Patterns of European Urbanization Since 1500*. London: Croom Helm. Region-by-region surveys and syntheses.

Skinner, G. W. (1964): "Marketing and Social Structure in Rural China," *Journal of Asian Studies* 24: 3–43. Skinner, ed. (1977): *The City in Late Imperial China*. Stanford: Stanford University Press. (1985): "The Structure of Chinese History," *Journal of Asian Studies* 44: 271–292. Cumulatively, a striking analysis of the intersection between top-down and bottom-up hierarchies.

Smith, Alan K. (1991): *Creating a World Economy: Merchant Capital, Colonialism, and World Trade, 1400–1825*. Boulder: Westview. Well-documented narrative of interaction between Europe and the rest of the world.

Smith, Carol A. (1976): "Analyzing Regional Systems," in Carol A. Smith, ed., *Regional Analysis*. Vol. 2: *Social Systems*. New York: Academic Press.

Smith, Michael Peter, ed. (1984): *Cities in Transformation: Class, Capital, and the State*. Beverly Hills: Sage. Critical and neo-Marxist analyses of contemporary cities.

Stoianovich, Traian (1970): "Model and Mirror of the Premodern Balkan City," in Institut d'études Balkanique of the Académie Bulgare des Sciences, *Studia Balcanica*. III. *La Ville balkanique XVe–XIXe siècles*. Sofia: Editions de l'Académie Bulgare des Sciences.

Sundin, Jan, and Erik Soderlund, eds. (1979): *Time, Space, and Man: Essays on Microdemography*. Stockholm: Almqvist & Wiksell. A sampler of European historical demography, with more Scandinavian material than usual.

Taylor, John G. (1979): *From Mobilization to Modes of Production: A Critique of the Sociologies of Development and Underdevelopment*. Atlantic Highlands, N.J.: Humanities Press. Beginning with critiques of Parsons, Baran, and Frank, Taylor proceeds to his own construction of frames for the Third World modes of production.

Tilly, Charles (1983): "Flows of Capital and Forms of Industry in Europe, 1500–1900," *Theory and Society* 12: 123–143.

Tilly, Louise A. (1992): *Politics and Class in Milan, 1881–1901*. New York: Oxford University Press. How industrialization, population change, and transformations of the Italian state interacted to produce Milanese working-class politics.

Timberlake, Michael, ed. (1985): *Urbanization in the World-Economy*. Orlando, Fla.: Academic Press. Papers on cities, urbanization, and power.

Tracy, James D., ed. (1990): *The Rise of Merchant Empires: Long-Distance Trade in the Early Modern World, 1350–1750*. Cambridge: Cambridge University Press. The state of play in a rapidly changing field of knowledge.

Trexler, Richard C. (1981): *Public Life in Renaissance Florence*. New York: Academic Press. Includes, among other things, a compelling analysis of public ceremonies as political struggle.

Verhulst, Adriaan (1989): "The Origins of Towns in the Low Countries and the Pirenne Thesis," *Past and Present* 122: 3–35.

Vetter, Klaus (1986): "Die Stadt in der Mark Brandenburg und in Brabant vom 15. bis 17. Jahrhundert—Ein Vergleich," in Wim P. Blockmans and Herman Van Nuffel, eds., *Etat et Religion aux XVe et XVIe siècles*. Brussels: Archives Générales du Royaume de Belgique.

Vovelle, Michel, ed. (1987):*Bourgeoisies de province et Révolution*. Grenoble: Presses Universitaires de Grenoble. Suggestions that a bourgeois revolution did, after all, occur.

de Vries, Jan (1976): *The Economy of Europe in an Age of Crisis, 1600–1750*. Cambridge: Cambridge University Press. Graceful description and synthesis, well informed in the relevant economics and demography. (1978): "Barges and Capitalism: Passenger Transport in the Dutch Economy, 1632–1839," *A.A.G. Bijdragen* 21: 33–398. (1984): *European Urbanization, 1500–1800*. Cambridge, Mass.: Harvard University Press. Urban hierarchies and population changes, deftly analyzed.

Waley, Daniel (1969): *The Italian City-Republics*. New York: McGraw-Hill, World University Library. Compact and informative.

Walker, Mack (1971): *German Home Towns: Community, State, and General Estate, 1648–1871*. Ithaca: Cornell University Press. How German social life organized in and around the lesser cities.

Weber, Adna F. (1899): *The Growth of Cities in the Nineteenth Century*. New York: Macmillan. An important early compendium that is still surprisingly useful.

Wolf, Eric R. (1982): *Europe and the People Without History*. Berkeley: University of California Press. The expansion of capitalism, as seen by the conquered and as mythologized by the conquerors.

Wrigley, E. A. (1987): *People, Cities, and Wealth: The Transformation of Traditional Society*. Oxford: Blackwell. The tight interplay of population, resources, and economic activity.

Zunz, Olivier, ed. (1985): *Reliving the Past: The Worlds of Social History*. Chapel Hill: University of North Carolina Press. A guide to reading and research across the world.

STATES IN GENERAL

Abu-Lughod, Janet (1989): *Before European Hegemony*. New York: Oxford University Press. Grand examination of the world's connectedness during the thirteenth century.

Ames, Edward, and Richard T. Rapp (1977): "The Birth and Death of Taxes: A Hypothesis," *Journal of Economic History* 37: 161–178.

Amsden, Alice H. (1989): *Asia's Next Giant: South Korea and Late Industrialization*. New York: Oxford University Press. How, contrary to free-market prescriptions, the American-backed South Korean state organized low-wage, high-precision industrialization.

Anderson, Benedict (1983): *Imagined Communities: Reflections on the Origin and Spread of Nationalism*. London: Verso. Nationalisms and other invented deformities.

Anderson, James, ed. (1986): *The Rise of the Modern State*. Brighton, Sussex: Wheatsheaf Books. A bright, clear Open University coursebook, mostly on Europe and the period since 1650.

Anderson, Lisa (1986): *The State and Social Transformation in Tunisia and Libya, 1830–1980*. Princeton: Princeton University Press. Well-played comparison.

Andreski, Stanislav (1968): *Military Organization and Society*. Berkeley: University of California Press. Dense, neologistic, propositional argument about the correlates of different kinds of military arrangements.

Ardant, Gabriel (1971–1972): *Histoire de l'impôt*. 2 vols. Paris: Fayard. Provocative general history of taxation.

Armstrong, John A. (1982): *Nations Before Nationalism*. Chapel Hill: University of North Carolina Press. The relations between national identification and both religion and politics. Subtle and learned.

Badie, Bertrand, and Pierre Birnbaum (1979): *Sociologie de l'Etat*. Paris: Bernard Grasset. Rethinking political development by rejecting developmental and evolutionary accounts of the state and drawing heavily on historical analyses.

Barfield, Thomas J. (1989): *The Perilous Frontier: Nomadic Empires and China*. New York: Blackwell. Clears away many misconceptions about the Mongols and their relations with China.

Barkey, Karen, and Sunita Parikh (1991): "Comparative Perspectives on the State," *Annual Review of Sociology* 17: 523–549.

Barnett, Michael N. (1992): *Confronting the Costs of War: Military Power, State, and Society in Egypt and Israel*. Princeton: Princeton University Press. Financing war does not always, it turns out, strengthen state power or make the state more efficient.

Batchelder, Ronald W., and Herman Freudenberger (1983): "On the Rational Origins of the Modern Centralized State," *Explorations in Economic History* 20: 1–13.

Baynham, Simon, ed. (1986): *Military Power and Politics in Black Africa*. New York: St. Martin's. Expert discussions of contrasting patterns.

Bean, Richard (1973): "War and the Birth of the Nation State," *Journal of Economic History* 33: 203–221.

Bendix, Reinhard (1964): *Nation-Building and Citizenship*. New York: Wiley. (Revised edition, Berkeley: University of California Press, 1977.) Varied essays within a Weberian comparative mode.

Bensel, Richard (1990): *Yankee Leviathan: The Origins of Central State Authority in America, 1859–1877*. Cambridge: Cambridge University Press. An attempt to reconcile state theory and political-economic interpretations of the American Civil War and Reconstruction period.

Berry, Mary Elizabeth (1986): "Public Peace and Private Attachment: The Goals and Conduct of Power in Early Modern Japan," *Journal of Japanese Studies* 12: 237–272.

Binder, Leonard et al. (1971): *Crises and Sequences in Political Development*. Princeton: Princeton University Press. Flawed but energetic effort to locate standard sequences in historical and contemporary experience.

Birnbaum, Pierre (1982): *La logique de l'Etat*. Paris: Fayard. Sophisticated and comparative essays on the social bases of different kinds of national politics.

Black, C. E. (1966): *The Dynamics of Modernization*. New York: Harper & Row. Historically informed sorting out of alternative development paths.

Block, Fred (1987): *Revising State Theory: Essays in Politics and Postindustrialism.* Philadelphia: Temple University Press. Block's semi- and post-Marxist inquiries, chiefly on capitalism and the American state.

Bollen, Kenneth A., Barbara Entwisle, and Arthur S. Alderson (1993): "Macro-comparative Research Methods," *Annual Review of Sociology* 19: 321–351.

Boswell, Terry (1989): "Colonial Empires and the Capitalist World-Economy: A Time Series Analysis of Colonization, 1640–1960," *American Sociological Review* 54: 180–196.

Bowen, Roger W. (1980): *Rebellion and Democracy in Meiji Japan: A Study of Commoners in the Popular Rights Movement.* Berkeley: University of California Press. Structural bases of uprisings and social movements.

Bratton, Michael (1989): "Beyond the State: Civil Society and Associational Life in Africa," *World Politics* 41: 407–430. Wide-ranging review essay.

Braud, Philippe, ed. (1993): *La violence politique dans les démocraties européennes occidentales,* special issue of *Cultures et Conflits,* nos. 9–10 (Spring/Summer). Equal time to official, unofficial, and interactive uses of violent means.

Breuer, Stefan, and Hubert Treiber, eds. (1982): *Entstehung und Strukturwandel des Staates.* Opladen: Westdeutscher Verlag. Maurice Godelier, S. N. Eisenstadt, and others reach for great generality.

Brewer, John D. et al. (1988): *The Police, Public Order and the State: Policing Great Britain, Northern Ireland, the Irish Republic, the USA, Israel, South Africa and China.* New York: St. Martin's. Putting the police in political context.

Bright, Charles, and Susan Harding, eds. (1984): Statemaking and Social Movements. Ann Arbor: University of Michigan Press. Historians and social scientists try to put social movements squarely into connection with the changing forms of states.

Calhoun, Craig (1993): "Nationalism and Ethnicity," *Annual Review of Sociology* 19: 211–239.

Callaghy, Thomas M. (1985): *The State-Society Struggle: Zaïre in Comparative Perspective.* New York: Columbia University Press. Analogies between the creation of absolutism and contemporary African state-making.

Campbell, John L. (1993): "The State and Fiscal Sociology," *Annual Review of Sociology* 19: 163–185.

Campbell, John L., J. Rogers Hollingsworth, and Leon N. Lindberg, eds. (1991): *Governance of the American Economy.* Cambridge: Cambridge University Press. Power within and between U.S. economic organizations, including the national state.

Canak, William L. (1984): "The Peripheral State Debate: State Capitalist and Bureaucratic-Authoritarian Regimes in Latin America," *Latin American Research Review* 19: 3–36.

Caporaso, James A., ed. (1989): *The Elusive State: International and Comparative Perspectives.* Newbury Park, Calif.: Sage. Thoughtful essays, chiefly by political scientists who have again started thinking of states as powerful actors with distinctive profiles.

Cardoso, Fernando H., and Enzo Faletto (1979): *Dependency and Development in Latin America.* Berkeley: University of California Press. (First published in Spanish in 1969.) Influential statement of dependency theory.

Cerny, Philip G. (1990): *The Changing Architecture of Politics: Structure, Agency, and the Future of the State.* Newbury Park, Calif.: Sage. Unremittingly abstract, Cerny works out the implications of "structuration" for the analysis of politics, providing a useful inventory of recent literature in the process.

Chambliss, William J. (1989): "State-organized Crime—The American Society of Criminology, 1988 Presidential Address," *Criminology* 27: 183–208.

Chase-Dunn, Chris (1989): *Global Formation: Structures of the World-Economy.* New York: Blackwell. An original variant, with extensive statistical analysis, of world-system thinking. (1990): "World-State Formation: Historical Processes and Emergent Necessity," *Political Geography Quarterly* 9: 108–130.

Choucri, Nazli, and Robert C. North (1975): *Nations in Conflict.* San Francisco: Freeman. Modeling, measurement, and estimation of major nineteenth- and twentieth-century international conflicts.

Claessen, Henri J.M., and Peter Skalnik, eds. (1978): *The Early State.* The Hague: Mouton. By "early," these authors, primarily anthropologists, mean early in some evolutionary sequence.

Clark, Gordon L., and Michael Dear (1984): *State Apparatus: Structures and Language of Legitimacy.* Boston: Allen & Unwin. Attempts to frame a general conception, including space.

Clemens, Elisabeth S. (1993): "Organizational Repertoires and Institutional Change: Women's Groups and the Transformation of U.S. Politics, 1890–1920," *American Journal of Sociology* 98: 755–798.

Cobban, Alfred (1969): *The Nation State and National Self-Determination.* London: Collins. (First published in Fontana Library, a Collins series, 1945.) A distinguished historian's analysis of the emergence of sovereignty.

Cohen, Ronald, and Elman R. Service, eds. (1978): *Origins of the State: The Anthropology of Political Evolution.* Philadelphia: Institute for the Study of Human Issues. Handy introduction to a larger literature.

Cohen, Youssef (1989): *The Manipulation of Consent: The State and Working-Class Consciousness in Brazil.* Pittsburgh: University of Pittsburgh Press. Co-optation of workers by the ideological apparatus.

Cohen, Youssef, Brian R. Brown, and A.F.K. Organski (1981): "The Paradoxical Nature of State Making: The Violent Creation of Order," *American Political Science Review* 75: 901–910.

Colbourn, Forrest D. (1988): "Statism, Rationality and State Centrism," *Comparative Politics* 20: 485–492.

Collier, Ruth B. (1982): *Regimes in Tropical Africa: Changing Forms of Supremacy, 1945–1975.* Berkeley: University of California Press. Inventory and description.

Collier, Ruth Berins, and David Collier (1991): *Shaping the Political Arena: Critical Junctures, the Labor Movement, and Regime Dynamics in Latin America.* Princeton: Princeton University Press. The variable processes by which organized labor found a regular place in national politics.

Connell, R. W. (1990): "The State, Gender, and Sexual Politics: Theory and Appraisal," *Theory and Society* 19: 507–544.

Corrigan, Philip (1980): *Capitalism, State Formation and Marxist Theory: Historical Investigations.* London: Quartet Books. More abstract and conceptual than its title suggests.

Cumings, Bruce (1989): "The Abortive Abertura: South Korea in the Light of Latin American Experience," *New Left Review* 173: 5–32.

Dahl, Robert A. (1975): "Governments and Political Oppositions," in Fred I. Greenstein and Nelson Polsby, eds., *Handbook of Political Science,* vol. 3. Reading, Mass.: Addison-Wesley.

Dalton, Russell J., ed. (1993): "Citizens, Protest, and Democracy," July 1993 issue of *The Annals of the American Academy of Political and Social Science.* Late-breaking news from citizen protests in Europe and America.

Denis, Claude (1989): "The Genesis of American Capitalism: An Historical Enquiry into State Theory," *Journal of Historical Sociology* 2: 328–356.

Donald, David (1984): *The Politics of Reconstruction, 1863–1867.* Cambridge, Mass.: Harvard University Press. How they put the American state back together.

Doyle, Michael W. (1986): *Empires.* Ithaca: Cornell University Press. Largely an explication of definitions and concepts; within those limits, useful.

Duchacek, Ivo D. (1986): *The Territorial Dimension of Politics: Within, Among, and Across Nations.* Boulder: Westview. Extended demonstrations of ways that space makes a difference.

Dudley, Leonard (1990): "Structural Change in Interdependent Bureaucracies: Was Rome's Failure Economic or Military?" *Explorations in Economic History* 27: 232–248.

Eisenstadt, S. N. (1963): *The Political Systems of Empires: The Rise and Fall of the Historical Bureaucratic Societies.* New York: Free Press of Glencoe. Self-consciously Weberian, Eisenstadt treats the tension of centralization and devolution in China, the Byzantine Empire, and elsewhere.

Evans, Peter, Theda Skocpol, and Dietrich Rueschemeyer, eds. (1985): *Bringing the State Back In.* New York: Cambridge University Press. Self-conscious attempts to integrate theories of state formation with historical and comparative studies of particular states.

Fatton, Robert (1988): "Bringing the Ruling Class Back In: Class, State, and Hegemony in Africa," *Comparative Politics* 20: 253–264.

Forrest, Joshua B. (1988): "The Quest for State 'Hardness' in Africa," *Comparative Politics* 20: 423–442.

Fried, Morton H. (1967): *The Evolution of Political Society: An Essay in Political Anthropology.* New York: Random House.

Friedmann, David (1977): "A Theory of the Size and Shape of Nations," *Journal of Political Economy* 85: 59–78.

Gallo, Carmenza (1991): *Taxes and State Power: Political Instability in Bolivia, 1900–1950.* Philadelphia: Temple University Press. At last, someone sees—and very brightly—the significance of the interplay between taxation and class structure for political conflict.

Galtung, Johan (1972): "A Structural Theory of Imperialism," *The African Review* 1: 93–138.

Geertz, Clifford, ed. (1963): *Old Societies and New States.* New York: Free Press. Influential collection of essays from the days of modernization. Geertz (1980): *Negara: The Theatre State in Nineteenth-Century Bali.* Princeton: Princeton University Press. The state as perilous cultural construction.

Giddens, Anthony (1985): *The Nation-State and Violence.* Berkeley: University of California Press. Like much of Giddens's writing, frequently suggestive but often maddeningly vague and short of evidence.

Gillis, John R., ed. (1989): *The Militarization of the Western World.* New Brunswick, N.J.: Rutgers University Press. General essays on the creeping influence of military activity since about 1870, by Geoffrey Best, Gordon Craig, Michael Geyer, and others.

Gledhill, John, Barbara Bender, and Mogens Trolle Larsen, eds. (1988): *State and Society: The Emergence and Development of Social Hierarchy and Political Centralization.* London: Unwin Hyman. Anthropological and archaeological views thereon.

Goldstein, Joshua S. (1988): *Long Cycles: Prosperity and War in the Modern Age.* New Haven: Yale University Press. Careful, comprehensive, and well documented.

Graubard, Stephen, ed. (1993): "Reconstructing Nations and States," *Daedalus* 122, entire issue. Katherine Verdery, John Hall, Liah Greenfeld, Michael Mann, Tom Nairn, Ernest Gellner, and other students of nationalism speak out, often eloquently.

Grew, Raymond, ed. (1978): *Crises of Political Development in Europe and the United States.* Princeton: Princeton University Press. The last of the famous Studies in Political Development, this one much more historical—and even less decisive—than most.

Gurr, Ted Robert (1988): "War, Revolution, and the Growth of the Coercive State," *Comparative Political Studies* 21: 45–65.

Gurr, Ted Robert, Keith Jaggers, and Will H. Moore (1990): "The Transformation of the Western State: The Growth of Democracy, Autocracy, and State Power Since 1800," *Studies in Comparative International Development* 25: 73–108.

Haas, Ernst (1986): "What Is Nationalism and Why Should We Study It?" *International Organization* 40: 707–744.

Hall, John A., ed. (1986): *States in History.* Oxford: Blackwell. Michael Mann, Peter Burke, and other analysts lay the historical and theoretical ground for systematic studies of the state.

Hall, John A., and G. John Ikenberry (1989): *The State.* Minneapolis: University of Minnesota Press. Valuable survey of concepts and theories.

Hall, John W. (1966): *Government and Local Power in Japan, 500–1700.* Princeton: Princeton University Press. Knowledgeable synthesis.

Hein, Jeremy (1993): *States and International Migrants.* Boulder: Westview. How differently Indochinese refugees fared in France and the United States as a function of deeply different state policies and bureaucracies.

Heper, Metin (1985): "The State and Public Bureaucracy: A Comparative and Historical Perspective," *Comparative Studies in Society and History* 27: 86–110.

Hobsbawm, E. J. (1990): *Nations and Nationalism Since 1789: Programme, Myth, Reality.* Cambridge: Cambridge University Press. The phases and follies of nationhood, elegantly displayed.

Hooks, Gregory (1990): "The Rise of the Pentagon and U.S. State Building: The Defense Program as Industrial Policy," *American Journal of Sociology* 96: 358–404.

(1993): "The Weakness of Strong Theories: The U.S. State's Dominance of the World War II Investment Process," *American Sociological Review* 58: 37–53.

Howard, Michael, ed. (1959): *Soldiers and Governments*. Bloomington: Indiana University Press. See especially his introduction.

Hsiao, Kung-Chuan (1960): *Rural China: Imperial Control in the Nineteenth Century*. Seattle: University of Washington Press. A detailed study of crucial mechanisms in a vast empire's survival.

Johnston, R. J. (1982): *Geography and the State: An Essay in Political Geography*. New York: St. Martin's. A general discussion of states from the perspectives of space and political economy.

Kearney, Michael (1991): "Borders and Boundaries of State and Self at the End of the Empire," *Journal of Historical Sociology* 4: 52–72.

Kennedy, Paul (1987): *The Rise and Fall of the Great Powers: Economic Change and Military Conflict from 1500 to 2000*. New York: Random House. The best-seller turns out to be more thoughtful and tentative than expected.

Keohane, Robert O., and Joseph S. Nye, Jr. (1975): "International Interdependence and Integration," in Fred I. Greenstein and Nelson W. Polsby, eds., *Handbook of Political Science*, vol. 8. Reading, Mass.: Addison-Wesley.

Khazanov, Anatoly M. (1993): "Muhammad and Jenghiz Khan Compared: The Religious Factor in World Empire Building," *Comparative Studies in Society and History* 35: 461–479.

Kick, Edward, and David Kiefer (1987): "The Influence of the World System on War in the Third World," *International Journal of Sociology and Social Policy* 7: 34–48.

Kim, Kyung-Won (1970): *Revolution and International System: A Study in the Breakdown of International Security*. New York: NYU Press. Deals with the war-making of the revolutionary French, in one of the few attempts that have been made to rigorously relate domestic politics and international conflict via real cases.

Kirby, Andrew (1993): *Power/Resistance: Local Politics and the Chaotic State*. Bloomington: Indiana University Press. A geographer's fresh reflections on the modes of government.

Kirby, Andrew, and Michael D. Ward (1991): "Modernity and the Process of State Formation: An Examination of 20th Century Africa," *International Interactions* 17: 113–126.

Krader, Lawrence (1968): *Formation of the State*. Englewood Cliffs, N.J.: Prentice-Hall. An anthropologist's synthesis.

Krasner, Steven (1984): "Approaches to the State: Alternative Conceptions and Historical Dynamics," *Comparative Politics* 16: 223–246. (1985): *Structural Conflict: The Third World Against Global Liberalism*. Berkeley: University of California Press. How politics modifies short-run economic interest.

Kriesi, Hanspeter (1993): *Political Mobilization and Social Change: The Dutch Case in Comparative Perspective*. Aldershot, England: Avebury. Social movements and routine politics related to the distinctness of the Dutch state and economy.

Lang, James (1975): *Conquest and Commerce: Spain and England in the Americas*. New York: Academic Press. The economic and political bases of distinctly different forms of rule. (1979): *Portuguese Brazil: The King's Plantation*. New York: Academic Press. Colony- and state-formation in a long comparative perspective.

Laumann, Edward O., and David Knoke (1987): *The Organizational State: Social Choice in National Policy Domains*. Madison: University of Wisconsin Press. The detailed networks and coalitions that make a difference in U.S. government.

Launius, Michael A. (1985): "The State and Industrial Labor in South Korea," *Bulletin of Concerned Asian Scholars* 16: 2–10.

Lee, Su-Hoon (1988): *State-building in the Contemporary Third World*. Boulder: Westview. Systematic, quantitative examination of alternative theories.

Lerner, Adam J., ed. (1991): "Reimagining the Nation," *Millennium* 20, entire issue. Anthony Smith, Richard Falk, Jean Bethke Elshtain, William Connolly, Partha Chatterjee, and others take variously postmodern looks at nationalism.

Lonsdale, John (1981): "States and Social Processes in Africa: A Historiographical Survey," *African Studies Review* 24: 139–226.

Lowi, Theodore J. (1992): "The State in Political Science: How We Became What We Study," *American Political Science Review* 86: 1–7. How changes in the American state have shaped the agenda of political science in the United States.

Lustick, Ian S. (1993): *Unsettled States, Disputed Lands: Britain and Ireland, France and Algeria, Israel and the West Bank-Gaza*. Ithaca: Cornell University Press. What is really at issue in struggles like those over Palestinian territory.

Mandel, Robert (1980): "Roots of the Modern Interstate Border Dispute," *Journal of Conflict Resolution* 24: 427–454.

Mann, Michael (1988): *States, War and Capitalism*. Oxford: Blackwell. (1986, 1993): *The Sources of Social Power*. Vol. I: *A History of Power from the Beginning to A.D. 1760*; Vol. II: *The Rise of Classes and Nation-States, 1760–1914*. Cambridge: Cambridge University Press. Massive synthetic effort in the first two of a projected four volumes. Chips off the great block include (1988): *States, War and Capitalism*. Oxford: Blackwell. Mann, ed. (1990): *The Rise and Decline of the Nation State*. Oxford: Blackwell. More precisely, how particular states—especially Britain and the United States—gained and lost power.

Markovitz, Irving Leonard (1977): *Power and Class in Africa*. Englewood Cliffs, N.J.: Prentice-Hall. Overview of shifting class formations and political power in Africa from the precolonial to postcolonial periods. Markovitz, ed. (1985): *Studies in Power and Class in Africa*. New York: Oxford University Press. Thirteen case studies analyzing contemporary African politics from a perspective that lays heavy emphasis on the concept of social class—and in two of them, on the role of gender issues.

Marshall, T. H. (1950): *Citizenship and Social Class*. Cambridge: Cambridge University Press. One of the outstanding statements of the (debatable) view that the modern state tends increasingly to equalize its citizens and draw them into political life.

Mastanduno, Michael, David A. Lake, and G. John Ikenberry (1989): "Toward a Realist Theory of State Action," *International Studies Quarterly* 33: 457–474.

Mayo, James M. (1988): *War Memorials as Political Landscape: The American Experience and Beyond*. New York: Praeger. Historical review of meanings, symbols, and political contexts.

McNeill, William H. (1982): *The Pursuit of Power: Technology, Armed Force and Society Since A.D. 1000*. Chicago: University of Chicago Press. Quick, thinly documented, and provocative.

Mellor, Roy E.H. (1989): *Nation, State, and Territory: A Political Geography*. London: Routledge. Blessedly concrete discussion of boundaries, relations between nations and states, territorial administration, and similar issues.

Migdal, Joel S. (1988): *Strong Societies and Weak States: State-Society Relations and State Capabilities in the Third World*. Princeton: Princeton University Press. Why and how the Israeli state exerts a lot of control over its population, the state of Sierra Leone very little, and Egypt, India, and Mexico lie between the extremes.

Mitchell, Timothy (1991): "The Limits of the State: Beyond Statist Approaches and Their Critics," *American Political Science Review* 85: 77–96.

Modelski, George (1978): "The Long Cycle of Global Politics and the Nation-State," *Comparative Studies in Society and History* 20: 214–235.

Modelski, George, and William R. Thompson (1988): *Seapower in Global Politics, 1494–1993*. Seattle: University of Washington Press. Data-packed analysis of changing hegemony.

Morgan, Edmund S. (1988): *Inventing the People: The Rise of Popular Sovereignty in England and America*. New York: Norton. Whence and wherefore the idea of government by the consent—and in the interest—of the governed.

Moul, William Brian (1988): "Balances of Power and the Escalation to War of Serious Disputes Among the European Great Powers, 1815–1939: Some Evidence," *American Journal of Political Science* 32: 241–275.

Mouzelis, Nicos P. (1986): *Politics in the Semi-Periphery: Early Parliamentarism and Late Industrialization in the Balkans and Latin America*. New York: St. Martin's. Oligarchic parliamentarism and its successors in Bulgaria, Greece, Chile, Argentina, and Brazil.

Nelson, Joan M. (1979): *Access to Power: Politics and the Urban Poor in Developing Nations*. Princeton: Princeton University Press. Hard blows against theories of marginality.

O'Connor, James (1973): *The Fiscal Crisis of the State*. New York: St. Martin's. Marxist analysis of the role and activity of the state in capitalism.

O'Donnell, G. A. (1972): *Modernización y autoritarismo*. Buenos Aires: Paidos. General analysis of the emergence of "bureaucratic-authoritarian" regimes, especially in Latin America. See also his even more general article (1980): "Comparative Historical Formations of the State Apparatus and Socioeconomic Change in the Third World," *International Social Science Journal* 32: 717–729.

O'Donnell, Guillermo, and Philippe C. Schmitter (1986): *Transitions from Authoritarian Rule: Tentative Conclusions About Uncertain Democracies*. Baltimore: Johns Hopkins University Press. Where we stand on studies of democratization.

Olson, Mancur (1982): *The Rise and Decline of Nations: Economic Growth, Stagflation, and Social Rigidities*. New Haven: Yale University Press. The author of *The Logic of Collective Action*, which caused a stir in its own right, spells out the implications of different forms of collective action for the structure of power and the state of the economy.

Orloff, Ann Shola (1993): "Gender and the Social Rights of Citizenship: The Comparative Analysis of Gender Relations and Welfare States," *American Sociological Review* 58: 303–328.

Paddison, Ronan (1983): *The Fragmented State: The Political Geography of Power.* Oxford: Blackwell. Eclectic, concept-mongering, data-filled discussion of relations between national and local governments in twentieth-century capitalist democracies.

Parker, Geoffrey (1988): *The Geopolitics of Domination.* London: Routledge. Precisely, the geopolitical requisites for expansion and domination.

Pinheiro, Paulo Sérgio (1992): *Estratégias da Ilusão: A Revoluçao Mundial e o Brasil, 1922–1935.* São Paulo: Companhia das Letras. How revolutions elsewhere affected Brazil's revolutionary conflicts.

Poggi, Gianfranco (1990): *The State: Its Nature, Development and Prospects.* Stanford: Stanford University Press. With no clear theory of state formation but a reflective sense of the literature, Poggi puts the contemporary Western state in its historical context.

Poulantzas, Nicos (1973): *Political Power and Social Classes.* London: New Left Books. Imprecise but influential effort to improve Marx with long-run instead of short-run instrumentalism.

Przeworski, Adam, and Fernando Limongi (1993): "Political Regimes and Economic Growth," *Journal of Economic Perspectives* 7: 51–69. Against the view that authoritarian regimes assure faster growth than democratic ones.

Ramsay, G. D. (1975): *The City of London in International Politics at the Accession of Elizabeth Tudor.* Manchester: Manchester University Press. (1986): *The Queen's Merchants and the Revolt of the Netherlands.* Manchester: Manchester University Press. The interplay of economics and politics on an international scale.

Rasler, Karen A., and William R. Thompson (1990): *War and State Making: The Shaping of the Global Powers.* Boston: Unwin Hyman. How global wars reshaped states and relations between them from 1100 A.D. to the recent past.

Rokkan, Stein, and Derek W. Urwin, eds. (1982): *The Politics of Territorial Identity: Studies in European Regionalism.* Beverly Hills, Calif.: Sage. Case after case, with tentative—very tentative—generalizations.

Rosecrance, Richard (1986): *The Rise of the Trading State: Commerce and Conquest in the Modern World.* New York: Basic Books. How, in the world of the 1980s, trade became more attractive than force as an instrument of foreign policy.

Rueschemeyer, Dietrich, Evelyne Huber Stephens, and John D. Stephens (1992): *Capitalist Development and Democracy.* Chicago: University of Chicago Press. How industrialization generated uncontainable popular demands and thereby opened the way to democracy.

Ruggie, John Gerard (1993): "Territoriality and Beyond: Problematizing Modernity in International Relations," *International Organization* 47: 139–174.

Rupert, Mark Edward (1990): "Producing Hegemony: State/Society Relations and the Politics of Productivity in the United States," *International Studies Quarterly* 34: 427–456.

Schapera, I. (1956): *Government and Politics in Tribal Societies.* London: Watts. An anthropologist's reflections on African government before and beside colonialism.

Schieder, Theodor (1969): *Zum Problem des Staatenpluralismus in der modernen Welt.* Cologne: Westdeutscher Verlag. Why and how plural states, including the various Habsburg empires, evolved.

Schram, Stuart, ed. (1985): *The Scope of State Power in China.* Schram, ed. (1987): *Foundations and Limits of State Power in China.* Both volumes published for the European Science Foundation by the School of Oriental and African Studies, University of London, and the Chinese University Press of Hong Kong. Authoritative manuals.

Schurmann, Franz (1974): *The Logic of World Power: An Inquiry into the Origins, Currents, and Contradictions of World Politics.* New York: Pantheon. A founding statement for realist analyses of U.S., Soviet, and Chinese foreign policies.

Schwartz, Mildred A. (1974): *Politics and Territory: The Sociology of Regional Persistence in Canada.* Montreal: McGill-Queens University Press. Systematic and analytic, from a Canadian perspective.

Seeldrayers, Edmond-Pierre (1958): *Les Composants de l'Etat moderne.* Brussels: Librarie Encyclopédique. An analysis of the interaction of states and other organizations around them.

Segal, Daniel A. (1988): "Nationalism, Comparatively Speaking," *Journal of Historical Sociology* 1: 301–321.

Sen, Amartya (1991): "What Did You Learn in the World Today?" *American Behavioral Scientist* 34: 530–548. On the relative effectiveness of states and markets in delivering different sorts of goods.

Shue, Vivienne (1988): *The Reach of the State: Sketches of the Chinese Body Politic.* Stanford: Stanford University Press. Penetrating, theoretically informed studies.

Silberman, Bernard S. (1993): *Cages of Reason: The Rise of the Rational State in France, Japan, the United States, and Great Britain.* Chicago: University of Chicago Press. Why, *pace* Max Weber, very different sorts of bureaucracies formed in these four countries.

Skocpol, Theda (1980): "Political Response to Capitalist Crisis: Neo-Marxist Theories of the State and the Case of the New Deal," *Politics and Society* 10: 155–201. (1982): "State Capacity and Economic Intervention in the Early New Deal," *Political Science Quarterly* 97: 255–278. (1992): *Protecting Soldiers and Mothers: The Political Origins of Social Policy in the United States.* Cambridge, Mass.: Harvard University Press. How organized women and opportunistic politicians interacted to create a "maternalist" welfare state.

Skowronek, Stephen (1982): *Building a New Administrative State: The Expansion of National Administrative Capacities, 1877–1920.* Cambridge: Cambridge University Press. Taking the American state seriously.

Snider, Lewis W. (1988): "Comparing the Strength of Nations: The Arab Gulf States and Political Change," *Comparative Politics* 20: 461–484.

Spuler, Bertold (1977): *Rulers and Governments of the World.* 3 vols. London: Bowker. Catalog, running far back in time.

Stepan, Alfred (1978): *The State and Society: Peru in Comparative Perspective.* Princeton: Princeton University Press. Stepan always theorizes his cases provocatively.

Strang, David (1990): "From Dependency to Sovereignty: An Event History Analysis of Decolonization, 1870–1987," *American Sociological Review* 55: 846–860.

(1991): "Global Patterns of Decolonization, 1500–1987," *International Studies Quarterly* 35: 429–454.

Tainter, Joseph A. (1988): *The Collapse of Complex Societies*. Cambridge: Cambridge University Press. How marginal returns from complexity do in big structures, especially empires.

Tarschys, Daniel (1971): *Beyond the State: The Future Polity in Classical and Soviet Marxism*. Swedish Studies in International Relations 3. Stockholm: Laromedelsforlagen. Careful review of doctrines and fantasies.

Taylor, Peter J. (1981): "Political Geography and the World-Economy," in Alan D. Burnett and Peter J. Taylor, eds., *The Politics of Territorial Identity*. New York: Wiley.

Theobald, Robin (1990): *Corruption, Development and Underdevelopment*. Durham, N.C.: Duke University Press. Prudent, well-informed survey of corruption and state formation on a world scale.

Therborn, Goran (1978): *What Does the Ruling Class Do When It Rules?* London: NLB. If you don't like the title, you won't like the book; it's a thoughtful, widely documented, ultimately inconclusive pair of essays on (1) the dictatorship of the proletariat and (2) states and class power.

Thompson, William R. (1988): *On Global War: Historical-Structural Approaches to World Politics*. Columbia: University of South Carolina Press. Another culmination, complement to the Rasler-Thompson and Modelski-Thompson books listed earlier.

Thomson, Janice E. (1989): "Sovereignty in Historical Perspective: The Evolution of State Control over Extraterritorial Violence," in James A. Caporaso, ed., *The Elusive State: International and Comparative Perspectives*. Newbury Park, Calif.: Sage. (1990): "State Practices, International Norms, and the Decline of Mercenarism," *International Studies Quarterly* 34: 23–48.

Tibi, Bassam (1989): *Konfliktregion Naher Osten: Regionale Eigendynamik und Grossmachtinteressent*. Munich: Beck. Placing the Middle East wars of 1967 and 1973 firmly in the perspectives of international relations and state structure.

Topalov, Christian (1991): "Patriotismes et citoyennetés," *Genèses* 3: 162–176.

Tracy, James D., ed. (1990): *The Rise of Merchant Empires: Long-Distance Trade in the Early Modern World, 1350–1750*. Cambridge: Cambridge University Press.

Turner, Bryan S. (1986): *Citizenship and Capitalism: The Debate over Reformism*. London: Allen & Unwin. (1988): "Religion and State Formation: A Commentary on Recent Debates," *Journal of Historical Sociology* 1: 322–333. (1990): "Outline of a Theory of Citizenship," *Sociology* 24: 189–218. Critique and elaboration of T. H. Marshall. The article summarizes and extends the book.

Wakeman, Frederick, Jr. (1985): *The Great Enterprise: The Manchu Reconstruction of Imperial Order in Seventeenth-Century China*. 2 vols. Berkeley: University of California Press. Massive and informative.

Wallensteen, Peter, Johan Galtung, and Carlos Portales, eds. (1985): *Global Militarization*. Boulder: Westview. Militarism and the threat of war.

Wallerstein, Immanuel (1974–1989): *The Modern World System*. 3 vols. to date. New York: Academic Press. First three of a projected series of volumes portraying the birth and spread of the capitalist world system. These volumes cover the sixteenth to nineteenth centuries. (1991): *Geopolitics and Geoculture: Essays on the*

Changing World Systems. Cambridge: Cambridge University Press. Provocative and often prophetic essays published in the 1980s.

Waltz, Kenneth N. (1979): *Theory of International Politics.* New York: Random House. For retrospect, see his 1988 work: "The Origins of War in Neorealist Theory," *Journal of Interdisciplinary History* 18: 615–628.

Webber, Carolyn, and Aaron Wildavsky (1986): *A History of Taxation and Expenditure in the Western World.* New York: Simon and Schuster. A bit haphazard but packed with information.

Wendt, Alexander E. (1987): "The Agent-Structure Problem in International Relations Theory," *International Organization* 41: 335–370. Exactly who acts in international relations?

Whitney, Joseph B.R. (1970): *China: Area, Administration, and Nation Building.* Research Paper 123. Chicago: Department of Geography, University of Chicago. Geopolitical strategy of Chinese government.

Wittman, Donald (1991): "Nations and States; Mergers and Acquisitions; Dissolutions and Divorce," *American Economic Review* 81, Papers and Proceedings: 126–129.

Zolberg, Aristide (1987): "Beyond the Nation-State: Comparative Politics in Global Perspective," in Jan Berting and Wim Blockmans, eds., *Beyond Progress and Development: Macro-Political and Macro-Societal Change.* Aldershot, England: Avebury.

EUROPEAN STATES

Aarebrot, Frank H. (1974): "Regional Differences in Political Mobilization in Norway: Local Infrastructure Development, Political Polarization, and Suffrage Extension, 1868–1897," *International Journal of Politics* 4: 91–140.

Alapuro, Risto (1988): *State and Revolution in Finland.* Berkeley: University of California Press. Theoretically informed political history with implications far beyond the Nordic countries.

Anderson, Eugene N., and Pauline R. Anderson (1967): *Political Institutions and Social Change in Continental Europe in the Nineteenth Century.* Berkeley and Los Angeles: University of California Press. Well-packed handbook, subject by subject, period by period.

Anderson, M. S. (1988): *War and Society in Europe of the Old Regime, 1618–1789.* London: Fontana. Eminently useful general survey.

Anderson, Perry (1974): *Passages from Antiquity to Feudalism.* London: NLB. (1974): *Lineages of the Absolutist State.* London: NLB. Two books to conjure with.

Andreucci, Franco, and Alessandra Pescarolo (1989): *Gli spazi del potere: Aree, regioni, Stati:—Le coordinate territoriali della storia contemporanea.* Florence: Istituto Ernesto Ragionieri. Essays on regions and space in political change.

Andrews, Kenneth R. (1984): *Trade, Plunder and Settlement: Maritime Enterprise and the Genesis of the British Empire, 1480–1630.* Cambridge: Cambridge University Press. Rampant capital in the making of empire.

Armstrong, John A. (1973): *The European Administrative Elite*. Princeton: Princeton University Press. Theoretical and historical analysis.

Arrighi, Giovanni, ed. (1985): *Semiperipheral Development: The Politics of Southern Europe in the Twentieth Century*. Beverly Hills: Sage. Marginal states in the world system.

Artéus, Gunnar (1982): *Krigsmakt och samhälle i Frihetstidens Sverige*. Stockholm: Militarhistorika Forlaget. Systematic examination of historical evidence to establish the extent and social bases of militarization in eighteenth-century Sweden. English summary.

Ballbé, Manuel (1983): *Ordén púeblico y militarismo en la España constitucional (1812–1983)*. Madrid: Alianza Editorial. Standard treatment of nineteenth-century struggles.

Barkey, Karen (1991): "Rebellious Alliances: The State and Peasant Unrest in Early Seventeenth-Century France and the Ottoman Empire," *American Sociological Review* 56: 699–715.

Bearman, Peter S. (1993): *Relations into Rhetorics: Local Elite Social Structure in Norfolk, England, 1540–1640*. New Brunswick, N.J.: Rutgers University Press. Changing networks of kinship and patronage as a key to political transformation.

Beik, William H. (1985): *Absolutism and Society in Seventeenth-Century France*. Cambridge: Cambridge University Press. Analytic and thorough.

Best, Geoffrey (1982): *War and Society in Revolutionary Europe, 1770–1870*. London: Fontana. Another valuable survey.

Birnbaum, Pierre (1988): *States and Collective Action: The European Experience*. Cambridge: Cambridge University Press. Lucid, energetic essays on connections between collective action and states' organization. (1993): *"La France aux Français": Histoire des haines nationalistes*. Paris: Seuil. The ugliness of xenophobia, especially as seen in French anti-Semitism.

Black, Jeremy, ed. (1987): *The Origins of War in Early Modern Europe*. Edinburgh: John Donald. Specialized essays.

Blickle, Peter (1988): *Unruhen in der ständischen Gesellschaft, 1300–1800*. Vol. 1. Munich: Oldenbourg. Enzyklopädie Deutscher Geschichte. Learned and opinionated.

Blockmans, Wim P. (1978): "A Typology of Representative Institutions in Late Medieval Europe," *Journal of Medieval History* 4: 189–215. (1988): "Princes conquérants et bourgeois calculateurs: Le poids des réseaux urbains dans la formation des états," in Neithard Bulst and Jean-Philippe Genet, eds., *La ville, la bourgeoisie et la genèse de l'état moderne*. Paris: Editions du Centre National de la Recherche Scientifique. (1988): "Alternatives to Monarchical Centralisation: The Great Tradition of Revolt in Flanders and Brabant," in Helmut Koenigsberger, ed., *Republiken und Republikanismus im Europa der Frühen Neuzeit*. Munich: Oldenbourg, 1988.

Blum, Jerome (1978): *The End of the Old Order in Rural Europe*. Princeton: Princeton University Press. Sweeping survey of the emergence of a rural world dominated by capitalism and large states.

Bonham, Gary (1983): "State Autonomy or Class Domination: Approaches to Administrative Politics in Wilhelmine Germany," *World Politics* 35: 631–651.

Bonney, Richard (1991): *The European Dynastic States, 1494–1660.* Oxford: Oxford University Press. Encyclopedic and analytical.

Bossenga, Gail (1988): "City and State: An Urban Perspective on the Origins of the French Revolution," in Keith Michael Baker, ed., *The French Revolution and the Creation of Modern Political Culture.* Vol. I: *The Political Culture of the Old Regime.* Oxford: Pergamon. (1988): "La Révolution française et les corporations: Trois exemples lillois," *Annales: Economies, Sociétés, Civilisations* 43: 405–426.

Braddick, Michael (1991): "State Formation and Social Change in Early Modern England: A Problem Stated and Approaches Suggested," *Social History* 16: 1–18.

Brady, Thomas A., Jr. (1985): *Turning Swiss: Cities and Empire, 1450–1550.* Cambridge: Cambridge University Press. Forming states to ward off imperial power.

Braudel, Fernand (1966): *La Méditerranée et le monde méditerranéen à l'époque de Philippe II.* 2 vols. 2d ed. Paris: Colin. Inspiration to a generation of European scholars for its breadth, method, and analytic intelligence.

Brewer, John (1976): *Party Ideology and Popular Politics at the Accession of George III.* Cambridge: Cambridge University Press. Includes a rich, reflective analysis of popular politics in London and its implicit political theory. (1989): *The Sinews of Power: War, Money and the English State, 1688–1783.* New York: Knopf. Remarkable recasting of our understanding of the eighteenth-century British state.

Broeker, Galen (1970): *Rural Disorder and Police Reform in Ireland, 1812–36.* London: Routledge & Kegan Paul. How the British experimented with repression across the Irish Sea before installing it in England.

Brogden, Mike (1987): "The Emergence of the Police: The Colonial Dimension," *British Journal of Criminology* 27: 4–14.

Brubaker, Rogers (1992): *Citizenship and Nationhood in France and Germany.* Cambridge, Mass.: Harvard University Press. Sustained comparison from the seventeenth century onward brings out the difference between "inclusive" French and "exclusive" German principles of citizenship as a function of state formation.

Bruckmüller, Ernst (1990): "Ein 'deutsches' Bürgertum? Zu Fragen nationaler Differenzierung der bürgerlichen Schichten in der Habsburgermonarchie vom Vormärz bis um 1860," *Geschichte und Gesellschaft* 16: 343–354.

Bulpitt, Jim (1983): *Territory and Power in the United Kingdom.* Manchester: Manchester University Press. Center versus periphery, court versus country, internal colonialism discussed in general and in terms of the formation of the United Kingdom.

Bulst, Neithard, and Jean-Philippe Genet, eds. (1988): *La ville, la bourgeoisie et la genèse de l'Etat modern (XIIe–XVIIIe siècles).* Paris: Editions du Centre National de la Recherche Scientifique. Important new studies of burghers and states.

Busch, Otto (1962): *Militarsystem und Sozialleben im alten Preussen 1713–1807: Die Anfänge der sozialen Militarisierung der preussisch-deutschen Gesellschaft.* Berlin: de Gruyter. How the military permeated Prussia.

Carr, Raymond (1966): *Spain, 1808–1939.* Oxford: Clarendon Press. One of the best standard histories.

Carsten, F. L. (1954): *The Origins of Prussia.* Oxford: Clarendon Press. One of the big state-making experiences, well analyzed. See also his 1967 book for later development: *The Rise of Fascism.* Berkeley: University of California Press.

Chapman, Brian (1970): *Police State.* London: Pall Mall. The concept and the reality.

Church, Clive H. (1981): *Revolution and Red Tape: The French Ministerial Bureaucracy, 1770–1850*. Oxford: Clarendon Press. What repeated revolutions did to state structure.

Clark, Sir George (1969): "The Social Foundations of States," in F. L. Carsten, ed., *The New Cambridge Modern History*. Vol. V: *The Ascendancy of France, 1648–88*. Cambridge: Cambridge University Press: 176–197. Good summary essay on a pivotal period for European state-making. *The New Cambridge Modern History* as a whole is an excellent resource for facts, interpretations, and bibliographies.

Cohen, Stanley, and Andrew Scull, eds. (1983): *Social Control and the State: Historical and Comparative Essays*. Oxford: Martin Robertson. Primarily critical views of the hoary sociological concept of social control, with special reference to Britain since 1700.

Contamine, Philippe (1984): *War in the Middle Ages*. Oxford: Blackwell. (French version published in 1980.) Important synthesis for the major powers of western Europe.

Cooper, J. P. (1960): "Differences Between English and Continental Governments in the Early Seventeenth Century," in J. S. Bromley and E. H. Kossman, eds., *Britain and the Netherlands*. London: Chatto & Windus.

Corrigan, Philip, and Derek Sayer (1985): *The Great Arch: English State Formation as Cultural Revolution*. Oxford: Blackwell. Imprecise but challenging.

Corvisier, André (1976): *Armées et sociétés en Europe de 1494 à 1789*. Paris: Presses Universitaires de France. The art and organization of war in a belligerent era.

Coveney, P. J., ed. (1977): *France in Crisis, 1620–1675*. Totowa, N.J.: Rowman & Littlefield. Standard texts on seventeenth-century conflicts and changes, translated and introduced.

Cronin, James E. (1991): *The Politics of State Expansion: War, State and Society in Twentieth-Century Britain*. London: Routledge. A lucid, original combination of history and political criticism.

Cruz, Rafael (1993): "Crisis del Estado y acción colectiva en el periodo de entreguerras, 1917–1939," *Historia Social* 15: 119–138.

Dann, Otto, and John Dinwiddy (1988): *Nationalism in the Age of the French Revolution*. London: Hambledon. Thoughtful survey.

Downing, Brian M. (1992): *The Military Revolution and Political Change: Origins of Democracy and Autocracy in Early Modern Europe*. Princeton: Princeton University Press. As the subtitle hints, an extended and well-documented argument for the revision of Barrington Moore's classic theses by considering the financing of military organization and the survival of medieval representative institutions.

Duffy, Michael, ed. (1980): *The Military Revolution and the State, 1500–1800*. Exeter Studies in History 1. Exeter, England: University of Exeter. How the expansion of armed forces and the rise of expenditures affected European states.

Dunn, James A., Jr. (1972): "Consociational Democracy and Language Conflict: A Comparison of the Belgian and Swiss Experiences," *Comparative Political Studies* 32: 51–78.

Elliott, J. H. (1963): *Imperial Spain, 1469–1716*. London: Edward Arnold. Spain in its greatness and (only relative) decline.

Emsley, Clive (1983): *Policing and Its Context, 1750–1870*. London: Macmillan. Lucid, well-documented comparisons of England, France, and Prussia.

Evans, Eric J. (1983): *The Forging of the Modern State: Early Industrial Britain, 1783–1870*. London: Longmans. Industrialization and changes in national politics.

Fedorowicz, J. K., ed. (1982): *A Republic of Nobles: Studies in Polish History to 1864*. Cambridge: Cambridge University Press. Authoritative collection of essays on that elusive state.

Fullbrook, Mary (1993): *National Histories and European History*. Boulder: Westview. Well-informed reviews both of general issues and particular countries, oriented toward the understanding of nationalism.

Genet, Jean-Philippe, ed. (1990): *L'Etat moderne: Genèse*. Paris: Editions du Centre National de la Recherche Scientifique. Summaries by region plus specialized studies.

Genet, Jean-Philippe, and Michel Le Mené, eds. (1987): *Genèse de l'état moderne: Prélèvement et Redistribution*. Paris: Editions du Centre National de la Recherche Scientifique. Well-informed essays on fiscal structure and state formation in medieval and early modern Europe.

Goldstein, Robert J. (1983): *Political Repression in 19th Century Europe*. London: Croom Helm. A catalog, using a broad definition, for all of Europe, 1815–1914.

Greenfeld, Liah (1992): *Nationalism: Five Roads to Modernity*. Cambridge, Mass.: Harvard University Press. How ideas of the nation formed and changed in England, France, Germany, Russia, and the United States.

Greengrass, Mark, ed. (1991): *Conquest and Coalescence: The Shaping of the State in Early Modern Europe*. London: Edward Arnold. The Papal State, Portugal, Béarn, Flanders, Ireland, Scotland, the Ukraine, and other presumed peripheries offer another perspective on state formation.

Grillo, R. D. (1980): *"Nation" and "State" in Europe: Anthropological Perspectives*. New York: Academic Press. How European states interact with ethnic minorities, poor regions, and social change.

Guénée, Bernard (1985): *States and Rulers in Later Medieval Europe*. Oxford: Basil Blackwell. Informative survey from a French perspective.

Guilmartin, John, Jr. (1988): "Ideology and Conflict: The Wars of the Ottoman Empire, 1453–1606," *Journal of Interdisciplinary History* 18: 721–748.

Gutmann, Myron P. (1980): *War and Rural Life in the Early Modern Low Countries*. Princeton: Princeton University Press. Under what conditions did war cause irreparable damage to population growth?

Hamilton, E. V. (1947): *War and Prices in Spain, 1650–1800*. Cambridge: Cambridge University Press. One of the most influential early statements of the theme of dominant economic cycles closely tied to changes in the European money supply. (1950): "Origin and Growth of the National Debt in France and England," in *Studi in onore di Gino Luzzato*.Vol. I. Milan: Giuffrè.

't Hart, Marjolein (1993): *The Making of a Bourgeois State: War, Politics and Finance During the Dutch Revolt*. Manchester, England: Manchester University Press. As the open sesame of state formation, fiscal history becomes magically effective.

Hay, Douglas et al. (1975): *Albion's Fatal Tree: Crime and Society in Eighteenth-Century England*. New York: Pantheon. Essays on crime, repression, and the use of legal means to hold back the working class.

Headrick, Daniel R. (1981): *The Tools of Empire: Technology and European Imperialism in the Nineteenth Century.* New York: Oxford. How technical change facilitated hegemony.

Hechter, Michael (1975): *Internal Colonialism: The Celtic Fringe in British National Development, 1536–1966.* Berkeley: University of California Press. Pioneering, however much subsequent work has whittled away its arguments and findings.

Hechter, Michael, and William Brustein (1980): "Regional Modes of Production and Patterns of State Formation in Europe," *American Journal of Sociology* 85: 1061–1094.

Henshall, Nicholas (1992): *The Myth of Absolutism: Change & Continuity in Early Modern European Monarchy.* London: Longmans. France and England viewed realistically, theories of absolutism viewed skeptically.

Hernández, Francesc, and Francesc Mercadé, eds. (1986): *Estructuras Sociales y cuestión nacional en españa.* Barcelona: Ariel. Thoughtful essays on state and social organization in Spain.

Hernes, Helga (1988): "Scandinavian Citizenship," *Acta Sociologica* 31: 199–215.

Herr, Richard (1989): *Rural Change and Royal Finances in Spain at the End of the Old Regime.* Berkeley: University of California Press. How fiscal policy and changes in the rural economy interacted in the collapse of the old state.

Hill, Christopher (1966): *The Century of Revolution, 1603–1714.* London: Nelson. Mildly Marxist analysis of seventeenth-century England, centering on its revolution.

Hintze, Otto (1962): *Staat und Verfassung.* 2d. ed. Göttingen: Vandenhoeck & Ruprecht. One of the most important statements from the German "historical school" of the early twentieth century.

Hroch, Miroslav (1985): *Social Preconditions of National Revival in Europe: A Comparative Analysis of the Social Composition of Patriotic Groups Among the Smaller European Nations.* Cambridge: Cambridge University Press. Painstaking and informative, if somewhat undigested, compilation of those who actually became patriotic activists.

Ingrao, Charles W. (1987): *The Hessian Mercenary State: Ideas, Institutions, and Reform Under Frederick II, 1760–1785.* Cambridge: Cambridge University Press. Close look at an important vendor of troops.

Jelavich, Charles, and Barbara Jelavich (1977): *The Establishment of the Balkan National States, 1804–1920.* Seattle: University of Washington Press. How the Ottoman Empire broke up.

Jespersen, Leon (1985): "The *Machtstaat* in Seventeenth-Century Denmark," *Scandinavian Journal of History* 10: 271–304.

Kaiser, David (1990): *Politics and War: European Conflict from Philip II to Hitler.* Cambridge, Mass.: Harvard University Press. How the character of war changed as a consequence of alterations in the organization of states and vice versa.

Keeney, Barnaby C. (1947): "Military Service and the Development of Nationalism in England, 1272–1327," *Speculum* 4: 534–549.

Kettering, Sharon (1993): "Brokerage at the Court of Louis XIV," *The Historical Journal* 36: 69–87. One of a series of articles neatly delineating patron-client and brokerage relationships in France.

Kiernan, V. G. (1973): "Conscription and Society in Europe Before the War of 1914–18," in M.R.D. Foot, ed., *War and Society: Historical Essays in Honour and Memory of J. R. Western, 1928–1971*. London: Elek Books. (1980): *State and Society in Europe, 1550–1650*. Oxford: Blackwell. Urbane, Left-leaning synthesis.

Klaveren, Jan van (1957): "Die historische Erscheinung der Korruption," *Vierteljahrschrift für Sozial- und Wirtschaftsgeschichte* 44: 289–324. (1960): "Fiskalismus—Merkantilismus—Korruption: Drei Aspekte der Finanz- und Wirtschaftspolitik während des Ancien Regime," *Vierteljahrschrift für Sozial- und Wirtschaftsgeschichte* 47: 333–353.

Koch, Koen (1993): *Over Staat en Statenvorming*. Leiden: DSWO Press. Explication, criticism, and synthesis, with special reference to Dutch state formation.

Konvitz, Joseph W. (1990): "The Nation-State, Paris and Cartography in Eighteenth- and Nineteenth-Century France," *Journal of Historical Geography* 16: 3–16.

Kristeva, Julia (1993): *Nations Without Nationalism*. New York: Columbia University Press. Passionate, original reflections on racism, patriotism, and related evils.

Kuhnle, Stein (1973): *Social Mobilization and Political Participation: The Nordic Countries, c. 1850–1970*. Bergen, Norway: Institute of Sociology. Detailed, data-based comparisons.

Lachmann, Richard (1989): "Elite Conflict and State Formation in 16th- and 17th-Century England and France," *American Sociological Review* 54: 141–162.

Ladero Quesada, Miguel Angel (1970): "Les finances royales de Castille à la veille des temps modernes," *Annales: Economies, Sociétés, Civilisations* 25: 775–788.

Ladewig Peterson, E. (1975): "From Domain State to Tax State: Synthesis and Interpretation," *Scandinavian Economic History Review* 23: 116–148.

Lane, Frederic C. (1973): *Venice, a Maritime Republic*. Baltimore: Johns Hopkins University Press. A classic. (1975): "The Role of Government in Economic Growth in Early Modern Times," *Journal of Economic History* 35: 8–17. Likewise.

Lempert, David (1993): "Changing Russian Political Culture in the 1990s: Parasites, Paradigms, and Perestroika," *Comparative Studies in Society and History* 35: 628–646.

Levack, Brian P. (1987): *The Formation of the British State: England, Scotland, and the Union, 1603–1707*. Oxford: Clarendon Press. No-nonsense tracing of the legal process.

Levy, Jack S. (1983): *War in the Modern Great Power System, 1495–1975*. Lexington: University Press of Kentucky. (1989): "The Causes of War: A Review of Theories and Evidence," in Philip Tetlock et al., eds., *Behavior, Society, and Nuclear War*. New York: Oxford University Press. Both the monograph and the review are dense, thoughtful, and valuable.

Lewis, Archibald R., and Timothy J. Runyan (1988): *European Naval and Maritime History, 300–1500*. Bloomington: Indiana University Press. Helpful survey.

Lindegren, Jan (1985): "The Swedish 'Military State,' 1560–1720," *Scandinavian Journal of History* 10: 305–336.

Linz, Juan (1992): "Los nacionalismos en España: Una perspectiva comparada," *Historia y Fuente Oral* 7: 127–136.

Liublinskaya, A. D. (1968): *French Absolutism: The Crucial Phase, 1620–1629*. Cambridge: Cambridge University Press. An outstanding Russian scholar offers a more or less Marxist synthesis.

Lüdtke, Alf (1989): *Police and State in Prussia, 1815–1850.* Cambridge: Cambridge University Press. (Translation of German version published in 1982.) Police as a prism for the state's imposition of order. (1992): *"Sicherheit" und "Wohlfahrt": Polizei, Gesellschaft und Herrschaft im 19. und 20. Jahrhundert.* Frankfurt: Suhrkamp. Political contexts and meanings of police activity, especially in the various Germanies since 1850.

Mager, W. (1990): "Die Beseitigung des Feudalregimes in Frankreich und die Bauernbefreiung in Deutschland: Ein Vergleich," in J. Craeybeckx and F. Scheelings, eds., *De Franse Revolutie en Vlaanderen.* Brussels: VUB Press.

Mallet, M. E., and J. R. Hale (1984): *The Military Organization of a Renaissance State: Venice, c. 1400 to 1617.* Cambridge: Cambridge University Press. Two masters of the subject team up.

Mandel, Robert (1980): "Roots of the Modern Interstate Border Dispute," *Journal of Conflict Resolution* 24: 427–454.

Maravall, Jose Antonio (1972): *Estado moderno y mentalidad social siglos XV a XVII.* 2 vols. Madrid: Ediciones de la Revista de Occidente. Conceptions and realizations of the Spanish state in a tumultuous age.

Martínez Dorado, Gloria (1993): "La formación del Estado y la acción colectiva en España: 1808–1845," *Historia Social* 15: 101–118.

Meyer, Jean (1983): *Le poids de l'Etat.* Paris: Presses Universitaires de France. Mostly on the French state, eighteenth to twentieth centuries: opinionated and well informed.

Mjøset, Lars (1990): "The Turn of Two Centuries: A Comparison of British and U.S. Hegemonies," in David P. Rapkin, ed., *World Leadership and Hegemony.* Vol. 5, International Political Economy Yearbook. Boulder: Lynne Rienner.

Monnier, Alain, and Jitka Rychtarikova (1992): "Comment l'Europe s'est divisée entre l'Est et l'Ouest," *Population* 46: 1617–1650.

Motyl, Alexander J., ed. (1992): *Thinking Theoretically About Soviet Nationalities: History and Comparison in the Study of the USSR.* New York: Columbia University Press. A superb guide to available theories, an introduction to the complexities of Russian imperialism.

Moul, William Brian (1988): "Balances of Power and the Escalation to War of Serious Disputes Among the European Great Powers, 1815–1939: Some Evidence," *American Journal of Political Science* 32: 241–275.

Namier, Lewis (1957): *The Structure of Politics at the Accession of George III.* 2d ed. London: Macmillan. A classic of Namierism, aka prosopographical psephology.

Nef, John U. (1965): *Industry and Government in France and England, 1540–1640.* Ithaca: Cornell University Press. (First published in 1940.) Brief and stimulating comparisons of the two great powers-in-the-making.

Nilsson, Sven A. (1988): "Imperial Sweden: Nation-Building, War and Social Change," in Sven A. Nilsson et al., *The Age of New Sweden.* Stockholm: Livrustkammaren.

Noiriel, Gérard (1991): *La tyrannie du National: Le droit d'asile en Europe, 1793–1993.* Paris: Calmann-Lévy. How the rights of political refugees, declared by the French Convention in 1793, bent in response to the interests of consolidating national states.

Nordlinger, Eric A. (1972): *Conflict Regulation in Divided Societies.* Occasional Papers in International Affairs 29. Cambridge, Mass.: Harvard University Center for International Affairs.

North, Douglass C., and Barry Weingast (1989): "Constitutions and Commitment: Evolution of Institutions Governing Public Choice in Seventeenth-Century England," *Journal of Economic History* 49: 803–832.

Ostergard, Uffe (1991): "'Denationalizing' National History: The Comparative Study of Nation-States," *Culture and History* 9–10: 9–41. (1992): "Peasants and Danes: The Danish National Identity and Political Culture," *Comparative Studies in Society and History* 34: 3–27.

Padgett, John F., and Christopher K. Ansell (1993): "Robust Action and the Rise of the Medici, 1400–1434," *American Journal of Sociology* 98: 1259–1319.

Parker, Geoffrey (1988): *The Military Revolution: Military Innovation and the Rise of the West, 1500–1800.* Cambridge: Cambridge University Press. The major synthesis so far.

Peacock, Alan T., and Jack Wiseman (1967): *The Growth of Public Expenditure in the United Kingdom.* 2d ed. London: Allen & Unwin. Budgets as clues to big political processes.

Plumb, J. H. (1967): *The Growth of Political Stability in England, 1675–1725.* London: Macmillan. Take the title at its full meaning: an analysis of how stable government arrived in England after a period of enormous instability.

Poggi, Gianfranco (1978): *The Development of the Modern State: A Sociological Introduction.* Stanford: Stanford University Press. What distinguishes the nineteenth-century constitutional state from its predecessors.

Pounds, Norman J.G., and Sue Simons Ball (1964): "Core-Areas and the Development of the European States System," *Annals of the Association of American Geographers* 54: 24–40.

Powers, James F. (1988): *A Society Organized for War: The Iberian Municipal Militias in the Central Middle Ages, 1000–1284.* Berkeley: University of California Press. Conquest as the bone and sinew of state formation.

Prak, Maarten (1991): "Citizen Radicalism and Democracy in the Dutch Republic: The Patriot Movement of the 1780s," *Theory and Society* 20: 73–102.

Putnam, Robert D. (1993): *Making Democracy Work: Civic Traditions in Modern Italy.* Princeton: Princeton University Press. Embedding democratic institutions in civic reciprocity and sociability makes them work.

Raeff, Marc (1983): *The Well-ordered Police State: Social and Institutional Change Through Law in the Germanies and Russia, 1600–1800.* New Haven: Yale University Press. What it's like to impose top-down order on sprawling, bottom-up chaos.

Reynolds, Susan (1984): *Kingdoms and Communities in Western Europe, 900–1300.* Oxford: Clarendon Press. How aspiring monarchs confronted constituted communities.

Rian, Oystein (1985): "State and Society in Seventeenth-Century Norway," *Scandinavian Journal of History* 10: 337–363.

Riemersma, Jelle C. (1950): "Government Influence on Company Organization in Holland and England (1550–1650)," *The Tasks of Economic History,* supplementary issue of the *Journal of Economic History* 10: 31–39.

Rosanvallon, Pierre (1990): *L'État en France de 1789 à nos jours*. Paris: Seuil. Sophisticated top-down history of the state apparatus. (1992): *Le sacre du citoyen: Histoire du suffrage universel en France*. Paris: Gallimard. Voting rights as doctrine and reality.

Rosenberg, Hans (1958): *Bureaucracy, Aristocracy and Autocracy: The Prussian Experience, 1660–1815*. Cambridge, Mass.: Harvard University Press. The standard general work about the origins of the nineteenth-century bureaucratic state.

Scammell, G. V. (1981): *The World Encompassed: The First European Maritime Empires c. 800–1650*. London: Methuen. How Europeans, long landbound, turned seaward with a vengeance.

Schulze, Hagen, ed. (1987): *Nation-building in Central Europe*. Leamington Spa, England: Berg. More specialized than the title implies.

Schwartz, Robert M. (1988): *Policing the Poor in Eighteenth-Century France*. Chapel Hill: University of North Carolina Press. The turn toward repression ... although not in the way that Michel Foucault conceived it.

Schwartzman, Kathleen C. (1989): *The Social Origins of Democratic Collapse: The First Portuguese Republic in the Global Economy*. Lawrence: University Press of Kansas. How the fragmentation of a semiperipheral state's bourgeoisie made a democratic regime vulnerable.

Searle, Eleanor (1988): *Predatory Kinship and the Creation of Norman Power, 840–1066*. Berkeley: University of California Press. Original and well argued.

Shennan, J. H. (1974): *The Origins of the Modern European State, 1450–1725*. London: Hutchinson University Library. Great on description, less so on analysis.

Somers, Margaret R. (1993): "Citizenship and the Place of the Public Sphere: Law, Community, and Political Culture in the Transition to Democracy," *American Sociological Review* 58: 587–620.

Steinmetz, George (1993): *Regulating the Social: The Welfare State and Local Politics in Imperial Germany*. Princeton: Princeton University Press. Exquisitely tuned to current theoretical discussions, Steinmetz nonetheless does yeoman work in accounting for regional variations within the empire.

Strayer, Joseph (1970): *The Medieval Origins of the Modern State*. Princeton: Princeton University Press. An outstanding medieval historian steps back to survey the entire field. (1971): *Medieval Statecraft and the Perspectives of History*. Princeton: Princeton University Press. More specialized essays on the same theme as in the 1970 book.

Tacke, Charlotte (1993): "Les lieux de mémoire et la mémoire des lieux: Mythes et monuments entre nation et région en France et en Allemagne au XIXe siècle," in Dominique Julia, ed., *Culture et Société dans l'Europe moderne et contemporaine*. Florence: European University Institute. Hermann and Vercingetorix memorialized.

Tenenti, Alberto (1967): *Piracy and the Decline of Venice, 1580–1615*. Berkeley: University of California Press. How other piratical states outpirated Venice.

Thompson, I.A.A. (1976): *War and Government in Habsburg Spain 1560–1620*. London: Athlone Press. A crucial period of Habsburg power—and a good book on it.

Tilly, Charles, ed. (1975): *The Formation of National States in Western Europe*. Princeton: Princeton University Press. The extractive, coercive side of European states as a critique of political development theories. (1990): *Coercion, Capital, and European States,* A.D. 990–1990. Oxford: Blackwell. Synthesis and comparison of alternative processes by which states took shape in Europe. (1993): *European Revolutions, 1492–1992.* Oxford: Blackwell. Broad survey of difference and change.

Vallée, Aline (1987): "Etat et sécurité publique au XIVe siècle: Une nouvelle lecture des archives royales francaises," *Histoire, Economie et Société* 6: 3–15.

Veblen, Thorstein (1966): *Imperial Germany and the Industrial Revolution.* Ann Arbor: University of Michigan Press. (First published in 1915.) Veblen is always worth reading (see his sardonic work on U.S. universities); here he gives us important insights into statism and capitalism.

Verdery, Katherine (1983): *Transylvanian Villagers: Three Centuries of Political, Economic and Ethnic Change.* Berkeley: University of California Press. Remarkable blend of local history, ethnography, and theoretical synthesis concerning state, economy, and ethnicity. (1993): "What Was Socialism and Why Did It Fall?" *Contention* 3: 1–24. With commentaries by Reginald Zelnik and Valerie Bunce.

Viner, Jacob (1948): "Power Versus Plenty as Objectives of Foreign Policy, in the Seventeenth and Eighteenth Centuries," *World Politics* 1: 1–29.

Walker, Mack (1971): *German Home Towns: Community, State, and General Estate 1648–1871.* Ithaca: Cornell University Press. How local power structure made a difference.

Watkins, Susan Cotts (1990): *From Provinces into Nations.* Princeton: Princeton University Press. How European states became distinctly different in demography after 1870.

Werner, Ernst (1985): *Die Geburt einer Grossmacht—die Osmanen (1300–1481).* Vienna: Böhlhaus. The strident entry of the Ottomans into the European system.

Will, Pierre-Etienne, and R. Bing Wong (1991): *Nourish the People: The State Civilian Granary System in China, 1650–1850.* Ann Arbor: University of Michigan Press. Close examination of one crucial institution that tells us much about the state as a whole.

Witt, Peter-Christian, ed. (1987): *Wealth and Taxation in Central Europe.* Leamington Spa, England: Berg. Specialized essays.

Woolf, Stuart (1992): "The Construction of a European World-View in the Revolutionary-Napoleonic Years," *Past & Present* 137: 72–101. Part of an important special issue on "The Cultural and Political Construction of Europe."

Zagorin, Perez (1982): *Rebels and Rulers, 1500–1660.* 2 vols. Cambridge: Cambridge University Press. Well-informed, if antitheoretical, survey of rebellions in England, France, Germany, and the Spanish Empire.

Zolberg, Aristide R. (1980): "Strategic Interactions and the Formation of Modern States: France and England," *International Social Science Journal* 32: 687–716.

About the Book and Editors

THE RISE OF LARGE, powerful states in Europe after 1000 A.D. transformed life across the Continent and eventually through the whole world. The new European states disposed of unprecedented stores of capital and vast military capacities.

In recent decades, scholars have often drawn general models of state formation from the European experience after 1700, then applied them with only partial success to other parts of the world. Although such studies of modern Europe improved on early theories of modernization and development, they failed to accommodate the varied ways in which city-states, empires, federations, centralized states, and other forms of government evolved and the pivotal role that cities played in the multiple paths to state formation.

In a sweeping, original work detailing eight centuries of city-state relations, Charles Tilly, Wim P. Blockmans, and their contributors document differences in political trajectories from one part of Europe to another and provide authoritative surveys of urbanization in nine major regions; they also suggest many correctives to previous analyses of state formation. They show that the variable distribution of cities significantly and independently constrained state formation and that states grew differently according to the character of urban networks in a given region. Their systematic study shows that unilinear models of state transformation underestimate the contingency and variability of popular and elite compliance with state-building activities. The book's findings offer important implications for the nature of economy, sovereignty, warfare, state power, and social change throughout the world.

Charles Tilly is University Distinguished Professor and director of the Center for Studies of Social Change at the New School for Social Research. His most recent books are *Coercion, Capital, and European States* (1992) and *European Revolutions* (1993). He has just completed a book on popular contention in Great Britain, 1758–1834, and (with his son Chris) is now writing a book on capitalist work and labor markets, to be published by Westview. **Wim P. Blockmans** is professor of medieval and European history at Leiden University. He has published, with Walter Prevenier, *The Burgundian Netherlands* (1985) and *Under the Spell of Burgundy* (1995). Currently he is co-editor of the seven-volume series *Origins of the Modern State in Europe, 1300–1800*, forthcoming.

About the Contributors

Anders Andrén is an archaeologist who has written several works on medieval urbanization. He is currently a reader in historical archaeology at the Univerity of Lund in Sweden.

Giorgio Chittolini is professor of medieval history at the University of Milan and member of the board of editors of *Società e storia*. He has worked primarily on the political institutions of the Renaissance state. With D. Willoweit he is editor of *Statuten, Städte und Territorien zwischen Mittelater und Neuzeit in Italien und Deutschland* (1992).

Pablo Fernández Albaladejo is professor of modern history at the Autonoma University, Madrid. His works include *La crisis del Antiguo Régimen en Guipúzcoa, 1766–1833* (1975) and several articles on the political and constitutional history of the Spanish monarchy during the sixteenth and seventeenth centuries, recently collected in the book *Fragmentos de Monarquía* (1992).

Marjolein 't Hart teaches economic and social history at the University of Amsterdam. Recently she published *The Making of a Bourgeois State: War, Politics and Finance During the Dutch Revolt* (1993).

Antonio Manuel Hespanha is researcher at the Instituto de Ciencias Sociais in Lisbon and professor of history at the Universidade Nova de Lisboa. He is the author of *A história do direito na história social* (1978) and *História das instituições: Épocas medieval e moderna* (1982). His main research interest is the legal and institutional history of the early modern ages.

Peter Moraw is professor in Landesgeschichte (regional history) at the Justus-Liebig University at Giessen and published a history of Germany in the late Middle Ages, *Von offener Verfassung zu gestalteter Verdichtung: Das Reich im spüten Mittelalter 1250 bis 1490* (1985) and is co-editor of the ten-volume *Neue Deutsche Geschichte* (New German History), currently published by Beck, Munich.

Traian Stoianovich is professor emeritus at Rutgers University where he has taught since 1955; he has also taught at New York University, the University of California at Berkeley, Stanford University, and Sir George Williams University (Montreal). He is the author of *A Study in Balkan Civilization* (1967), *French Historical Method: The "Annales" Paradigm* (1976), *Between East and West: The Balkan and Mediterranean Worlds* (1992–1994), and *Balkan Worlds: The First and Last Europe* (1994).

Sergij Vilfan served as director of the town archives of Ljubljana (Slovenia) 1950–1970 and was professor of legal history at the Faculty of Law (University of Ljubljana) until 1989. He is now Honorary Professor of the Faculty of Law in Graz

(Austria) and member of the Slovenian Academy of Sciences and Arts. His work deals with legal, social, and economic history as well as legal ethnology and historical metrology; he has published books and articles in several languages and countries.

Andrzej Wyrobisz is professor of early modern history at the Institute of History, Warsaw University, Poland. He is the author of several works on the history of material culture and on the social and economic history of towns in the late Middle Ages and early modern times. Editor of "Przegląd Historyczny" ("Polish Historical Review"), he also serves as overseas correspondent of "Urban History."

Index